Also in the Variorum Collected Studies Series:

ANGELIKI E. LAIOU
Gender, Society and Economic Life in Byzantium

NICOLAS OIKONOMIDES
Society, Culture and Politics in Byzantium

NICOLAS OIKONOMIDES
Social and Economic Life in Byzantium

ATHANASIOS MARKOPOULOS
History and Literature of Byzantium in the 9th–10th Centuries

PAUL SPECK
Understanding Byzantium
Studies in Byzantine Historical Sources

MILTON V. ANASTOS
Aspects of the Mind of Byzantium
Political Theory, Theology, and Ecclesiastical Relations with the See of Rome

ALICE-MARY TALBOT
Women and Religious Life in Byzantium

JEAN-MICHEL SPIESER
Urban and Religious Spaces in Late Antiquity and Early Byzantium

R.J. MACRIDES
Kinship and Justice in Byzantium, 11th–15th Centuries

AVERIL CAMERON
Changing Cultures in Early Byzantium

CÉCILE MORRISSON
Monnaie et finances à Byzance: analyses, techniques

ALEXANDER KAZHDAN
Authors and Texts in Byzantium

BRIAN CROKE
Christian Chronicles and Byzantine History, 5th–6th Centuries

VARIORUM COLLECTED STUDIES SERIES

Women, Family and Society in Byzantium

Angeliki E. Laiou

Angeliki E. Laiou

Women, Family and Society in Byzantium

Edited by Cécile Morrisson
and Rowan Dorin

Routledge
Taylor & Francis Group
LONDON AND NEW YORK

First published 2011 by Ashgate Publishing

Published 2016 by Routledge
2 Park Square, Milton Park, Abingdon, Oxon OX14 4RN
52 Vanderbilt Avenue, New York, NY 10017

Routledge is an imprint of the Taylor & Francis Group, an informa business

British Library Cataloguing in Publication Data
Laiou, Angeliki E.
Women, family and society in Byzantium.
– (Variorum collected studies series)
1. Women – Byzantine Empire – Social conditions.
2. Families – Byzantine Empire. 3. Domestic relations (Byzantine law)
4. Byzantine Empire – Civilization – 527–1081.
5. Byzantine Empire – Civilization – 1081–1453.
I. Title II. Series
949.5'02'082–dc22

ISBN 978-1-4094-3204-3

Library of Congress Control Number: 2011924281

ISBN 13: 978-1-4094-3204-3 (hbk)

VARIORUM COLLECTED STUDIES SERIES CS988

CONTENTS

Law, Politics and Society

This volume contains xiv + 276 pages

PUBLISHER'S NOTE

The articles in this volume, as in all others in the Variorum Collected Studies Series, have not been given a new, continuous pagination. In order to avoid confusion, and to facilitate their use where these same studies have been referred to elsewhere, the original pagination has been maintained wherever possible. Article IV has been reset, with the original page numbers in square brackets within the text.

Each article has been given a Roman number in order of appearance, as listed in the Contents. This number is repeated on each page and is quoted in the index entries.

PREFACE

Daß wir erschraken, da du starbst, nein, daß
dein starker Tod uns dunkel unterbrach,
das Bisdahin abreißend vom Seither:
das geht uns an; das einzuordnen wird
die Arbeit sein, die wir mit allem tun.

Rilke, *Requiem für eine Freundin* (1908)

Angeliki Laiou (1941–2008) was among the leading Byzantinists of her generation.[1] Armed with a penetrating intellect and graced with an uncommon clarity of thought and expression, she broke new ground in the field of Byzantine social and economic history. Fruitfully drawing on the insights of other historical periods and scholarly disciplines, but always sensitive to the specificities of the Byzantine experience, she published pioneering studies of topics ranging from family structure to economic ideology.

The articles gathered here bear witness to these qualities, as well as to her readiness to revisit her own earlier work in light of new insights and discoveries. They testify equally to the tragedy of her swift and unexpected passing, which left Byzantine Studies bereft of one of its most eloquent defenders and robbed her colleagues and students of a beloved friend and mentor. It is on behalf of these colleagues and students that we have undertaken the task of preparing three collections of her articles to be published posthumously in the Variorum series.[2] Though the vitality of her presence is now but a treasured memory, it is our hope that these volumes will ensure that her scholarly legacy remains alive and well.

We are particularly grateful to David Jacoby for suggesting this project in the first place, to John Smedley for shepherding it through the publication process with patience and good humour, and to Vassili Thomadakis for his support and encouragement. We would also like to thank Joëlle Beaucamp for generously agreeing to write the Introduction to this volume, and Gilbert Dagron, Michael McCormick, Nevra Necipoğlu, and the staff at Dumbarton Oaks for their assistance.

CÉCILE MORRISSON & ROWAN DORIN

---

[1] For a detailed account of her life and achievements, as well as a full bibliography, see the obituary by Cécile Morrisson and Alice-Mary Talbot in *Dumbarton Oaks Papers* 63 (2011): 1–14.

[2] *Women, Family and Society in Byzantium*, *Byzantium and the Other: Relations and Exchanges*, and *Economic Thought and Economic Life in Byzantium*.

ACKNOWLEDGEMENTS

Grateful acknowledgement is made to the following institutions, journals and publishers for their kind permission to reproduce the papers included in this volume: Dumbarton Oaks Research Library and Collection, Washington DC (for articles I and VI); the Association des amis du Centre d'histoire et civilisation de Byzance, Paris (II, VIII); Verlag Roman Kovar, Egling, and the Institut für Rechtsphilosophie, Religions- und Kulturrecht, Vienna (III); Koninklijke Brill N.V., Leiden (IV); John Wiley and Sons, Ltd, Chichester (V); and Vittorio Klostermann GmbH, Frankfurt am Main (VII).

INTRODUCTION*

In much of her work, and particularly in the studies gathered here, Angeliki E. Laiou sought to unravel the complex relationships between law (imperial or ecclesiastical), dominant ideologies, and social practice in Byzantium, using relatively abundant sources. As she herself emphasized, "the multidimensional picture that results may be a jurist's nightmare, but it is reality as it is lived" (Article II, p. 151). One could not better express the goals that she set for herself, a historian first and foremost of Byzantine society. Most articles reprinted in this volume date from the period in which Laiou was bringing to fruition the work that will endure as her principal achievement, *The Economic History of Byzantium*, testifying thereby to the persistently broad range of her scholarly concerns.

Laiou's interest in the history of women in the Byzantine world of the eleventh through fourteenth centuries was first displayed in her 1981 report to the XVI International Congress of Byzantine Studies on "The Role of Women in Byzantine Society." Over the following decade, she dedicated numerous articles to this subject, most of which were assembled in *Gender, Society, and Economic Life in Byzantium* (Variorum Collected Studies Series CS370), published in 1992. That same year, the volume entitled *Mariage, amour et parenté à Byzance aux XIe-XIIIe siècles* gathered together the five lectures she delivered in French at the Collège de France in Paris. The importance that Laiou placed on this field of research continued to manifest itself in subsequent years, resulting in the five articles reprinted here in chronological order under the heading "Women in Byzantine Law and Practice."

Article IV ("Women in the marketplace of Constantinople, 10th–14th centuries") further develops her earlier research into the economic role of women, whether of poor, middle class or aristocratic backgrounds. Here again, Laiou insists on the necessary distinction between an ideology (ever-present in our sources) that disparaged markets and retail and condemned the women who were active in these spheres, and a social reality that varied widely according to their milieus, and which can be glimpsed only in rare and scattered sources. This distinction notwithstanding, the dominant ideology left a firm imprint on the commercial activity of women, whether through the weight of family networks or the importance of marital property.

* Joëlle Beaucamp would like to thank the editors for translating this introduction from the original French.

In the four other articles in this section, Laiou considers new approaches and expands her investigation beyond the period of the eleventh through fourteenth centuries that had been at the heart of her work since 1981. This is especially true of "Sex, consent and coercion in Byzantium" (Article I), which appeared in 1993. In this 112-page study, she came to distinguish two attitudes in the Byzantine world: on one side, that of "civil" law (though "imperial" would probably be more appropriate here) and, less sharply, of canon law, in which the consent of a woman to a sexual act outside of marriage is taken into consideration (in the establishment of penalties, for instance); and on the other, that of society, reflected by ecclesiastical and literary sources, in which notions of dishonor and pollution and the value placed on virginity predominate, with the question of consent relegated to a secondary position.

While one might occasionally harbor some reservations over her treatment of late Antique legislation or the compilation of the Basilika and its scholia (as she herself conceded [Article I, p. 126, n. 39]) Laiou's analysis of the twelfth-century canonical commentaries, together with the cases reported in both the Peira and the responsa of Demetrios Chomatianos, is notably acute and apposite. The same is true of the conclusions she draws from the different versions of the epic poem *Digenes Akrites*, as well as twelfth-century novels, which offer evidence not for actual behavior but for mental attitudes. Her insistence on relating these norms to social practice and political considerations is conspicuous throughout, especially regarding the strategies of the aristocracy. She incorporates too the contributions of anthropology, particularly the importance of honor and dishonor in Mediterranean societies. It is worth noting that the considerable latitude that Laiou discerns in the application of the law (which is apparent above all in the Peira) is not reserved only to sexual matters, but rather seems to characterize Byzantium in general, as Dieter Simon has shown.

Laiou returned to some of these themes in her 1999 presentation to the congress of the *Gesellschaft für das Recht der Ostkirchen*, published in *Kanon* in 2000 as "The evolution of the status of women in marriage and family law" [Article III]. However, as well as dealing with the question of extra-marital sex, she confronts here the question of the formation of marriage, in which the Church played an ever-more dominant role (thus leading to an increasing intervention of ecclesiastical courts in matrimonial affairs). She looks too at divorce, and especially at divorce on grounds of adultery, at least in theory the sole grounds accepted by the Church. According to Laiou, the canonical commentaries (if not the canons themselves) moved toward a certain equality between men and women. But the influence exercised by the Church was complex. If the suppression of concubinage by the Ecloga was indeed due to such influence, as Laiou argues, the requirement (imposed soon afterward) that a marriage must be blessed in order to be valid reduced many unions to the level of concubinage. The complexity of the Church's influence was no less pronounced in the matter of divorce. The article's principal contribution to this particular issue lies in its study of the cases submitted to the ecclesiastical courts, and the decisions that were subsequently rendered. Ecclesiastical judges developed a notion of divorce "for implacable hatred," which could serve as a replacement for the now-forbidden divorce by mutual consent, and also offered a way to avoid divorce for adultery, which was very unfavorable toward the woman. Civil courts did not enjoy the flexibility of such recourse to *oikonomia*, but even here we find deviations from the norms established by law.

Laiou's concern with understanding the system of inter-generational property transfers among Byzantine families through a sociological and anthropological lens is particularly prominent in her 1998 article on "Marriage prohibitions, marriage strategies and the dowry in thirteenth-century Byzantium" (Article II). She starts from the premise that Byzantium practiced a divergent devolution of property between the male and female lines, which, according to anthropologists, has as a corollary a tendency toward close marriage. This type of marriage, however, was forbidden in Byzantium and became increasingly so over the centuries. This ought therefore to have led to a fragmentation of family patrimonies. The study of individual cases, known for the most part through Chomatianos's writings, suggests that such a result was only partially true, since one had to take into account the formation of new households (and hence new patrimonies) as well as strategies specifically aimed at alleviating this fragmentation, for instance the joint exploitation of property regardless of its formal ownership.

Her 2009 contribution to a volume on the *Social History of Byzantium*, entitled "Family structure and the transmission of property" (reprinted here as Article V), returns to the questions of the prevailing Byzantine practice of divergent devolution of property and the increasingly strict prohibition on close marriages (whereby other societies were able to address this problem). Several new themes can nevertheless be identified. To begin with, Laiou attempts to embrace the whole of Byzantine history from the seventh century onward, though it runs up against the difficulty of the paucity of sources concerning social practices prior to the eleventh century. She also seeks to compare Byzantium with the Latin West, stressing in this regard that the ongoing intervention of the state and the church, to which was added the heritage of Roman law, was responsible for the specificity of Byzantine developments. She notes too that the transmission of property occurred, for the most part, upon the marriage of one's children and was therefore closely tied to marriage strategies. As far as the aristocracy is concerned, Laiou believes that it is possible to argue that women were disadvantaged in terms of property transfers until the tenth century, but not thereafter. Regarding the peasantry, she dissects a legal commentary on the Novel of Romanos Lekapenos on the right of preemption, discovering therein a strategy aimed at limiting patrimonial fragmentation, namely the joint exploitation of lands, with the limits of the community defined by the degree of first cousin (as with the aristocracy). She also reexamines a much-disputed topic: the collation of the dowry (the requirement that a dowered woman return her dowry in order to participate in the inheritance). From her point of view, such a disposition was socially disruptive, and custom therefore prevailed over law.

The final three articles in the collection touch on diverse aspects of the Byzantine world, but they all share their author's trademark commitment to rendering the evidence offered by the sources more intelligible by elaborating a typology of cases and resituating them in their full context (whether synchronic or diachronic), as well as by uncovering the biases in contemporary accounts and searching for transformations in society that could explain shifts in ideology.

This is exemplified by her article, "Law, justice, and the Byzantine historians: ninth to twelfth centuries" (Article VI), in which Laiou discusses the persistent ties between justice and fiscality in Byzantium. In particular, she observes a marked constrast in the accounts of historians. While the enduring importance accorded to justice, and especially to the figure of the just sovereign, is obvious, law itself is rarely mentioned and virtually never appears as a constitutive element of justice. In these narratives, the emperor and the courts judge according to equity rather than according to the laws. Starting in the late eleventh century, however, there is a perceptible shift, notably in the writings of Michael Attaleiates, for whom justice was to be carried out in accordance with the laws and the good emperor was one who respected the laws. Laiou offers a hypothesis for understanding the rising importance granted to law in the rendering of justice: the growing complexity of society no longer permitted judgments based on simple principles alone – the institutionalization of these principles was required instead.

The 1995 study entitled "Peasant rebellion: notes on its vocabulary and typology" (Article VII) is based mainly on the *History* of George Pachymeres, which describes a number of peasant rebellions in Asia Minor in the second half of the thirteenth century. According to the analysis offered by Laiou, Pachymeres's narrative is relatively favorable to the rebels, thus setting its author apart from the perspective of the ruling classes of the period. In it she does not find revolts driven by misery; rather it is political motivations (legitimacy or lack of confidence in the state) or fiscal ones that predominate. Laiou identifies certain constant features within these events, such as the fear of mass uprisings among the powerful, who were nevertheless aware of the military weakness of the peasants, and the opposition between capital and province or between urban and rural dwellers. Yet she also discerns a shift, whose importance she stresses: there appears during this period a right to rebellion, since the people have come to be the guarantors of the political order. The opposition made in the sources between peasants and the army also strikes Laiou as a new development. Seeking therefore to understand why such revolts do not appear before the thirteenth century, she proposes an explanation in the composition of the thematic armies, which were made up of soldier-peasants (at least until the tenth century).

The final article in the collection, "The emperor's word: chrysobulls, oaths and synallagmatic relations in Byzantium (11th–12th C.)" (Article VIII) returns to the other social category to which Laiou devoted so much of her attention – the aristocracy – focusing on its relations with the imperial power. Here again she scrutinizes the ambiguous relationships between ideology and practice as they are played out in the sources. In order to illuminate Byzantine realities, she studies both the documents attesting agreements between the emperor and foreign allies and those between the sovereign and his subjects (generally aristocrats). She sees the increasing role of the oath as an internal evolution of the Byzantine world and not as an influence from the West. Besides, whenever the emperor agrees to a bilateral accord, it takes the form of a chrysobull, that is to say a unilateral act of donation: the very rare exceptions all concern foreign powers. This evolution of the chrysobull, which turns a unilateral document into the mere mask of a bilateral relationship, is also seen as an internal development.

A final remark: Laiou's understanding of the position of Byzantine women – especially aristocratic ones, whose lives are better known – is more optimistic than that of other historians, a difference of opinion of which she was fully conscious (see Article V, p. 57, n. 24). This divergence can undoubtedly be explained by the fact that her research stressed more the social practice discernable in the sources than the weight of ideology and juridical norms. It can also be explained by the fact that she was particularly interested in the final centuries of Byzantine history and in a social milieu (the aristocracy) of which her knowledge was unrivalled. One should not exclude the possibility, however, that the force of her own personality played a certain role: for Angeliki Laiou, there was neither any consonance nor any connection between "women" and "weakness."

JOËLLE BEAUCAMP

Aix-en-Provence
March 2011

I

Sex, Consent, and Coercion in Byzantium

Preface

In Byzantium of the late twelfth century, a lively debate took place, primarily among canonists, on the question of the validity of coerced consent to monastic life. The question arose out of specific and actual situations, in which force, violence, or duress were used to persuade individuals to enter the monastic life, a decision whose validity by definition depended on the free consent of the individual. The occasions were many and varied: a bishop was forced, by imperial officials, and for reasons which remain unclear, to become a monk; many members of the aristocracy, male and female, were coerced into monastic life by emperors who wanted to reduce their political power; women in particular were tonsured unwillingly, so that their marriages would be dissolved; the wives of men elevated to the episcopate were forced to become nuns, as opposed to simply living in a monastery, immediately after their husband's ordination.[1] The last two issues were the ones which were most hotly debated. The forced tonsure and divorce of women was of particular importance to aristocratic society, since it was a way for emperors, and occasionally others, including members of the families of the spouses, to break up marriages and therefore political alliances. Used since at least the early eleventh century specifically for this purpose, forced tonsure became, during the brief reign of Andronikos I (1183–85), a relatively frequent means of dissolving the marriages of the aristocracy. After his deposition and death, both the civil courts and the canonists were faced with political questions as

[1] For a discussion of a number of these cases, see A. Laiou, *Mariage, amour et parenté à Byzance, XIème–XIIIème siècles* (Paris, 1992), chap. 4.

well as with the theoretical question of what constitutes and what establishes free and coerced consent, and in what circumstances the validity of monastic vows was undermined by coercion. It was, I think, because of these very real problems that the debate then took place among canonists on the second issue, that is, on the coerced tonsure of the wives of bishops, a question which in the end produced imperial legislation, namely, a Novel of Emperor Isaac II Angelos.[2] The debate was real, and quite sophisticated.

In the course of investigating these twelfth-century developments, I became interested in the general question of free and coerced consent, and the ways in which Byzantine society dealt with it. As far as the twelfth century is concerned, the issue clearly came to the fore as a result of the increasing effort of Comnenian emperors to control society, especially aristocratic society, and therefore the matrimonial alliances of its members. The other side of this coin is the desire of members of the aristocracy to control and further their own interests; the combination led both to political clashes and to the debate of more general issues. However, the posture of the aristocracy did not in itself mean a greater respect for the free will of the individual, but rather an insistence on control by the family rather than by the state. It was the canonists, and perhaps the civil judges, faced with specific issues in court, who generalized and brought the question of free and coerced individual consent to the forefront of the discussion. Although the debate centered around the question of free consent to monastic life, the interplay of individual free will and the limiting factors of state, church, family, and custom governed and governs many other aspects of life, including the transfer of property and intervention in religious and political life.

In this effort to approach the issue insofar as Byzantium is concerned, I have concentrated on the question of consent to sexual and matrimonial relations. In some ways, this aspect of the larger question is the easiest to treat, since free consent, at least to marriage, was an element society explicitly recognized as necessary, and equally explicitly circumscribed by the just as necessary consent of the parents of the spouses. It is also an issue to whose subtleties we have become sensitive because of current debates concerning sexual harassment and rape, debates now taking place in both western Europe and North America. While one must be cautious not to superimpose current concerns on past societies, nevertheless it would be absurd not to recognize

[2] J. and P. Zepos, *Jus Graecoromanum* (hereafter *JGR*), I (Athens, 1931), 435–36.

the fact that historians are moved and informed by the debates of their own day.

In Byzantium, as in Rome and much more than in Rome, sexual activity was to be confined within institutional limits defined by law. In the Roman Empire, these institutions consisted of marriage and concubinage. In Byzantium, monogamous marriage was the ideal promulgated by the church, and to some extent adopted by the state. In the eighth century, the Isaurian emperors promoted productive and stable unions to the extent of assimilating long-term cohabitation with marriage, while early in the tenth century Emperor Leo VI finally forbade concubinage.[3] Concubinage was far from abolished by these measures, and the woman who had a long-term cohabitation with a man outside the confines of marriage even enjoyed some protection which seems to have been customary rather than legal.[4] Nevertheless, sexual activity outside of marriage, as well as adultery, was considered illicit in various degrees. The purpose of this study is to examine the role of consent in establishing legal categories, and, further, the role of consent in the determination of culpability and punishment, not only in the law but, more importantly, in social thought and practice. Was consent the main factor distinguishing various aspects of illicit sexual activity, or were other factors, such as social position or marital status, more important? Was society conscious of and interested in how free one's consent was, and in the elements which constitute or prove coercion? Was coerced consent considered valid?

The illicit sexual activities to which the question is pertinent are several. In Roman law, and in Byzantium, the categories included adultery, that is, intercourse with a married woman; *stuprum,* or φθορά, which involves a man with a woman unmarried or no longer married; and *per vim stuprum,* which is *stuprum* with the addition of coercion or force. Incest, whatever its specific definition, was certainly an illicit sexual relationship, but the question of consent does not enter as a defining factor, and incest therefore will not be treated here. On the other hand, abduction, which was, strictly speaking, the forcible removal of a woman (or, indeed, a man) came very quickly to acquire sexual connotations, since it was thought either to be attended by

[3] *Ecloga,* L. Burgmann, ed., *Ecloga: Das Gesetzbuch Leons III. und Konstantinos' V.* (Frankfurt, 1983), 2.6; P. Noailles and A. Dain, *Les Novelles de Léon VI le Sage* (Paris, 1944), p. 91, and *Procheiros Nomos* 4.25–26.

[4] A. Laiou, "Contribution à l'étude de l'institution familiale en Épire au XIIIème siècle," *Fontes Minores* 6 (1984), 284 ff.

intercourse or to be occasioned by a desire to marry. Since force or the presumption of force is by definition inherent in at least some stages of abduction, the issue of consent does arise here, and will be discussed.

Many strains of thought, past elaborations, and inherited and new attitudes informed the Byzantine approach to these issues. From the Roman past, the Byzantines inherited legal categories as well as the important idea that consent was a differentiating factor in the categorization of actions. But the further elaboration of the problem depended on non-Roman antecedents. Shame and honor, so important in Greek Antiquity, played an important role.[5] So did ideas of sexual pollution, which were very old, but which were given new form by Christianity. The church, with its own ideas regarding sin, its expiation, and personal responsibility, played a fundamental role. The result of the combination and sometimes the opposition of ideas stemming from these different traditions was the creation of a new system, medieval in aspect and specific to Byzantium.

The subject could be treated in a number of ways. My own interests do not lie in the philosophical concepts that may underlie definitions of consent, but rather in social history. The present study is an effort to elucidate how the various issues connected with free or coerced consent were dealt with in Byzantine society, both formally and informally. Thus legal definitions, legal practice, and social attitudes and practice will all be considered, as will the literary treatment of these issues. While this is not a study in legal history, it does address legal issues. I am grateful to many people who, over the years, have helped me to understand the intricacies involved in such matters.

I am also grateful to the participants in the seminar for the lively discussion which helped me to clarify my thoughts, and for the insights which they contributed on a number of points, as well as for the occasional contribution of source references. I would like to thank particularly Hélène Ahrweiler, Robert Browning, Alexander Kazhdan, Jelisaveta Allen, Alice-Mary Talbot, Alexander Alexakis, and Denis Sullivan for their contributions. Some of the research on which this work is based was carried out in 1988–89, when I was on leave from my regular duties. I am grateful to the American Council of Learned Societies and the National Endowment for the Humanities for a grant which made that year possible.

[5] Hugh Lloyd-Jones, "Ehre und Schande in der griechischen Kultur," *Antike und Abendland* 33 (1987), 1–28.

1. The Legal Categories

Is law the proper place to start such an investigation? It can easily be argued that if the purpose is to understand social attitudes, formal legal pronouncements are not very useful and can, in fact, be misleading. Such an argument has a certain force. To some extent, undoubtedly, law reflects social attitudes; it also, surely, seeks to shape them. But legal systems can and do incorporate many laws which are capricious, or outdated, or unenforced because unenforceable. Furthermore, legal pronouncements have a subtext which is essential for understanding both their letter and their spirit and which one ignores at one's peril. It may be argued that less formal sources, literary and other, can be more useful than legal texts in providing information about the complexities, subtleties, and ambiguities which render this subject interesting. On the other hand, one of the first questions to be addressed is whether consent served to create legal categories insofar as sexual and matrimonial relations were concerned, and for an answer to such a question one must surely turn to the legal texts. Furthermore, the vocabulary of consent and coercion is a legal vocabulary, even though the elaboration of the concepts may be undertaken in the course of non-legal debates, primarily theological or philosophical, and even though the vocabulary itself is shaped by attitudes which originate from people other than the legislator or the legal commentator. It has, therefore, seemed best to start with the formal legal texts, and then bring other sources to bear upon the issue in order to help illuminate and interpret both the legal vocabulary and the utility and import of the legal system.

The Roman Background

In Roman law, there were certain sexual unions that were accepted and encouraged, and others that were tolerated. Marriage, the union of free Roman citizens, into which the partners entered with their free consent and that of their parents or those who had them in their authority, was the one fully accepted and recognized form of cohabitation. The regulations surrounding marriage had in view primarily the marriage of the upper class, which Augustus is known to have wished to safeguard and encourage. Concubinage was an accepted form of sexual union between social unequals. Categories of sexual behavior which were known to law, and which were condemned with varying degrees of severity, include *stuprum,* that is, sexual relations with those categories of women with whom *stuprum* could be committed. These categories consisted of women of good repute and social class, whether unmarried or *matres familiae* who were no longer married, that is, who were widowed or divorced.[1] Adultery, strongly condemned by the *lex Julia de adulteriis coercendis,* could, properly speaking, be committed only with and by a married woman. The category *per vim stuprum* would seem, at first glance, to consist of forced sexual intercourse, that is, rape. But it was somewhat ill-defined, and left many questions unanswered, such as the degree of force necessary to qualify an action as *per vim stuprum,* as well as the type of woman against whom this action could be committed.[2] Finally, abduction, whatever its origins, acquired an implication of sexual coercion, certainly by the time of Constantine I and possibly already at the time of Augustus. Seen as a crime against public order, it was punished by the *lex Julia de vi publica.*[3] Its characteristics were forcible removal to another place and the use of arms.

The intricacies and ambiguities of the Roman legal categorizations have been treated elsewhere in this volume. Here, a few observations will suffice. First, although the sources permit one to make the above statements, they themselves recognized the ambiguities. In particular, the difference between *stuprum* and adultery was blurred in people's minds. The difference should be clear: "Adultery is committed with a married woman; *stuprum* is committed with a widow, a virgin, or a boy."[4] But it was not quite clear, as Papinian acknowledged.[5] The confusion perhaps reflects the fact that the major concern

[1] Susan Treggiari, *Roman Marriage:* Iusti Coniuges *from the Time of Cicero to the Time of Ulpian* (Oxford, 1991); Diana Moses, "Livy's Lucretia and the Validity of Coerced Consent in Roman Law," in Part I of this volume. For the Roman background I am indebted to Diana Moses, who brought up a number of important issues in our seminar, and also collected and made available to me various relevant texts.

[2] For *per vim stuprum,* see Moses,"Livy's Lucretia." See also Aline Rousselle, *Porneia: On Desire and the Body in Antiquity* (Oxford, 1988), 78 ff. Cf. *D.* 48.5.30 (29).9, *D.* 48.6.3.4.

[3] *D.* 48.6.5.2.

[4] *D.* 48.5.35 (Modestinus) = *Bas.* 60.37.34: "Adulterium in nupta admittitur; stuprum in vidua vel virgine vel puero committitur."

[5] *D.* 48.5.6: "Lex stuprum et adulterium promiscue et καταχρηστικώτερον appellat. sed proprie adulterium in nupta committitur . . . stuprum uero in uirginem

was with adultery, which endangered the institution the legislation most aimed to protect, that is, marriage. This concern then led people to subsume the lesser crime of *stuprum* under the greater one of adultery, which thus became a generalized category. The confusion, however, seems to have affected common attitudes, and perhaps the attitudes of some lawyers, rather than the legal pronouncements themselves. Even so, there are other instances where qualifications refine the original statement. Thus, for example, while adultery involves primarily married women, a concubine, too, could be accused of adultery, even though her union was not considered a valid marriage.[6]

Second, for Roman law, social status, especially of the woman, was an important factor in defining the legal categories. It is clear that a slave, for example, could not be accused of adultery, since slaves could not contract marriages. At another level, social class also governed the categorization of *stuprum:* one could have sexual relations with a woman either of ill repute or of a low social class (e.g., a prostitute, a procuress, an innkeeper, or an actress) without committing *stuprum; stuprum* with a slave was considered to constitute property damage to her owner.[7] Social status is intimately connected to mores or perceived mores, since the legislation is explicitly made for the virgin and the *mater familias,* the latter being defined as one who lives honorably (*quae non inhoneste vixit,* the σεμνὴ γυνή of the Greek sources).[8] On the other hand, *stuprum* could be committed against another man's concubine. For, if Roman law made of social class a defining factor in its categorizations, so it also dealt with the marital status of a woman. In the all-important category of adultery, it was the marital status of the woman, not of the man, that defined the category. It can thus be argued that the legal categories of sexual crimes in Roman legislation were established according to

---

uiduamue committitur, quod Graeci φθορὰν appellant. In the *Basilics* 60.37.8 this is rendered as: Λέγεται μὲν μοιχεία καὶ ἡ πρὸς παρθένον ἢ χήραν φθορά, κυρίως δὲ μοιχεία μὲν ἐστὶν ἡ τῆς ὑπάνδρου, φθορὰ δὲ ἡ τῆς παρθένου καὶ χήρας. Roman law states that a "widow" signifies either a widowed or a divorced woman.

[6] *D.* 48.5.14 (13). The *Basilics* (60.37.14) state this differently: "there can be accusation of adultery in an *improperly constituted marriage,*" perhaps because by then Leo VI had forbidden concubinage.

[7] Rousselle, *Porneia,* 85; cf. *D.* 47.10.25. About the *stuprum* of slaves, see Diana Moses, "Livy's Lucretia," note 31.

[8] See Ulpian in *D.* 50.16.46, no. 1.

relationships between men: the perpetrator and the woman's husband, or lover, or father.[9] Punishment was relative to the social position of the culprit and the victim. The age of the woman involved (i.e., the question of whether she is under the age of consent or not) did not loom large.

As for consent, the only consent or absence of it that is envisaged is that of the woman. In Roman legislation, it serves to differentiate principally between the categories of *stuprum* and *per vim stuprum*. It is the only place where it makes a difference, that difference being in the severity of the punishment of the man (and possibly in the punishment of the woman). But if this differentiation is connected only with *stuprum*, it probably applies only to widows and virgins; it is nowhere specifically stated, for example, that a married woman may have withheld her consent from an adulterous act of sexual intercourse. Furthermore, none of the subtleties of establishing consent or defining force is evident in the various laws connected with sexual crimes, although some do appear in other connections.

It should be noted here that although Roman law does have different categories of illicit sexual behavior, these are somewhat fuzzy and punishments are sometimes not spelled out, often being implicit rather than explicit.[10] This being the case, one is left with the impression that the consent of the woman plays a role that is secondary to that of her marital and social status (and to the social status of the man) in the definition of legal categories. The point is made with crystal clarity in a late Roman text, the Novel of Constantine I on abduction (326), where the consent of the woman is explicitly said not to affect the categorization of the crime although, exceptionally, it does affect the punishment of the woman.[11]

It will be evident to the naked eye that Roman law has been discussed here in an entirely superficial way. Indeed, this short summary cannot accommodate the complexities and ambiguities, let alone the development, of Roman law. My purpose has been simply to provide a telescoped background to

[9] See also the remarks of Joëlle Beaucamp, "La prostitution féminine," in *Die Reaktion der Normalen*, Max-Planck-Institut für europäische Rechtsgeschichte (Frankfurt, 1988), 80 ff.

[10] See, for example, C. 9.9.20 on the (unspecified) punishment of women guilty of *stuprum*.

[11] *Codex Theodosianus*, ed. Th. Mommsen (hereafter *CTh*) (Berlin, 1905; repr. Hildesheim, 1990), 8.24.1.

the discussion of Byzantine law and practice. Perhaps one final comment is in order. The late Antique period, especially but not only under the Christian emperors, saw an increase of concern and therefore legislation about matters pertaining both to marriage and to sexual relations outside marriage. Studied in the last instance by Joëlle Beaucamp, the legislation is, according to this author, both a sign of repression where women are concerned and a measure of protection.[12] This is a period of legislative strictness on moral and sexual matters. Instead of detailing one more time the moral concerns of the emperors and the pertinent legislation, one could perhaps refer to an epigram of Agathias Scholastikos, who complains about the constraints thus imposed upon a man who also, it must be admitted, had claims to unusual fastidiousness in sexual matters. What is a man to do, he laments, to find love? In the streets, one meets with the prostitute's inordinate love of gold. The bed of a virgin is approachable only through marriage, else one is subject to the law on *stuprum* (ποινὰς τὰς περὶ τῶν φθορέων). At the same time, it is no fun to sleep with one's legitimate wife, for she claims it as her due. The couch of adultery is evil, and strange to love, as is that of a boy. A widow is too easy; a prude is too difficult, and prone to remorse. If one turns to his own slave, he feels degraded; if to the slave of another, he is guilty of a crime against the master's property. The conclusion? Πάντ' ἄρα Διογένης ἔφυγεν τάδε, τὸν δ' ὑμέναιον/ ἤειδεν παλάμῃ, Λαΐδος οὐ χατέων.[13]

The *Ecloga*

Although late Roman and early Byzantine emperors (Constantine I, Constans II, Theodosios II, and Justinian I) legislated on specific sexual crimes, such as adultery and, primarily, abduction, the categorization of illicit sexual activity is not renewed until the time of the *Ecloga*. The Isaurian law code, promulgated by Leo III and Constantine V in 741, introduced into the topic of illicit sexual relations innovations that were to last for a long time, since they were repeated with only a few changes in the ninth-century legal compilations, the *Procheiros Nomos* and the *Eisagoge,* and from there passed into the official codification, the *Basilics* (tenth century) and eventually into the

[12] Joëlle Beaucamp, *Le statut de la femme à Byzance (4e–7e siècle)*, I, *Le droit impérial* (Paris, 1990), 17 ff, 92 ff, 170 ff, 195 ff, 246 ff.

[13] *Anthologia Palatina,* V, ed. P. Waltz (Paris, 1928), 133. I owe this reference to Hélène Ahrweiler.

late Byzantine compilations of Harmenopoulos and Vlastares. The first and most obvious innovation is that the different categories of illicit sexual behavior seem much clearer in the *Ecloga* than they do in the Justinianic codification of Roman law. This is due to the fact that virtually all these categories are grouped together in the section on punishments. They no longer appear under the rubric of the *lex Julia de adulteriis coercendis* or the *lex Julia de vi publica,* nor must they be culled from individual laws and legal opinions, but form a coherent part of the penal code of the compilation. The one exception is adultery, which appears in both section 17 (on punishments) and section 2 (on marriage), since it is also, when the woman is guilty of adultery, one of the few recognized grounds for divorce.[14] The new grouping, which is repeated in the *Procheiros Nomos* and the *Eisagoge,* is perhaps occasioned by the purpose of the compilation, meant to serve as a practical guide to judges, especially those of the provinces, who could no longer understand or deal with the complex Justinianic corpus.[15] In the *Basilics,* the provisions of the *Ecloga,* as modified by the *Procheiros Nomos,* appear as an appendage to the rubric Νόμος Ἰουλίου περὶ τῶν ἐν μοιχείᾳ ἐνεχομένων καὶ περὶ φθορᾶς παρθένων καὶ χηρῶν.[16] Abduction is treated both under this rubric and in a special section (*Bas.* 60.58). Nevertheless, the grouping and definition of the categories as they appear in the *Ecloga* remain intact in the *Basilics*. This technical regrouping serves to point out one important fact and has one important effect. It makes clear that the differentiation of the categories had as a practical result, and perhaps as a purpose, the establishment of criteria for the punishment of the (male) culprit. Furthermore, marriage is even more important than in the Augustan legislation; it is not by chance that the very first chapter of the *Ecloga* is on betrothal and the second on marriage. With marriage assuming such an importance, all sexual activities outside it are seen as illicit, in various degrees, and so are grouped together. The effect is that, once the various categories of illicit sexual activity are grouped together, they come into sharper focus, as does the differentiation between them; and, whether for this reason or for other ones, so does the issue of consent as a differentiating factor.

[14] *Ecloga* 2.9.1, 2.9.2, 17.27. For the date, see Burgmann, *Ecloga,* pp. 10–12. All references will be to this edition.

[15] *Ecloga,* Prooimion, p. 162. The emperors mention specifically their desire to make plain in a detailed fashion the punishments appropriate to each crime.

[16] *Bas*. 60.27.

A first matter to notice concerns vocabulary. The term *stuprum,* as the Romans themselves said, rendered the classical Greek term φθορά.[17] The word φθορά reappears in the *Basilics* as the proper translation of *stuprum.*[18] In the *Ecloga,* derivatives of φθορά (e.g., ὁ φθείρων, ὁ φθορεύς, ἡ φθαρεῖσα) do indeed appear where we would expect them if *stuprum* is meant; but there is also the appearance of a new term, and possibly a new category. That is the term πορνεία, which means fornication generally, and seems to include sins of the flesh without further specification. It appears as a legal category for the first time in the *Ecloga,* and the punishments associated with it are in the first instance differentiated by the marital condition of the man, a new phenomenon. A married man who fornicates is punished by twelve lashes; the unmarried fornicator suffers half of this punishment.[19] Special provisions regarding fornication with a slave woman, whether one's own or that of another, add financial penalties to the corporal punishment, since the man either loses his own slave or remits to her master the sum of 36 nomismata (half a pound of gold), if he has slept with the slave of another man.[20] The same term, πορνεία, is used to describe fornication with a consecrated nun; this crime is then equated with adultery, at least as far as the punishment is concerned, and, exceptionally, the woman is punished as well as the man.[21] The importance and meaning of the category of πορνεία will be discussed later.[22] For the moment, suffice it to say that, although differentiation of the punishment according to the social condition of the woman is close to the spirit of Roman law, the use of the marital condition of the man

[17] Papinian in *D.* 48.5.6: "stuprum uero in uirginem uiduamue committitur, quod Graeci φθορὰν appellant."

[18] See, for example, *Bas.* 60.37.34 = *D.* 48.5.35 and *Bas.* 60.37.8 = *D.* 48.5.6.

[19] *Ecloga* 17.19, 17.20.

[20] *Ecloga* 17.21 and 17.22. The *Procheiros Nomos* adds corporal punishment in the case of the man who sleeps with his slave (39.60; cf. *Eisagoge* 40.58). The *Ecloga,* the *Procheiros Nomos,* and the *Eisagoge* all specify that if a man is poor, he should be beaten and remit as much as he can of the sum of 36 nomismata. The *Procheiros Nomos* and the *Eisagoge,* which also incorporate parts of the Justinianic corpus, have provisions, originating in Roman law, which punish a woman who sleeps with her slave: *Procheiros Nomos* 39.43 and 44; *Eisagoge* 40.49–50, and cf. *Bas.* 60.37.72 and 73. The penalties are different from those stated in a law of Constantine I: C. 9.11.

[21] *Ecloga* 17.23. Both are punished by the slitting of the nose.

[22] Below, pp. 128–32.

as a means of differentiating punishment, which appears in this section, is novel.

Let us now turn to the various categories of illicit sexual behavior as they appear in the *Ecloga*. *Adultery,* that is, intercourse with a married woman, is a relatively straightforward category; both the man and the woman involved are punished by the slitting of the nose and the woman is divorced, being allowed to take back "the things which she brought in to her husband and nothing more." The adulterer is not divorced from his wife.[23] As with the case of Roman law, the issue of consent to the adultery is not raised.[24]

The most important innovations of the *Ecloga* have to do with φθορά, which is dealt with in chapters 17.29, 17.31, and 17.32. The term φθορά is difficult to render into English; its original meaning is corruption, and sometimes this is retained.[25] At other times it has connotations which can be rendered variously as seduction, deflowering, or sexual intercourse even with a woman who is not a virgin. All of the relevant chapters of the *Ecloga* deal exclusively with the seduction of a virgin. That of a married woman comes under the rubric of adultery, but that of a widow is not envisaged at all, unless it is subsumed in the general statement about fornication in 17.19–20. It will be seen below that the consent or otherwise of the seduced girl looms large, since it establishes the level of punishment of the man.

The first case the *Ecloga* treats is that of *consensual stuprum,* where the girl is willing but her parents are not.[26] While the text literally speaks of "lack of knowledge" rather than lack of consent of the parents, I take the meaning to be that the parents were unwilling to give their consent not, certainly, to

[23] *Ecloga* 17.28; cf. 2.9.1, 2.9.2 on divorce. The translation is that of E. H. Freshfield, *A Manual of Roman Law: The Ecloga* (Cambridge, 1926). On adultery in Roman society, see Treggiari, *Roman Marriage*, 262 ff.

[24] Roman and Byzantine law hint at the fact that consent was important. Both state that the five-year proscription for accusation of adultery lapses if there is rape. In such a case, the crime can be prosecuted without limit of time: *D.* 48.5.29; *Eisagoge* 40.44; *Procheiros Nomos* 39.26; *Bas.* 60.67.29 and scholia. The Byzantine sources stress the difference between consensual adultery and rape. See, for example, *Eisagoge* 40.44: ἀλλὰ τοῦτο λέγομεν περὶ τῶν εἰς ἑκοῦσαν ἡμαρτηκότων. Ἐὰν δέ τις βιασάμενος . . . ἁμάρτῃ . . . ἀπροσδιορίστως δύναται κατηγορεῖσθαι.

[25] As such, it is strongly connected with ideas of pollution, on which cf. below, IV.

[26] *Ecloga* 17.29: προαιρέσει μὲν τῆς κόρης, ἀγνοίᾳ δὲ τῶν αὐτῆς γονέων.

the girl's deflowering, but rather to a marriage between her and the man who seduces her. If, after the fact, the man wishes to marry the girl, and her parents assent, the marriage is permitted. It is important to note that the girl's consent to the seduction is assumed to signify also consent to the marriage: it is nowhere stated that this consent must be sought, and since it was essential for a valid marriage, it must have been assumed. If the man is unwilling to marry the girl, or if her parents do not agree, he is subject to a fine or to what we would call civil damages: a well-off man will give the girl (not the fisc or her parents) one pound of gold; a poorer man will give half his property, and a man who has no property (πένης καὶ ἀνεύπορος) will be beaten, shorn, and exiled. The financial penalties are, *mutatis mutandis,* similar to those envisaged for the *stuprum* of a virgin or widow in *Institutes* 4.18.4, that is, the *lex Julia de adulteriis*. This punished the man guilty of *stuprum* without force (*sine vi*) with a fine of half his property if he were well-off or corporal punishment and exile if he were of a humble status. The important difference lies in the remedy envisaged in the first instance, that is, marriage, which is not presented as a remedy in the *Institutes*. Influenced perhaps by Christianity and canon law, the legislation seeks first to remedy the seduction of a virgin by having recourse to the institution of marriage, and only secondarily to punish the action by giving the girl a compensation which could, presumably, serve to increase her dowry for an eventual marriage. This, too, is an innovation, since in Roman legislation any compensation went to the fisc. The ecclesiastical influence on this legislation is highlighted by the scholia to *Basilics* 60.37.78, which add canon 67 of the Apostles and canons 25 and 26 of St. Basil, encouraging or permitting the marriage of a seducer with the girl he had seduced.

These provisions regarding consensual *stuprum* were slightly revised by the *Procheiros Nomos,* which made the marriage contingent on the consent of the parents of the man as well, and in this form it passed into the *Basilics*.[27] The emendation of the *Procheiros Nomos* was, in legal terms, a reasonable one, since once the possibility of marriage is broached, the consent of all the important parties, that is, the future spouses and their parents, becomes nec-

[27] *Procheiros Nomos* 39.65; cf. *Bas*. 60.37.78. On the change introduced by the *Procheiros Nomos,* as well as on the Isaurian legislation regarding φθορά, see the very good comments of M. A. Tourtoglou, *Παρθενοφθορία καὶ εὕρεσις θησαυροῦ* (Athens, 1963), 20 ff.

essary. In real terms, of course, it adds to the number of people who could put an end to the marriage plans. It was a law that remained well known and was quoted in judicial decisions including the *Peira* and the decisions of Chomatianos. It seems, from the text of the *Ecloga,* that the provisions for the corporal punishment of fornicators (17.19 and 17.20) were not cumulative, that is, they were not added to the punishment of those guilty of seducing virgins; those provisions, therefore, must apply to *stuprum* with widows, divorced women, and generally with those who were neither currently married nor marriageable virgins.[28]

There is one exception to the provisions concerning consensual *stuprum,* and it has to do with the case of a man who sleeps with the fiancée of another. In such a case, the man is punished by having his nose slit, *even if the girl had consented.* The punishment of the man here is the same as for adultery, which must still be due to ecclesiastical influence, especially after the Council in Trullo, where betrothal was almost equated with marriage, although the civil legislation did not adopt such a measure until the time of Leo VI.[29] It is to be noted, however, that the girl is not punished, as a married woman would have been (*Ecloga* 17.32). The *Procheiros Nomos* (39.68) adds that if the seducer acted without the consent of the girl, his punishment will be increased by a monetary penalty and the girl will receive one-third of his property. The penalty is thus equal to the penalty for rape of an unmarried girl (*Procheiros Nomos* 39.66).

In the *Ecloga,* it is the girl's consent and her age that serve to differentiate the punishment of the seducer. Thus rape of an unmarried girl is punished by the slitting of the nose,[30] a penalty which in the *Procheiros Nomos* is increased since the man is to give the girl one-third of his property (39.66). The commentary to the *Basilics* insists on the matter of consent by repeating ἄκουσαν (*Bas.* 60.37.79 = *Procheiros Nomos* 39.66). The heaviest penalty is reserved for the seduction of a girl under the age of thirteen, that is, under the age at which she was allowed to contract a marriage. The man is punished by the slitting of the nose and by giving the girl one-half of his property; he

[28] Cf. below, II.

[29] Council in Trullo, canon 98, states that a man who marries the fiancée of another while the first man is still alive is guilty of adultery. For this purpose, therefore, betrothal is equivalent to marriage.

[30] *Ecloga* 17.30: ὁ βιαζόμενος κόρην καὶ φθείρων αὐτὴν ῥινοκοπείσθω.

is thus subject to both exemplary punishment and civil damages (*Ecloga* 17.31 and *Procheiros Nomos* 39.67). The scholion to the pertinent passage of the *Basilics* (60.80, repeating *Procheiros Nomos* 39.67) makes this punishment also dependent on the consent of the girl; it states that if the girl had been unwilling, the man should be punished according to the provisions of *Basilics* 60.51.35, no. 3, which legislate exile for a man of the upper class, while a lower-class man is sent to the mines.[31] It is my view, however, that the commentator misunderstood the spirit of this law, carried away perhaps by an overzealous attempt to reconcile the Isaurian legislation with those parts of the Justinianic corpus which were still preserved in the *Basilics*. Given the stricter provisions of Roman legislation, he thought that they should apply to the seduction of a girl before puberty, and thus he used the issue of consent to indicate the most severe form of that crime. My view is that, as far as the *Ecloga* and the *Procheiros Nomos* are concerned, the girl's absence of consent is inherent in the fact of her impuberty, in other words, consent is immaterial. A girl under the age of thirteen was incapable of contracting a marriage, and a marriage thus contracted could be dissolved, because the consent of the girl did not legally exist. By extension, this would apply also to sexual intercourse, because, as we have seen in *Ecloga* 17.29, the woman's consent to sexual intercourse was assumed to include her consent to marriage. Thus I would argue that for the Isaurians the impuberty of the girl makes the question of her consent moot, since she is legally incapable of giving it. If this is so, we have here a clear concept of what modern law recognizes as statutory rape, where age is the only relevant factor, impuberty creating a "conclusive presumption of force," and consent is immaterial.[32]

In the late Antique world, abduction (*raptus*) had been a subject of much imperial concern, and had occasioned extremely severe legislation on the part of Constantine I and slightly less severe pronouncements by Justinian I. The church fathers had also been much exercised about it.[33] By contrast, the

[31] *D.* 48.19.38, no. 3, which is the source for *Bas.* 60.51.35, no. 3, states these punishments for those who "nondum viripotentes virgines corrumpunt," *without* reference to the girl's consent. There is no mention of consent either in the *Digest* or in the *Basilics*.

[32] *Corpus Juris Secundum, A Complete Restatement of the Entire American Law,* vol. 75 (New York, 1952), "Rape," § 13.

[33] See below, II.

Ecloga barely deals with abduction. The term appears only once, in 17.24, a chapter which deals with a rather specific case, namely, with the abduction "from any place" of a nun or a παρθένον βιωτικήν, whom I take to be simply an unmarried girl. There is no stated punishment for abduction itself; but if the woman is seduced, that is, if there is sexual intercourse, the man is punished by having his nose slit. The punishment is the same one as for the rape of a virgin (*Ecloga* 17.30). Thus the legislator is much more interested in illicit sexual intercourse, a crime against persons, than in the violent crime of abduction; and he seems to assume that intercourse that follows abduction is equivalent to rape. Both of these elements concerning abduction will be seen in cases judged by Eustathios Romaios in the eleventh century.[34]

Interest in abduction revived under the Macedonian dynasty. The *Eisagoge* incorporates a summary of a law of Justinian I, while Leo VI legislated further on the issue.[35] The *Basilics,* too, has a section on abduction. This legislation, especially the Novel of Leo VI, was known to jurists in the eleventh century. It was summarized by Psellos, and commented upon by Eustathios Romaios. Whether it was applied or not is another question, which will be discussed below.

It is evident, then, that the *Ecloga* innovates in a number of ways in the matters of concern to us. Unlike Roman law, the legislation of the Isaurians seems to affect equally persons of any social status, with the exception of slaves (on whom see *Ecloga* 17.21 and 17.22). There is, thus, a blurring of social distinctions in such matters. Just as a valid marriage may be contracted by anyone (except slaves), so relations outside marriage are treated in the same manner, whether the persons involved are members of the aristocracy or not. The one case where punishment is differentiated according to economic, not social status, is the case of consensual *stuprum,* where the penalty imposed on the man differs according to his ability to pay it. As for the social position of the woman, that too does not loom large; nuns are treated differently from other women, but that is a matter not of the woman's social status but of her condition: she is a bride of Christ. Again unlike Roman legislation, the emphasis is very clearly on *stuprum,* seduction and rape; even abduction

[34] See below, III. On abduction, see P. Karlin-Hayter, "Further Notes on Byzantine Marriage: Raptus—ἁρπαγή or μνηστεῖαι?" *Dumbarton Oaks Papers* 46 (1992), 133–54.

[35] *Eisagoge* 40.45.

is seen as secondary to the seduction of the abducted girl. Once *stuprum* has been established, the consent or otherwise of the woman plays a much greater and clearer role than in Roman law. It serves to establish the legal category of rape, which is illicit carnal knowledge without consent, and statutory rape; and it is the telling factor that differentiates the punishment of the man. The consent of the woman, however, does not have legal consequences for her. Consensual sex with an unmarried woman carries penalties for the man, but not for the consenting woman. Only the adulteress, and, by extension, the nun who engages in sexual intercourse, is punished. That is not to say that the consenting woman was not punished at all; she was, by the church and by society, in ways which are not included in the law. The church established a concept of personal responsibility in the matter of sins, which was to affect what happened to a woman who consented to illicit sexual activity. But we will return to this.

As far as rape is concerned, it may be pointed out that the *Ecloga* envisages it only in certain cases: an unmarried girl or a nun who is abducted. It does not arise in the case of the adulterous woman or of a widow, which, of course, is different from our own concept and legislation. It is only in the Macedonian legislation that the rape of a married woman is envisaged, in a somewhat more precise form than it had been in the *Digest*.[36] James Brundage has shown the evolution of a medieval definition of rape that approximates the modern one. He traces this in the writings of the great canonists, starting with Gratian. Rape becomes a crime against persons, and in its medieval definition involves both abduction and sexual intercourse. By the end of the Middle Ages, coitus with a child is equated with rape, because of the absence of the possibility of consent.[37] The law of the *Ecloga* has many of these elements and in some ways comes closer to the modern definition of rape as unlawful "carnal knowledge of a female by force or forcibly" and against her will. Rape is a legal category here, and abduction is not a necessary element in its definition. On the contrary, the use of force, which is common in abduction, is presumed to make non-consensual (as far as the woman is concerned) any intercourse subsequent to it. Statutory rape, although there is no term for it, is also a legal category in the Isaurian law code. Finally, while

[36] *Eisagoge* 40.44, and see above, note 24.

[37] J. A. Brundage, "Rape and Marriage," *Revue de droit canonique* 28 (1978), 62 ff.

the possibility of marriage between a raped woman and the man who raped her is not envisaged in the Isaurian legislation, as it apparently is in the medieval West, marriage is indeed encouraged as a remedy for seduction.

Thus both the issue of the consent of the woman and the encouragement of marriage play an important role in both the *Ecloga* and, many centuries later, in medieval canon law. One of the sources of these changes is common to both situations: it is the influence of Christianity and the church, which will be discussed below. The other is specific to the Isaurian emperors: they were very much interested in encouraging marriage. This may be seen in a number of their measures: the prerequisites for marriage were greatly simplified, and the impediments on marriage between unequal partners were lifted; divorce was made very difficult; Constantine V, in his struggle against the monasteries, apparently attacked the celibacy of monks and nuns, possibly as a symbolic gesture.[38] The innovations in the *Ecloga* are due to both social policy and the influence of the church.

I have concentrated on the *Ecloga* because its provisions form the basis of the medieval Byzantine definition of categories of illicit sexual behavior. Through the thirteenth century, most discussions of such matters quoted the law of the *Ecloga,* as incorporated in the *Basilics* with the slight emendations brought about by the Macedonians. The one exception to this statement is the legislation on abduction, so briefly treated in the *Ecloga,* and the subject of concern to the Macedonian emperors. As for the *Basilics,* they did, of course, include many elements of the Justinianic compilation, changing in the process both the vocabulary and, to some degree, the substance. The commentaries on the *Basilics* also refer to canonical legislation on these issues. A study of the pertinent passages of the *Basilics,* to test the coherence of a legislation that incorporated such disparate elements, would be a highly meritorious and rewarding exercise. It is not undertaken here, because the primary concern of this study is neither antiquarian nor is it with internal legal history,[39] but rather with those aspects of the law which were invoked in court or in other ways influenced perceptions and behavior; and that is the law of the *Ecloga.* It is, however, to be noted that the *Ecloga* gives a fairly schematic definition of what constitutes the crimes. It provides us with no rules of procedure or evidence, no guidance for seeking proof. That was left to the courts, and we will examine some court decisions in due course.

[38] See *Ecloga* 2.9.1–4; Theophanes, *Chronographia,* I (Bonn, 1839), 675–81.

[39] Besides, I have no competence to do such a study.

The Name of Seduction

The terminology of seduction, deflowering, in short, of φθορά, presents a certain interest, for it changes and develops over time. The Romans had explained the term *stuprum* by reference to the ancient Greek word φθορά.[40] When the Byzantines then created their own legal texts that were based on Roman law, they normally translated *stuprum* by two terms: στοῦπρον (στροῦπτον, στροῦπτρον) or φθορά. Thus *Basilics* 60.37.34 (rendering *D.* 48.5.35) uses the term φθορά in the text, but στροῦπτον in the commentary; at one point the commentator uses both terms: Σημείωσαι, τί ἐστὶ μοιχεία καὶ τί ἐστὶ στροῦπτον ἤτοι φθορά.[41] The two terms do not have a distinguishable difference in meaning.

On the other hand, there are also very broad definitions of *stuprum*, and some of the Greek equivalents given to the term are surprising. This is evident in the legal dictionaries, compilations which have several different strata and which therefore are difficult to place with chronological accuracy. The broadest definitions appear in the Lexicon αὐσηθ, a compilation whose archetype apparently dates from before the tenth century. In this lexicon, *stuprum* is translated as στοῦπτρον, ἀθεμιτογαμία, and further defined as follows: μοιχεία λέγεται ἐπὶ ὑπάνδρου, στροῦπτρον δὲ ἐπὶ παρθένου καὶ χήρας ἀθεμίτως συνευναζομένων. Finally, the broadest meaning for *stuprum* is ἁμάρτημα.[42]

The Lexicon Μαγκίπιουν, whose original, according to the editor, dates to the eleventh century, and which sometimes draws on material as far back as the sixth century, also has interesting translations and definitions: Σ 44: στούπρουμ: πορνεία; Σ 55: στούπρουμ: φθορὰ χήρας. λέγεται καὶ

[40] *D.* 48.5.6.

[41] Cf. *Bas.* 60.37.8 = *D.* 48.5.6. Although the text distinguishes between adultery and φθορά, the commentator, at another point, having said that στροῦπτον is committed with a widow or an unmarried girl, proceeds to add, strangely, τὸ δὲ στροῦπτον οἱ Ἕλληνες καλοῦσι μοιχείαν. In general, the commentaries on the *Basilics* and the Byzantine sources try to distinguish more clearly between *stuprum* and adultery, and the commentary on the *Basilics* (888) clarifies the issue of consent.

[42] L. Burgmann, "Lexicon αὐσηθ," *Fontes Minores* 8 (1990), 283, 284, 285. The word ἁμαρτία is also used in the *Eisagoge* (40.57), to describe the fornication of an unmarried man: ὁ ἔχων γυναῖκα καὶ πορνεύων, διὰ ιβ′ ἀλλακτῶν σωφρονιζέσθω· καὶ ὁ μὴ ἔχων δὲ καὶ τῇ αὐτῇ περιπίπτων ἁμαρτίᾳ, διὰ στ′ ἀλλακτῶν σωφρονιζέσθω.

ἀσέλγεια, φθορὰ παρθενίου, which must be translated as: "*Stuprum:* the corruption (seduction) of a widow; the corruption of a young man and of a virgin girl is also called *stuprum,*" a good Roman definition.[43]

With the exception of the last entry mentioned above, the others are very broad definitions, the broadest being "sin" (ἁμάρτημα). The second broadest is ἀθεμιτογαμία, which generally has the meaning "illicit (or, eventually, incestuous) marriage," but which here must rather mean illicit sexual intercourse. Thus the Byzantine concept of *stuprum* includes both a narrow sense, of illicit intercourse with a woman who is not married, or with a man, and a much wider sense of sins of the flesh. The second perhaps begins with the use of the word πορνεία to refer to *stuprum;* the first such use of the word in a text of civil law appears in the *Ecloga.*

Committing Fornication

As has already been mentioned, *Ecloga* 17.19 and 17.20 punish with beating the man who commits fornication (ὁ πορνεύων), doubling the punishment when the man is married. There are two points to be noted here: the use of the term itself and the fact that it is the marital status of the man that determines the level of the punishment, along with the condition of the woman, that is, whether she is a slave or a nun (17.22, 17.23).

Porneia is a term which can mean either fornication generally or, more specifically, prostitution or having commerce with a prostitute. In the language of the Justinianic corpus it carries both meanings, retaining for the most part that which is connected with prostitution.[44] Interestingly, a passage of the *Basilics* obscures the connection with prostitution which is clear in the Latin text, by using the term πορνεύω in a way that suggests the generalized meaning, by then current, of fornication. Thus, where the Latin text has: "Si ea quae tibi stupro cognita est passim venalem formam exhibuit ac prostituta meretricio more vulgo se praebuit, adulterii crimen in ea cessat" (*CJ* 9.9.22), the Greek text has: Ἐάν τις μοιχείαν ἁμαρτήσῃ πρὸς ἐκείνην πρὸς ἣν ἤδη πολλοὶ ἐπόρνευσαν, οὐκ ἐγκαλεῖται περὶ μοιχείας (*Bas.* 60.37.61). Thus incapacities which in the Roman text befell prostitutes now touch all women who have fornicated with many men.

In the *Ecloga,* the term is used a number of times. In 17.36, the topic is

[43] B. H. Stolte, "Lexicon Μαγκίπιουν," *Fontes Minores* 8 (1990), 355, 373, 374.

[44] Justinian, Novels, 18.5.41; 14 Praef. 1.31; 22.37; 18.5.41; 89.12.5.4.

abortion. Whereas the Justinianic Novel which is the basis of this text simply discusses the abortion and the punishment of the woman, with no reference to the sexual activity that resulted in pregnancy, the *Ecloga* says ἐὰν πορνεύσῃ, and if she then becomes pregnant and attempts to kill her fetus, she is to be beaten and exiled. The meaning of the term here is the general one of illicit sexual activity, since it seems to apply to all women, whether they are married (in which case the term adultery would have been more appropriate) or not. Similarly, chapter 2.9.2 states that a marriage is dissolved if the wife πορνεύσῃ. Here too the term has a general meaning, since the legally accurate word would have been μοιχεύσῃ. The inaccuracy, or, more correctly, the generalized meaning, does not come from the late Antique past: Justinian had used the correct term "adultery" when speaking of this type of divorce.[45]

The generalized meaning of the word πορνεία owes much to the Scriptures and to the church fathers. This is abundantly clear in the text concerning divorce for adultery, which is directly connected to the pertinent passages in the New Testament, namely, Matt. 5:32 (πᾶς ὁ ἀπολύων τὴν γυναῖκα αὐτοῦ παρεκτὸς λόγου *πορνείας* ποιεῖ αὐτὴν μοιχευθῆναι) and Matt. 19:9.[46] Besides, the word, as used in the New Testament and by the church fathers, frequently carries the general meaning of fornication.[47] Ecclesiastical literature uses the term the same way: the demon of fornication (ὁ δαίμων τῆς πορνείας) is responsible for feelings of lust, whether the object is a married woman, an unmarried woman, or indeed a man.[48] Thus in the *Pratum Spirituale* of John Moschos, compiled in the 630s, the verb πορνεύω is used to denote illicit sexual activity, as in the case of the man who fornicated with the wife of the tavern-keeper (ἐπόρνευσεν εἰς τὴν γυναῖκα τοῦ καπήλου), and in a sense that is connected with the older meaning of going to a whorehouse or having commerce with a prostitute.[49] No differentiation is made between fornication and adultery. Thus fornication is a sin of the flesh rather

[45] Novels 22.15.1 and 117.8.2.

[46] See *Ecloga* 2.9.1, 1.276.

[47] See 1 Cor. 7:2: διὰ τὰς πορνείας (to avoid fornication) ἕκαστος τὴν ἑαυτοῦ γυναῖκα ἐχέτω, and 1 Cor. 6:18: φεύγετε τὴν πορνείαν. Πᾶν ἁμάρτημα ὃ ἐὰν ποιήσῃ ἄνθρωπος ἐκτὸς τοῦ σώματος ἐστιν, ὁ δὲ πορνεύων εἰς τὸ ἴδιον σῶμα ἁμαρτάνει. Cf. also St. John Chrysostom, *De Virginitate*, passim.

[48] See Laiou, *Mariage, amour et parenté*, chap. 2.

[49] *Pratum Spirituale*, ed. J.-P. Migne, Patrologia Graeca (hereafter PG), 87.3, nos. 14, 45, 97, 136, 188. See also PG 99, col. 1728 and G. A. Ralles and M. Potles,

than a legal category in the ecclesiastical sources (for the canonical ones, see below), and this sense eventually passed into legal texts as well, for example, in the passages of the *Ecloga* (17.36 and 2.9.2) mentioned above.[50]

Since both men and women are prone to sin, the question arises whether the appearance of a category of sins of the flesh has an influence on the development of the concept of individual consent and responsibility, especially in the case of women. We have seen that civil legislation of the Roman and late Antique periods for the most part considers the man as the actor in and initiator of sexual crimes, with one exception, connected with abduction, which will be discussed in the next chapter; and that the consent of the woman is invoked primarily in order to determine the level of punishment of the man. In the *Ecloga,* the situation is somewhat different. In the two passages already mentioned (17.36 and 2.9.2), the verb πορνεύω is used in the active voice, and its subject is the woman, who is thus responsible for her actions and punished for them. In *Ecloga* 17.29, the consent of the girl (circumscribed, however, by that of her parents) can erase the crime. Is this a real rather than an illusory phenomenon, and do we have a new concept of the responsibility of the woman in sexual activity?

The last set of sources to which we must turn are the canonical sources, which may provide at least partial answers to these questions. The canons of the fourth-century Fathers are, indeed, instructive. Canon 21 of St. Basil does differentiate between πορνεία and μοιχεία, in terms which are consistent with the principles of Roman law, if *porneia* is taken as equivalent to *stuprum*. The married man who has intercourse with an unmarried woman is guilty of πορνεία, not μοιχεία. St. Basil does not agree with this principle, but, he says, it has been established by custom, and so he is forced to accept it.[51] Canon 38 of St. Basil establishes the principle that girls who follow (their lovers), even though their parents are unwilling to have them marry, commit fornication. If subsequently the parents agree, it is permitted for them to

---

Σύνταγμα τῶν θείων καὶ ἱερῶν κανόνων (hereafter Ralles-Potles), 6 vols. (Athens, 1852–59; repr. 1966), IV, 438.

[50] On a similar difference between Roman *stuprum* and Christian fornication, see Treggiari, *Roman Marriage,* p. 11 and chap. 9.

[51] P.-P. Joannou, *Discipline générale antique (IVe–IXe s.),* II, *Les canons des pères grecs* (Rome, 1963), canon 21. Cf. Ralles-Potles, IV, 149–51, with the 12th-century commentaries.

marry; but the girl is subject to three years' penance. This must be the direct antecedent of the provision in *Ecloga* 17.29 on consensual *stuprum* and the remedy of marriage. Canon 9 is a commentary on Matt. 5:32 and Matt. 19:9, which forbid divorce except for reason of fornication (παρεκτὸς λόγου πορνείας). Once again, St. Basil insists, as in canon 21, that the spirit of the Gospel would argue that a marriage should be dissolved whether the man or the woman is guilty of fornication, but custom has decreed otherwise, so that women are expected to retain their husbands, whether these are guilty of fornication or adultery (καὶ μοιχεύοντας ἄνδρας καὶ ἐν πορνείᾳ ὄντας). It then proceeds to discuss the circumstances in which a woman may be labeled an adulteress, circumstances that include the case of a woman who left her husband because he beat her or was a fornicator, if she subsequently lived with another man. Finally, when it comes to establishing the ecclesiastical penalties for various sexual crimes, the canons distinguish clearly between fornication and adultery, adultery carrying the heavier penalty, and the penalty for fornication being dependent on the marital status of the man. Canon 21 of St. Basil says that a married man who is guilty of fornication should be subjected to longer punishment than the (unmarried) man. The twelfth-century canonists elaborate on the rationale, saying that the unmarried man has some extenuating circumstances "because of the natural need" (Zonaras), and that the exact determination of the length of penance for a married man is left to the discretion of the confessor (Balsamon). The ecclesiastical punishment for fornication and adultery differ from one church father to another. St. Basil punishes fornication with the penance of a seven-year exclusion from communion, and adultery with fifteen years (canons 58, 59). This is exactly the spirit adopted by the *Ecloga* (17.19, 17.20). For St. Gregory of Nyssa, fornication is punishable with penance for five years, while other sins that also do injustice to others should receive double the punishment.

The contribution of the church to the development of the concept of sexual crime and that of individual responsibility is very important. *Porneia*, fornication, is almost a legal category in the canonical writings; but it also becomes a sin, and an all-embracing one: it is the complex of sins of the flesh, and so it appears in non-canonical writings.[52] St. Gregory of Nyssa, speaking of the various sins of the flesh, makes the point clearly: "whatever

[52] St. John Chrysostom, *In illud, propter fornicationes uxorem*, PG 51, cols. 213–17.

is not legitimate is fully illegitimate" (πᾶν τὸ μὴ νόμιμον παράνομον πάντως), which Balsamon glossed by saying that there is only one form of legitimate sexual relationship between man and woman; everything outside that is illegitimate.[53] At the same time, the general sin is subdivided into particular and different ones. As Balsamon put it in his commentary to canon 21 of St. Basil, fornication is not of a single type, nor is it always punished in the same manner. The level of punishment is a function of a number of things: the marital status of both partners, age, the sincerity of contrition, and so on.[54] The sanctity of marriage is safeguarded, as is made quite clear by the fact that the married fornicator is punished more severely than the unmarried one. And the woman is almost as responsible for her actions as the man is. Her consent to a course of action not only helps establish the level of punishment for the man, but also determines her own punishment.

Let us now return to the *Ecloga*. The Isaurians introduce several differentiations into the old category of *stuprum:* sexual relations between men are called ἀσέλγεια (17.38); sex with an unmarried girl is a category to which much attention is given, and where the consent and the age of the girl play a primary role. The term *porneia* embraces other categories of sexual activity, either implicitly or explicitly: explicitly for intercourse with a slave woman (17.21 and 17.22) and a nun (17.3); implicitly with widows or divorced women and possibly with prostitutes (17.19 and 17.20). The use of the term and the increased punishment for the married man are similar to what we find in ecclesiastical sources and probably derive from them; but "porneia" as a legal category in civil law first appears in the *Ecloga*. The increased importance of the woman's consent as a differentiating factor may also be due to ecclesiastical influence. In the *Ecloga,* the woman's consent does not bring direct punishment upon her, except in the case of adultery. The question must now be asked whether the consenting woman was truly not punished by Byzantine society.

[53] Ralles-Potles, IV, 312; commentary on canon 4 of St. Gregory of Nyssa.

[54] Cf. Laiou, *Mariage, amour et parenté,* chap. 2.

2. With Her Consent

We have seen that the consent or absence of consent of the woman to illicit sexual activity plays quite an important role both in canonical statements and in the *Ecloga*. The question of consent is, of course, a vexed one. It is important to determine how consent is established, what constitutes free consent, what the role of coerced consent is, and what level, if any, of coercion is deemed acceptable. These questions will be treated in subsequent chapters. For the moment, our investigation will focus on the consequences of consent for the woman. It is, after all, possible for consent to be a primary factor in establishing the nature of a crime and the penalties for the man, but without immediate and overt consequences for the woman. What was the situation in the Byzantine Empire? Was the woman who consented to unlawful sexual acts punished, and if so, how and in what circumstances? Since our focus here is on consent, the categories of illicit sexual activity will not be treated separately, as they would be if one were simply trying to list the penalties involved for each one. Adultery will be kept out of the investigation, since consent was not of capital importance in the legal approach to it. The topics that best lend themselves to our investigation are consensual sex outside marriage and abduction. These were two situations in which unlawful sexual activity could take place, and in which a woman might give her consent to it, or might be thought to give her consent to it. The issues involving consent are (a) whether there is punishment of the woman who consents to elopement, or abduction, or sex with the man with whom she runs away or who abducts her and (b) whether the woman's consent to marry the man is acceptable, and thus whether a marriage may result from elopement or abduction.[1]

Let us start with ecclesiastical legislation. Canon 38 of St. Basil, already mentioned,[2] bears closer investigation, and must be studied together with

[1] For a discussion of abduction and betrothal, see Karlin-Hayter, "Further Notes on Byzantine Marriage." My concern here is less with abduction itself and more with the effects of consent on the woman.

[2] See above, pp. 130–31.

the canons concerning abduction.[3] The situation envisaged by canon 38 is the following: a girl follows a man without the consent of her parents. If the parents then change their views, a marriage can take place. Nevertheless, the girl, who is considered guilty of fornication, is punished by not being able to take communion for three years. This seems to refer to what we would call elopement; the canon itself does not state explicitly that the elopement was attended by intercourse, although the word "fornication" suggests it. The twelfth-century commentators do not mention elopement in such a case, concentrating rather on consensual sexual intercourse, in the absence of agreement of the girl's parents, that is, a situation similar to that envisaged by *Ecloga* 17.29. The canons on abduction try to differentiate between abduction by force, without the consent of the girl, abduction with her consent, and feigned abduction, properly speaking elopement.

When the canonical legislation of the fourth century was being enacted, civil law punished abduction extremely harshly, especially after the law of Constantine I of 326, which punished with death the abductor and the consenting woman as well as all accomplices. The ecclesiastical legislation, while keeping the civil legislation in mind, was much less harsh. Indeed, canon 30 of St. Basil is exceedingly lenient, punishing the abductor and his accomplices with a three-year abstention from communion; compare this to the same Father's provision for punishment of the fornicator, who is to be excluded from communion for seven years (canon 59). Canon 30 then proceeds to differentiate between willing and unwilling abduction: if the abduction does not involve force, if the woman is a widow under her own authority (αὐτεξουσία), and if there is no *stuprum* beforehand, then there is no punishment for the man or the woman. Thus there are three factors which allow abduction to go unpunished: that there be no injury to the rights of others (those who might have the woman in their authority and who thus had the power to arrange her marriage), that the woman be willing, and that there be no intercourse attendant on the abduction. This is abduction with intent to marry. What must be stressed is that for ecclesiastical legislation the crime of abduction, so heinous to civil law, was not a crime of grave consequence. It could easily be remedied by marriage, unless the abducted girl was someone else's fiancée (canon 22 of St. Basil). Much more serious, for the canonical

[3] The canons on abduction are canons 22, 30, 53 of St. Basil; canon 27 of Chalcedon; canon 92 of the Council in Trullo; canon 11 of the Council of Ankyra.

legislation of the fourth century, was illicit sexual intercourse or fornication, even though it might be a marriage strategy, and a way of forcing unwilling parents to give their consent to marriage. St. Basil admitted that this situation too could be remedied by marriage; but it was punishable by *epitimia* of four years, whether the woman had consented to intercourse or not (canons 22 and 25). The combination of canons 22, 25, and 38 suggests that in the case of fornication, even if marriage was intended, both the man and the woman suffered ecclesiastical punishment. The marriage itself was somewhat tainted, since its origins were improper, involving unlawful sex (canon 26 of St. Basil). The relative leniency toward abduction and the condemnation of sexual intercourse before marriage runs through canonical legislation, particularly that of St. Basil, and the decisions of Byzantine judges throughout the history of the empire. Perhaps it reflects a more general social attitude that places a very great value on the girl's virginity at marriage, an attitude characteristic of Mediterranean societies.[4]

The canonical legislation of the early centuries, however, is not consistent, especially with regard to the effects of abduction, that is, whether the consent of the woman to abduction permits marriage or not. While St. Basil allows the marriage, other canons, such as canon 27 of the Council of Chalcedon and canon 92 of the Council in Trullo forbid it, being consonant with the civil legislation. Clearly, the church had difficulty reconciling a number of imperatives: that of consistency with civil law, the need to discourage the violence inherent in abduction, the need on the other hand to correct an existing illegal situation through the institution of marriage. The matter became particularly complex when the woman consented either to elopement, abduction, or illicit intercourse. In turn, twelfth-century canonists tried to make sense of the set of situations that the canons had envisaged. In the process, of course, the canonists also brought to bear the experience and the concerns of contemporary society. The principal differentiation in the commentaries is between abduction without sexual intercourse on the one hand, and fornication before marriage on the other; a strenuous but barely successful effort is further made to differentiate between elopement and abduction with the consent of the woman.

The twelfth-century canonists also had to take into account the civil

[4] See Jack Goody, *The Development of the Family and Marriage in Europe* (Cambridge, 1983), 29–30.

legislation which had developed in the meantime. That legislation made no mention of elopement, which could, however, be subsumed under the provisions governing φθορά with a consenting woman. As for abduction, the laws were relatively clear. If a man abducts a woman forcibly, with the use of arms, and sleeps with her, he is to be killed. His property and that of his accomplices will be confiscated and given to the woman. If arms are not used, the punishment is less harsh. The consent of the woman to the abduction is immaterial in fixing the man's punishment; indeed the punishment is the same even if a man abducts his own fiancée. Marriage between a woman and her abductor is strictly forbidden, even if the woman, her parents, and the man wish it.[5] Clearly, a problem arises because these provisions do not permit the regularization of irregular situations. The twelfth-century commentators tried to deal with some of the problems.

Zonaras is perhaps the most coherent. In his commentary on canon 30 of St. Basil, he explains the circumstances in which a voluntary abduction will go unpunished: a woman is *sui juris,* she surrenders herself voluntarily, no coercion is involved, and there has been no previous seduction (φθορά) or secret copulation. In such a case, there is no punishment of the man, and, it is implied but not stated, a marriage may be contracted.[6] The words of the canon, "let us not concern ourselves with appearances," allow Zonaras to give an example of what situation is being envisaged. The canon refers explicitly to a widow *sui juris,* in words that are ambiguous, and Zonaras explains that some commentators have taken this to mean that widows wore a distinctive dress.[7] However, he says, the better explanation is that a woman, ashamed to give herself to her lover perhaps because he is lowborn, pretends to be abducted but in truth follows him voluntarily. In such a case, the provisions on abduction do not apply, since the abduction is only a pretext. He then refers the reader to canon 53 of St. Basil, which speaks of the feigned abduction of

[5] These provisions, as outlined here, are a combination of *Bas.* 60.58.1 and Novel 35 of Leo VI. The *Basilics* does not refer to sexual intercourse but only to the abduction itself. Michael Psellos, in his versification of the laws, also conflates the provisions of the *Basilics* and the Novel of Leo VI: G. Weiss, "Die juristische Bibliothek des Michael Psellos," *Jahrbuch der Österreichischen Byzantinistik* 26 (1977), 91.

[6] If the woman is not *sui juris,* those who have her under their authority may dissolve the marriage; Ralles-Potles, IV, 169–71.

[7] The word σχῆμα may mean either "appearance" or "pretense."

a slave woman (a freed slave?) and allows the marriage because there is no real abduction. On the other hand, the unmarried girl who sleeps with her lover is guilty of fornication; her consent earns her an *epitimion* of three years, but she may marry her lover if the parents give their assent (commentary on canon 38 of St. Basil). Thus marriage is the remedy for both voluntary abduction and consensual fornication. Indeed, both actions seem to be paths leading to marriage; the rights of the parents or persons who have authority over the woman are safeguarded, since their consent is essential for the marriage. Zonaras does not much exercise himself about the differences between voluntary abduction and elopement. For him, the important point is the woman's consent.

Balsamon, on the other hand, who has a much stricter attitude toward illicit sexual activity and who also has a stronger concern for harmonizing civil and ecclesiastical law, is forced to do somersaults that have a certain elegance, but are hard to duplicate in reality. He, too, recognizes the reality that voluntary abduction is in truth a way for people to force their parents' hand and get married. In a *responsum* to Patriarch Mark of Alexandria, he deals with an example from real life either presented by the patriarch or made up by Balsamon himself: a woman was being forced by her father to marry someone she did not want; her father actually betrothed her, not in a church, but by written contracts (δι' ἐγγράφων δεσμωτικῶν). She then sent word to her lover who came, one night, with some low-class (ἀπαιδεύτων) companions of his, abducted her with her consent (ἥρπασε θέλουσαν), and took her to his house in another village. The question is whether they may marry, since the parents are now willing to have the marriage take place. Balsamon's answer is uncompromising: they may not marry, according to the provisions of *Bas*. 60.58.1, which also states that the parents, if they agree to the marriage, are to be exiled. Furthermore, the abductor and his accomplices will be anathematized, according to the provisions of canon 27 of the Council of Chalcedon.[8] Thus the consent of the woman does not at all alleviate the penalty, as indeed it does not in formal civil law, but she herself is not punished. And yet this case has all the elements of elopement: the girl wishes to marry a man and the abduction is only a feint, presumably to protect her reputation; the parents' hand is forced, as it often is in such cases; in the end, all the relevant parties want the marriage. It might be thought that Balsamon ob-

[8] Ralles-Potles, IV, 495–96.

jected to the marriage because the girl was already engaged, but he does not at all mention this in his argumentation and, since the engagement was a civil one, not an ecclesiastical one, he perhaps did not find it binding in this respect.[9] His objections, therefore, are on the formalistic grounds that this was abduction, and the civil laws absolutely forbade marriages resulting from abduction.

This position is evident in his other commentaries as well. His commentary on canon 30 of St. Basil deals with the punishment of a man who abducts a woman (*epitimia* for three years). The canon also says that if the abduction was voluntary, and there has been no sexual intercourse, the man shall go blameless. Unlike Zonaras, Balsamon differentiates between civil and ecclesiastical punishment. The girl's consent frees the man only of ecclesiastical punishment; he remains subject to the severe penalties of *Bas.* 60.58.1. For Balsamon, consent of the woman is irrelevant, as it was in civil law. He further adds that a case which came before the imperial tribunal, concerning the abduction of the daughter of Neophotistos by a man named Seth, was adjudicated according to the provisions of civil law.[10]

A problem arises when Balsamon then tries to deal with the part of the canon that refers to the voluntary abduction of a woman *sui juris,* which Zonaras considered to be equivalent to elopement. Balsamon, in an embarrassed statement, says that, "if you should wish to say that there was no true abduction of the woman but a pretence . . . , then neither the *epitimia* will apply, nor the laws that punish the abductors." This is formally acceptable, but it gives no handle on how to treat real situations, for it does not state the conditions that would differentiate an elopement from a voluntary abduction: presumably, the difference would be whatever the various parties and the confessor stated them to be. The matter reappears in the commentary on canon

[9] Canon 22 of St. Basil, among others, states that a betrothed girl who has been abducted must be returned to her first fiancé. He is then free to marry her or not. Betrothal was a civil contract until the time of Leo VI; nevertheless, the church increasingly assimilated it to marriage, as may be seen in canon 98 of the Council in Trullo. When the early church legislation on abduction was being elaborated, the (civil) betrothal was considered binding for these purposes. But by the time of Balsamon, one could argue that only a betrothal with ecclesiastical blessing was binding.

[10] Cf. Balsamon's commentary on canons 67 of the Apostles, 27 of Chalcedon, and 92 of Trullo, where he insists on the provisions of civil law, the punishment of the man, and the prohibition of marriage. The woman's consent remains irrelevant.

38 of St. Basil, concerning the penalties imposed on a woman who "follows her lover" without the consent of her parents. Both Zonaras and Balsamon specify that this means that the girl had sexual intercourse with the man. Balsamon, but not Zonaras, then specifically explains that this does not refer to abduction, and therefore the remedies pertinent to it are not pertinent to abduction. In this case of consensual sex, when there is no abduction involved, the consent of the parents, obtained after the fact, can validate the marriage that had taken place, and that was considered fornication in the absence of parental consent.[11] But, says Balsamon, the situation is now different from what it was in the fourth century. Then, marriages were contracted by consent alone; this meant that the couple could marry and the girl could suffer the ecclesiastical punishment (three years without communion) subsequently. In his own day, where no marriage could take place without the benediction of the church, he submitted that a valid marriage could be contracted only after the three years (or, the saving statement, whatever length of punishment the bishop had ordered) had elapsed.

This embarrassment, and Balsamon's very strict interpretation of the canons regarding abduction, resulted from the development of marriage strategies among the aristocracy of the twelfth century, some of which very clearly had Balsamon's approval. Abduction and elopement were not unknown in the eleventh century. Then, as in the fourth century, and as in parts of Greece until recently, this kind of action could be taken in order to force the hand of unwilling parents. The fact, noted by anthropologists and historians of Antiquity, does not really need elaboration, beyond the mere notice that it evidently existed in Byzantine times as well, although I do not think it was widespread.[12] But the twelfth century was eminently the century in which the marriages of the aristocracy were very tightly controlled by the families, the

[11] It may be noted again that this is the situation, and the solution, envisaged by *Ecloga* 17.29. The canonists never refer to this law code, promulgated by Iconoclastic emperors and abrogated by the Macedonians.

[12] See, among others, Judith Evans-Grubb, "Abduction Marriage in Antiquity: A Law of Constantine (*CTh* IX.24.1) and Its Social Context," *Journal of Roman Studies* 79 (1989), 59–83; Michael Angold, "The Wedding of Digenes Akrites: Love and Marriage in the Eleventh and Twelfth Centuries," *Πρακτικά του Α΄ Διεθνούς Συμποσίου, η Καθημερινή Ζωή στο Βυζάντιο* (Athens, 1989), 201–15; Michael Herzfeld, "Gender Pragmatics: Agency, Speech and Bride-Theft in a Cretan Mountain Village," *Anthropology* 9 (1985), 25–44; and Karlin-Hayter, "Further Notes on Byz-

state, and the church, each trying to establish its preeminent right. This was, furthermore, a period when mésalliance was abhorred and severely punished by none other than Emperor Manuel I, with whose measures, extending to the mutilation of the guilty men, Balsamon apparently agreed.[13] Abduction for the purpose of, at worst, mésalliance or, at best, marriage to someone of whom the parents disapproved was not in the interest of aristocratic society. Balsamon's own statements make his concern clear: in his commentary on canon 92 of the Council in Trullo, he specifically connects abduction with mésalliance: "some say that he who abducts a woman for the purpose of marriage, perhaps because she was unworthy of his family, . . . does no wrong." He insists that marriage cannot be allowed in such cases, because it destroys social order (τὴν εὐταξίαν τῶν πόλεων). As for sexual intercourse before marriage, it is, as we have seen, the major concern of all ecclesiastical law. Balsamon allows marriage to correct this act, because he cannot do otherwise, but he makes it very difficult.

Let us now recapitulate the canonical regulations insofar as the consent of the woman is concerned. The canons of St. Basil give the consent of the woman the greatest role: it is what differentiates between abduction and elopement; the woman's consent to marriage, always subject to the consent of the parents, can correct the crimes of abduction and fornication. The church's effort is to strengthen marriage, and by that token the role of the consent of the woman is strengthened, although a different position is taken by the Council of Chalcedon and the Council in Trullo. This importance of the consent of the woman is preserved in the commentary of Zonaras, but weakened by the statements of Balsamon, which reflect the twelfth-century concerns of aristocratic society with tightly controlled marriages. Churchmen did not speak with a single voice any more than laymen did. The consent of the woman to illicit intercourse also carries punishment for her, both in the canons of St. Basil and in the twelfth-century commentaries. Thus consent, in this case, establishes legal categories, differentiates the penalties involved, and recognizes the responsibility of the woman by punishing her. It is true that these illicit activities could lead to love matches, otherwise not provided for either by the law or by custom, which revolved around arranged mar-

---

antine Marriage." I argue below against the notion that abduction was a common phenomenon in Byzantium, especially in the 11th–12th centuries.

[13] See Laiou, *Mariage, amour et parenté,* chap. 1.

riages. However, it was not, as has been argued for Western medieval societies, "rape" that permitted this relative freedom of choice to women (and men), but rather elopement, however nebulously defined, which forced the parents to give their consent because of the fear of social stigma attached to a woman who had lost her virginity.[14]

Where civil law is concerned, there appear to be two strains of thought with regard to the effects of consensual sexual intercourse on the consenting (unmarried) woman. One strain, which proved not to be a prevalent one, is represented by the enactment of Constantine I on abduction (326).[15] This law, the harshest ever passed, provides for the execution in a degrading and horrible manner (by crucifixion, burning, or being thrown to the beasts) of the man who seizes a girl ("invitam . . . vel volentem abduxerit").[16] The consent or otherwise of the woman plays no role in the punishment of the man, nor, indeed, does her consent make it possible to correct the crime by marriage. Constantine invokes the foolishness and inconstancy of the female mind, which caused ancient lawgivers to deny women the right to testify. However, the same disadvantages do not protect her if she consented to her abduction. If the consent was overt, she is to suffer the same punishment as the man. If she claimed that she had been forced, this too will avail her only a little. Constantine does not admit the possibility of non-complicity of the girl in abduction for, as he puts it, girls should stay indoors or scream for help if they are attacked outside the house; if they did not do so, then they consented to the abduction even if they claimed they did not. The punishment, however, is lighter, the girl merely losing the right to inherit from her parents.

There are several points of interest in this piece of legislation, whose gruesome provisions (including, among other things, the execution of the girl's nurse by pouring molten lead down her throat) have excited the interest and even passion of a number of scholars.[17] First, the consent of the girl is

[14] For the idea that rape created greater freedom of action, see Brundage, "Rape and Marriage," 74–75.

[15] *CTh* 9.24.

[16] This is the interpretation of Evans-Grubb, "Abduction Marriage," 66, with which I agree. This part of the law was made somewhat less harsh in 349, when simple capital punishment (execution by the sword) was substituted: ibid., 66, with reference to *CTh* 24.2.

[17] Apart from Evans-Grubb, see Denise Grodzynski, "Ravies et coupables," *Mélanges de l'École française de Rome* 96 (1984), 697–726, who believes that Constantine wanted primarily to punish the consenting girl, and for that reason assumed her

indeed important, not for the abductor but for her. Second, there are two levels of consent that are envisaged here: active (and admitted?) consent and the absence of evident opposition, which is taken to imply consent. No woman is presumed innocent here. Third, the statements about the girl essentially inviting abduction by her behavior (not staying indoors) or not proving her opposition (by crying out to alert the neighbors) smacks of folk wisdom rather than jurisprudence. Judith Evans-Grubb suggests, undoubtedly correctly, that the assumptions of the Constantinian legislation about the girl's overt or covert consent are no different from those of Mediterranean societies generally, which consider that all abducted girls have agreed to the abduction.[18] In that sense, the edict is revealing, although its unrelieved harshness suggests that it was promulgated for a particular reason and provoked by a particular case, perhaps close to the emperor's family.[19] It is revealing precisely because it brings to the fore a certain concept of the woman's guilt and a concept of consent which we will find elsewhere, though rarely in official documents.[20]

The attitude toward the consenting woman which is expressed in Constantine's law was short-lived. The tenor of his legislation was progressively weakened, and his law was finally replaced by an edict of Justinian I on abduction (533).[21] In this piece of legislation, the consent of the woman plays no role at all: the man and his accomplices are punished by death, whether the woman had been willing or not. Furthermore, a woman who appears to have consented did not truly consent, for "unless a man solicited her and deceived her by his detestable arts, he would not have been able to induce her to submit to such dishonor: "nisi etiam eam sollicitaverit, nisi odiosis artibus circumvenerit, non facit eam velle in tantum dedecus sese prodere." Thus the woman's (or the girl's) consent to abduction is considered from the

---

to be responsible before the law; and Beaucamp, *Le statut de la femme à Byzance*, 111 ff.

[18] Evans-Grubb, "Abduction Marriage," 64–65.

[19] A. H. M. Jones, *Constantine and the Conversion of Europe* (London, 1948), 243 ff, suggests a connection with the fate of Constantine's son Crispus, without, however, any evidence.

[20] See below, especially V.

[21] See *CTh* 9.24.2 and 9.24.3, and *CJ* 9.13.1, *D.* 1.3.53; cf. Evans-Grubb, "Abduction Marriage," 76 ff.

beginning uninformed and therefore valueless. This provides protection for the woman; but since marriage is not allowed, there is certainly dishonor involved. As far as consent is concerned, it is not at all taken into consideration. It reappears with the *Ecloga,* not in the case of abduction but in the case of consensual sex, and it does play a role there, although it carries no punishment. Macedonian legislation on abduction admits that the woman may have consented, but gives no legal weight to her consent.

The only time, after 326, that the woman who consents to sex outside of marriage is held responsible to the extent of being punished is in the fourteenth century, in a Novel of Andronikos II (1306). The Novel is short, and may thus be quoted in full.[22]

> Let it be declared and obeyed, that a woman, and especially a virgin, should not throw her honor at the feet of the first comer, but if anyone should force her in the wilderness, let her be avenged according to the laws; if, however, she should give herself willingly, let her be chastened by having her hair shorn and by a dishonorable parade. Nor should the seducer be allowed to go unpunished in either case,[23] but he will certainly pay to the Fisc the legal fine. And if he cannot, still he will be held responsible according to the law.

The legal aspects of this text have already been discussed by Tourtoglou. Some points, however, should be brought out here. On the issue of consent, we note a reference to the ancient distinction, enunciated in Deut. 22:23–24, between seducing a woman in the city (where she is assumed to have consented) and in the country (where the absence of consent is assumed). In case of rape, the man would suffer the legal punishment, presumably the one in *Basilics* 60.37.79, by which the man gives the girl one-third of his property and is further punished by having his nose slit. If the girl was willing, he is punished by a fine, to be paid to the fisc: we notice that the remedy of marriage is not accepted here. The fine is the well-known fine for *partheno-phthoria,* which appears in the documentary sources soon afterwards. What

[22] I am using the edition in *JGR,* I, 535; this is Novel 26 of Andronikos II, para. 3.

[23] Tourtoglou, *Παρθενοφθορία,* 75–76, quite rightly says that the law as published in this edition makes no sense, since in the first case the seducer's punishment has already been mentioned ("according to the laws"). He prefers another reading, namely, τῷ δέ γε φθορεῖ μὴ τὸ ἀζήμιον ᾖ, which would be translated "nor should the seducer go unpunished," and I have adopted this reading here.

is of particular interest for us here is the punishment of the woman, who is publicly shamed. If imposed, the parade and public shearing of the hair could be a very harsh punishment indeed.[24] It is evident that this law is an anomaly, both in its language and in the penalties it imposes. Indeed, in the form in which it is published, it is, in the first instance, a decision of the synod, which Patriarch Athanasios I proposed to Andronikos II, who then promulgated it as law. Its ecclesiastical provenance, and especially its attribution to a patriarch of strict morals whose purpose was the moral purification of society, explains its tone and the culpability attributed to the woman. The spirit of it, however, was probably very close to the informal punishment that women who had engaged in consensual sex outside marriage could suffer: if marriage did not take place, the girl was most probably shamed and dishonored, even if there were no public parading involved. This would have been a deterrent more powerful than the law was for men, and it may be the reason why the law does not, usually, mention a specific punishment for the woman; the woman's punishment would have taken place outside the realm of law, the man's inside it.[25] This statement, of course, refers to the majority of women, not to members of the aristocracy, whose mores varied with the times. In the twelfth century, aristocratic mores were nothing to boast about, but people were not punished for them, either formally or informally. By contrast, Zoe Zaoutzaina, who had been Leo VI's mistress and later became his second wife, did suffer public shame after her death, for her tombstone read "the poor woman was a daughter of Babylon."[26]

There are thus two strains of thought in civil legislation with regard to the woman who consents to illicit sexual activity. One (Justinian I's) is that a woman is not fully responsible for her actions in this respect and must be protected. The other strain (Constantine I's) is that she is fully responsible for what takes place, even if her consent is not overt and admitted, and must be punished. I have suggested here that in reality there are forms of punishment,

[24] On this, see Ph. Koukoules, *Βυζαντινῶν βίος καὶ πολιτισμός*, 6 vols. (Athens, 1948–57), III, 187 ff.

[25] For an inkling of such a social attitude, see canon 34 of St. Basil, which specifies that the ecclesiastical punishment of a repentant adulteress should not be made public, so as to spare her life.

[26] George the Monk, "De Leone Basilii Filii," *Theophanes Continuatus*, ed. I. Bekker (Bonn, 1938), 857. On all this, see Laiou, *Mariage, amour et parenté*, chap. 2.

mostly shame and dishonor, which the law does not enunciate, with the exception of Novel 26 of Andronikos II, which codifies them.

The Evidence of the Courts

A certain amount of evidence, both on how the law actually functioned and on the treatment of the consenting woman, may be found in court records. How much a reflection these are of reality is a vexed question, the answer to which must depend on the kind of reality one has in mind. It can certainly be argued that court cases do not reflect a statistical reality, since the majority of cases, especially those regarding sexual matters, would have been resolved informally and without recourse to the courts. I do indeed assume that any case that appeared in court was, in some way, extraordinary and thus not reflective of everyday reality. A second possible objection is more difficult to evaluate. The compilations we have—essentially the eleventh-century *Peira* and the thirteenth-century dossier of Demetrios Chomatianos—were undoubtedly made selectively, and the exact purpose of the compiler remains obscure. Thus it is theoretically possible that only those solutions which held a particular interest or curiosity for the compiler were included. If this is the case, it introduces a second remove from reality, since the compiler may have excluded from the collection those solutions which were exactly according to the law, and left us only the more complex solutions, which would be of interest to lawyers but would not be nearly so instructive in terms of social history.[27] To this argument I have no general answer. Each case must be taken as it stands, and the conclusions drawn from it can be instructive only to the degree that they show a gamut of legal possibilities, or to the degree that they encapsulate thoughts and concepts that are also present elsewhere, either in jurisprudential, ideological, or literary statements. The final caveat is connected with chronology: the legal cases that have survived, namely, the *Peira,* and the decisions of Chomatianos and Apokaukos, are concentrated in the eleventh through early thirteenth centuries, while the register of the acts of

[27] For a study of the possible purpose of the *Peira,* see N. Oikonomides, "The 'Peira' of Eustathius Rhomaios: An Abortive Attempt to Innovate in Byzantine Law," *Fontes Minores* 7 (1984), 169–92. The register of the acts of the Patriarchate of Constantinople is not, I believe, selective in the same way. As for the acts of John Apokaukos, they have survived in a haphazard fashion, and I do not believe that they form a compilation with any particular purpose in mind.

the Patriarchate of Constantinople is richest for the eleventh through fourteenth centuries, with only a few extant cases from earlier periods. This must be kept in mind, but there is nothing much to be done about it.

Three cases will be examined below, all referring to illicit sexual activity to which the woman had consented. The first case took place in Epiros in the thirteenth century.[28] A man named John, son of Rados, from the theme of Devol, presented to Demetrios Chomatianos a question about the following case. A married man had deflowered (φθείρας) Rados' sister, Stanna, who was unmarried and a virgin, with her consent but without the knowledge of her brother (προαιρέσει μὲν αὐτῆς, ἀγνοοῦντος δὲ τοῦ αὐταδέλφου αὐτῆς). The brother requested a written opinion as to whether the man was punishable. Chomatianos' court functioned both as a civil and as an ecclesiastical tribunal, and he himself was deeply learned in the civil law. His *responsum* to this query took into account both civil and ecclesiastical legislation. First he turned to the civil law, and explained that it punishes differently the rape of a betrothed girl, that of a single girl, and that of an underage girl; it also differentiates between the abduction of a single and a betrothed girl, and the seduction of a consenting unmarried girl. Having listed these categories, and having heard from John what the circumstances of the seduction were, Chomatianos then turns to the case: the girl, he says, was seduced willingly and, the man being already married, there is no question of a marriage between the two. The man must be punished according to the laws which are *Bas*. 60.37.78 (the seducer must give to the girl a pound of gold or, if he is not wealthy, half his property; if he is poor, he is beaten, shorn, and deported) and *Bas*. 60.37.82, which says that a married man who fornicates is subject to beating. As for ecclesiastical legislation, Chomatianos quotes canon 21 of St. Basil, and finds that canon 59 is applicable, which provides for a seven-year abstention from communion.

His final response is that the man should pay to the girl, if he is wealthy, "as many nomismata of local currency as the law requires" (τῶν κατὰ χώραν ἐμπολιτευομένων καὶ πραττομένων νομισμάτων ὅσον ὁ νόμος δηλοῖ), and if he is not wealthy, half his property. The local prelate must subject him to the ecclesiastical punishment mentioned above.

[28] See the edition of J. B. Pitra, *Analecta sacra . . .*, 7 vols. (Paris, 1876–82), no. 74. The faults of this edition are well known; some necessary corrections will be incorporated in the discussion of the case.

A number of points of interest arise from this *responsum*. First, the question of the brother, which is not quoted but summarized, sets out clearly the factors that legally define the case: the seducer was married; the girl was a virgin; she was not betrothed; she was willing, but her brother was not aware of the affair. While this clarity may be due to the archbishop's secretary rather than to the brother, it is interesting that someone elicited sufficient facts to establish the legal category. The mention of the brother's ignorance seems to have been included precisely in order to establish the legal category; for, since the seducer was already married, even if the brother had known (and consented), there could not in any case have been a marriage of the girl and her seducer. Second, the brother is handling the affair, presumably because the girl is an orphan. Third, Chomatianos treats *Bas.* 60.37.82 (= *Ecloga* 17.19–22) as cumulative punishment, to be added to the compensation that is due to the girl. This is an interpretation which is not self-evident, and which was probably not the intent of the lawgiver. Chomatianos' interpretation makes fornication into a general category, affecting all sins of the flesh, and independent of the other subdivisions of sexual crimes. But it must be noted that the corporal punishment established by *Bas.* 60.37.82 is not to be applied. Interestingly, in his response Chomatianos also ignores the possibility that the man was poor, which would have led to his being punished by beating. Perhaps the corporal punishments originally legislated by the *Ecloga* for sexual crimes were no longer being applied. Finally, the consenting woman is not punished; on the contrary, she is to receive some property.

A second case, also from Chomatianos' court, takes a different attitude toward the woman. A potter named Chrysos had left Kastoria and his lawfully wedded wife and gone to Ochrid. There he lived with a Vlach woman named Tzola who, according to the description of the facts, was a seductive and tempting woman; she is called his concubine. Chrysos' wife learned of the matter, went to Ochrid, and managed to extract him from Tzola's "whorish embrace, helped by the law and by the might of the government according to Christ" (τῶν πορνικῶν ἐκείνης ἀπέσπασεν ἀγκαλῶν καὶ δεσμῶν, τῷ τε νόμῳ βοηθουμένη καὶ τῇ ἰσχύι τοῦ κατὰ Χριστὸν πολιτεύματος). Eventually, Tzola presented demands, presumably to Chomatianos' court: she argued that all of Chrysos' property in Ochrid had been acquired by their common labor, something that Chrysos admitted and against which his wife had nothing to say. A compromise was reached, whereby Tzola received a share of this common property, pronouncing herself satisfied. It was written that if

Tzola should ever again, by open or occult means (a reference to magic?), persuade Chrysos to sleep with her, or if she raised further property demands, she would lose the things she had received from him, and she would be punished by the civil authorities, "so as to be chastened" (εἰς σωφρονισμὸν αὐτῆς).[29]

Although the title of this case, "On those men who are married and fornicate" (περὶ τῶν ἐχόντων γυναῖκας καὶ πορνευόντων), is a direct reference to *Bas.* 60.37.82, it will be noticed that the man is not at all punished for his transgression. It is, on the contrary, the consenting woman who is threatened with punishment, even though the law nowhere provides for such punishment. Evidently, the case was resolved not by legal criteria but by social ones: the woman is identified as a Vlach, she is described by the pejorative term γυναικάριον, and she was obviously not a virgin, since she is described as a temptress of men; thus the crime of *parthenophthoria* is not relevant, although clearly the man should have been punished by beating, according to *Bas.* 60.37.82. It appears that he was threatened by the law and thus broke up his affair. The not so covert reference to Tzola's use of occult machinations may have been made in order to justify further this legally unorthodox but socially acceptable disposition of the case. The woman here appears as the seductress, the initiator of the illicit sexual activity, and is held responsible for it.

Such attitudes were, I think, more widespread than a single case suggests; they underlie much of the literature of monastic provenance that deals with sex and temptation. As an example, one may mention almost at random a striking little tale. It is a story told in the *Pratum Spirituale,* a seventh-century compilation of cautionary tales written for and by monks. It concerns a woman who lived the life of a nun in her own house, spending her days fasting, praying, and giving alms. The devil instilled a demonic desire in the heart of a young man, who kept vigil outside her house, and importuned her every time she left to go to church. As a result, *she was forced to stay inside.* Finally, she sent her maidservant to invite him into the house, where he went eagerly, thinking he had achieved his purpose. The woman, sitting at her loom, asked him what it was about her that made him so enamored. He replied that it was her eyes which had tempted him, at which point she took

[29] Pitra, no. 136. On this case, see also Laiou, "Contribution à l'étude de l'institution familiale en Épire," 286.

her shuttle and pierced her eyeballs.[30] The moral of the story is that this action cured him of his passion, and he became a monk.

The story is, of course, full of commonplaces, including the commonplace about passion being inspired by the devil, and that about the woman sitting at her loom, which is a shorthand statement denoting a good woman engaged in a proper female pursuit.[31] Precisely because it is so full of clichés, it provides a useful insight into the assumptions of that kind of milieu. The most powerful assumption is that, although the active role in the incident is played by the man, the cause of the man's passion and of the potential crime is the woman. Connected to this is the first solution adopted by the woman in question, namely, her staying indoors. The point made here is similar to the one that Constantine I makes explicitly in his Novel on abduction: if the woman really did not want to be bothered, she would have stayed home. Finally, it is to be noted that the only person punished here is the woman, although she had not committed any crime. She punishes herself, ostensibly to remove the temptation; but is it not also the case that she is punished privately for an unofficial crime, namely, for having brought the man into temptation? While this is a morality that is specifically monastic, it is likely that an attenuated form of it was pervasive in society, and must be taken into account when one discusses the treatment of the woman who consents to, or initiates, illicit sexual activity.

The next case we will examine is much more complex, has many interesting aspects, and for that reason has been frequently commented upon.[32] However, the story bears repeating here for the purpose at hand. We are in Constantinople, in the years 1025–28, probably closer to the later date, and the people involved are all members of the upper class, the civil aristocracy.[33]

[30] John Moschos, *Pratum Spirituale,* PG 87.3, no. LX, cols. 2912–13. The text says that she pierced her eyes and took them out: ἔδακεν καὶ ἐξέβαλεν τοὺς δύο ὀφθαλμοὺς αὐτῆς.

[31] See A. Laiou, "The Role of Women in Byzantine Society," in eadem, *Gender, Society and Economic Life in Byzantium* (London, 1992), pt. V, 243–44.

[32] See J. Beaucamp, "La situation juridique de la femme à Byzance," *Cahiers de civilisation médiévale* 20 (1977), 169; Laiou, *Mariage, amour et parenté,* chap. 3; D. Simon, *Ἡ εὕρεση τοῦ δικαίου στὸ ἀνώτατο Βυζαντινό δικαστήριο* (Athens, 1982), 15.

[33] The case is in the *Peira* 49.4. The text says that it was first judged by "the late Argyropoulos, who not much later came to the throne." This is Romanos Argyros,

The *protospatharios* Imerios, son of Solomon, fell in love with the daughter of a *protospatharios* and *teichiotes* (officer guarding the palace walls). He deflowered her (διεπαρθένευσεν αὐτὴν λάθρᾳ), without her father's knowledge and consent. The girl became pregnant, and thus her father found out about the affair. The two young people went to church and declared their intention to marry; however, Imerios was still in his father's authority, and thus he delayed the marriage, presumably because Solomon was opposed (διὰ τὴν ὑπεξουσιότητα τὸν γάμον ὑπερετίθετο). But after Solomon died, Imerios refused to marry the girl, and proposed to make another marriage.

At this point, someone, presumably the girl's father, brought action against Imerios, before the court of the Hippodrome. The case was judged, in the first instance, by Romanos Argyros, Tornikios, and other judges. Eustathios Romaios was not present. There was much dispute, the judges found the case very complex, and they could not resolve it. At this point, the emperor (presumably Constantine VIII) intervened with two letters. One ordered Imerios to marry the daughter of the *protospatharios* Gregory Solomon (a relative of his?), and the other ordered the court to judge the case of the *teichiotes'* daughter. Once again, there was much dispute among the judges, and various points of view were expressed regarding the punishment of Imerios. Argyros took the strictest position, proposing that Imerios be punished by both the corporal punishment to which seducers are subject and a monetary fine, while the others proposed that he pay a fine of one pound of gold, according to the law governing the seduction of a consenting girl (*Bas.* 60.37.78). The solution, described by the compiler as an admirable one, was eventually found by Eustathios Romaios, who read the record of the first trial and also heard the case as presented at that moment. He considered corporal punishment to be too harsh, especially since the emperor himself had ordered Imerios to marry the other girl; as for the fine of one pound of gold, that seemed to him too picayune. He judged the case as a case of insult (ὕβρις) against the girl's father, and decided that the *teichiotes* should receive 150

---

later emperor. At the time he was, perhaps, prefect of the city, an office he reached in the late years of Constantine VIII; for his *cursus honorum*, see Laiou, *Mariage, amour et parenté*, chap. 4. Eustathios Romaios is mentioned as *patrikios*, a title with which he appears after 1025: Oikonomides, "Peira," 171–72. The case was written up after 1034, since Argyros was already dead.

nomismata, "according to the law."[34] As for the girl, who was seduced and deflowered (ἐφθάρη καὶ διεπαρθενεύθη), Eustathios produced a law which said that compensation for destruction (of property? τὰς φθορὰς καὶ τὰς ὑποφθοράς) should be estimated by the judge, and he decided that the girl should receive a compensation of 210 nomismata, so that the total fine, due to the girl and her father, came to five pounds of gold. The decision was then presented to the emperor, who confirmed it.[35]

There follows a description of Eustathios' opinion and argumentation. He explained, first of all, why he turned to the law on *injuria* (ὕβρις) and used it to compensate the father for the seduction and deflowering of the daughter. He then proceeded to argue by showing that Imerios' infraction was greater than the one to which the law applied. The law said that even entering a house without the master's consent in order to bring someone to court constitutes *injuria* (*Bas*. 60.21.23 = *D*. 47.10.23); how much greater an *injuria* it is, then, for a man to enter someone's house in order to destroy the entire household (ἐπὶ διαφθορᾷ οἰκίας ὅλης) and deflower a virgin. Having shown the greatness of the crime, he then invoked the law that says that punishments should be milder rather than harsher; the same case may be judged on several different grounds, according to the discretion of the judges; he chose to apply the law on *injuria*. He also explained why he did not apply the law on seduction and impose the penalty of one pound of gold. That law, he said, is an abstract law, which does not take account of specific circumstances; its application depends on the desire of two parties to marry, and it does not exclude even actors, or poor or unfree men, all of whom are expected by this legislation either to marry the girl or pay a fine, even though the actor or the unfree man may not marry the daughter of a senator, even if he should desire to do so. In the present case, the girl is the daughter of a senator, and the case could have been judged according to several different

[34] For the law on *injuria*, see *Bas*. 60.21.

[35] The summary of the case in the commentary on *Bas*. 60.37.78 says that the emperor was Romanos Argyros. However, the longer and more circumstantial description in the *Peira* does not name the emperor, and I see no reason to suppose that it was anyone other than Constantine VIII. Perhaps the commentator was carried away by the statement in the *Peira* that the first time around the case was judged by, among others, Romanos Argyros who "not much later came to the throne." The point does not in any way affect those parts of the case which are pertinent to our topic, but it might be of interest for an eventual biography of either of these two rulers.

laws, including seduction and *injuria;* if the lesser law (on seduction) had been invoked, the stricter one would have been ignored. Finally, he said that Imerios could, while his father was alive, have many times invoked the father's authority in order to avoid marriage and punishment, and this would have set a bad example. Hence, it is implied, the punishment should be more severe than that imposed by the law on seduction. Eustathios' brief was, says the compiler, greatly admired by all.

This fascinating case was, it would seem, a cause célèbre in Constantinople, widely discussed among legal circles; but the legal circles were no different from the circle of the two principal parties, so that it must have been a matter of heated discussion among the aristocracy of the city. And how could it have been otherwise? The people involved were all members of the aristocracy; Imerios must have been a dashing fellow, who had managed to seduce one girl in her father's house and perhaps had also seduced Gregory Solomon's daughter, whom the emperor finally ordered him to marry. Undoubtedly, although the record does not mention this, the interests of different members of the aristocracy were engaged, and the dissension among the judges may well have been due to political reasons, not only to legal disagreements. The very fact that the girl's father chose to bring the case to court, with all the attendant publicity, suggests that there was more to this than meets the eye, and in any case it must have constituted a fairly unusual course of action. Finally, the intervention of the emperor not once but three times shows the importance attached to the case.

As far as our topic is concerned, the following points of interest arise. First of all, the affair between Imerios and the daughter of the *teichiotes* is a clear case of seduction of a consenting girl. After the girl's father gave his consent (the words "the father became aware" must be interpreted to mean that he gave his consent to the match), an effort was made to resolve the matter in the most convenient way allowed by law, that is, by marriage. The formal declaration of intent, made in church, must have been undertaken in an effort to bypass the objections of Imerios' father, but it was unsuccessful: the consent of the parents of both parties was still a necessary precondition of a valid marriage. Second, it is probable that Imerios was also guilty of the seduction of the daughter of Gregory Solomon, since the emperor intervened and ordered him to marry her. This undoubtedly introduced a further complication into the affair, since there were competing claims of two girls and their families. Then one must note that Romanos Argyros, who demanded the harshest punishment of the seducer, seems to have treated *Bas.* 60.37.82 (*Ecloga* 17.19–20 = *Procheiros Nomos* 39.59), which decreed the beating of the fornicator, as a cumulative punishment, which would be added to the punishment for the seduction of a virgin. Eustathios Romaios did not dispute the idea, but he found the corporal punishment too harsh. It must be deduced that in the eleventh century the corporal punishment for fornication was not applied, at least where the members of the aristocracy were concerned, although the relevant law was known and could be invoked. Of great interest is Eustathios' judgment on the applicability of the law on the seduction of a consenting virgin: he thought this law inoperable because it was "abstract." His further explanation suggests that the inapplicability lay in the fact that a law passed in the eighth century was no longer appropriate to eleventh-century society, where the aristocracy was strong and was claiming for itself privileges for which it could find support in those parts of the *Basilics* which had their origins in Roman law. The fact that the girl and the man were both members of the aristocracy played an explicit role in Eustathios Romaios' eventual decision. Thus the incoherence of the *Basilics,* which incorporated both late Roman legislation and laws that originated under very different conditions in the eighth century, was recognized by Eustathios, who used his discretionary powers as judge to correct the incoherence. The fact that he found the penalty of one pound of gold too small also undoubtedly was due to the changed economic circumstances of the empire: the sum was negligible for members of the aristocracy in the eleventh century.

The freedom of the judge in choosing the law by which a case would be prosecuted is discussed with charming candor by Eustathios Romaios. The implications of this for the legal system are explored in a pathbreaking article by Dieter Simon.[36] For our purposes, it is only a certain part of this discretionary power that needs commentary. Specifically, when Eustathios Romaios decided to award the *teichiotes* the sum of 150 nomismata as compensation for the insult he had suffered, he was not doing so "according to the law," as he claimed, for the law nowhere states the size of the penalty. It seems quite clear that the judge first decided that the compensation should be five pounds of gold and then proceeded to apportion the sum between the girl and her father, as he saw fit. The decision was probably predicated upon the social position of the injured family more than upon anything else. It is also because

[36] Simon, *Ἡ εὕρεση*, 25 ff.

of the fact that the *teichiotes* was a member of the aristocracy that the case was ultimately judged as a case of insult.[37] It must also be noted that the case must have been notorious enough and of sufficient legal interest that a summary of it appears as part of the commentary on *Bas*. 60.37.78 (on the seduction of a consenting virgin). The summary emphasizes the reasoning that led to the appeal to the law on insult, which seems to be the most interesting aspect of the case in legal terms.

Finally, it is of interest to us to find out what the effects of consent were on the woman, according to this case. Certainly, the woman was not punished. However, in the first round of the trial, some of the judges wanted to impose such a paltry penalty on the man (in strict application of the law, to be sure) that this would by itself be a form of punishment for her. Eustathios Romaios' description of the heinous aspect of the crime of deflowering, and his likening of the seducer of virgins to the insects who destroy crops is undoubtedly a flowery rhetorical phrase; but it serves to remind us that even in the relatively easygoing eleventh century virginity was a highly prized commodity, and the girl involved in a notorious case like this one was publicly shamed. Whether the daughter of the *teichiotes* was subsequently married, entered a monastery, or lived with her family we do not know; nor do we know whether any adjudication was made on the matter of the child. If any arrangements did exist, they must have been either included in a different (and not extant) decision or made privately. What remains is the fact that the girl was not formally punished for her consent to the seduction, but the social condemnation seeps through the description of the case.

Not surprisingly, it is in literature that one gets the full flavor of this informal condemnation of girls who agree to their own seduction. The twelfth-century poem of *Digenes Akrites* shows the hero engaging in a number of illicit sexual activities. Interestingly enough, the only case of seduction of a consenting virgin is also the only one where the woman is punished. It

[37] There is no connection between Eustathios' reasoning on this point and the invocation of the law on insult in a different set of circumstances by Balsamon, in his commentary on canon 30 of St. Basil. Referring to the case where there is a fake abduction, that is, an elopement, Balsamon says that in such a case neither the civil nor the ecclesiastical punishments on abduction apply; however, if the couple was married against the wishes of the parents, the marriage will be dissolved, and the parents of the girl, assuming that she is under their authority, can bring an action for insult against him: Ralles-Potles, IV, 172.

is the case of Maximo, and the punishment is certainly not one that owes anything to any law, but it is severe indeed: in a fit of remorse, Digenes kills her. There is a discussion of the treatment of sexual crimes in literary texts in the last part of this essay. For the moment, suffice it to say that the punishment inflicted on Maximo is an exaggerated version of attitudes that one finds primarily in ecclesiastical texts, in which seduction is at least as much the fault of the woman as it is of the man.

Conclusion

In this, as in all other aspects of the topic under discussion, it is important to remember that the sources speak in different voices and that even within the same type of source there are divergent views. While it is generally true to say that a woman's consent to illicit sex outside marriage (adultery has been excluded from this discussion) does not create legal consequences for her, there are, as we have seen, specific points in time when legal consequences did indeed exist. As far as the man is concerned, the cases we have examined have shown that there was considerable latitude in the application of the law. Social class, which was almost wholly absent as a consideration in the *Ecloga*, when the prevalent provisions for sexual crimes were established, reappears as an important factor, certainly by the eleventh century.

The formal, that is, canonical ecclesiastical sources treat the woman's consent differently. It does have consequences for the woman, who is thus treated as responsible for her actions. The informal ecclesiastical sources, stemming from a monastic milieu, ascribe even greater responsibility to the woman. In the end, the spirit which imbues the ecclesiastical sources must be considered as generally prevalent. For we have seen that shame was an informal but nevertheless telling punishment, which was formalized by Andronikos II, acting under the influence of the patriarch. And we have also seen that as learned a jurist as Chomatianos did not hesitate to consider punishing a woman, when the combination of her low social status and her bad name made it unnecessary to give her the full benefit of the law. This being so, it is now time to turn to another set of questions and try to find out what, in the mind of the Byzantines, constituted consent, free, coerced, or otherwise.

3. The Meaning of Force

The consent or absence of consent of the woman to illicit sexual activity has been seen to have legal consequences insofar as the categorization of the crime is concerned, and also with regard to the punishment of the man. The consenting woman was also subject to punishment, probably at all times in an unofficial and private way, and sometimes by law. The question then becomes how the consent of the woman or its absence was established and what was recognized as constituting force in a legal sense. Consent can be stated and conscious, or it can simply mean the absence of objection. Which of these was recognized as valid consent? Insofar as marriage was concerned, absence of opposition was considered tantamount to consent.[1] Was it the same in the case of consent to sexual intercourse? On the other side, what was the type and level of force necessary to prove coercion? What circumstances proved the presence of force, and how did people seek to establish that such circumstances existed? Was the absence of consent sufficient to prove coercion, or did one have to show resistance? Consent can be the result of physical or mental force, but the way coerced consent is treated is not self-evident. It is entirely possible that coercion, even if established, does not invalidate the consent that was given under duress; it is also possible for a society to accept that coerced consent is invalid, and the acts that are its consequence also have no legal validity. These are thorny problems, whose solution varies with time and place. In this chapter we will investigate what the Byzantines thought constituted force, violence, duress. In the next chapter we will address the problem of the validity of coerced consent.

In answer to the first question asked above, namely, whether the absence of opposition is tantamount to consent, one may invoke the law of Constantine I on abduction. His assumption appears to be that a woman who could not prove opposition had consented to the act. However, even in this harsh

[1] *Bas.* 28.1.10 (*D.* 23.1.12): δοκεῖ δὲ τῷ πατρὶ συναινεῖν ἡ μὴ ἀντιλέγουσα.

law, the circumstances had to be such that the woman's opposition or absence of it was capable of being established.

When one seeks to establish whether someone was coerced into an act or undertook it out of his/her own free will, there are several ways the question may be addressed. In Byzantium the simplest way was to seek objective criteria; to ask, in other words, whether the circumstances or the external evidence were such that they justified a presumption of force. To take an example from modern legal systems, rape is assumed if there was physical force whose signs are evident, bruises or torn clothing being considered as signs.[2] What one needs to do in systems where such objective criteria are used is to look for those criteria which are accepted as establishing the existence or presumption of force, and examine also the ways in which the presence of such circumstances was proved. A second concept embraces subjective criteria: there are no circumstances which prove by themselves the use of force, but nevertheless consent to the act was not given. The problem of date rape, in contemporary American society, falls into this category. Each society has particular attitudes with regard to these approaches, and in our own society both the objective criteria and the legal weight given to subjective factors are in the process of changing. As an example, one may turn to the question of sexual harassment, where rules recently adopted by a number of institutions, universities in the first instance, incorporate the assumption that there is no free consent between two people when an inequality of hierarchical status exists.

Arms and the Woman

When we try to approach these issues in Byzantium, the law gives us no guidance, for it does not deal explicitly with them. One must, instead, seek enlightenment from court cases, which, indeed, would be the most useful source even for a study of similar phenomena today. The first case we will examine is deceptively simple: it involves an abduction with the use of arms, which in itself is proof of force; it is more difficult to establish whether there was also sexual intercourse with the use of force.

The case was judged in Constantinople, in the first quarter of the elev-

[2] *Corpus Juris Secundum: A Complete Restatement of the Entire American Law,* "Rape," § 55, 72, 80.

enth century, by the famous jurist, Eustathios Romaios. A translation of it is provided in the Appendix to this chapter, but, since it is a rather subtle and complex legal document, its elements will be reconstructed below.

A man named Theoktistos had, at a certain point, abducted, with the force of arms (ἐνόπλῳ βίᾳ), Maria, the fiancée of his nephew John. Eventually he returned her to her own house, either before or after a court case was brought against him. By imperial command, that case had been judged by Petros, *protospatharios* and prefect of the city of Constantinople, as well as by Eustathios Romaios.[3] An investigation was made, a decision was taken, and the culprit was punished, both "according to the laws and by imperial decision" (νόμοις τε καὶ βασιλικῇ κρίσει). The court decision (not extant) had described in detail the crime, the legal examination of the case, and the decision. The case had been judged as a pure case of abduction.

After Maria had returned to her own house, her parents and her fiancé called in certain reputable women, who examined Maria for physical evidence of deflowering, and found none. They gave sworn testimony, registered in a document (ἐκμαρτύριον) that Maria was a virgin. As a result of this testimony, the marriage of Maria and John could and did take place.[4]

Subsequently a certain Niketas Gypsokopos, whose relationship to John and Maria is not known, brought a case against John, and this is the document we have. Gypsokopos was seeking the divorce or annulment of John's marriage to Maria, on two grounds, both of them connected with incest. First,

[3] The circumstances of the first case, brought against Gypsokopos, are briefly discussed in the record of a second court case, which is the only one extant today: A. Schminck, "Vier Eherechtliche Entscheidungen aus dem 11. Jh.," *Fontes Minores* 3 (1979), 224 ff, with a German translation. The date of this text is established by the editor as being after 1028. As for the first case, against Theoktistos, since it was judged while Petros was *eparchos* (prefect of Constantinople), it must have taken place between June 1023 and November 1028 or possibly between June 1023 and sometime in 1026: Laiou, *Mariage, amour et parenté,* chap. 4.

[4] It is not stated whether the examination took place before or after the court case against Theoktistos. Eustathios Romaios, however, insists that in that first court case there was no mention of deflowering, so that one must assume that the examination preceded the accusation against Theoktistos. The course of events thus must be: abduction, discussions between the abductor and the girl's family (this is my assumption: the text does not mention it), return of the girl to her home, examination of the girl by the women, case against Theoktistos, marriage of John and Maria either before or after the decision had been issued by the court.

he charged that Maria had slept with John's uncle, Theoktistos, and that therefore her marriage to John was invalid because incestuous: Theoktistos was first cousin of John's father, and thus the two were related to the fifth degree.[5] The second charge was that the marriage was incestuous anyway, because John's brother had married a girl who was the daughter of Maria's first cousin. This second part of the accusation is of no concern to us here. It must be assumed that Gypsokopos wanted the marriage dissolved because he had some interest of his own; he may, for example, have wanted Maria as a bride for himself or for one of his close relatives.

The point at issue here was whether Theoktistos had slept with Maria, as charged, or not. Eustathios Romaios argued that no intercourse had taken place, on the following grounds. First, he said, the original accusation had made no mention of deflowering but only of abduction. Nor did the original court decision mention deflowering. He argued further that if there had been sexual intercourse, the plaintiffs would have brought such an accusation, which would have greatly aggravated Theoktistos' crime and increased his punishment. Against a possible (or actual: we don't know) argument that

[5] *Bas.* 60.37.74 (= *Procheiros Nomos* 39.69, *Ecloga* 17.33) forbids the marriage of a nephew with his aunt; the *Tomos* of Patriarch Sisinnios had forbidden marriages between people variously related by affinity to the fifth or sixth degree. It did not cover the type of relationship charged by Gypsokopos, but in this period there were efforts to extend the prohibitions of the *Tomos* to cover a considerable number of different circumstances: Laiou, *Mariage, amour et parenté*, chap. 1. The question of whether illicit intercourse could establish sufficient kinship to create impediments was open. A *responsum* of Patriarch Alexios Stoudites, contemporary with the case judged by Eustathios Romaios, can enlighten us as to contemporary ecclesiastical thinking on this issue. The archbishop of Thessaloniki brought to the attention of the patriarch a case eerily resembling the one at hand. The daughter of Theodore Karmalikios had been engaged to the son of Basil Kalos Kairos. Before the marriage had taken place, a relative of Basil abducted the girl; the fiancé wished the marriage to proceed, and the opinion of the patriarch was sought, apparently because there were others who wanted to dissolve the marriage; the grounds, though unstated, would have been incest. The patriarch was of the opinion that if there was only abduction, the marriage could take place; if there was also sexual intercourse, it could not; V. Beneševich, in *Vizantijskij vremennik* (hereafter *VizVrem*) 12 (1906), 516–17. The date of the document is 1027. Finally, it should be noted that, according to Novel 93 of Leo VI, Maria's betrothal to John would have been dissolved anyway, if she had slept with anyone (other than John) while being engaged. The Novel is not invoked in the decision.

parents would shirk at making such an accusation because it would have brought shame on the girl, he concedes the disgrace, but says that any hesitation stemming from fear of disgrace would have been overridden by people's desire to bring the maximum punishment on their enemies.

The second argument (and the only solid one) concerns the testimony as to Maria's virginity. Apparently the testimony was disputed by Gypsokopos, because women are not allowed to bear witness, and because the women who had testified had died in the interim (and so their testimony could not be reconfirmed). Eustathios Romaios said, quite properly, that the testimony of women is, in fact, allowed by law in matters where men cannot testify (*Bas.* 21.1.17). Furthermore, he said, Gypsokopos had not brought into question the qualifications of these women; therefore, their testimony would remain valid, and it had established that the girl was indeed a virgin.

Eustathios then abandons himself to his usual rhetorical argumentation. He may, once again, be responding to an argument of Gypsokopos, to wit, that deflowering should be assumed, since it always follows an abduction; it is also possible that he may simply be preempting such an argument. Eustathios treats Gypsokopos' argument as conjecture, and argues, on the other side, that rape does not necessarily follow abduction. His own assumption, at least for the purposes of this argument, seems to be that there are two possible reasons for abduction: a man who is carried away by passion alone may indeed sleep with the woman. But if abduction is undertaken with the purpose of marriage (which apparently was the case here), then a man does not rape the girl, because he knows that women are more amenable to flattery than to force, and because he wishes to elicit the girl's consent (to marriage). What this argumentation leaves out of consideration, of course, is the possibility of consensual sex between a girl and her abductor: he is only arguing that rape need not follow abduction. This is a logical leap, since he uses the word φθορά.

Finally, he turns from logical arguments, which are inconclusive, back to the law, stating that evidence must almost always be preferred to conjecture. The evidence, in this case, is that there was no deflowering, and so the marriage was valid.

The case presents a multiple interest, both in terms of the functioning of Byzantine courts and of the topic that concerns us here. Clearly the affair continued for some years, since the "reputable women" who testified on Maria's virginity died between one court case and the next. Clearly, too, the disputes were between social equals, and in fact the original crime, the abduction, had been committed by a close relative of the bridegroom. The people involved must have been important in some way. Although the names give few clues, it is evident that Maria must have been an interesting bride, since her hand was disputed by her bridegroom, his uncle, and probably Gypsokopos; she must have been an heiress of some importance. The imperial interference also suggests that we are dealing with important people. The only useful name for determining the social status of the parties is that of Niketas Gypsokopos (chalk-maker, plasterer?); it is certainly not an aristocratic name, denoting rather someone associated with the crafts. So it must have been wealth rather than aristocratic lineage that defined the importance of the parties in question. The fact that Gypsokopos tried to use the evolving legislation on incest to dissolve a perfectly valid marriage is interesting but far from unique in this period.[6]

Insofar as our topic is concerned, the following observations may be made.

1. The use of arms by the abductor in itself establishes the fact that there was force involved; in such a case, the consent or otherwise of the girl is irrelevant. Indeed, both the *Basilics* (60.58.1) and Novel 35 of Leo VI state explicitly that the consent of the girl plays no role in determining the punishment of the man and his eventual accomplices, and no role in the treatment of the case. Whether, therefore, the woman was willing or unwilling, the use of arms creates a presumption of force.[7] The punishment, according to the law, of an abductor who used a sword was death by the sword. What this means for our purposes is that if it could be established that a man abducted

[6] See Laiou, *Mariage, amour et parenté,* chap. 1, passim. For Western European medieval evidence that abduction was a marriage strategy and that the parties involved tended to be social equals, see R. Benveniste, "Γαμήλιες στρατηγικές στό Μεσαίωνα: οἱ ἀπαγωγές," *Τά ἱστορικά* 5 (1988), 103–14. Among the Sarakatsanoi, studied by J. C. Campbell, abduction (with the use of arms) takes place when a man is offended by the refusal of a girl's family to accept his offer of marriage. The offensive presumption is that he is not equal to the girl's family: J. C. Campbell, *Honour, Family and Patronage* (Oxford, 1964), 129 ff.

[7] See also G. Weiss, "Die Synopsis legum des Michael Psellos," *Fontes Minores* 2 (1977), 193: ὁ κόρην *βιασάμενος* καὶ *βιαίως ἁρπάσας* μετὰ ξιφῶν βαρβαρικῶς ξίφει τιμωρητέος. Cf. *Corpus Juris Secundum,* "Rape," § 74: the "display of weapons" is a threat that "would cause the prosecutrix to yield."

a woman with the use of arms, this would incur the heaviest penalty of the law, the consent of the woman being irrelevant.

2. The question then arises, and was discussed in court, whether abduction and the use of force also necessarily implies rape. The law of the *Basilics,* which is essentially that of Justinian I, refers exclusively to abduction and makes no mention of sexual intercourse. On the other hand, the law of Leo VI, which was known in the eleventh century, specifically ties abduction with rape, and the punishment it envisages strikes the man who abducts and violates a virgin: τὸν δι᾽ ἁρπαγῆς καὶ βίας φθορέα γεγονότα κόρης θανάτῳ ὑπάγεσθαι.[8] It is the assumptions of this law that Eustathios Romaios contests in his rhetorical argument, although he does not refer to the law itself. In the case at hand, Gypsokopos may have argued that, since Leo VI's Novel treats rape as part of abduction, rape must always follow upon it. Eustathios Romaios, on the other hand, argued that rape is not a necessary corollary of abduction: he distinguished between the two, whereas the Novel of Leo VI did not. The basis on which he made the distinction, however, must owe more to practice than it does to law. For he argued that sometimes men abducted women in order to marry them; and this was expressly forbidden by civil law, both that of the *Basilics* and that of Leo VI, as indeed it was by canon law.[9] Eustathios Romaios seems willing to assume that, unless there is evidence to the contrary, every abduction is a feigned abduction, which he himself said was no abduction at all.

3. The description of the case states that Theoktistos was punished, "according to the laws," for the crime of abduction, but that he was spared the heavier punishment to which he would have been subjected if he had also slept with the girl. The question arises, under which law Theoktistos was punished. Certainly, neither *Bas.* 60.58.1, on abduction, nor Novel 35 of Leo VI could have been applied, since both of these imposed the death penalty;

[8] Noailles and Dain, Novel 35, p. 141, lines 14–15. Cf. *Bas.* 60.58.1, p. 3110: οἱ ἁρπάσαντες γυναῖκα . . . ξίφει τιμωρείσθωσαν. The commentaries on the *Basilics,* perhaps because of Novel 35 of Leo VI, do speak of the abducted woman as if she had been raped: *Bas.* 60.58.1.1: ὁ ἁρπάζων. . . . τῇ βιασθείσῃ. The relevant part of the *Basilics* repeats *Procheiros Nomos* 39.40. Leo VI innovated when he explicitly tied abduction to rape; the law of Basil I, in the *Procheiros Nomos,* speaks only of abduction.

[9] See Balsamon, on canon 91 of the Council in Trullo: Ralles-Potles, II, 521 and Nomocanon 9.30 (Ralles-Potles, I, 214 ff).

and there is no other law punishing abduction without sexual intercourse. What must, therefore, have happened, is that there was a different form of punishment, outside the legal provisions, which may be why an imperial decision was necessary. There was clearly a mitigation of the law, perhaps because of an argument that Theoktistos' motive in abducting the girl was marriage, with which motive Eustathios Romaios seems sympathetic. The only thing we can say with certainty is that the law on abduction was not applied, and that, if the girl had been deflowered, the punishment would have been more severe.

4. We thus see once again[10] that, at least in this period, there was more concern with the seduction of a virgin than with abduction. At the same time, it remains a fact that seduction could still be corrected by marriage; and it is in this light that one must see Eustathios Romaios' differentiation between abduction and elopement. Elopement is punishable as seduction, to be sure, but by allowing certain cases of abduction to be treated as seduction, Eustathios makes it possible for marriage to correct the crime.

5. A question, important for our purposes, is not explicitly addressed by our text. If Maria had been found not to be a virgin, would it have been *assumed* that she had been raped, or would she have had to *prove* that she had been forced and not been a willing participant in the act? Eustathios' argumentation, as that of Leo VI, envisages only the possibility of rape, not of consensual sex. Thus it appears that once abduction had been proved, any sexual contact attendant upon it would have been considered forced. The external circumstance of abduction, with the violence which is a defining element of it, would also have been sufficient to establish the crime of rape. It would not have been admitted that the woman was capable of free consent in such circumstances.

The use of arms, then, is one circumstance which establishes *ipso facto* absence of consent, both to the abduction and to sexual intercourse.[11] The

[10] Cf. above, pp. 120–21. J. C. Campbell observes that, among the Sarakatsanoi, when a girl is abducted, she is held for three days and three nights, after which her abductor presents himself to the police. The girl is asked three times whether she wishes to marry him, and most often she does, for during those three days and nights she has been told, among other things, that no one will believe she is still a virgin after having been in the company of armed men for so long: Campbell, *Honour,* 130.

[11] Other sources show an age-old assumption that a woman, when in the company of armed men, must expect rape. See, for example, the case of St. Pelagia,

investigative aspect of all this is not stated; the testimony of witnesses is the only mechanism of establishing facts that is apparent in the case.

The Use of Accomplices

In the eleventh century the courts had elaborated another rule of thumb for determining that there was a crime of abduction, which by definition is a violent crime. Eustathios Romaios stated that the use of accomplices by itself establishes the crime of *raptus* (abduction) and renders irrelevant the consent of the woman. On the other hand, if a man takes a woman away without accomplices, but secretly and with her consent, that is not considered abduction, but rather seduction of a virgin, for which the punishment was more lenient, and marriage could be a remedy.[12] This, apparently, was the decision of a court case rendered by the old *censor* against a certain Protokaravos. Surprisingly, we find this judicial determination quoted as *the law* in a *Tomos* of Patriarch Kosmas (1081), which summarizes certain canonical provisions on aspects of marriage. Having brought forth several canons on *raptus,* he turns to "the civil law," and quotes, verbatim, *Peira* 63.5, omitting only the last sentence, which establishes that this was a judicial decision. I find this an extraordinary text, first because of the use of precedent as law, and second because it seems that the patriarch is using legal texts selectively to strengthen the possibility of marriage following elopement. The *Tomos* makes no mention either of *Bas.* 60.58 or of Novel 35 of Leo VI.[13] Accomplices thus create a presumption of force, while the lack of accomplices suggests that the woman consented to the abduction/elopement.

Crying in the Wilderness

Another objective factor which is taken into account in determining the presence or absence of consent is whether a woman's outcry could be heard. In

mentioned in the *Synaxarium Ecclesiae Constantinopolitanae* (hereafter *SynCP*), ed. H. Delehaye (Brussels, 1902), col. 120, and discussed at length by St. John Chrysostom, PG 50, cols. 579–84.

[12] *Peira* 63.5. This was incorporated into the *Scholia* to *Bas.* 58.60. Cf. Karlin Hayter, "Further Notes on Byzantine Marriage," 139, with a faulty citation to the *Peira*.

[13] A. Papadopoulos-Kerameus, *Varia Graeca Sacra* (St. Petersburg, 1909), xxxiv–xxxvi. On some problems with this document, see J. Darrouzès, *Les Regestes des Actes du Patriarcat de Constantinople,* I (Paris, 1989), no. 919.

Byzantium this is a function of the locality in which the crime was committed. We have already seen that Novel 26 of Andronikos II differentiates between a woman being forced "in the wilderness" and one who gives herself willingly. The distinction, as we have noted, is an ancient one, stemming from Deuteronomy. What it means, in effect, is that the benefit of the doubt goes to the woman who is seduced in a place where her outcry cannot be heard or noticed: that fact by itself establishes presumption of force. Thus, since the external circumstances in which consent might be established are absent, the woman is held not to have consented. She need not prove absence of consent; she need only prove that the circumstances existed which rendered it impossible for her objections to be registered.

This type of circumstantial proof appears in the civil legislation only with the Novel of Andronikos II, but it seems to have been used earlier either in ecclesiastical courts or possibly in provincial courts. This, at least, is suggested by a case discussed by John Apokaukos. The text is a *semeioma* of Apokaukos, written in the presence of witnesses.[14] It is not a court decision, but rather a description of an affair that was brought to his attention by chance.

The pertinent circumstances are as follows. One day, when Apokaukos was visiting the bishop of Vonitza, a man named Symeon Sgouropoulos came to them and complained of his troubles. He explained that in the previous year, his daughter, Vlasia, who was young and a virgin, had gone out to a spring, very near her house, to draw water. There she was found by a Vlach, Constantine Avrilionis, who took her to a crevice, "where he thought that no help could come to her from anywhere, nor would she be heard if she cried out," and deflowered her. After that, every time he found her he would rape her (ἐπάγων βίαν ἐμίγνυτο). Eventually, she became pregnant and bore a child. This, said Sgouropoulos, was the first offense of Avrilionis. A few days before the birth, Avrilionis and about thirty other Vlachs had met Sgouropoulos and his son-in-law (who had married another of his daughters), and beat them up severely, either because he was angry at Sgouropoulos' efforts on behalf of his daughter, or because he thought that Sgouropoulos was too poor and inconsequential, and thus an easy prey. The son-in-law was now at the point of death, while Sgouropoulos was suffering from terrible wounds. The

[14] N. A. Bees, "Unedierte Schriftstücke aus der Kanzlei des Johannes Apokaukos des Metropoliten von Naupaktos (in Aetolien)," *Byzantinisch-Neugriechische Jahrbücher* 21 (1971–74), no. 5, pp. 60–62.

metropolitan then launches into a graphic description of the wounds, which upset both him and the bishop. The bishop of Vonitza advised Sgouropoulos to turn to the civil authorities and bring his case to the *protovestiarios;* Apokaukos wrote up the circumstances, so that Sgouropoulos could bring the letter to the civil authorities.

One is here confronted with a situation where reality has the upper hand, and the law has very little chance of being heard. True, the circumstances are specific: this was in the country, in an area and at a time of uncertainty and troubles. It is, therefore, not surprising that private vengeance seems more in evidence than legal arrangements. Nor is it astonishing that the bishop of Vonitza and Apokaukos were much more concerned with the life-threatening attack on Sgouropoulos and his son-in-law than with the rape, which is treated almost as a prelude to the attack. It is, therefore, all the more interesting to discover what it was that the girl's father (or, more likely, Apokaukos) wanted to establish with regard to the sexual crime.

Indisputably, the main element that the girl's side wanted to establish was the use of force. It was thus stressed that the first encounter took place in a spot where she could not be heard if she cried out, and that the subsequent encounters took place by force. The explanation of the girl's presence in a lonely spot serves the same purpose: it is explained that she was out on a legitimate errand (the good biblical errand of drawing water), and that the spring where she went was the one closest to the house. No one could argue that she courted disaster.[15] It was further stated that the girl was young and had been a virgin. By law, Avrilionis should have been punished by having his nose slit and giving the girl one-third of his property. But no mention is made of that. What is of interest here is that the locality in which the crime occurred is the primary factor in establishing presumption of force. It is, for our purposes, irrelevant to ask why the crime was not reported the first time around, or under what circumstances it was repeated. It is relevant to note that no mention of marriage is made, which may be why the girl's father was eventually moved to take steps, as is implied in the description of the sequence of events.

In terms of our inquiry, two things are especially notable. First, that once it had been stated that the encounter took place in a lonely spot, the question of the girl's consent appeared moot: she would not have been heard if she had

[15] The point was made by Alice-Mary Talbot.

cried out, and therefore she got the benefit of the doubt. Second, it is reasonable to assume that private solutions, peaceful or otherwise, were sought before the parties had recourse to the authorities, and not only in the wilds of Epiros.

The chronicle of Skylitzes preserves the story of a woman who was raped by a Varangian soldier in the theme of Thrakesion, where the Varangians were spending the winter. The soldier found her in the "wilderness" and, unable to persuade her to sleep with him, raped her (βίαν . . . ἐπῆγεν). She grabbed his sword and killed him. The other Varangians, hearing of the story, gave her all of the dead soldier's property and left him unburied, "according to the law regarding suicides" (κατὰ τῶν βιοθανάτων τὸν νόμον).[16]

Here force is established by two circumstances, the location and the use of arms. The private justice exacted by the woman (and by the other soldiers) is more severe than the provisions of the law regarding rape, but is very close to the spirit of the law governing abduction and rape. That law, of Leo VI, it will be remembered, posits death for the man, and gives his property to the abducted and raped maiden.

As far as locality is concerned, it should be noted that "the wilderness" and the spring of water have a significance beyond that which stems from Deuteronomy. These are liminal areas, where extraordinary events can occur and danger lurks. It is, perhaps, this ambiance of liminality that lifts the woman's guilt. It will be remembered that brooks and streams were the seduction spot of choice in the case of the gods of ancient Greece.[17]

The Factor of Age

In Chapter I we saw that, according to the *Ecloga,* followed by the *Procheiros Nomos* and the *Basilics,* the seduction of a virgin before puberty is tantamount to rape in terms of the punishment involved.[18] There was, then, the

[16] John Skylitzes, *Ioannis Scylitzae Synopsis historiarum,* ed. I. Thurn (Berlin and New York, 1973), 394 (in 1034). The Madrid manuscript of Skylitzes has a miniature illustrating the incident.

[17] I thank Professor Stanley Tambiah for pointing out the importance of liminality. For ancient Greece, see Mary Lefkowitz, "Seduction and Rape in Greek Myth," in Part I of this volume.

[18] See above, I. The modern definition of statutory rape is the unlawful carnal knowledge of an underage girl.

concept of statutory rape, according to which age is an external, objective factor which by itself makes the question of consent immaterial, if the woman has not attained puberty. It will not escape notice that the age limitation is the same for marriage and for sexual intercourse: an underage girl is legally incapable of consent to marriage, as she is to consent to sexual intercourse.

Curiously enough, we are better informed about statutory rape than about any other sexual crime, with the exception of adultery. The matrimonial policies of the Byzantines, at least as they emerge with some clarity in the eleventh century, meant that marriage arrangements were made when the girls were very young.[19] Whereas both civil and ecclesiastical law forbade the marriage of a girl below the age of puberty, it was often a short step from negotiating an arrangement to actually performing the marriage ceremony before the statutory age of thirteen years for the girl. Even when no marriage had been contracted, sometimes the fiancé would live in the house of the bride-to-be; and although Alexios I tried to forbid the free and unsupervised congress of betrothed young people, specifically in order to reduce the risk of a sexual encounter, it is not at all certain that his legislation was followed.[20] The preconditions thus were often present for illicit sexual activity in a family setting. Sometimes the fiancé might sleep with his prospective mother-in-law, who might be closer to his age than was his betrothed.[21] And sometimes the girl was deflowered by her fiancé long before puberty. A well-known historical example is the case of Simonis, daughter of Andronikos II, who was married, at the age of five, to the Serbian kral Stefan Uroš II Milutin, then about forty years old. He apparently consummated the union while Simonis was still under age, and she became sterile as a result.[22] John Apokaukos in the thirteenth century, Patriarchs Athanasios I and Kallistos I in the fourteenth century, and the moralist Joseph Bryennios in the fifteenth, all

[19] Among the numerous reported cases, I mention almost at random *Peira* 49.34 (seven-year-old girl), 42.5; Ralles-Potles, V, 381 (a girl engaged at five and seven), and 32–36; Bees, "Apokaukos," nos. 9, 10. A longer list may be found in M.-T. Fögen, "Rechtsprechung mit Aristophanes," *Rechtshistorisches Journal* 1 (1982), 77 note 10.

[20] *JGR*, I, 309, 325.

[21] See the responsa of Niketas of Herakleia, *VizVrem* 2 (1895), 167–69.

[22] Angeliki E. Laiou, *Constantinople and the Latins: The Foreign Policy of Andronicus II, 1282–1328* (Cambridge, Mass., 1972), 95–96.

complained about the crime of παιδοφθορία, the deflowering of girls before puberty.[23]

As can be readily seen, this type of illicit sexual activity could create a number of serious problems, quite apart from the infraction of the laws of church and state. If the man subsequently decided not to marry the girl, she could well find herself unmarriageable. In any case, she might suffer physical damage, including sterility, as well as damage to her reputation. The situation became vexed if the parents of the girl had in some way contributed to the circumstances leading up to the crime. It is, perhaps, for these reasons that the courts tried such cases in ways that are intriguing. The two cases discussed below were chosen because they address, albeit indirectly, the question of the consent of the girl, which is our primary interest here.

In the *Peira* (49.22), we find the story of a girl who was betrothed at the age of seven, although her father lied and pretended that she was ten years old. It should be remembered that, according to the law, a simple engagement could be made when the girl (or the boy) was seven years old, but it could not be confirmed by a church ceremony until the age of thirteen for the girl and fourteen for the boy. In our case, there was a church ceremony one year later, presumably the ceremony of betrothal rather than marriage, since the man is still called the girl's fiancé. The man raped the girl (ἐβιάσατο τὴν κόρην); she resisted, so he held her down and covered her mouth so violently that blood rushed from her ears. The text says that the girl was damaged (ἐβλάβη), for she became afraid even to look at a man. The judge dissolved the marriage (the word γάμος is used), calling it a φθορά (seduction of a virgin), and invoking the law which punished the seduction of a virgin before puberty by the slitting of the nose and by the transfer to the girl of one-half of the man's property. The girl did, indeed, receive the monetary compensation, but the corporal punishment was not imposed. On the other hand, the judge ordered the man to be beaten and shorn, since he did not hold imperial office (διὰ τὸ μὴ τετιμῆσθαι βασιλικῷ ἀξιώματι).

The most important decision taken by the judge was the dissolution of the engagement/marriage, undoubtedly on the basis of the fact that it was invalid because the girl was below the statutory age at which a marriage could

[23] F. Miklosich and J. Müller, *Acta et diplomata graeca medii aevi*, 6 vols. (Vienna, 1860–90), I, 397–99; Bees, "Apokaukos," nos. 9, 10; Koukoules, *Βυζαντινῶν βίος καὶ πολιτισμός*, IV, 77 note 45.

be contracted. The subsequent seduction thus was not a case of a man forcing his wife. Therefore, the judge could treat it as φθορά, not because of the force involved but because there was no marriage. He could then apply, although only in part, the provisions of *Bas.* 60.37.80, coupled with a punishment not envisaged by the law, that is, ordering the man to be beaten and shorn. It should be noted that this corporal punishment could be imposed only on a man who was not an imperial official.

What about the role of violence and of the girl's absence of consent? In fact, the decision formally depended only on the girl's age, which was sufficient to invalidate the marriage. Furthermore, the legislation invoked assumes the absence of (legal) consent to sexual activity if the girl is under age. And yet the judge goes to some lengths to describe vividly the force involved, and its consequences. Is it possible that evidentiary proof of force was necessary to establish statutory rape, or can the matter be explained in other ways? To start with, there is a practical explanation. It is evident that the case was brought to court by the girl's parents or guardians, and that for it to reach the court private efforts at accommodation must have failed. It may have been the parents who justified their complaint by mentioning the fact that force was used, and it must have been an important part of their suit: they could not simply appeal to the law that forbids an engagement (with church ceremony) or a marriage before the age of thirteen, since the girl's father himself had allowed it to take place. Second, the judge may have used the issue of force in order to show that the crime was aggravated, and thus to impose the maximum penalty.[24] Possibly the argumentation may have been influenced by other cases of rape, where the girl was not under age and force played an important legal role. All of the above are possible and plausible.

What seems most important, however, is a factor which is quite outside formal law, but very important in real terms. The permanent injury to the girl was the fact that she became afraid of men; thus it was no longer possible to remedy the situation by an eventual marriage, either to her fiancé or to another man, or at least it could so be argued. That, in fact, was the factor that truly aggravated the crime of rape, and that was what was established by the insistence on the use of force.

To summarize, it is clear that in this particular case the factor of age,

[24] In modern American law, evidence of force in statutory rape, while immaterial to the crime, is admissible in order to determine civil damages.

which legally would have established absence of consent, and even circumstantial force,[25] was not considered adequate. The actual use of force, as proven by the physical violence involved, was considered important, primarily, it would seem, because of its effects: it had the socially undesirable consequence of making marriage impossible for the girl. This is further illuminated by a case which was judged by the patriarchal court of Constantinople in 1325.[26]

The affair engaged members of the clergy of the metropolis of Ainos, and was brought to court by John Manglavites. He reported that he had betrothed his eleven-year old daughter to the son of the *archon ton ekklesion* of Ainos, Argyros.[27] Since the girl was under age, the *dikaiophylax* of the church of Ainos did not allow her to live in the same house as the groom. Her father, Manglavites, on the other hand, did allow her to live in the bridegroom's house, but only, as he insisted, after having received guarantees from his father that no sexual intercourse would take place until she came of age. But then, Manglavites charged, the young man forced her, and slept with her,[28] causing her great harm (παντελοῦς βλάβης καὶ ἐρημώσεως ταύτῃ γενόμενος πρόξενος). The injury, in this case, was physical. So, since the girl was also present when the case was brought, the court ordered her examined by a midwife, who testified that she had indeed suffered physical injury, with the result that she could no longer sleep with a man.

After the examination, the court decided to dissolve the betrothal, and granted to Manglavites the return of the dowry which he had promised, plus the θεωρετρούπόβολον, that is, the man's marriage gifts to her. The disso-

[25] Cf. *Peira* 42.5: Βία ἐστὶν οὐ μόνον τὸ στρεβλῶσαι καὶ ἐγκλεῖσαι, ἀλλὰ καὶ τὸ παρὰ γνώμην τινός, ὅτε μάλιστα κύριος θελήματος οὐκ ἐστὶ διὰ τὸ ἀνήλικον, πρὸς συνάλλαγμα συνωθεῖσθαι.

[26] H. Hunger and O. Kresten, *Das Register des Patriarchats von Konstantinopel*, I (Vienna, 1981), no. 89, pp. 510–13.

[27] The term used is ἠγάγετο γαμβρόν. Since Manglavites then proceeds to state that the girl was not of a legal age to contract a marriage, it would logically follow that the arrangement was a simple betrothal, without the church blessing. However, logic is not always the best guide, and by this period betrothal in church was a practice long established; so it is entirely possible that it is to such a betrothal that Manglavites refers.

[28] ἐμίγη παρὰ φύσιν αὐτῇ. The words "against nature" in all probability refer to the fact that she was too young for sexual intercourse, rather than to "unnatural" intercourse.

lution was granted on two grounds: the girl's age, which is the first ground mentioned in the decision, and the injury she had sustained and her inability to have sex, which was the ground to which the court gave the heavier weight. The court further took notice of the responsibility of the groom's father, who allowed the girl to come to harm, even though she had gone to his house under his protection and guarantee.

Once again, the basic decision is the dissolution of the matrimonial arrangement, and the financial penalty imposed upon the groom and his father—since presumably the man's marriage gifts were given by the father. The court which, it must be remembered, was an ecclesiastical court, gave two grounds for the dissolution. The first was the girl's impuberty; this would not invalidate a simple betrothal but it would invalidate one blessed by the church. Ecclesiastical courts had also established the principle that a church betrothal or marriage would be dissolved if there was sexual intercourse before the girl reached puberty.[29] The court's further decision, that the son of Argyros should not, in future, go near the girl, is interesting. In other circumstances, it would have been possible to keep the betrothal or to dissolve the current engagement but envisage the possibility of its being renewed once the girl had come of age. That, at least, would seem to be the tenor of canons 22 and 25 of St. Basil, which permits the marriage of a man with the girl he has deflowered, even where force was involved.[30] Indeed, canon 67 of the Apostles insists that a man who has violated a virgin must marry *her* and no other; admittedly, the reference is to a virgin who is not engaged, but it could easily be thought to cover the rape of one's own fiancée.[31] So the girl's impuberty by itself would not seem to justify the decision as it stands. In any case, according to the law, the decision was up to the parents.

At the same time, the civil law on rape was not applied, nor was the case fully treated as a case of rape. The court imposed a punishment ad hoc, and justified it primarily by reference to the injury sustained by the girl and

[29] See, for example, Ralles-Potles, V, 109.

[30] Ralles-Potles, IV, 150–54, 157–59. The Σύνταγμα κατὰ στοιχεῖον of Matthew Blastares states that if a man seduces (φθείρας) his fiancée before her thirteenth year, the resolution is up to the parents of the girl. They can allow the betrothal to stand; if they prefer to break it, because of the seduction (διὰ τὴν φθοράν), the fiancé has to give the girl one-third of his property (Ralles-Potles, VI, 374). The reference derives, in a remote way, from *Procheiros Nomos* 39.65. Cf. *Eclogadion* 17.28.

[31] See the commentary of Balsamon, in Ralles-Potles, II, 86.

her inability to contract a marriage in the future. Thus the girl's absence of consent per se was not treated as a legal issue in this case. The punishment was decided, rather, on the basis of the effect of the sexual intercourse on the future of the girl. Once again, it becomes clear that marriage was considered to be the remedy for a number of sexual crimes, and when marriage was impossible, the severity of the crime increased. At the same time, it is interesting that the patriarchal court did not apply the law on rape, nor did it insist on the issue of rape, as Eustathios Romaios had done.

It is also noteworthy that the court castigated the groom's father for his carelessness in allowing sexual intercourse to take place. This had been a matter of concern for a long time, and a Novel of Alexios I addressed the issue directly. In dealing with betrothal, he said that the engaged couple should not be allowed to meet unsupervised until they had reached puberty. The parents were charged with following this prescription diligently. In case of sexual intercourse before puberty, both the young man and his parents were to be considered guilty of *parthenophthoria*.[32] This Novel was not applied by the patriarchal court to the letter, but a memory of it may well have remained.

Conclusion

As far as sexual crimes are concerned, it seems that the Byzantines placed great importance on objective rather than subjective factors. There are a number of circumstances—the use of arms and accomplices, the locality—which are understood to make it impossible for free consent to be given, and equally impossible to establish whether consent was given or not. In these circumstances, consent is assumed to be absent. In such circumstances, too, it would seem that consent was considered to be the absence of objection: and when this could not be freely exercised or ascertained, the advantage was with the violated woman. On the other hand, sometimes an effort was made to prove the girl's absence of consent: this was so in *Peira* 49.22, where the physical evidence of a struggle was brought forth and accepted by the court, even though it was not necessary for the categorization of the crime. Here something more than absence of objection was sought and proven, not for legal reasons, but rather so as to justify the punishment imposed by the court. The

[32] See *JGR*, I, 324. Elsewhere the emperor says that the parents of both parties would be guilty of *porneia*, and should suffer the appropriate ecclesiastical punishment as well as pay a penalty to the fisc: ibid., p. 109.

claim of psychological injury to the girl strikes a modern note, even though it is tied to a thoroughly medieval and Byzantine concept: the importance of marriage and the evaporation of the girl's hopes for a future marriage. Both the *Peira* 49.22 and the decision of 1325 leave one with the impression that if the marriage had been found valid, the use of force would not have justified an accusation of rape. This question requires further examination, as does the question of coerced consent, that is, consent which was not freely given.

Appendix

Legal Opinion of Eustathios (Romaios) the Magistros (after 1028) (ed. A. Schminck, *Fontes Minores* 3 [1979], 224–28)

In two ways[1] Niketas Gypsokopos tried to shake and destroy a properly constituted marriage, putting forward like siege engines and palisade stakes arguments which, he thought, were excellent. But he was shown under cover of piety and propriety to be insolently attacking John, who had taken in marriage Maria, to whom he had first been legally betrothed.

The accusation was as follows: Theoktistos, who had as his nephew[2] John, the son of his cousin, abducted by armed force John's fiancée, and he "knew" her, even though illegally and by force. And the unholy act had already been punished by law and imperial decision. And the girl is taken from her abductor, being returned to her own home and her mother. But John, on the pretext that he stood by the betrothal and remained faithful to the marriage agreement, took no umbrage at his uncle's congress with Maria, although he brought shame on himself, but for his own part also he stained with condemnation and horror the unlawful union.

So with this first action the accuser pounced on John, but he responded that the attack was false; that during the entire action for abduction the topic of carnal knowledge (φθορά) was never raised.

And indeed this was true; for the legal opinion, which was written by imperial order by the then *protospatharios* and eparch Petros and by us who judged the case, and which described from beginning to end the crime committed, the investigation of the case, and the decision, made no mention at all of deflowering, although such a grave offense would not have been overlooked by the plaintiffs if it actually happened, as it could make the accusation much more terrible and serious and harm the culprit, even if it would add disgrace to the dishonored woman. For nothing which harms an enemy seems shameful to those in the heat of passion.

Furthermore, evidence was also brought forward by well-reputed women who met and confirmed by physical examination and testimony that the girl was untouched.

[1] Only the account of the first attempt is translated here.

[2] Greek uses nephew and uncle to describe what in English would be "first cousins once removed" or, in popular usage, "second cousins."

And their evidence is not to be discarded; for what must be hidden from the eyes of men, in these (matters) it is not forbidden for women to be witnesses, and the law relates as follows: "a woman cannot be a witness to a will, but in other matters she may bear witness." In what other (matters)? Clearly "in matters in which men are not called." Thus, as their testimony was not invalidated according to legal regulation, there is no ground for complaint against the marriage.

For if someone following conjectures may be carried away to assume that it is likely that a girl separated from her family and staying with her abductor will suffer something undesirable, yet another who uses secure reasoning and knows that the possible is between what happens and what does not, will find that carnal knowledge (φθορά) does not of absolute necessity follow abduction. For the man who is smitten by the sight of physical beauty, embracing an insane desire and being love-sick with passion, such a man when he gains control of what he desires may be led down to a slip. But a man whom concern for marriage and for living together as a prelude (to marriage) drives to such an attack, this man does not think it necessary to use force at all, knowing well that a woman's nature is won more by flattery than by force, so as not to have the girl accusing him with the others, but by kindness he may draw her to consent.

Reasoning which considers opposites knows how to create these (possibilities), but the law, which leads matters which are indeterminate and initially hanging in the balance through evidence to clear knowledge, proceeds to the truth, which it respects and prefers to supposition except in some (few) instances.

As the women who were called to testify by the betrothed man and the family of the betrothed girl and who testified to the virginity of the girl were not discredited by the accuser, the marriage already constituted through this testimony will not be dissolved, but will have validity, the women, although they have since died, being believed to have given sworn testimony.

Translation by Denis Sullivan.

4. Coerced Consent

Subjective criteria for establishing consent and its absence are notoriously more difficult to deal with than objective criteria. It is debatable whether, if the circumstances themselves do not prove absence of consent but the woman nevertheless claims that she did not give her consent, this internal absence of consent can be accepted. But the most difficult problem, both to define in theory and to deal with in practice, is connected with consent given under duress. There are a number of questions that modern scholars can raise. The one which seems of primary importance today is the validity of coerced consent: if one agrees to take a certain action under duress, physical or moral, is that action valid? If coercion is established, is the act and its consequences invalidated? Is someone responsible for actions taken under duress? At what point can one claim coercion and expect legal consequences to follow? What are the circumstances in which consent can be said to have been coerced, and do some of them have greater weight than others? And how is coercion proved? The problems are more complex than is apparent at first glance. To take a perfectly contemporary example, the problem is posed if a man persuades a woman over whom he holds some kind of power to sleep with him: an employer and his employee, or a teacher and his student. Can the consent of a woman in such a situation be considered free, or is it to be assumed that the relationship in and by itself is such that an element of force exists or may be feared, thus rendering suspect (and potentially invalid) the consent of the woman?[1] How much force has to be used or threatened for consent to be considered coerced? Does the woman's life have to be threatened, and in what way? Or is fear of much lesser consequences, such as loss of a job, or a threat (real or imagined) to one's career, sufficient to establish coercion? Legal thinking on such issues is evolving in our day, and has been posed differently in different societies. In some societies these problems are not considered to exist, and thus do not give rise to any debate. By extension, it must not be assumed that because such questions are evident in some modern societies

[1] The male and female roles can be reversed in our society.

they were also present in societies of the past; the evidence for each society under discussion must be examined.

The difficulty of dealing with coerced consent can, perhaps, be best understood by a look at some twentieth-century positions. American law, as of 1952, posited that, in cases of alleged rape and except when the woman was under age, instructions to the jury must state that "consent on the part of the female, however reluctantly given, prevents the act from being rape." However, the judge must also know that "where there is evidence not only of force, but of threat of serious bodily harm, an instruction that force may be exerted not only by physical violence but also by threats of serious bodily harm, so as to overpower the female and cause her to yield against her will, is not erroneous."[2] It cannot be said that such instructions are crystal clear.

Insofar as Byzantine society is concerned, the issue of coerced consent was indeed debated, and with some force, but not necessarily in connection with circumstances that are of particular relevance today. Coerced consent to marriage was certainly a matter which was considered grave and which would dissolve a marriage, whether the coercion was due to force, fraud, or fear. The consent extracted from a boy or a girl before puberty was considered *ipso facto* invalid, but this is somewhat different from coerced consent. A number of court cases indicate the types of coercion that were, at various times, thought to invalidate the act. In thirteenth-century Epiros, the lady Theodora tou Indanou, a woman who seems to have been a person of power in Malaina, forced a man and a woman, who were under her authority, to marry. The man was unwilling, resisted, and was imprisoned. His unwillingness was well known in the region, so that the local clerics refused to perform the marriage ceremony. Eventually a priest was called from outside the region, and the wedding took place; although the text does not say so, the young man must have given some sort of consent which the priest found acceptable. However, John Apokaukos, to whom the young man later presented his case, found that the groom had not consented to the marriage, which was dissolved for that reason.[3] In this case, both the authority of the lady Theodora over the young man and her use of physical force invalidated whatever consent he had given

[2] *Corpus Juris Secundum,* "Rape," § 82. For the difficulties posed by coerced consent in Roman society, see Moses, "Livy's Lucretia."

[3] Bees, "Unedierte Schriftstücke," no. 19, and cf. Laiou, "Institution familiale," 308–9.

under duress. A similar case was heard before the patriarchal court of Constantinople in 1401: the *chartophylax* of the church of Thessalonike was powerful enough to force a man named Glavas to marry one of his nieces, despite the fact that Glavas was unwilling to do so. The circumstances, as reported, are rather suspicious: Glavas, we are told, had already been engaged to another niece of the *chartophylax* and had slept with her, when the *chartophylax* accused him of having deflowered the second niece and forced him to marry her; at that point, Glavas slept with his wife once, to prove that she was a virgin, and then disappeared! The story, as related, does not make intuitive sense; nevertheless, what is of interest here is that Glavas' (assumed) consent was considered by the court to have been invalid because he was unwilling and acted under duress.[4]

Less clear is the validity ascribed to consent which was given because the person was fraudulently misinformed. Such was the case of Constantine Palates, who became betrothed to a woman with serious physical flaws of which he was unaware. When he recognized the "fraud" (τὴν ἀπάτην), he withdrew his consent and left the area. Eventually the betrothal was dissolved by the patriarchal court, not because Palates' consent was extracted from him fraudulently, but rather because his parents had not consented, and he himself had developed a violent hatred of his fiancée.[5]

Forced marriage, then, was one area in which the question of free consent was considered important by the Byzantines, and where consent given under duress would invalidate the marriage. The matter did not, as far as I know, give rise to much debate, perhaps because the law was quite unambiguous: no marriage could be valid that was not undertaken with the consent of the future spouses and those who had them under their authority. Whereas questions might arise as to the circumstances in which consent was obtained, and it was possible for the desires of parents and children to differ, the theoretical issues that could be raised did not engage the Byzantines. On the other hand, the eleventh and twelfth centuries saw quite a heated debate on the validity of coerced consent to monastic life and on two other issues connected

[4] Miklosich-Müller, *Acta*, II, 522–23.

[5] Hunger and Kresten, *Das Register des Patriarchats von Konstantinopel*, I, no. 11 (Sept.–Dec. 1315). The fiancée's extreme ugliness or unhealthiness are the only acceptable grounds for breaking an engagement among the modern Sarakatsanoi: Campbell, *Honour*, 128–29.

with it: the forced tonsure of women in order to dissolve their marriages, and the forced tonsure of the former wife of someone who was elected bishop.[6] In principle, monastic life could only be entered upon with the free will, freely exercised, of the person in question. In practice, however, some people were forced to enter a monastery, often by imperial command. Balsamon, a well-known advocate of imperial prerogative, argued that such tonsures were valid, precisely because they were mandated by imperial command.[7] Otherwise, coercion, in the form, for example, of force exercised by an official, invalidated the act. A subtler form of duress, namely, fear of death, which frequently caused men or women to take monastic vows when they were sick, was recognized as duress but was not thought to be a circumstance which invalidated the vow. The forced tonsure of women (or, more rarely, men) as a form of divorce was not easily accepted, although it was practiced. The debate on the validity of such acts centered on the question of whether the divorce that was achieved by the forced tonsure of one of the spouses was valid or not. Opinions were split on the issue, which sometimes had important political overtones. The implicit assumption of those who accepted that the divorce was valid must have been that tonsure, even when forced, was irreversible. In the late twelfth century, a new element was injected, which sought to investigate, even though in a cursory fashion, whether there might be consent after the fact: thus if a woman remained cloistered after the force had been removed, it could be argued that she was acting freely. The implicit assumption of those who did not accept such divorces as valid was that consent obtained by force invalidated the monastic vow and so also the divorce attendant upon it.

The debate on the forced tonsure of the wives of elected bishops had the most interesting theoretical overtones, partly because the canonists who carried out the debate were very eager to establish that these women were, in fact, acting freely. The most coherent argument was that if one freely consents to a course of action, one consents equally freely and fully to its consequences. Thus a woman who consented to divorcing her husband so that he could ascend to the episcopate was held to consent as well to the consequences, that is, to the monastic life.[8]

[6] Laiou, *Mariage, amour et parenté,* chap. 4.

[7] Ibid., and Ralles-Potles, IV, 203.

[8] For the documentation, see Laiou, *Mariage, amour et parenté,* chap. 4.

If there were theoretical debates by civil jurists on the validity of coerced consent to sexual intercourse, they have not survived. The issue of coerced consent, closely connected with internal, subjective criteria of force, was debated only in canonical sources, and raised in literature from a monastic milieu, as we shall see below.

Before discussing the pertinent texts, it will be useful to try to establish a distinction between rape and coerced consent to sexual intercourse, although the boundaries between the two are hazy. In a formal sense, it could be argued that rape in Byzantium was intercourse in conditions that clearly indicated the use of force, or where consent could not be exercised or could not be proved. There are, however, other circumstances, where the woman consented to the act, but her consent was not freely exercised because she acted under duress. The distinguishing line is fine, and sometimes the distinction depends on whether our sources decide to raise the question of consent or not: such is the case of the rape of a woman in captivity. In other cases, the distinction is clear, as, for example, when a woman assents to sexual intercourse although she does not want to, under the force of circumstances such as poverty.

The Legitimation of Coercion

The documents emanating from the court or the hand of John Apokaukos preserve a curious and unique case of coercion sanctioned by society. The people involved were a married couple, Constantine and Irene, peasants who lived in the village of Govlastou, which was, apparently, part of the landed property of the see of Naupaktos.[9] They were married, but a year later Irene had still not allowed the marriage to be consummated. This clearly offended the community, and the inhabitants of the village exercised pressure—through ridicule—on Irene, to no good effect. The administrators of the church tried to threaten her into submission, again without result. They then locked the couple in a hut, repeatedly, so that Constantine would sleep with Irene, *"even though she was unwilling"* (καὶ μὴ θελούσῃ). She fought him, and he bore the scars of her scratches and bites on his hands. Eventually, the dumbfounded Apokaukos pronounced the marriage dissolved, on the grounds of Irene's evident hatred of her husband.

[9] Bees, "Unedierte Schriftstücke," no. 7; cf. Laiou, *Mariage, amour et parenté,* chap. 3.

The affair is, of course, what we would today call marital rape, although the word is not mentioned, and, from the description, the concept could not be further from the mind of Apokaukos. Among the many interesting facts of the case, one may mention the evident interference of the community in the marital affairs of its members. We get a rare glimpse into that aspect of village society, which has been studied in some detail in Western Europe where the documentation is much richer.[10] Of greater interest to us here is the fact that the community, the church administrators, and Apokaukos all considered forced intercourse with equanimity and indeed tried to impose it on an unwilling married woman. What does this legitimation of force within the context of marital sexual activity imply?

The first question that must be asked is whether there is the concept of marital debt, and whether that duty is considered more important than the absence of consent of one of the partners to sexual intercourse. A related question is whether the woman and, indeed, the man, surrenders the free disposition of her/his body at marriage. The sum of these two questions is whether the concept of marital rape existed in Byzantine society. The formal legal statements about marriage do not specifically mention sexual intercourse as a duty, but every presumption of the legislator indicates that sexual intercourse was considered to be a constituent element of marriage. The fact that the legal age of marriage was directly tied to puberty, and the fact that impotence in a man was considered grounds for divorce even in the strict anti-divorce legislation of the *Ecloga* (2.9.3) make the point with some force. Furthermore, Christian theologians and moralists, from St. John Chrysostom on, and starting with St. Paul's grudging statement, "let every man have his own wife to avoid fornication,"[11] had attributed two purposes to marriage: procreation and a legal outlet to sexual urges, although the two carried a different weight at different times.[12]

Canonists had discussed not so much the positive argument that husband and wife had a duty to sleep with each other, but the negative argument that

[10] I am thinking of the Charivari, on which see, for example, Natalie Zemon Davis, *Society and Culture in Early Modern France* (Stanford, Calif., 1975), 97–123, esp. 104–9.

[11] 1 Cor. 7:1. On the marital debt in Western medieval Europe, see James A. Brundage, "Implied Consent to Intercourse," in Part III of this volume.

[12] Laiou, *Mariage, amour et parenté*, chap. 2.

spouses should abstain from intercourse only by common consent. The main text is canon 3 of St. Denys of Alexandria, and especially the twelfth-century commentaries. The canon refers to 1 Cor. 7:5 which says: "defraud ye not one the other, except it be with consent for a time, that ye may give yourselves to fasting and prayer," and adds that they must control this period of abstinence themselves. The twelfth-century commentators insist on the idea that the abstinence must be by mutual agreement. Otherwise, says Zonaras, the partner who does not desire intercourse is depriving the other partner of what Zonaras clearly considers to be his/her legitimate due. He also refers to the statement that "the wife hath not power of her body but the husband; and likewise also the husband hath no power of his own body, but the wife" (1 Cor. 7:4), to argue that the partner who does desire intercourse is the master of the body of his/her spouse. The argument further goes that if one is forced into abstinence, he/she may fall into sin by engaging in illicit sexual activity.[13] Indeed, there is good historical evidence that the clergy counseled wives against abstinence, even when undertaken in the cause of piety, precisely because it endangered the soul of the husband. Thus Patriarch Euthymios advised Theophano, the pious first wife of Leo VI, to rethink her desire to enter a monastery, since this would tempt her husband into adultery. The patriarch referred specifically to 1 Cor. 7:4.[14] Whereas neither the canon of St. Denys nor the commentaries take the further step of sanctioning the use of force, it would not be impossible to argue that this mode of thinking made the use of force acceptable, at least unofficially. Perhaps the issue would have been seen less as forcing the unwilling partner and more as ensuring the payment of the marital debt. In a permutation of this, a woman named Athanasia, who wanted to leave her husband, a man of lewd disposition, and enter a monastery, did her best to persuade him to let her go, even offering him large sums of money. She feared that, if she left him, she could be branded an adulteress, and he would go searching for her in the monastery.[15] A systematic review of hagiographic sources would perhaps yield some interesting information on the topic.

[13] Ralles-Potles, IV, 10. Balsamon repeats the same arguments. The further statement, that the period of abstinence refers only to major times of prayer, and not to every time one prays, is not relevant to our topic.

[14] P. Karlin-Hayter, *Vita Euthymii patriarchae CP* (Brussels, 1970), 37–39.

[15] The story of Athanasia may be found in the *vita* of the 5th-century St. Matrona, *Acta Sanctorum,* Nov. III, 810B.

The case reported by Apokaukos also raises the question of whether sexual intercourse was considered to be a necessary constituent element of a valid marriage. Byzantine law, following Roman law, was formal in stating that it was intent, not intercourse that made a marriage.[16] In the twelfth century, Emperor Manuel I insisted that this was the case. Nevertheless, such a position was hard to maintain in practice, and was undermined by the law itself which considered impotence after three years of marriage sufficient grounds for divorce. The problem became evident in the debate on marriage impediments deriving from consanguinity or affinity. The question was raised, for example, whether it was marriage or sexual intercourse which created relationships that could pose impediments, and the answers were far from consistent. In 1183, when Andronikos I wanted to wed his illegitimate daughter Irene to Manuel I's illegitimate son Alexios, the synod took a highly disputed decision which allowed the marriage on the basis of the argument that illegitimate unions do not create recognizable relationships.[17] The decision was rescinded after Andronikos' demise. On the contrary, Demetrios Chomatianos informed the kral of Serbia that a certain marriage arrangement was impossible because the parties were related, even though by a sexual relationship outside marriage: "for the law does not cast aside the relationships created by fornication."[18] The insistence of the community of Govlastou that Irene and her husband sleep together is undoubtedly an illustration of a general phenomenon: whatever the formal law might say, intercourse was the element which people considered to be the constituent element of a marriage.

In a previous chapter we have seen the concern of the Byzantine legislator with the seduction of unmarried girls and the considerable incentives offered to the man to marry the seduced girl. We have further seen that the law and the courts were primarily concerned with the crime of seduction (rather than abduction, for example) and with its remedy, marriage. We also saw that if a woman consented to the seduction the law seems to assume that she also consented, *ipso facto,* to marriage. Her formal consent to the marriage was undoubtedly essential, but her consent to sexual intercourse created a presumption of consent to marriage. The examination of the issues involved

[16] *D.* 50.17.30 and Justinian, Nov. 22.3.

[17] Niketas Choniates, *Historia,* ed. J. L. van Dieten (Berlin and New York, 1975), 260–62, 309–10; cf. Laiou, *Mariage, amour et parenté,* chap. 1.

[18] Pitra, no. 16.

in sexual intercourse between man and wife seems to establish that consent to marriage also implies necessary consent to sexual intercourse, except when the spouses agree to abstain; thus the very concept of marital rape seems to be absent.

"I will agree to it unwillingly" or, the Consent of the Virtuous Woman

The moralizing literature of the Byzantines contains quite a number of little tales of the following sort. A virtuous woman finds herself in straitened circumstances; her husband is in deep debt or in jail. A rich or powerful man approaches her and offers to rescue her, in return for sexual favors. She hesitates, and then consents with or without the permission of her husband; but before the act can take place, the rich man realizes the error of his ways, and rescues her anyway, for which he is compensated in one way or another.[19] These stories were, one supposes, interesting to their audience because of the inherent tension and drama of the situation, increased by the very mildly salacious sexual element. For us, the interest lies in the attitude of the sources toward coerced consent in such circumstances.

Perhaps the most telling story of this genre is one related by Paul of Monembasia. According to the editor, the story was elaborated between the sixth and the tenth centuries, probably closer to the later date.[20] An old monk describes his meeting with Sergios, *demotes* of Alexandria, whom he found in a tavern, disporting himself with prostitutes whose pimp he was. The monk persuaded Sergios to tell him of at least one good thing he had done in his life, and after demurring at first, Sergios obliged. He related how one day he had gone into a shop and seen a very beautiful woman seated at the loom. He wanted to sleep with her, but was told by the mistress of the shop that this was not possible: the woman was noble, albeit in reduced circumstances since her husband, who owed one hundred gold coins to the governor of Alexandria, was in jail and her two children reduced to slavery. She herself toiled

[19] See, for example, *Pratum Spirituale,* nos. 186, 189. Ibid., no. 39, has a variant case where a young woman feigns consent to her own rape, but argues the amorous monk out of his intention, by waving his responsibilities before him: he could not possibly afford to marry her, and if he insists on violating her he will be responsible for her death, for she will hang herself. The monk, of course, is dissuaded.

[20] John Wortley, *Les récits édifiants de Paul de Monembasie,* (Paris, 1987), 18, 23.

day and night to free them. The shopowner thought that the woman would never agree to sleep with Sergios, even though he offered to pay the hundred gold coins. However, when the woman was approached, she consented (συνέθετο) fairly readily, after an initial outburst of tears. Her reasoning was that God would forgive her because of her *prior blameless life,* and because she would sleep with the man unwillingly. She would surrender her body *moved by necessity* (ἐξ ἀνάγκης), the necessity being the fact that she wanted to free her husband and children, but was unable to manage it. Sergios, having been apprised of her consent, paid her the agreed sum, and she came to his bedroom with tears and sighs, "but still, she came." He, however, seeing her distress, thought that it would be just as easy (and as sinful) for him to sleep with a prostitute; so he let her go but let her keep the cash.[21]

The narrator of this story sets out clearly the circumstances of coerced consent, and insists on both the consent and the coercion. It must be said that his use of language suggests the possibility of a certain tongue-in-cheek attitude toward the woman's protestations. The phrases Εἰ καὶ μετὰ στεναγμοῦ καὶ δακρύων, ὅμως συνέθετο ("even though she sighed and cried, still she agreed"), and ἦκε μετὰ στεναγμῶν καὶ δακρύων οὐ μετρίων, ἀλλ' οὖν εἰσῆλθεν εἰς τὸν κοιτῶνα μου ("she came, with many sighs and tears, but still she entered my bedchamber") suggest that the tears and the sighs may have simply been to save appearances; so does the fact that the woman consented even though the shopkeeper had been sure that she would not. Be that as it may, the point is that the "necessity" or *force majeure* here invoked is economic and family necessity. The woman's consent, although given unwillingly, is valid, that is, there is no hint that the man forced her, although she was forced by circumstances; in other words, the act, had it taken place, would have been fornication rather than rape. Consent, therefore, was valid, even though it was unwilling, indeed forced. In the end, the day was saved by the change of heart of the man, so we never get to learn what the narrator's attitude would have been toward the woman if sexual intercourse had taken place: would she, for example, have suffered some sort of punishment?

In fact, this story, and the others similar to it, are not very useful for our inquiry. The main fact they establish is that economic necessity was seen as a kind of force that produced coerced consent. But, although the circumstances are presented as attenuating the sin, the point is never tested since the

[21] Wortley, *Récits édifiants,* 129–32.

act does not take place. Other evidence suggests that the kind of necessity presented here might not be accepted as sufficient to excuse the consent.

The Limits of Coercion

The Byzantine canonical sources do address the question of the coerced consent of a woman to sexual activity. The most prominent issues here are, first, the kind and degree of coercion that has to be established before it can be proven that consent was really forced; and second, assuming that the woman did not act freely, does this excuse her entirely, in part, or not at all? In other words, does consent, even if extracted by force, make the woman culpable, and does the act itself have consequences for the woman even if she acted under duress?

The issue arose in various contexts, for example, in the matter of sexual relations between a slave woman and her master (canon 49 of St. Basil). The most important context, however, was connected with the circumstances of the early church, which was concerned to establish the limits of punishment for those who had acted under duress in other circumstances: people who had, during the time of persecutions, been forced to sacrifice to the idols, or who had been captured by pagans in a war context and had been forced to eat forbidden food or perform sacrifices to the idols. The consent of women to sexual intercourse in similar circumstances is treated as part of this problem. Although early canonical legislation arose out of specific realities, the broad issue remained important in the twelfth-century commentaries. The advance of the Turks in Asia Minor created once again situations in which men became renegades, and the church had to define its position toward apostasy under duress.[22] Second, the arbitrary and authoritarian actions of twelfth-century emperors, who intervened with a heavy hand in matrimonial affairs and sometimes forced people to enter monastic life, also gave the canonists the occasion to comment on the validity of actions undertaken under duress.[23]

Roman law had also contended with the problem of married women who slept with their captors in the context of war. The relevant legislation is pro-

[22] On this, see N. Oikonomidès, "La brebis égarée et retrouvée: l'apostat et son retour," in D. Simon, ed., *Religiöse Devianz, Jus Commune,* no. 48 (Frankfurt, 1990), 143–57; on the 12th century, see esp. pp. 147–54. The reader will also find in this article the various canons that deal with apostasy.

[23] See above, pp. 139–40, and Laiou, *Mariage, amour et parenté* chap. 4.

cedural, that is, it has to do with what happens to the woman's marriage, and what action the husband can bring against her when she returns. The marriage is dissolved, since captivity deprives the woman of her free status, and it is renewed when she returns. The husband, then, may bring an action of adultery against her, though not by right of being her husband, since he was not married to her during the period of her captivity. However, if she was *forced* to commit adultery, no action may be taken against her.[24] It would thus seem that according to civil law captivity itself was not proof of coercion, but that if the woman could somehow prove that she was forced to sleep with her captor(s), she was restored to her former position and suffered no punishment. It is interesting that the commentary on the *Basilics* includes canon 1 of St. Gregory of Neocaesareia and canon 49 of St. Basil, which discuss how one should deal with women who had sexual intercourse with a man under duress. Thus the commentators saw that, although civil and canon law treat the matter very differently, they address the same general problem.

For our purposes, the first important text is canon 1 of St. Gregory of Neocaesareia, which is interesting in itself and is also a point of reference in the commentaries on other canons. The canon discusses two related topics: the treatment of people who ate forbidden foods when in captivity, and of the women who slept with their captors. The context is barbarian invasions. On the first issue, the resolution is that this act did not entail sin, especially since the barbarians in question did not sacrifice to idols, so that the forbidden foods were not sacrificial meats. On the second issue, involving women, the saint is not quite so sanguine. Here he wishes to examine whether the act really took place under duress, and the criterion is simple: it is the woman's prior life. If she was known to have led a virtuous life, and "now she has suffered an insult under violence and duress," the presumption will be that she is blameless. The presumption is justified by an appeal to Deut. 22:26, which speaks of rape that takes place in the wilderness. Thus the act is, for all intents and purposes, equated to rape, and the woman is not subject to

[24] *Bas*. 60.37.14 = *D*. 48.5.13.14: καὶ ἡ παρὰ τοῖς πολεμίοις μοιχευθεῖσα καὶ ὑποστρέψασα κατηγορεῖται παρὰ τοῦ ἀνδρὸς οὐ δικαίῳ ἀνδρός, εἰ μὴ βίᾳ τοῦτο πέπονθεν. The commentary says that there are two divergent readings, οὐ δικαίῳ ἀνδρὸς and δικαίῳ ἀνδρός, with the second reading being the most frequent, and proceeds to explain the meaning of both readings. Cf. Moses, "Livy's Lucretia."

punishment. On the other hand, a woman whose prior life was not virtuous must be suspected of a propensity to fornication in times of captivity as well, and such a woman should not be easily readmitted to communion.[25] Thus the woman's prior life is made the criterion on the basis of which one differentiates between (presumed) coerced consent and (presumed) free consent to the act. The focus of attention is not on whether the woman acquiesced or not to a particular act, but on whether she was of good character or not; an extension of this argument would be that a woman of suspect morals always consented to sexual intercourse, and could not be raped.

The commentaries on this canon are particularly interesting. Zonaras starts with a historical statement, setting the canon within the historical circumstances of the barbarian invasions. On the matter of those who ate forbidden foods, he proceeds to elaborate and make a distinction which the canon had not made, between eating out of gluttony and eating in order to sustain life; the prisoners who ate these foods, being enslaved (and therefore, it is presumed, not having freedom of action), if they did it to sustain life, will be excused. By the same token, he makes the even clearer distinction between women whose prior life was not virtuous, and who must suffer ecclesiastical punishment, and those who had led a virtuous prior life and who, "having been enslaved because of the captivity, suffered the barbarians' insult by force"; they did not sin and will not be punished. Zonaras introduces here the concept that a war captive is enslaved, and therefore by definition incapable of free will and subject to the consent of the master. The corollary of this position (which owes a good deal to Roman law) would be that *all* women captives who slept with their captors must be assumed to have been forced. Therefore, the exception concerning the woman whose prior morals were suspect is even more anomalous than it was in the canon. The explanation lies in Zonaras' gloss of the words "whorish habit" (πορνικὴ ἕξις). "Habit," he says, "is long-term behavior which has been solidified by time, so that it becomes second nature." Presumably, then, these women acted according to their nature, and their nature is to consent to sexual intercourse in all circumstances.

[25] Joannou, *Les canons des pères grecs*, 19–21; Ralles-Potles, IV, 45–46. On the connection between food pollution and sexual pollution, see Mary Douglas, *Purity and Danger: An Analysis of Concepts of Pollution and Taboo* (New York and Washington, D.C., 1966), 123 ff.

Balsamon's position was more subtle, and stricter, both in the case of those who ate forbidden food and in the case of the women who slept with their captors. After having repeated Zonaras' commentary, he goes on to establish distinctions of his own. His premise is that St. Gregory had said that the sin of those who eat sacrificial meats is not great, not that it should not be punished at all. For his part, Balsamon divides people among those who ate sacrificial meats willingly and with pleasure; those who ate because they were forced by the barbarians; those who ate because of natural need; and those who were forced by barbarians who did not sacrifice to the idols. All of them must be punished, but with different degrees of severity, depending on consent and duress, the heaviest punishment going to those who ate willingly, the lightest to those who were forced by the need to survive. The most important distinction he makes is between being forced by circumstances to take a certain action, and performing the action itself under clear force: thus, in the case at hand, someone who has food or drink pushed or poured down his throat by force is blameless. By contrast, those forced by general circumstances (captivity, the need to survive) to eat forbidden meats did so with a certain measure of consent (ὑποκύψαντες τῷ θελήματι τοῦ τυράννου) and thus must be punished to some extent. These distinctions, not mentioned in the canon under discussion, are nevertheless made by other canons. Balsamon is here glossing the relatively mild dispositions of St. Gregory by introducing the more severe attitude of other canons.[26]

Having discussed the matter of forbidden foods, Balsamon adds that, by the same token, the women who slept with the barbarians by force (τὸ ὑποστῆναι φθορὰν βαρβαρικὴν κατὰ βίαν) must suffer some ecclesiastical punishment, although a mild one. Here he departs quite clearly from the

[26] Ralles-Potles, IV, 47–49. The Council of Ankyra dealt extensively with the question of those who were forced to sacrifice or to eat forbidden meats, and the 12th-century commentators also discuss the distinction between various degrees of force: canons 3, 4–6, 8, 12. Balsamon takes the opportunity presented by canon 3 of the Council of Ankyra to discuss the case of the forced tonsure of a bishop and the forced tonsure of noble ladies by Emperor Andronikos I. None of these canons refer to women who might have been violated by pagans or while they were captive; nor do the other relevant canons, for example, canons 73 and 81 of St. Basil, canon 2 of Gregory of Nyssa, canons 1–14 of St. Peter of Alexandria, and canons 11 and 12 of the Council of Nicaea. Note that pollution is expiated by the ecclesiastical punishment, and cf. Douglas, *Purity,* 134.

canon, and seeks to support his position by simply reiterating that canon law, unlike civil law, will not suffer the polluted (μολυνθεῖσαν) woman to go unpunished. Unfortunately for the logic of his argument, the canon law he invokes is the one he is trying to establish. Of the civil laws he invokes, Novel 33 (not 103 as in the text) of Leo VI the Wise has nothing to do with the topic, and *Bas.* 60.37.14 does not support his position, as he himself recognizes.

Balsamon's commentary on this canon shows him to be much stricter than the canon itself and stricter than Zonaras in his attitude toward the woman who is violated while in captivity. Since he uses variants of the word "force" (βία, κατὰ βίαν, βιασθεῖσαι), it is quite clear that he is speaking of a situation in which the women acted under duress. But he also establishes that the woman nevertheless consented, even though under duress (she could, one supposes, have opted for death). So he is speaking of coerced consent, which he pronounces punishable. In the case of women whose prior behavior was immoral, he concurs with the canon and with Zonaras that this establishes the presumption of a consent freely given: prior behavior supersedes the duress of the woman's present situation. In the case of a woman of blameless prior morals, coercion does not entirely absolve her from punishment either, although the punishment would be milder. If he is arguing from analogy with the case of people who ate forbidden foods under duress, it would seem that the telling point is the degree of force the person suffered, the residual being a degree of consent: she would have had to prove lack of consent to the act itself, not to the circumstances. However, Balsamon does not explicitly develop the analogy; in the end, it would seem that for the woman it is the act itself which is punishable, as well as her intention.

A similar position may be discerned in the commentary on canon 49 of St. Basil. The canon itself is short and, it would seem, clear: "The seductions (fornications) which are carried out by force carry no guilt; thus the slave who is forced by her master is innocent."[27] Zonaras elaborates somewhat on the lack of consent, stressing that the slave woman who is forced, and who submits to her master's desires *unwillingly,* will not be subject to the ecclesiastical punishment given to fornicators. He then extends the provisions of the

[27] Ralles-Potles, IV, 202: αἱ πρὸς ἀνάγκην γενόμεναι φθοραί, ἀνεύθυνοι ἔστωσαν· ὥστε καὶ ἡ δούλη, εἰ ἐβιάσθη παρὰ τοῦ ἰδίου δεσπότου, ἀνεύθυνος ἐστίν. The commentaries are on pp. 202–3.

canon to those women who were abducted against their will and to "the others who were seduced (ἐφθάρησαν) in similar ways," with specific reference to the canon of St. Gregory of Neocaesareia which was discussed above. Thus he assimilates all sexual intercourse in which the woman was under duress, physical or formal, and finds the woman blameless, always, presumably, subject to the restriction of a virtuous prior life which was enunciated in the canon of St. Gregory.

Balsamon takes a different attitude. He, too, extends the canon to cover all involuntary seductions, including that of free women who are somehow under the authority of a governor or official (ἀρχοντικῶν προσώπων). He refers one to the first canon of St. Denys of Alexandria, which, however, has nothing to do with the topic; the reference may be to the first canon of St. Peter of Alexandria, concerning those who abjured the Christian faith after torture, and which does mandate a mild ecclesiastical punishment. The careful reader of Balsamon's text would, perhaps, have seen this discrepancy. The canonist then proceeds to add some refinements to the canon and, it seems to me, to change its intent. He says that the woman violated under the conditions mentioned above will not suffer the *epitimia* proper to fornicators; however, the woman who was taken by force, if she had been a deaconess, will not be allowed to continue in this office.

Balsamon's argument is based on both analogy and an appeal to the inscrutable ways of God. The argument from analogy states that a priest who has been forced to do something that prohibits him from exercising the priestly function (or has done so through ignorance) will be deposed.[28] By an analogy that is not at all evident to the modern reader, Balsamon extends this to the case of people who became monks because the emperor forced them to: they will remain monks, "even though they were shorn by force." Equally by analogy, more evident in this case, the deaconess who has been violated will not be able to exercise that office.

In fact, slave women were never able to become deaconesses, and the office itself did not exist in Balsamon's time. Therefore, unless his argument deals with an anachronistic situation, which would not be typical for this canonist, the message he wishes to convey is general and not specific. That message is, quite simply, that the woman who has been forced to sleep with

[28] Balsamon is referring, correctly, to canon 1 of the Council of Ankyra and canon 27 of St. Basil.

someone is tainted, polluted. It is the act itself which changes the status of the woman, not her consent or absence of consent. In this case, as in the case of women violated by their captors, as, by an analogy of our own, in the case of any woman who is forced into sexual intercourse, her consent is only one of the factors which govern the consequences for her: she is thought in any case to have given some sort of consent; coercion does not fully excuse her consent; and she remains tainted by the act. Whatever might seem to Balsamon's contemporaries problematic about punishing someone who has not consented freely to an act is resolved by the appeal to the inscrutable ways of God: "God allowed her to suffer an evil thing" (διὰ τὸ παραχωρήσει Θεοῦ ἐμπεσεῖν αὐτὴν εἰς κακόν).

Balsamon is, arguably, the most important Byzantine canonist. Although some of his opinions were later disputed by less eminent figures like John of Kitros, and although his own writings recognize the fact that certain issues were hotly debated by other canonists, he was not *sui generis,* and his statements are worthy of serious consideration. He was, furthermore, deeply interested in the question of coerced consent, and his position can be discerned through his various statements. He upheld, on the whole, the right of imperial authority to force people into taking certain actions which were predicated upon a semblance, at least, of free consent; and he upheld that position even for an emperor who was widely considered a tyrant, namely, Andronikos I. But his attitude was also dependent on the gender of the person who gave coerced consent. Thus, when specific cases came up, he was much more ready to accept coerced tonsure when it happened to a woman than to a man. On the issue at hand, his attitude is also incoherent. It has been argued that he was particularly lenient to repentant renegades who acted under pressure from the Turks.[29] That, I think, is true, and a credit to Balsamon's political

[29] Oikonomidès, "La brebis égarée," 148–50. I do not, however, agree with the author that Balsamon is shocked by the very strict provisions of canon 62 of the Apostles for clerics who abjure the Christian faith (Ralles-Potles, II, 80). On the contrary, I would take Balsamon's argument not as sarcastic but at face value. The fact that he adduces the civil law, much more lenient than the ecclesiastical law on this issue, does not mean that he was favoring civil law. The point he is making here is exactly the same as in his commentary on canon 1 of St. Gregory of Neocaesareia (see above, pp. 190–91), where he does adduce the civil law, but only to say that the ecclesiastical law is stricter, and to follow the latter—even though his argument is specious, as I have tried to indicate.

acumen.[30] The liberal attitude does not, however, extend to women who were forced into sexual intercourse; here he is much less benevolent than Zonaras, and attaches a measure of culpability to the woman, however great the coercion may have been. The culpability is, it seems, primarily moral rather than legal.

I would suggest that Balsamon's less than watertight argumentation indicates a certain dissonance between legal principles and social assumptions. The legal principle, well established in Roman and Byzantine civil law, and adopted by ecclesiastical law, was that one is not responsible for actions undertaken because of violence or under duress; the validity of such acts was highly questionable. On the other hand, there seems to be a deeply engrained persuasion that a woman is never really and truly forced, but that an element of consent is present.[31] That may be why the judges who tried cases of statutory rape were so insistent on registering the evidence of violence. And this would explain why Balsamon finds it possible to hold the woman raped by someone who holds power over her guiltless legally but guilty morally (in his commentary on canon 49 of St. Basil).

It is, once again, literature which may give us an insight into the underlying assumptions. The source used here is, undoubtedly, specific to a particular, monastic milieu. But we shall see in the next chapter that similar assumptions appear in the poem of *Digenes Akrites,* written for an aristocratic, even court, audience. Paul of Monembasia relates the story of three women who lived in the theme of Anatolikon during the reign of Constantine VII, in

[30] As Oikonomidès has argued, the Byzantine church exhibited the same liberal attitude toward renegades in the 13th century. An interesting case appears in the acts of the Patriarchate of Constantinople in the late 14th century. A certain Merxes (Mrkša Žarković), "cousin" of Emperor Manuel II, had sent, through an intermediary, a request for the recognition of his marriage or, possibly, only for a confirmation that he was held blameless for it. The marriage was within the prohibited degrees of relationship (fourth degree by affinity), and the patriarch found the matter to be a vexed one. However, he recognized the marriage, and sent Merxes his blessing, because the marriage had been undertaken by necessity and force, exercised by the Turks. The duress was that if the marriage had not taken place, a great number of Christians stood in peril of their lives, although we do not know why. Thus the synod accepted the evident necessity, and held Merxes not only blameless but praiseworthy: Miklosich-Müller, *Acta,* II, pp. 230–31; Darrouzès, *Regestes,* no. 2975.

[31] For similar attitudes in classical Greece, see Lefkowitz, "Seduction and Rape in Greek Myth."

conditions sufficient to arouse anyone's pity: they inhabited a ravine, went naked for lack of clothing, and ate only the fruits brought them by a raven. One of the women explained to a newly arrived tax collector that she was the widow of a *protospatharios* from Constantinople. She was widowed at a young age, and a powerful man became enamored of her, so he sent his servants to abduct her by force (ἁρπᾶσαι με βίᾳ). She, on the other hand, tried to persuade them not to use force, and told them that she would go happily with them, except that she suffered from an ugly illness from which, however, she would be cured within forty days. They agreed to return after forty days, and she immediately distributed all her belongings to the poor, freed her slaves, and fled, with the two faithful servants whom she had kept. The tax collector and the abbot of a neighboring monastery were duly impressed, gave the women food and holy communion, and remained to bury them as they died, one after another, within three days.[32]

The moral of this story, and of others like it, is quite clear. Women can avoid rape or abduction. There are alternatives, hard ones to be sure, such as death or a form of living death, but nevertheless they are there for the woman who really does not consent.[33] It is a harsh position, and an ecclesiastical one. We saw in the previous chapter that civil law gave the benefit of the doubt to the woman who was raped in circumstances where she was incapable of giving a valid consent; and we have seen that this premise was, indeed, followed in some court cases. However, no society has a single, consistent attitude to such issues, and the other set of assumptions, which does not give the woman the benefit of the doubt, is also present, visible in ecclesiastical sources but lurking elsewhere, and not only in the famous edict of Constantine I.

Conclusion

Byzantine law recognized, at least since the time of the *Ecloga,* the consent of the woman as a very important factor in the differentiation of sexual crimes and the differentiation of punishment for the man. If a woman could establish that she was forced to have sexual intercourse, not only was the man punished more severely, but she profited from the punitive damages the man had to pay

[32] Wortley, *Récits édifiants,* 28–32.

[33] For death as an alternative to which the woman did not ultimately have to resort, see *Pratum Spirituale,* chap. XXXIX.

her. Thus, unless the situation was resolved informally and within the family setting, as most of the cases must have been, a woman and her family had every incentive to claim that she was forced; the law was not applied to the letter, but damages were, in fact, paid. Thus the courts had to address, in practice, the issue of what constitutes consent and what constitutes force. Civil law recognized a number of circumstances which established presumption of force, and thus the woman was, to some extent, protected.

The role of the church was rather complex. By insisting on the importance of the inner life, Christianity and the Christian church were an important force in developing the principle of individual responsibility and thus of consent. The church, at the same time, embraced older and widespread ideas about the importance of purity and the dangers of pollution. Anthropologists have taught us that pollution is independent of intentionality: "the distinctions of voluntary, involuntary, internal, external, are not relevant." What is relevant is simply whether a contact involving pollution has taken place.[34] Hence the ambivalent position of the church and the canonists. In some respects, the church was more sophisticated than civil law, for it was willing to go beyond appearances and face the issues of internal, subjective consent or absence of consent. On the other hand, it stated the fear of pollution which other sources may hint at, and at that level responsibility, intentionality, consent are less relevant. The end result is that in some ways women were less protected by ecclesiastical law than by civil law. For the church, the final proof of non-consent was always stark: the alternatives were recognized as death, living death, or some other extreme measure; furthermore, the criterion of a blameless prior life judges a woman's general behavior and not the particular act in question: finally, the church, which had recognized crying in the wilderness as a presumption of force, was unwilling to extend this to all similar circumstances. Balsamon undoubtedly was much stricter than others in this respect, but he was building upon an ideological substratum which recognized a subliminal responsibility of the woman who has been polluted. The role of the church in the development of the theory of consent thus has several different

[34] Douglas, *Purity,* 59 ff, 99 ff, 130 ff. I am grateful to Professor Tambiah for guiding me to the anthropological literature. The reader should note, however, Mary Douglas' statement that ideas of pollution form a part of society's general views and values. Since there is no analysis of Byzantine society in anthropological terms, one should be cautious about using the results of research that stem from other societies.

aspects to it. And when they have all been taken into account, it may be stated that canon law helped develop the idea of personal responsibility but that civil law, by recognizing intentionality as always pertinent, was often more beneficial to women.

5. The Evidence of Literature

What can literature contribute to an inquiry such as ours? If handled carefully, it can instruct us as to contemporary concerns and underlying attitudes. It can also be vastly misleading, for literature is not necessarily a reflection of reality, indeed it can be and often is a reversal of reality, and that too, if identified, is valuable information. But a straight reading of literary sources can lead us down a primrose path to lands that never were. Above all, one must remember that literature has its own rules and its own concerns: tension, conflict, taut situations are at a premium, as is their resolution. Abduction, rape, seduction, adultery, and temptation of all sorts make for a tense plot and good reading. Their presence in literary sources does not mean that they were rampant in society; it does mean that they provide a juicy plot, but what they reflect may be the very opposite of social practice.

In the Byzantine context, the pertinent sources are hagiography and tales of morality, to the extent that they can be considered literature, and, of course, the romances of the twelfth and fourteenth centuries, starting with the romance of *Digenes Akrites*. If one examines them internally, one would look primarily at the issues the authors choose to discuss and the terms in which the issues are presented. What is also of interest here are the attitudes that are projected and, since we are concerned with legal issues, the authors' knowledge and use of the laws. In what follows, I will concentrate on the romance of *Digenes Akrites* and the learned romances of the twelfth century.[1]

The story of *Digenes Akrites*, on which many studies have been written, is a romance set in a quasi-epic form, if only because the geographic setting of the story is the Arab-Byzantine frontier in Asia Minor, and we have been

[1] On the romances in general, see H.-G. Beck, *Byzantinisches Erotikon* (Munich, 1986); Roderick Beaton, *The Medieval Greek Romance* (Cambridge, 1989); L. Garland, "'Be Amorous but Be Chaste': Sexual Morality in Byzantine Learned and Vernacular Romance," *Byzantine and Modern Greek Studies* (hereafter *BMGS*) 14 (1990), 62–120. On *Digenes Akrites*, see H.-G. Beck, *Geschichte der byzantinischen Volksliteratur* (Munich, 1971), 62–97, and C. Galatariotou, "Structural Opposites in the Grottaferrata *Digenes Akrites*," *BMGS* 11 (1987), 29–68.

taught to consider such frontiers as giving rise to epic songs. The story starts with the raid of an Arab emir into Byzantine territory and the capture of a Byzantine maiden whom he eventually marries. This part of the narrative is full of conflicts and reconciliations, memories of past wars between Byzantines and Arabs and the Byzantine armies and the Paulicians. It is the most martial part of the story, even if the wars are told at one or more removes and belong to a past recalled by the emir. The child of the emir and the Byzantine maiden, Digenes Akrites, the hero of the second part of the story, is a prodigy from a young age. A valiant young man, he falls in love with a girl, abducts her, marries her, and proceeds to have exciting adventures, both amorous and martial, all in single combat. He eventually builds a palace on the Euphrates and dies at the significant age of thirty-three, his loving wife dying of grief before him.[2] The original version of *Digenes Akrites* must have been written in the first half of the twelfth century, given the mention in the Ptochoprodromic poem.

[2] See Beaton, *Romance,* 29–32, for a fuller summary of the story. The romance is extant in a number of versions. The best edition is by Erich Trapp, *Digenes Akrites—synoptische Ausgabe der ältesten Versionen,* Wiener byzantinistische Studien 8 (Vienna, 1971). For an English translation, see J. Mavrogordato, *Digenes Akrites, Edited with an Introduction, Translation and Commentary* (Oxford, 1956). The vernacular Escorial version is now considered to be closest to the original, although the Grottaferrata version, in a more learned style, preserves parts of the story that are not extant in the Escorial version. For the primacy of the Escorial version, see St. Alexiou, *Vasileios Digenes Akrites kai to asma tou Armoure* (Athens, 1985), passim; on the matter, cf. Beaton, *Romance,* 40–41. It is not quite clear when the two extant versions (as opposed to the prototype) were written, although we do know that a version of the story was known in aristocratic circles in Constantinople during the reign of Manuel I Komnenos (1143–80): St. Kyriakides, "Forschungsbericht zum Akritas-Epos," *Berichte zum XI. Internationalen Byzantinisten-Kongress,* II (Munich, 1958), 22, quoting a poem of Ptochoprodromos which mentions Manuel I as τὸν νέον τὸν 'Ακρίτην. On the identity of the author of the Ptochoprodromic poems and Theodore Prodromos, and the dates of Theodore Prodromos, see A. Kazhdan and S. Franklin, *Studies on Byzantine Literature of the Eleventh and Twelfth Centuries* (Cambridge, 1984), 90–93. The manuscripts are not helpful for establishing the dates of the two versions, since the Escorial manuscript is of the 15th century and the Grottaferrata one of the 14th. Scholars have usually discussed both versions as if they were of the 12th century, and there is no reason to challenge that assumption. Fortunately, the two versions do not differ significantly in what concerns the most important part of the story for my purposes, that is, for the scene of the abduction of Digenes' bride. Those differences which may be significant will be noted below.

Scholars have noticed, usually in shocked tones, that this Byzantine story, which they variously classify as epic and romance, is replete with sexual misdeeds. The two most important couples (Digenes' father and mother as well as the hero and his bride) are created by abduction. There is a case of seduction and elopement, admittedly of an Arab girl, one rape and one adultery, both committed by the hero. Hans-Georg Beck, commenting on the evident disjunction between the laws of church and state on the one hand and the behavior of the hero on the other, takes the story at face value and gives it probative value for the statement that Byzantine legal norms were not followed in the provinces.[3] But the poem as we have it, whatever the origins of its kernel, was probably written in Constantinople,[4] and in any case Beck has not made a careful examination of the legal problems incorporated in the story. Michael Angold, in a relatively recent study, concentrates on abduction. He, too, gives the story a place in social history, considering it to be a quasi-realistic although exaggerated reflection of two alternative positions toward marriage: a private affair, which could embrace abduction, and a public matter, in which abduction was severely punished.[5] A close look, however, suggests quite a different reading.

Let us look at abduction first. Roderick Beaton has recognized the importance of abduction, as a literary ploy, in all the twelfth-century romances. He has made the point that the heroes of these stories take only one decisive action, abduction, which in ancient romances is contemplated but not carried out.[6] This, then, would seem to be a real innovation of the otherwise highly derivative twelfth-century romances. The story of *Digenes Akrites* is, of course, not derivative; and it is here that abduction plays the most important role and is described in loving and significant detail.

There are, as I have already indicated, two abduction scenes in the story.

[3] H.-G. Beck, "Orthodoxie und Alltag," in *Byzantium: Tribute to Andreas N. Stratos*, II (Athens, 1986), 342 ff.

[4] I find the arguments presented by N. Oikonomidès, "L''épopée' de Digénis et la frontière orientale de Byzance aux Xe et XIe siècles," *Travaux et mémoires* 7 (1979), 375–97, and especially 396–97, persuasive, even though they have not been taken into account sufficiently by Alexiou, *Vasileios Digenes*.

[5] Angold, "The Wedding of Digenes Akrites," 201–15.

[6] Beaton, *Romance*, 60–61.

The most interesting and detailed is the abduction by Digenes of the girl of whom he is enamored. She is young, rich, of excellent family, and jealously guarded by her father, the *strategos* (general). Many noble young men desired to carry her off because of her beauty, but were killed by her father. Digenes courts her, seizes her, and after being pursued by her father's army and her brothers, is reconciled with her family and marries her, with the consent of both families. It is this story which has been explained as reflecting a reality that admits abduction as an alternative path to a properly arranged marriage, and has been seen by scholars as an illegal, but nevertheless accepted, act.

The terminology used in the text is, indeed, unequivocally that of abduction. Both of the oldest texts, the Escorial and the Grottaferrata, use the words which, in law, describe the crime of abduction, that is, the verb ἁρπάζω in its various forms, and the noun ἁρπαγή.[7] For such a crime, we know, the civil law mandated very severe punishment. According to Novel 35 of Leo VI, which is meant to replace *Bas.* 60.58.1, if a girl is abducted and raped, and if she is noble-born, as this one certainly was, the culprit is punished by death and the confiscation of his property, assuming that the abduction has taken place with force of arms. If no weapons were employed, the man's hands are mutilated, and his property is confiscated. The girl's consent is immaterial: it does not change the man's punishment, nor does it make marriage possible; in such circumstances, marriage is absolutely forbidden.

But if the language in *Digenes Akrites* is that of abduction, the situation, as described, tells quite a different story. The abduction scene is preceded by a discussion of love and how it makes people behave. Digenes and the girl fall in love, and she wants to marry him. It is her father who keeps her locked up and has killed her other suitors—surely a ballad-like motif. When Digenes pleads with his father to ask for the girl's hand, he learns that his father, behaving absolutely properly within the Byzantine context, had tried to arrange a marriage between her and his son, even before Digenes expressed his love, but he had failed.[8] Everyone is behaving properly, except for the girl's father who is being unreasonable.

[7] References will be to the Trapp edition. G refers to the Grottaferrata text, and E to the Escorial. E 1013: ἁρπαγὴ τῆς κόρης; G IV, 954: πῶς τὴν κόρην ἥρπαξε; 1552, 1554: ἤρθη, ἡρπάγη; 1675; κλεψίγαμον, ἥρπασας.

[8] G IV, 1205 ff, 1235, 1252–60; cf. E 853–55.

Then the couple take things into their own hands. Digenes asks the girl to marry him, and we are treated to another disquisition on love. She gives him a ring, the symbol of betrothal. Marriage is the purpose from the very beginning, a fact which is reaffirmed several times and confirmed by the girl who says that she will marry him for love, even though it is illegal for her to give herself to him: εἰ καὶ λίαν πάρανομον ἑαυτὴν προδοῦναι. He wants to establish the fact of her consent to running away, and she gives it: πείθομαι νῦν καὶ βούλομαι μετὰ σοῦ πορευθῆναι. So the act will fall under the rubric of elopement rather than abduction.[9] Furthermore, the poet takes care to establish the fact that the hero is acting alone in the enterprise. The only accomplices he wishes to have are God and the night; otherwise he will act all by himself:

> [He] was imploring God from all his heart:
> Saying "O God and Master, hear my prayer,
> Sink me the sun and make the moon to rise,
> To be my complice in this business,
> For I shall have to go one and alone."[10]

The word used to show that the hero is acting alone is the superlative form of the adjective, the rare word μονώτατος. The Escorial version (786) also mentions that Digenes was on his own, although here the point that is stressed is his heroic valor, since, alone that he is, he will meet and fight an army to win her. In the Grottaferrata version, on the other hand, the effort made is to establish that Digenes is carrying out the *abduction* by himself, that is, without accomplices. Valiant acts performed earlier in the narrative, for example, his exploits against bears and lions, were carried out in the presence of, although not with the help of, his father and uncle. I insist on this point, because the absence of accomplices removes one of the presumptions of force, at least as the matter was perceived in the eleventh century. Therefore, we have the following elements: the young couple voice their desire to marry, and the girl gives not only her clear consent but also a ring; the girl's father is the only one to object; the couple recognize that going against his will is illegal, but nevertheless they decide to run away. The hero is acting alone, a fact stressed by the poet. Finally, and most importantly, they do not sleep

[9] On the above, see G IV, 889–92, 1268, 1315, 1325, 1357, 1422, 1463, 1515. E 840 ff.

[10] G IV, 1322–25: μονώτατος; cf. G IV, 1357, μόνος; Mavrogordato, p. 97.

together, so no seduction of an abducted virgin has taken place. Would this have been considered abduction by a Byzantine judge in the twelfth century?

In the story, the parents behave as though there has been a real abduction (G IV, 1550 ff; E 910 ff). The girl's father, the *strategos,* and her brothers send out an army to avenge the crime and kill the hero. They are acting correctly and legally, for the law punished the parents who agreed to abduction, before or after the fact.[11] After Digenes has proven his prowess (by killing some of the people sent against him), the *strategos* agrees that the young man will make a good son-in-law. But the *strategos* insists on proper marriage contracts, a dowry, a church blessing, and an open wedding, so that the propriety of the marriage will be unquestioned. Digenes at first shuns the dowry, but eventually he accepts it. There is a reconciliation of the parents and the two families, symbolized by the fact that the poet insists on the presence of the girl's brothers.[12] In the Escorial version, the reconciliation seems endangered by the insistence of the *strategos* that the wedding take place in his house, and Digenes' own desire that he take the girl home to marry her. The Grottaferrata version makes the best of this by having what seems to be two weddings, one in each venue. In both versions, the episode ends with a perfectly proper and glorious wedding and with the exchange of wedding gifts of great value.[13]

If, for the purposes of the story, the girl's parents treat the affair as abduction, I submit that in a court of law, and in the minds of informed contemporaries, it would not have counted as abduction, especially as the story is presented in the Grottaferrata version. The poet takes great care to establish,

[11] Leo VI, Novel 35.

[12] G IV, 1820, 1893. This does not appear in the E version.

[13] Much has been made of the fact that the description of the wedding does not include a church ceremony, and no priests are visible. Angold ("Wedding," 203–4, 213–14) thinks that this is a reflection of a reality in which the church had not yet established fully its claim that the only valid marriage was accomplished by a church wedding. On the contrary, I think that this was so well established that there was no need to insist on it, while the poet has to insist on those aspects that were disputed in the story, namely, parental consent and the exchange of marriage gifts. In fact, both versions have Digenes' father-in-law use terms which are proper to a church wedding: νὰ σᾶς εὐλογήσωμεν (E 991) and τὴν ἱερολογίαν (G IV, 1674). For a present-day parallel, see the description of marriage among the Sarakatsanoi by an eminent anthropologist. There is a long description of the customs and a bare mention of the (necessary) church wedding: Campbell, *Honour,* 60 ff.

first of all, that the hero has the girl's full consent and that the aim is marriage. Second, the hero has no accomplices; and, although when he has to defend himself he draws his sword, the abduction itself is carried out without the use of arms. According to Novel 35 of Leo VI, an abduction can take place with or without arms, and is punished differently depending precisely on whether or not they are used; the consent of the girl is immaterial; rape seems to be a constituent element of the crime. But we have also seen that the eleventh-century courts gave different interpretations to the law, making it much more lenient and establishing other criteria that differentiated between abduction and elopement.[14] According to Eustathios Romaios, in the absence of sexual intercourse, the man is punished more leniently than the law required, even when arms were used. Furthermore, still in the opinion of the same judge, the presence of accomplices is a real differentiating factor between elopement and abduction: "If a man comes to the house of another with a mob, and seizes a woman, whether with her consent or not, he is guilty of abduction and is punished; but if he comes alone, with no accomplices, and dares to take secretly a woman who has already offered herself to him, he is guilty not of abduction but of the seduction of a virgin; thus it was adjudicated by the old censor in the case of Protokaravos."[15] The seduction of a virgin, as we know, can easily be corrected by marriage, assuming that the parents consent, which they eventually do in the case of Digenes.

The problem that Eustathios Romaios and others before him tried to address was the distinction between real force and consensual elopement. This is not easy to do, since in such situations the various parties can subsequently claim different intent. The canons and the canonists, as we have seen, had also tried to differentiate between the two, with varying degrees of success. The canonical texts that most conform to the situation as described in the Grottaferrata version of *Digenes Akrites* are the commentaries on canon 30 of St. Basil, where the embarrassed twelfth-century canonists try to posit a difference between voluntary abduction and elopement. The courts had to find ways of proving one or the other, and *Peira* 63.5 makes the issue hinge on the question of consent of the woman and the absence of accomplices. The author of the Grottaferrata version of *Digenes* has presented a situation which gave a double thrill to his audience: on the one hand, we have the

[14] Above, III.

[15] *Peira* 63.5.

tension, danger, and adventure of abduction; on the other, there is no abduction in legal terms but rather a "pretended abduction," that is, elopement. The marriage that eventually takes place would have been considered legal at least since the eleventh century, or it could be so argued by a Byzantine judge. Is this pushing the text of the poem too much? I think not. I have tried to show how the poem, although using the word "abduction," is talking about something which both the civil courts of the eleventh century and the canonists of the twelfth would have considered to be elopement.[16] The question does remain whether the poet argued this deliberately or unconsciously. I would suggest that it is deliberate, and would point in this connection to the somewhat different presentation of the same abduction scene in the Escorial version.

In the Escorial version, the situation is the same, but the poet does not stress all of the points that would show that there was no true abduction as the legal minds of the time perceive it. There is, unfortunately, a lacuna in the text, which starts *in medias res*. Apparently, the hero and the girl had already met and exchanged vows not to be separated, although it is not clear that the poet explicitly said that the vow was to marry (E 840 ff). The young man sets out alone (εἶμαι μοναχὸς καὶ μόνος θέλω ὁδεύειν: E 786), but arms himself as he sets out to go "to a terrible necessity, an abduction."[17] This is to be contrasted to the Grottaferrata version which does not mention arms in the abduction itself. Digenes does try to make sure that he has the girl's full consent, and this, somehow, is considered to give them rights over each other: "they kissed sweetly, as they had the right."[18] The army that pursues them includes a Saracen, which surely puts the hero in the right, and gives him the opportunity to kill a representative of the father-in-law's forces, without doing damage to the girl's family, since he spares her brothers.[19] Interestingly, in terms of the substratum of common opinion that we have been trying

[16] It is important to insist that, according to the views of the 12th-century canonists, this affair, as presented here, would have been elopement, and perfectly capable of being corrected by marriage. There is nothing here that would justify the view of some scholars that Digenes was acting against or outside ecclesiastical pronouncements: see, for example, Beck, "Orthodoxie," 342 ff, and Angold, "Wedding."

[17] E 790 ff: εἰς ἀνάγκην φοβερὰν κ' εἰς ἁρπαγὴν ὑπάγω; cf. E 820 ff.

[18] E 872 ff, 906; cf. G IV, 1539.

[19] The Saracen appears only in the Escorial version. On the matter, see the bibliography in Oikonomidès, "L' 'épopée' de Digénis," note 4.

to identify, the girl considers herself responsible for the threat to the hero's life from her father's army, and seeks her own punishment: "My sweet lord, let me die; I alone did this unfortunate thing, I alone should pay for it; you have a swift horse, save yourself" (E 945–47). As in the Grottaferrata version, the issue is resolved when all the parents consent to the marriage and the girl is given a great dowry by her family. Most of the elements that would make this an elopement are present here, but they are not stressed. Indeed, the description of Digenes' arming himself as he prepares for the feat gives a different flavor to this version and highlights the violence involved, although, as we have seen, the girl's consent is freely and fully given. The Escorial version is the more dramatic one, while the Grottaferrata poet sanitizes the story for his audience. We do not know who the author of the Grottaferrata version was; but whoever he may have been, he had a shrewd idea of the legal subtleties surrounding abduction and elopement, and took good care to show that this marriage had no legal problems. I, for my part, cannot believe that, whatever its origins, the story as we have it is an expression of frontier mores or practices, or that its author was anything like a retainer of a frontier aristocratic family. The entire treatment of abduction, marriage, social values is redolent of an aristocratic Constantinopolitan milieu.

What connection does this abduction story bear to reality? Does it indicate that abduction was commonplace or usual, does it have the elements of a formal and institutionalized bride-theft? It seems to me that it does not. The story takes place in a liminal environment, the eastern frontier, although the audience was the court of Constantinople. In that environment, things are supposed to happen which are, to some extent, a reversal of reality as it was known and practiced in high circles. True, there was, in the twelfth century, a documented case of elopement involving a member of the imperial aristocracy: this was the case of Andronikos Komnenos, eventually to become Emperor Andronikos I, who met in Acre Theodora, widow of Baldwin III, and persuaded her to flee with him and to roam for years all over the Near East. The story had an unhappy ending.[20] Yet this was a rare case, and he was a rare man, and besides, the event took place in another country. In the aristocratic society of the twelfth century, marriage was a highly regulated activity, and all that a romance such as *Digenes* provided was catharsis, and one de-

[20] Niketas Choniates, *Historia*, ed. van Dieten, 141–42, 226–27; Kinnamos, Bonn ed., 250; and cf. Laiou, *Mariage, amour et parenté*, chap. 1.

void of risk at that. For what looms large in the narrative is, above all, the eventual marriage of Digenes and the girl, attended by everyone's consent and all the proper festivities, as well as a large dowry. The consent of the girl's father was, indeed, forced, but nonetheless it was given. And the most stylized and formalized aspect of the poem lies in the description of the marriage arrangements.[21]

Indeed, the main straightforward (rather than reversed) connection the abduction story has with reality is the fear parents had of κλεψιγαμία: an improper marriage, tainted by the lack of consent of the parents, not confirmed by public ceremony, not grounded in good property relations symbolized by the dowry. As Balsamon suggests, this is what most elopements were about: inequality of social or economic status might cause people to elope, as it sometimes leads to abduction in Mediterranean societies studied by anthropologists. In such cases, the parents might know and secretly consent, for then the marriage can take place under a pretended *force majeure,* while preserving the social norms against mésalliance. This is the fear the girl's parents voice: that people might think Digenes had married someone beneath him, with all the attendant shame to the girl's family. Here is the girl's father speaking to Digenes after the hero had defeated the *strategos'* army:

> [I will] make your wedding famous in the world,
> The boys shall never cry you stole the match,
> And snatched a girl that had no share of goods,
> Which is disgrace to all are minded well.[22]

In fact, the poet has taken good care to establish the lineage and wealth of the girl at the very beginning of the incident; she, too, persuades herself that Digenes is fully worthy of her, in an exchange where she establishes the reassuring fact that the two are both from the eminent Doukas family and, therefore, kin (although, one hopes, distant kin). What is of importance here is that the parents are most afraid of the shame a marriage without a proper wedding and a dowry would bring on them and on the girl. That does seem to me to have the ring of reality, whereas the rest of the abduction story is a reversal of the truth regarding aristocratic marriages in the twelfth century.

[21] On aristocratic marriage, see Laiou, *Mariage, amour et parenté,* chaps. 1 and 3.

[22] G IV, 1675–78 (the translation is Mavrogordato's, 119). For the statement of the girl's mother, see E 1010–15.

This is not to argue that elopement and abduction did not occur. One supposes that they did, and the supposition is confirmed both by the twelfth-century commentaries on the canons and by occasional "true" stories, such as the by now well-known one of Alexios Kapandrites.[23] This has been interpreted several times in several languages, and there is no need to discuss it again here in detail. It is worth noting only one or two points. The affair took place in 1198 in Epiros, in a territory where all kinds of activities that were outside the law occurred, and concerns the second marriage of Kapandrites and Eudokia, both members of the local aristocracy. The woman's family disputed the marriage repeatedly, on two grounds, that of abduction and that of incest; only the first is of interest here. They charged that after the death of Eudokia's first husband, Kapandrites, already related to her by marriage, had abducted her, with armed accomplices, from the house of one of her relatives, had held her captive, and eventually married her, "by force and against the law." This charge was made twice, and the first time was dismissed by the emperor himself, on the testimony of Kapandrites' relatives and the bishop of Devol. Kapandrites himself charged that the woman's brother had abducted Eudokia from Kapandrites' home, by force, and married her "by force" to another. The issue went from court to court, with the question of incest playing a major role. The moral of the story is simple: force was not unknown, abductions took place, but subsequent interpretations of whether the woman had consented or not varied according to the interests of the parties, which in this case centered on the woman's property.[24]

What I am arguing is not that abduction and elopement did not exist; I am arguing that in the eleventh and twelfth centuries there is no evidence of institutionalized abduction as a recognized and therefore regulated alternative path to marriage. Certainly, the story of the abduction of Digenes' bride is no evidence of such an established and institutionalized social practice.

[23] See, for example, K. Pitsakis, *Τὸ κώλυμα γάμου λόγῳ συγγενείας ἑβδόμου βαθμοῦ ἐξ αἵματος στὸ Βυζαντινὸ δίκαιο* (Athens, 1985), p. 321 and note 110, which is the best study of this case.

[24] Ralles-Potles, V, 103–5, 395–96. On the Kapandrites story, see in the last instance Karlin-Hayter, "Further Notes on Byzantine Marriage," 143–44, and Laiou, *Mariage, amour et parenté,* chap. 1, note 150, with the earlier bibliography. It may be that the importance of abduction marriages has been exaggerated in other societies as well: see Louis Dumont, *Homo hierarchicus: The Caste System and Its Implications,* complete revised English edition (Chicago and London, 1980), 115.

As we have seen, the abduction of Digenes' bride turns out not to be an abduction in legal terms, but only in terms of literature; the eventual marriage is blameless by both aristocratic and ecclesiastical norms. Such is not the case with the treatment of the abduction of Digenes' mother by his father, the Arab emir. The objective situation described here is different and so, perhaps, is the origin of this part of the story, which may go back to a much earlier prototype.[25] Briefly, the girl is seized as a result of an enemy raid by the Arabs, along with other women and other spoils; her brothers try to find her; the youngest one engages the emir in single combat (a folk motif); eventually the situation is resolved with the emir's conversion and marriage to the young woman.

The terminology used by both versions is that of abduction and captivity: ᾐχμαλώτευσε . . . τυγχάνουσαν παρθένον; τὴν ἁρπαγὴν τῆς κόρης; κόρην τερπνὴν ἀφήρπαξας . . . πώλησον ταύτην πρὸς ἡμᾶς . . . κόρην τερπνὴν ἀφήρπαξεν εὐγενῆ τῶν Δουκάδων; ᾐχμαλωτεύσατε; τὸ ἔρπαξες.[26] A simile of the abductor and the hawk, which occurs both here and in the Digenes episode, must be a literary commonplace.[27] This abduction, taking place in the context of an enemy raid, has all the elements of force and violence, including the slain corpses of the young women who would not submit to the lust of the captors. The poet is not at all interested in justifying the actions of the emir, who in any case, being a foreigner, is outside the strictures of civil and ecclesiastical law. On the other hand, the actions of the girl herself, her family, and the other captive women are of interest to the poet, and to us insofar as the poet wishes to project the image that they behaved properly. Several aspects are worthy of note.

Interestingly, there has been no sexual activity, although the poet seems to suggest that it would have been expected. When the girl's brothers think she was killed, they say, "Thank the Lord, you died a virgin."[28] The other girls were, in fact, killed, "because they did not want to do what we told them."[29] Surely no one would argue that this is a reflection of reality; women

[25] Oikonomidès, "L' 'épopée' de Digénis," passim.

[26] G I, 32, 38, 76, 191–92; IV, 994; E 124, 635.

[27] G II, 465 and IV, 1538. Cf. the eagle in R. Hercher, *Erotici Scriptores Graeci,* II (Leipzig, 1859), 219.

[28] E I, 116.

[29] E 70.

captives were undoubtedly raped, and there was probably no wholesale killing of female captives. It is, however, a reflection of attitudes. Virginity is, as we have seen before, highly prized. And the passage may be the alternative (a stark one, to be sure) to coerced consent that Balsamon had in mind.[30] The girl's virginity is particularly useful, since it would remove some of the taint on her eventual marriage to the emir.

As for her family, the reaction is unimpeachable. The father being away at the time, the girl's mother sends her brothers to get her back. They give voice to the shame that has fallen on the family by saying that if they cannot recover her, they do not want to live any longer.[31] After they have offered the emir ransom money, and after the youngest brother's single combat with him, they eventually give in to his request and allow him to marry the girl.[32] So marriage sanitizes the abduction, although it was not originally intended; marriage is, in fact, the only honorable course that remains, after the brothers have failed to kill the captor.

The consent of the girl does not play a role, either in the original action or, explicitly, in the eventual resolution. It is only after her marriage that she is said to love the emir, and this, in a sense, is her consent after the fact. Surprisingly, the marriage is not as free of taint as one would expect in a piece of literature which seeks to give the hero a good pedigree. When the emir wants to go to Syria and his wife offers to accompany him, the brothers liken him to a hawk, which indicates that the original act had not been forgotten.[33] This is the one place where the question of her consent is raised, as the emir bitterly berates his wife, telling her that it was her desire to go with him to Syria, and he did not force her:

> Μὴ γάρ σε κατηνάγκασα, ἢ παρεβίασά σε·
> Μᾶλλον σύ με ἠνάγκασας μετ᾽ ἐμοῦ πορευθῆναι.[34]

[30] See above, Chap. IV. See, in this connection, the story reported in the Synaxarion of Constantinople, regarding St. Pelagia. It purports to date to the 4th century and speaks of a Christian virgin arrested for her religion. She feared for her virginity, "lest she be raped by the soldiers," and prayed to God that she die pure. God heard her, and St. John Chrysostom wrote an encomium celebrating the fact that she preferred to die rather than have her virginity sullied: *SynCP,* col. 120. For the encomium, see PG 50, cols. 579–84.

[31] G I, 192.

[32] G I, 275 ff, 299 ff.

[33] G II, 456 ff; cf. E 318 ff.

[34] G II, 490: "Did I constrain or do you violence?/ Rather you forced me you should go with me": Mavrogordato, p. 35. This does not appear in E.

The treatment of this abduction is much less sophisticated than that of the abduction of Digenes' bride, but then the situation is more clear-cut.[35] The civil and ecclesiastical laws on abduction would not apply in such a situation, and there is no response to their strictures on the part of the poet. What is particularly interesting for our purposes is that the only alternative to rape that the poet envisages is the death of the woman. We find similar positions in other pieces of literature, specifically in the tales of morality. In both the seventh-century *Pratum Spirituale* and the tenth-century tales of Paul of Monembasia, women escape rape or abduction (for the purpose of sexual contact) by death or by a form of living death.[36] Once again, the issue is not whether these stories reproduce reality or not; I doubt that they do in any statistically significant way. I further doubt that they represent any kind of morality that anyone could hope, or expect, would be followed. What they must represent is an extreme standard to set up against the woman who consents to sex under duress: ultimately, there are alternatives, and if the woman consented, under whatever duress, she bears a level of guilt. This is a contrived morality, contrived because the alternative it creates is hardly a viable one, as the stories themselves suggest by the very fact that some at least of the women (and the important ones to boot) do not take the alternative of death. It must therefore represent simply an underlying conviction that the woman sins by tempting the man, that she cannot be totally guilt-free, and that the fact of pollution remains. It is no accident that this attitude is most clearly expressed in texts of ecclesiastical provenance; but secular literature embraces it to some extent.

It is not irrelevant, in this connection, to say something about the problem as it appears in the other secular literature, the romances of the twelfth century. Written after *Digenes Akrites,* these are stories in the learned language, which owe a great deal to Hellenistic romances. It has already been observed that abduction plays a particular role here, being the one act in which the hero acts rather than being acted upon.[37] Compared with the sophisticated and lengthy discussion of abduction in *Digenes,* the treatment

[35] The lack of sophistication may also reflect a much earlier redaction of the original story which forms the first part of the extant narrative, a redaction before the elaborations of civil and canonical thought of the 11th and 12th centuries.

[36] *Pratum Spirituale,* chap. 39; Wortley, *Paul de Monembasie,* 32 ff; cf. above, IV.

[37] Beaton, *Romance,* 60–61, and above, p. 200.

here is trivial, which is useful because it points up the role of abduction as a literary device.[38] It is the action which starts the heroes on their adventures, and, unlike the story of *Digenes,* it creates the framework within which the misadventures can be justified. For every abduction is followed by disasters, captivity, threats to the girl's virginity (unsullied to the end, nevertheless),[39] and to the hero's own sexual purity, freedom, or life. Beaton has remarked that abduction is "only very cursorily motivated by the intelligence that the heroine has just been betrothed elsewhere."[40] That, indeed, is the excuse, but it is a perfunctory one. Nor is it possible to discern in these romances any elements which would justify the abduction, apart from the consent of the abducted girl. Thus in some cases the hero quite unabashedly has accomplices.[41] He also tries to persuade the girl to sleep with him without benefit of marriage, something which Digenes never did; the heroine, of course, resists virtuously, saying that she needs the consent of her father and mother.[42]

In the romance of *Ysmine and Ysminias,* abduction is treated at greater length, but not more elaborately. The abduction is preceded by omens, variously interpreted. According to the interpretation adopted by the lovers, it is Zeus himself who urged the abduction or elopement, which was certainly carried out with the full consent of the girl. The misadventures of the lovers are causally related to the abduction, both in Ysminias' view and in that of

[38] There are three complete romances which will be considered here: *Ysmine and Ysminias* by Eustathios Makrembolites, *Rodanthe and Dosikles* by Theodore Prodromos, and *Drosilla and Charikles* by Niketas Eugeneianos. They are all published in Hercher, *Erotici Scriptores Graeci,* II. The fourth romance survives only in fragments: O. Mazal, *Der Roman des Konstantinos Manasses: Überlieferung, Rekonstruktion, Textausgabe der Fragmente* (Vienna, 1967), and E. Tsolakis, *Συμβολή στη μελέτη του ποιητικού έργου του Κωνσταντίνου Μανασσή και κριτική έκδοση του μυθιστορήματός του 'Τα κατ' Αρίστανδρον και Καλλιθέαν;* Επιστημονική Επετηρίς της φιλοσοφικής Σχολής του Πανεπιστημίου Θεσσαλονίκης, Appendix X (Thessaloniki, 1967).

[39] In one of the romances, there is a quite extraordinary ceremonial ordeal by water to prove the heroine's virginity (and also, by the way, to fix the price of captive girls, since according to the story virgins were sold for a high price). When the heroine emerges unscathed, the people applaud and shout in loud and joyful tones, "the maiden is a virgin!" See *Ysmine and Ysminias,* Hercher, 241–42, 282–83.

[40] Beaton, *Romance,* 60–61.

[41] *Drosilla and Charikles,* 472–73 and 524; cf. *Ysmine and Ysminias,* 225.

[42] *Drosilla and Charikles,* 536–37.

the girl's parents. Ysmine's mother calls Ysminias a "wild beast" who seized the girl and carried her off. Her father, when he finally finds her, lays the blame squarely at her feet. He berates her for her false modesty and her reluctance to relate her adventures: "It is not a silent tongue that defines prudence, but, rather, orderly and seemly behavior. As for you, you had no shame when you behaved badly, but you are ashamed to speak about it."[43] Similarly, in the romance of Theodore Prodromos, Dosikles urges his beloved to tell her father that she had been abducted by force; and he himself admits that he abducted her (the verb "to steal" is used), that he was a wild beast, a robber, all in order to persuade the father to allow the marriage, which of course he does.[44]

In none of these romances is there any effort to present the (consensual) abduction as an elopement which would not be punishable. On the contrary, the young man essentially admits his fault, which is caused by love and by the fear of losing his beloved. The consent of the parents to the marriage is always sought and received, but the original act is unequivocally illegal, except perhaps in the realm of the laws of love. All of this simply points up the fictional character of the abduction scenes, and also serves to highlight the quite exceptional treatment of the subject in *Digenes Akrites*.

Of Rape, Adultery, and Punishment

Unlike the learned romances of the twelfth century, in which no sexual activity, apart from a kiss or coy caress, is seen to take place, the story of *Digenes Akrites* shows the hero engaging in feats of sexual valor, even though he professes to be deeply in love with his bride. There are two such episodes, both valuable in terms of the author's attitudes toward sex and the woman, consenting or not.

The story of the daughter of Aplorravdes, which appears in the Grottaferrata version but not in the Escorial manuscript, is almost a cautionary tale about what befalls girls who leave home to follow the wrong man. She was the daughter of an Arab emir who fell in love with a Greek captive of her father's and, with her mother's connivance, freed him and gave him presents and power. He eventually wanted to return to his homeland and persuaded

[43] *Ysmine and Ysminias*, 262, 268–70, 280.

[44] *Rodanthe and Dosikles*, 427–28.

her to follow him, promising her marriage. She took advantage of her mother's fatal illness and absconded with valuables from her home. While on the road, the couple made love "insatiably" for three nights, which is three times more than any other eloping couple did in the romances. Then the faithless lover left her, taking the money with him, and she dressed as a man and went on the road to find him. Digenes, who had already met the young man, then came upon the girl and expressed amazement at the depth of the girl's love and her sufferings. It was, indeed, her tale of love that aroused Digenes' own passion for her:

> This when I heard, friend, from the girl's mouth
> As it were a flame came up into my heart,
> Offered me love and lawless union.[45]

He proceeds to "lawless" actions (παράνομον μίξιν . . . ἁμαρτίαν . . . ἄθεσμος πρᾶξις . . . πράξεως παρανόμου . . . ἀπὸ τῆς ἀνομίας), even though the girl resists: "Although the woman much opposed the doing/ Calling on God and on her parents' souls." This rape is presented with a certain equanimity, which, however, is not difficult to understand. The girl was, after all, a foreigner, although she had converted to Christianity. Much more important, she was no longer a virgin and, moreover, she had already transgressed all sorts of boundaries for love: she had abandoned her parents' home and even her feminine dress. Would not all this, and her being alone on the road, be sufficient evidence of those depraved prior mores that the canonists thought justified the assumption that the woman had assented to the rape?[46] No rape at all, then, either in law, which spoke only of the rape of a virgin,[47] or insofar as the twelfth-century canonists were concerned. The act

[45] G V, 2275–78; Mavrogordato, 157. On this episode, cf. Galatariotou, "Structural Oppositions," 57–59.

[46] There is a hagiographic parallel to this in the *vita* of Lazaros Galeseiotes, as has already been noted by Kazhdan: A. P. Kazhdan, "Hagiographical Notes (Suite)," *Byzantion* 54 (1984), 182–84. The most striking parallel is that a girl who fled from her home with a man and found herself alone on the road would be assumed to be immoral and therefore fair game: *Acta Sanctorum*, Nov. III, sec. 7.

[47] Digenes' crime was, according to Byzantine law, fornication, punishable by beating according to the antiquated and no longer used provisions of *Ecloga* 17.19. Of course, if one were to consider that the girl was properly betrothed to her lover, Digenes was guilty of the much more serious crime of adultery, and indeed in one instance the poet says "[He has] fallen into the crime of adultery": G V, 2058. This,

remained, however, both illegal and a sin; although the Devil made him do it, the hero seeks to remedy the act. He forces the girl's lover to marry her, and goes through an internal process of repentance, which takes the external form of his abandoning his residence and moving elsewhere.

Insofar as the question of consent is concerned, the most important element of this story is the fact that the woman's avowed, illicit, and consummated love for a man takes her out of the protected world of virgins. Although she did not consent to sex with the hero, her prior life was such that sex was almost inevitable; interestingly, the attention of the poet is all concentrated on the remorse of Digenes, and not on the woman's reactions.

Digenes' encounter with the warrior Maximo has different and somewhat more complex elements.[48] She is a virgin, unvanquished in war, summoned by Digenes' adversaries to help them defeat him. The episode is replete with sexual overtones: the *apelatai,* Digenes' adversaries, want to defeat him and seize his wife (E 1399); Maximo, called a κούρβα, a whore, in the Escorial version, promises to cut off Digenes' head and bring the "girl" to the enemies who desire her; Digenes is reluctant to make war on a woman, but eventually is forced into it. In the single combat that follows, she is defeated, although Digenes refrains from killing her, saying that a man should not kill women, indeed should not even do battle with them.[49] This is, indeed, a battle of the sexes, for as soon as she is vanquished, Maximo declares that Digenes has won her. In a nice turn of phrase, the Escorial version equates the victory in battle to the winning of a woman: κ' ἐσὺ μόνος με κέρδισες κ' ἄλλος μὴ μὲ κερδίση ("you alone have won over me, and let no one else win me over," a wordplay on the two meanings of the verb). In the Grottaferrata version, the connection is explicitly spelled out: "I am a virgin still by none seduced. / You alone have conquered, you shall win me all."[50] Digenes

however, must be simply a careless use of the term, for there is no way that her relationship with her lover could have been considered a proper betrothal in the 12th century.

[48] The episode is recounted in G VI, 3089 ff, and E 1546 ff. A leaf is missing from the G manuscript at the point where Digenes slept with Maximo (at G VI, 3118). Beck thinks it may have been taken by a reader who was offended by its (presumably) salacious contents: Beck, "Orthodoxie," 342.

[49] Only in the Grottaferrata version, G VI, 2920 ff.

[50] Mavrogordato, 208; G VI, 3101–2: ἔτι παρθένος γάρ εἰμι ὑπὸ οὐδενὸς φθαρεῖσα· σὺ μόνος με ἐνίκησας, σύ με ἀποκερδίσεις.

tells her that he is married to a beautiful, rich girl from a powerful family, and so cannot marry her. In the Escorial version, he then makes an unequivocal proposition: "but if you want to fornicate, I'll do it to you" (εἰ δ' ἂν ὁρμῆς νὰ πορνευθῆς, ἐγὼ νὰ σοῦ τὸ ποίσω). The Grottaferrata version has, instead, the common motif that Digenes was seduced by her beauty and her sweet words; he sleeps with her, and dismisses her, asking her not to forget him. Again the Escorial version is brutally frank: "I dismounted, laid aside my arms, and quickly did to Maximo what she had wanted; and as soon as I did it to her, to Maximo, the whore, immediately I mounted my horse and went to the girl (his wife)."[51] Predictably, Digenes is then overtaken by remorse for his action, which the author of the Grottaferrata version, always more interested than the Escorial in defining sexual crimes, calls "adultery." The definition is not precise in legal terms, for he was really guilty of fornication and the seduction of a virgin, but we have seen that there was confusion in the common usage of the terms adultery and fornication since Roman times. The Escorial version is less interested in defining the crime and more involved in showing the total defeat of Maximo both in battle and in sexual terms—here is a woman who lost both her valor and her virginity: "After seducing Maximo, three injustices I did to her: first that I had her, second that she was shamed, and third and worst, that she lost her valor."[52]

The hero's conscience bothers him, especially after he has spoken with and lied to his wife. In the Grottaferrata version, he becomes enraged, goes back to Maximo, and "having caught her I slew her ruthlessly, after adultery performing the sorry murder."[53]

Neither version of the poem condones Digenes' actions in this episode, and neither explicitly states that Maximo, rather than Digenes, was the most culpable. But it does not take a very sophisticated reader to realize that, in the end, the blame falls primarily on the woman. It is she who declares her intention, honorable at first, to be sure. Her desire, or consent, to marry Digenes is taken to extend to a desire, or consent, to have sex with him. At

[51] E 1565–68: Κ' ἐπέζευσα τὸν μαῦρον μου καὶ λύω τ' ἄρματά μου/ καὶ τὸ ἐπεθύμα ἡ Μαξιμοὺ γοργὸν τῆς τὸ ἐποῖκα· / κ' ἀπῆτις τῆς τὸ ἔκαμα ἐγὼ τῆς Μαξιμοῦς τῆς κούρβας,/ εὐθὺς ἐκαβαλλίκευσα κ' ἐπῆγα εἰς τὸ κοράσιον.

[52] E 1586–88: Μετὰ τὸ φθείρειν τὴν Μαξιμοῦν τρία κακὰ τὴν ἐποῖκα· πρῶτον μὲν ὅτι εἶχα την, δεύτερον ὅτι ἐντράπη, τρίτον καὶ περισσότερον ἔχασε τὴν ἀνδρειάν της.

[53] I have changed somewhat Mavrogordato's translation (p. 215).

another level, she bears responsibility because it is her beauty and "her sweet words" that seduce the hero. In legal terms, Digenes is guilty of the seduction of a virgin with her consent, which would carry punishment for the man but not for the woman. In literature, the man emerges relatively unscathed, but the woman is punished very severely. Is she punished for her consent, or because she was polluted and therefore cannot be allowed to survive in her former role as a warrior virgin?[54] At still another level she is, of course, punished most severely because, having broken every code of female behavior, she is outside the pale.[55]

Some parallels with literature emanating from a religious or monastic milieu, namely, saints' lives and morality tales, are immediately obvious. The most obvious parallel lies in the fact that woman, with her beauty and wiles, leads man into temptation and cannot be held innocent for his crimes, whatever the law might say; equally, the woman is punished in some way, whether her punishment is self-inflicted or not. A more striking parallel has been brought to my attention by Alexander Kazhdan. The Synaxarion of the Church of Constantinople relates the story of the hermit Iakovos and the daughter of a rich man. The girl was possessed by a demon, who made her call out the hermit's name. Her parents brought her to Iakovos to be healed. After expelling the demon, the hermit began to be attacked by desire (πολεμεῖσθαι). He was defeated (ἡττηθείς) and slept with the girl, whom he subsequently killed. Such was his remorse that he buried himself in a grave and, through repentance, was so purified of the pollution (τοσοῦτον διὰ μετανοίας ἑαυτὸν καθῆρε τοῦ μύσους) that he was able to perform a miracle, assuring his sanctity. Thus his sin was corrected, and his saintliness increased. The girl's own punishment, for an unstated sin, was as irrevocable as that of Maximo who had transgressed in a number of ways.[56] Neither this story nor the story of Maximo can be taken as representing what people actually did; but they are powerful indicators as to the attitudes that suffused the legal system, especially in the implementation of the law, and influenced profoundly the lives of people.

[54] Note, however, that in the Escorial version that is precisely how she survives; she goes away "shamed."

[55] Cf. Galatariotou, "Structural Oppositions," 59–62.

[56] *SynCP,* 128–30. The date of the story unfortunately is not known, although it is placed in Samaria; the Synaxarion dates from the 10th century. The attitude reflected here is older and is preserved by the church and, it seems, by secular literature.

The literature of the twelfth century, on which we have concentrated, is, on the surface, a celebration of young love that conquers all; it is, further, a celebration of desire, most frequently the desire of the two young lovers for each other, but also desire *tout court*. However, our investigation has shown that this surface picture is painted on a sturdy canvas of quite a different texture. What is truly valued is virginity in the woman and a proper marriage for the two young people; transgressing the boundaries makes for a tense plot, but the resolution is always the same, and thus people do not challenge the norms, they affirm them. In my view, the clearest illustration of this is the story of the abduction of Digenes' bride. The poet covers every base, so he can have it all: the excitement of a seeming abduction and the clear understanding that no laws were truly broken, and the marriage stands perfectly valid in the end. So intent is the poet, especially of the Grottaferrata version, that one is tempted, despite all that has been said above, to seek here the reflection not of a common practice of abduction but of a particular event, a cause célèbre of its day, of which we now know nothing. But that, of course, is rank speculation.

The issue of consent is inscribed within this context. The consent of the woman is always present when there is an abduction/elopement; and it is always absent when the hero tries to persuade the girl to engage in premarital sexual relations, so these do not take place, except perhaps in an erotic dream.[57] It is her consent that legitimizes the abduction and the eventual marriage, but the consent is greatly circumscribed by that of the families. In *Digenes Akrites*, explicit consent to various illicit sexual relations is not an important factor in differentiating between crimes, or in establishing the punishment of the hero, which is always internal; it does, however, and significantly, play a telling role in the punishment of the virgin who willingly allows herself to be seduced.

[57] See one of Ysminias' erotic dreams, in which he presses the resisting girl with some force: Hercher, II, 185 ff.

Conclusion

This examination of the role of consent to sexual relations in the Byzantine legal system and in Byzantine society has shown that there were several different positions, conflicting at some points, agreeing in others. Consent was both a factor creating legal categories and an issue which was recognized by the church and by society. Its importance in establishing legal categories derives from Roman precedents, but the treatment of consent acquired greater clarity and therefore force in the Byzantine period, certainly since the eighth century. The consent of the woman served as the differentiating factor that created the category of rape. The emphasis on the importance of consent for the punishment of the man and the fact that the law, with very few exceptions, did not punish a woman who consented to illicit sexual intercourse outside marriage, create a situation that seems favorable to women, on the one hand; on the other, it reduces the woman's responsibility for her own actions. The emphasis on consent also led, in practice, that is, in the law courts, to the development of external criteria which created presumption of force. I would argue that the insistence on objective criteria, as these were defined in Byzantium, also served as a protection for the woman.

The other side of this argument is that subjective criteria for establishing consent or its absence functioned negatively for the woman in Byzantine society. As we have seen, subjective criteria were discussed primarily by the canonists, and in terms that bring out the complexities of the position of the church. The issue of personal responsibility, regardless of gender, looms large in the thinking of the church, and so, necessarily, does consent. The sinner, whether male or female, is punished, the punishment serving to expiate the sin. At the same time, the probing of the issue of internal consent, which at times becomes almost a psychological investigation, necessarily brings to the surface concepts regarding the true nature of women as well as ideas regarding purity and pollution. The canonists' efforts to investigate the deeper aspects of consent sometimes leads them to a position which almost considers immaterial the outward, visible signs of absence of consent on the part of the woman. There is, thus, a contrast between the acceptance of consent as the factor which establishes responsibility, culpability, punishment (as it does in civil and canon law) and the position that consent, particularly the consent of the woman, is irrelevant, since it is the action itself that is important. That second position is taken by some ecclesiastical and some literary sources. It is predicated upon a complex of ideas regarding shame, honor, and pollution which were shared by society generally and which serve to attenuate the importance of consent. A later text, which I have not discussed here, presents in a somewhat ghoulish fashion a farfetched logical conclusion of the attitude that focuses on pollution. It is a secular text, the treatise *On the Laws* of George Gemistos Plethon, and the severity of its provisions regarding the punishment of sexual crimes is closer to Western Renaissance societies than to Byzantine attitudes.[1] Those (males) engaging in homosexual activities, those guilty of bestiality, the adulterers, and those guilty of rape are to be burned, or "cleansed by fire" (πυρὶ καθαίρειν). Furthermore, they are to be burned not in the common cemeteries, but in special ones, designated for the most odious and polluting (ἐναγέσι) criminals. The only time the question of consent enters is in the case of consensual sex with an unmarried girl or woman who is still under a guardian's authority: the man is still to be burned, but he will be buried in the common cemetery.[2]

The importance given to φθορά by civil and canon law stems, undoubtedly, from such attitudes and from the value placed on virginity. Marriage, as we have seen, functions as a remedy to both seduction and elopement, and even to abduction if a formula can be found to make abduction resemble elopement. Marriage regularizes irregular situations and restores the honor of the family. The relative paucity of Byzantine (as opposed to late Antique) legislation regarding abduction may have the same causes as the somersaults of the canonists who tried to squeeze abduction into the more acceptable suit of elopement: the concern was less to maximize prosecutions for abduction, an irremediable crime, and more to allow as many cases as possible to be remedied by marriage. It should be reiterated, however, that although mar-

[1] For Western Europe, see, among others, Guido Ruggiero, *Boundaries of Eros: Sex, Crime and Sexuality in Renaissance Venice* (New York, 1985), and R. Carrasco,"Le châtiment de la sodomie sous l'Inquisition (XVIe–XVIIe siècle)," in A. Corbin, ed., *Violences sexuelles* (Paris, 1989), 53–69; for Dubrovnik in this period, see B. Krekić, "Abominandum Crimen: Punishment of Homosexuality in Renaissance Dubrovnik," *Viator* 18 (1987), 337–45.

[2] C. Alexandre, *Pléthon, Traité des Lois* (Paris, 1858), 124–28.

riage is vigorously promoted as a remedy for a number of illicit sexual relations, both partners must be willing to give their consent to it. And here the issue of the limits of individual consent becomes central, since it was always circumscribed by the interests and desires (and formal consent) of the family, the state, and the church, three institutions whose relative weight in regard to the control of marriages varied according to historical period and social class.

In this study I have tried to investigate the various parameters of the complex and sometimes contradictory Byzantine attitudes toward the issue of consent. The importance of this topic for social history and the history of women has, I hope, become evident in the text. Perhaps one more word may be said about a particularity of the subject treated here. If one were studying the role of individual consent in marriage or in property relations (for example, the alienation of land) one would have to address, in the first instance, the limitations placed upon the desires of the individual by the interests of others who must consent to his/her action in order for the action to be valid: the consent of the parents in marriage, the consent of neighbors and others in the sale of land. In the case of consent to sexual relations, the focus is different: what is at issue is less the limits placed on the individual by other interested parties, and more the question of the effects of certain actions upon the actors themselves. Hence the question of personal attitude, responsibility, culpability is paramount. Guilt is not merely legal guilt but a moral failure, stemming from the individual and reflecting on the family as well; and a crime is also a sin. While this may be the case with other crimes, for example, murder, it is most pointedly true of sexual activity, a fact which explains the ambiguities and the richness of the response to both actual and theoretical or fictitious situations.

II

MARRIAGE PROHIBITIONS, MARRIAGE STRATEGIES AND THE DOWRY IN THIRTEENTH-CENTURY BYZANTIUM

This study deals with two rather complex topics: the prohibition of close marriages, on the one hand; and, on the other, property relations within marriage in a system that incorporates both exogamy and the divergent devolution of property (or bilateral inheritance). The fate of the patrimony in this contradictory conjunction is sometimes presented as a fundamental problem.[1] More generally, the topic at hand is the role of the family and marriage in the preservation and reproduction of resources in thirteenth-century Byzantium. A recent study has stressed the importance of matrimonial strategies in the reproduction of socio-economic systems in pre-capitalist societies.[2] My discussion will focus on the dowry, taking into account the actions both of the natal families of bride and groom and of the new household formed by marriage.

Introduction

In what follows, my thinking is based on a few general premises. There is, first of all, a distinction to be drawn between incest and close marriage. Incest is something of a universal human taboo, with substantial differences between various societies as to which relationships are considered incestuous and condemned as such.[3] The mother-son union is, it seems, very rare indeed. But other incest prohibitions vary, although there are some interesting common grounds: thus the problem of « confusion of relationships » as a justification for treating marriages as incestuous, and therefore illicit, exists in China, as it does in the Byzantine Empire of the late 10th century.[4] When anthropologists speak

1. I am indebted to my colleague, Stanley J. Tambiah, for his help with the anthropological material. By « patrimony » I mean the parental property before any division takes place.

2. P. BOURDIEU, « Stratégies de reproduction et modes de domination », *Actes de la recherche en sciences sociales* 105, décembre 1994, p. 3-12. Bourdieu makes an important distinction between real, or material, capital, and symbolic capital; here I deal primarily with the former. On similar questions in western Europe, see J. GOODY, *The Development of the Family and Marriage in Europe*, Cambridge 1983.

3. The classic study of incest is by C. LÉVI-STRAUSS, *Les structures élémentaires de la parenté*, Paris 1949.

4. S. MOSCOVICI, *Society Against Nature: The Emergence of Human Society*, Atlantic Highlands N. J. 1976, p. 137; Patriarch Sisinnios, in G. RALLES and M. POTLES, *Σύνταγμα τῶν θείων καὶ ἱερῶν κανόνων*, Athens 1852, V, p. 14-15 (hereafter RALLES-POTLES).

of incest, they refer mostly to sexual relations. Prohibition of sexual relations may, of course, differ from prohibition of close marriage : in some societies, one may engage in sexual activity with people one may not marry. For this study, I confine myself solely to the prohibition of close marriage.

Neither the concept of incest nor the prohibition thereof nor impediments to close marriage is, as far as I can see, of a simple nature, that is, prohibitions do not only and do not always aim at preserving or changing a specific set of property relations or power relations; they certainly do that, but at the same time, appeals to religious precepts or to concepts of shame can play a real role. Therefore, the question must be what role prohibitions of incest or of close marriage play in each society, at any given point. Turning to property relations within the family or kinship group, I think it important to stress, as some anthropologists and sociologists have done, that whereas exogamy and endogamy have a different effect on property relations, the perpetuation of the family group does not travel down a single road, where the preservation of the original family patrimony is the ultimate good. Endogamy does lead to the concentration of property, and for that reason may be desired by a family or social group and opposed by other social groups or by the state. Alliances with other families, that is, exogamy, however, can be equally valuable and desirable.[5] The fact that in-marriage and out-marriage can both be parts of the same marriage strategy does not make for tidy formulations, but it is close to reality. It suggests a flexibility which I have tried to keep in mind when examining the institution of the dowry.

Dowry is, indeed, part and parcel of the diverging devolution of property. By necessity, it entails the diffusion of the property of the family, the clan or lineage, or at least so it seems at first glance ;[6] and therefore, according to some theories, marriage strategies are supposed to be informed by efforts to counter or turn into benefits the effects of bilateral inheritance. It is quite true to say that anthropologists have linked this system of inheritance to a tendency toward close marriage. As to why there is divergent devolution in the first place, some anthropologists have connected it to a desire on the part of the parents to guarantee that male and female children retain or improve their condition in life, and thus reproduce the social and economic or political position of the family or the lineage.[7]

5. Moscovici, *ibid.*, p. 9 ff, p. 95 for primitive societies; cf. P. Bourdieu, *Outline of A Theory of Practice*, Cambridge 1977, p. 57 ff; J. Goody, *The Oriental, the Ancient and the Primitive*, Cambridge 1990, p. 338. I use the terms « endogamy » and « exogamy » loosely here. It is evident that a society with well-defined groups may practice exogamy in that marriage within a part of the group may be forbidden, and endogamy in that the preferred marriage may be with members of a larger group (see the caste system in India). « Close marriage » is preferable to « endogamy » when one discusses the Byzantine Empire.

6. For qualifications on this statement, see *infra*, p. 144 ff.

7. See Goody, *op. cit.* (n. 5) ; Id., *Production and Reproduction : A Comparative Study of the Domestic Domain*, Cambridge 1976; J. Goody and S. Tambiah, *Bridewealth and Dowry*, Cambridge 1973; S. Tambiah, « Bridewealth and Dowry Revisited: The Position of Women in Sub-Saharan Africa and North India », *Current Anthropology* 30, 1989, p. 413-435.

The concomitants of divergent devolution of property, according to anthropological literature, are: close control of marriages by the parental generation; close control of sexuality, especially that of girls; late marriage; monogamy, because of the difficulty of duplicating complex arrangements, and therefore an aversion toward dissolving marriages by divorce; the possibility of uxorilocal marriages; the disadvantaged position of lateral kin insofar as rights of inheritance are concerned; a tendency towards endogamy in order to keep the property within the family, and a tendency toward hypergamy to benefit the whole family. The last two tendencies are different but can be complementary: hypergamy is linked to exogamy; the woman marries up for social mobility, and her family pays a high dowry for the privilege, but it benefits from the girl's improved social position, translatable, among other things, into better dowries received by her brothers. Many of these patterns are observable in Byzantine society; that some are not should not be surprising, since, as I have already suggested, flexibility in family arrangements is an important ingredient in all systems.[8]

Given that in the Byzantine Empire there was both divergent devolution of property and rules prohibiting close marriages, I am going to discuss how marriage strategies dealt with the inherent problem, and how the question of the dowry is inscribed into marriage strategies. That is, I shall try to suggest the specificities of the Byzantine answer to these questions which affect a number of societies. But since specificities exist at various levels, a few words should be said about the areas that will be examined, and also about the choice of chronology.

The geographic area involved is simply a function of the documentation. There is documentation about Asia Minor, especially the area around Smyrna, in the 13th century, although it is not the optimal kind of documentation for our purposes. It consists primarily of acts of sale, donation, testaments and other property transactions, where dowry goods may be implicated; similar documentation exists for a small area around the monasteries of Makrinitissa and Nea Petra in Thessaly. There are also data of quite a different kind for an area which broadly covers western Macedonia up to Thessaloniki, Corfu and Epirus. This is the dossier of the archbishop of Ochrid, Demetrios Chomatianos, and of John Apokaukos, metropolitan of Naupaktos, consisting of decisions or expert opinions on a number of legal problems among which questions of dowry and succession have an important place. These sources have the advantage of being precise in terms of the information they provide; they have the disadvantage, as Bourdieu has pointed out in another connection, of being, at some point, eccentric, since, by the time a case reaches the courts, normal social arrangements have already broken down.[9]

8. For a discussion of the characteristics of Byzantine marriage, see A. Laiou, *Mariage, amour et parenté à Byzance aux XIe-XIIIe siècles*, Paris 1992.

9. P. Bourdieu, « Les stratégies matrimoniales dans le système de reproduction », *Annales ESC* 27, 1972, p. 1107.

The population that this documentary base allows us to discuss is an important one for our purposes. The people involved are land-owning peasants and landlords of various means, some of whom belong to the local aristocracy. They are not inhabitants of a big city, like Constantinople, where dowries are often in cash, with all the flexibility that entails. They do not belong to the imperial aristocracy, where different rules may or may not have prevailed. Their major property consists of land, which brings us to the heart of the problem as defined for this Colloquium.

As to the chronology, i.e., the thirteenth century, it too is partly predicated by the accident of sources. But it has the added advantage, for our topic, of being a period when the system of impediments to marriage for reasons of consanguinity or affinity had been fully elaborated, and in place since the late 12th century (the impediment by reason of the seventh degree of consanguinity was finally made into law in 1166). Family strategies, therefore, were operating under the full system of marriage impediments.

The prohibition of close marriage

That having been said, it must also be added that, as far as Byzantium is concerned, the major impediments to close marriage had been established a good deal earlier. Two phases may be distinguished. One came in the late antique period, and the other was introduced by the legislation of the Patriarch Sisinnios, in 997. Insofar as the connection between property and marriage is concerned, surely the most important point came with the legislation of the first Christian centuries, when a number of innovations were introduced into the law of marriage. In 342, the Emperors Constantius and Constans threatened with the death penalty the man who married his niece, that is, the brother's daughter or the sister's daughter.[10] They were abrogating a senatorial decree of 49 AD, which had been passed to legalize the marriage of Claudius and Agrippina. This was a fortuitous decree, and the uncle-niece marriage was not habitual in Roman society.[11] But the uncle-niece marriage had been a preferred form of marriage in ancient Greece, and certainly performed the function of retaining the property within the woman's kin-group, and thus mitigating the effects of diverging devolution on the property.[12] In the Byzantine Empire, the prohibition of uncle-niece marriages was effective. The Emperor Heraclius did, shortly before 624, marry his niece Martina, but this marriage was generally regarded as incestuous by the Church and the people.

10. *CTh* III, 12, 1.

11. M. Corbier, « Constructing Kinship in Rome: Marriage and Divorce, Filiation and Adoption », in *The Family in Italy, from Antiquity to the Present*, D. I. Kertzer and R. P. Saller eds, New Haven-London 1991, p. 134; cf. Y. Thomas, « Mariages endogamiques à Rome: Patrimoine, pouvoir et parenté depuis l'époque archaïque », *Revue historique de droit français et étranger* 58, 1980, p. 347.

12. Goody, *op. cit.* (n. 5), p. 391.

Perhaps the most common form of preferred marriage in societies where endogamy is practiced for the reconcentration of property that becomes diffused by bilateral inheritance is the cross-cousin marriage (father's sister's daughter or mother's brother's daughter) or the parallel cousin marriage (father's brother's daughter).[13] The marriage to the father's brother's daughter is a preferred form of marriage in some societies, and is justified « in terms of the retention of property or other relatively exclusive rights by near kin. »[14] In the late antique system, relations were counted with no reference to the line of descent; that is, male and female kin were not differentiated, for what counted was the degree of kinship. First-cousin marriages were permitted in imperial Rome, although there is some disagreement among scholars as to how widespread they were.[15] They were still permitted in the Justinianic Code. Two hundred years later, they were expressly forbidden by the *Ecloga* (741), which extended the prohibition to second cousins. Ecclesiastical prohibitions had preceded the civil ones, first-cousin marriage being prohibited by the Council in Trullo (691-692).[16] The further extension along lines of consanguinity is to the seventh degree, that is, to second cousin's daughter. By the time we reach this point, the line of prohibited unions coincides with the line of heirs to the property.[17] The reconstitution of even a part of the original patrimony becomes formally impossible, although in real terms the possibility of reconstitution stops with the first cousins. It should be noted, however, that whereas cross-cousin or parallel marriages may be preferred in many societies, in reality the number of such unions is severely limited by demographic and other factors. Thus in some societies marriage to second or third cousins replaces first-cousin unions.[18] But it also seems to me that when we reach that level of kinship, the original patrimony has been very fragmented indeed. Thus, I would argue that the development of prohibitions in Byzantium to include the seventh degree of consanguinity owes less to an effort to hinder the concentration of property and more to the inherent logic of the moral, religious and legal precepts that governed the earlier prohibitions. A real break had come when uncle-niece

13. Mother's sister's daughter is also a parallel cousin, but the incidence of such unions is rare. In Kabyle society, the patrilineal parallel cousin, the « most masculine woman » is the preferred bride, while the matrilineal parallel cousin is considered a bad choice: BOURDIEU, *op. cit.* (n. 5), p. 44-45. Cross-cousin and parallel-cousin marriages have similar effects on the preservation of the patrimony.

14. GOODY, *Production* (cit. n. 7), p. 15. (On p. 16 Goody calls cross-cousin marriage the preferred form). Table 4 in his Appendix I plots father's brother's daughter marriages, and finds a positive correlation with systems of diverging devolution, although this form of marriage is more broadly practiced.

15. CORBIER, *op. cit.* (n. 11), p. 140 ff; S. TREGGIARI, *Roman Marriage*, Oxford 1991, p. 114; B. D. SHAW, « Close-kin Marriage in Roman Society », *Man* n.s. 19, 1984, p. 432-444.

16. *CJ* I, 10, 4; *Ecloga* II, 2; RALLES-POTLES, II, p. 432-433.

17. *Bas.* XLV, 3, 8; XLV, 3, 2: natural (consanguineous) kinship does not extend beyond the seventh degree; but cf. *Bas.* XLV, 2, 14, where relatives of the eighth degree (the children of second cousins) are called to the inheritance if there are no closer heirs.

18. The point was made by Stanley Tambiah. Cf. BOURDIEU, *op. cit.* (n. 9), p. 4.

marriages and first-cousin marriages were prohibited, since these are the marriages that tend to reconcentrate the family property. I would expect that these prohibitions resulted in a strengthening of the nuclear family, more careful and delicate marriage negotiations, and a greater importance of the affinal group. The subsequent prohibitions regarding consanguineous close marriage reinforced exogamous practices, but had little effect on the potential reconstitution of the original property.

Marriage between consanguineous kin is not the only means of ensuring the preservation of the original patrimony. Multiple marriages between two or more families create links of affinity and, eventually, consanguinity that can have the same effect. For this form of close marriage to be practiced, the social or status group has to be a large one. The prohibition of further alliances between people already connected with affinal links was an early concern of the Christian church and the Byzantine state.[19] The important change here came in the second stage of the development of incest prohibitions, with the issuing of the *Tomos* of the Patriarch Sisinnios (997). This dealt not with consanguinity but with affinity, clearly a consequence of the importance of affinal links. It forbade the marriage of two brothers (or two sisters) to two first cousins, the marriage of uncle and nephew with two sisters, as well as that of aunt-niece with two brothers.[20] I have discussed elsewhere the reasons for the promulgation of this decree, which chronologically came right in the middle of imperial efforts to reduce the power of the aristocracy, and was, I think, connected with them. I stress here only the fact that multiple marriages between members of the same two families were used, certainly by the aristocracy, including the aristocracy at the highest level, to form strong political alliances; in the eleventh century, the marriage of uncle and niece to aunt and nephew seems to have been a preferred – and problematic – form of marriage. At the same time, the marriage of two brothers with two first cousins might also lead to a certain re-concentration of the patrimony, since both brothers and first cousins could and did hold goods jointly, while the joint ownership and exploitation of landed property did not continue after the fourth degree of consanguinity.[21] Such marriages can be considered as functionally endogamous, and the fact that they were prohibited can also be expected to have some effects. However, the further prohibition of the marriage of a man successively with a woman and her second cousin is a moral/religious prohibition rather than anything else.

19. The Levirate and its parallel, that is, the successive marriage of a man to two sisters, was forbidden by Constantius and Constans and by Arcadius, in 355 and 396 respectively: *CTh* III, 12, 2-3. Cf. St. Basil, Ralles-Potles, IV, p. 259 ff, and Council in Trullo, canon 54, which forbids the marriage of a father/son to mother/daughter; of two sisters to father and son; of two brothers to mother and daughter; of two brothers to two sisters.

20. Ralles-Potles, V, 14-19; on the *Tomos* of Sisinnios, see Laiou, *op. cit.* (n. 8), p. 15.

21. Laiou, *ibid.*, chap. 1 and 5.

Three families and the dowry

A marriage, in Byzantium, implicated in the first instance three families, two in existence and one *in potentia*: the family of the bride, the family of the groom, and the new family *of* the bride and groom. Whereas usually discussions of marriage strategies concentrate on the interests of the first two families, the interests of the new family also played an important role, as we shall see. With regard to property arrangements, the family of the bride gave the dowry; the family of the groom gave the *hypobolon* (i.e., the husband's portion),[22] and the *theoretron*; and the combination of the dowry and the *hypobolon* formed the joint property (the conjugal estate) of the new family, which could then be augmented by a number of means, including purchase and inheritance.[23] From the point of view of the family of the bride, and from a purely economic angle, the dowry constitutes a net outflow of resources, since the counter-dowry does not enter into the resources of the bride's natal family; the only way the natal family can seek to recover the dowry is if the wife dies without heirs. From the point of view of the groom's family, whether its resources are increased through the incoming dowry depends on whether the residence is patri-virilocal, in which case they are, at least for a while. But a problem arises as well, when one of the two spouses dies intestate and without heirs. In the case of the death of the bride, the family of the groom may, and sometimes does, try to retain the dowry.

If a family has an equal number of sons and daughters, and all share the patrimony equally, the dowries of the girls constitute a real outflow of goods for their natal family, which is only to some degree counterbalanced by incoming dowries. At the same time, a good and expensive (in terms of dowry) marriage for one or more of the girls may bring positive net results by raising the position of the natal family, so that the sons can make better marriages (with more dowry); or, the improvement in social position may have globally beneficial results for the girl's natal family. Thus marriage strategies have to be quite delicate, and much depends on the resources and the timing of the marriages of the children. When we look at the new family, created by the marriage, the question is to what extent the nucleus of the family property, which consists of the marriage gifts on both sides, becomes an autonomous unit, and to what extent the natal families have rights on it. In the first case (that of the autonomous unit), the fragmentation of the original patrimony, especially of the bride's family, is more advanced than in the second case, in which the natal family retains some rights on the property. If one looks at these questions from the viewpoint of legal practice, they can be formulated as follows: what does the

22. Interestingly, a late Byzantine source calls the man's portion a dowry: M. GEDEON, « Βυζαντινὰ συμβόλαια », *Byzantinische Zeitschrift* 5, 1896, p. 114.

23. J. BEAUCAMP, « Προικοϋπόβολον-ὑπόβολον-ὑποβάλλω », in *'Αφιέρωμα στὸν Νίκο Σβορῶνο*, I, Rethymnon 1986, p. 153-161. Note, however, that the property acquired subsequently was subject to different rules from those governing the use and transmission of the dowry and the *hypobolon*.

dowry consist of, and more particularly, does it involve land? What share of the patrimony is it? What happens at the moment of the death of the bride's father – does the dowry get turned in for a share of the inheritance (i.e., is dowry an advance on the inheritance), or is the dowried woman excluded from the inheritance?[24] And what happens when the woman dies without heirs? Does the dowry return to the family of origin, or does it stay with the new household?

From the viewpoint of social practice, there is also the question whether the dowry can be disaggregated into its constituent parts. A proper dowry in the Byzantine Empire included a trousseau, household implements, jewelry, cash and/or land and other productive resources. In other societies, the first three items were the woman's own property, with which she could do as she wished.[25] This matter will not be discussed in any depth here; it should form the topic of a separate study. What is at issue in this essay is primarily the part of the dowry that is an outflow of important resources, i.e., land, although cash can also represent an important outflow.

The confused dowry

Let us consider the dowry in the areas we mentioned. In Asia Minor, few of the numerous acts of sale, donation and other transactions mention dowry goods specifically.[26] Where they do, the dowry consists of the major productive resources of the area, that is, olive trees, and also land. In most cases, it is unclear whether the woman had a brother or whether she was a sole heiress. If she had no brothers or sisters, in fact, she would be the sole heiress of her parents, according to Byzantine law; and on demographic grounds it may be expected that a not inconsiderable number of families would fall into this category. Wrigley, and Goody after him, has estimated that in pre-industrial societies about 40% of the families would have no male heir surviving the father, and half of these (i.e., 20% of the total) would have female heirs.[27] Our data cannot inform us as to the statistical likelihood of a woman receiving land as dowry in the presence of a brother; however, they do include cases where

24. On this question, see my Appendix and the study by J. Beaucamp, in this volume.

25. For the 12th century, see Ph. KOUKOULES, *Εὐσταθίου Θεσσαλονίκης τὰ Λαογραφικά*, I, Athens 1950, p. 477. For jewels, etc., see, for example, the will of Kale Pakouriane (1098), in J. LEFORT, N. OIKONOMIDÈS, D. PAPACHRYSSANTHOU, *Actes d'Iviron*, II, Archives de l'Athos XVI, Paris 1990, no. 47; for a lower social stratum, see GEDEON, *op. cit.* (n. 22), and G. FERRARI DALLE SPADE, « Registro Vaticano di atti bizantini di diritto privato », in *Scritti giuridici*, III, Milan 1956, no. X; ID., « Formulari notarili inediti dell'età bizantina », in *Scritti giuridici*, I, Milan 1953, no. 1, and the case discussed in LAIOU, *op. cit.* (n. 8), p. 158 ff. For the role of jewelry, clothing, etc. in India, see TAMBIAH, « Bridewealth... Revisited » (cit. n. 7), p. 420 ff.

26. They are published in F. MIKLOSICH, J. MÜLLER, *Acta et Diplomata Graeca medii aevi*, IV, Vienna 1871, p. 169-170, 32-34, 125-127, 132-133, 181, 133-134, 135-136, 140-141.

27. GOODY, *Production* (cit. n. 7), p. 87-88, and Appendix II.

this situation is observable.[28] In other cases, this is the most reasonable interpretation of the event described: thus a woman, member of the local aristocracy, donates land given her by her father in her (marriage) contracts, and performs this act with the consent of her two sons, her daughter and her future son-in-law, i.e., her immediate heirs and the man who might expect a dowry from her. Since her father is dead at the moment of the transaction, it may be reasonably assumed that she was not his sole heir, or she would have said so; but it may not necessarily be assumed that her siblings were male.[29] There is also mention of a woman who seems to have owned land, and she did have a brother; she is described as ἐξώπροικος in the document.[30] I know of nothing to suggest that women, with brothers, did not receive land as dowry in this area, although the proof, as I have indicated, is exiguous. Women do appear as owning land, which they sell or donate usually with the consent of other members of their families, but it is characteristic of this dossier that the proportion of mentions of dowry property even in cases which involve women is very low (7-8%).[31] I have suggested before that one explanation of this may be that property was given to women not as dowry but as property outside the dowry, which benefits the woman, by giving her greater leeway in the disposition of the property, but is not necessarily favorable to her natal family.[32] It is also suggestive that dowry goods are being donated without reference to the laws protecting dowry. My suggestion is that there is a *tendency*, although hard to say how strong, toward the unofficial assimilation of dowry property with hereditary property. If this is so, then the rights of the natal family with regard to the dowry become subject to the law of hereditary succession: in the absence of descendants from the woman's body, the ascendants and the lateral relatives (in the first instance brothers/sisters) are the heirs in intestate succession.[33] However, during her lifetime the woman can do as she wishes with the property, and she has testamentary discretion: thus, it is possible for the property to leave the natal family for good.

28. Such must be the case of Ioannes Pardoleon who, along with his wife, their two sons and their uncle (wife's brother, without a doubt) Varites, donate to the monastery of Lemviotissa olive trees which had been the wife's dowry; Varites was a *plesiastes* (close neighbour with rights of preemption), and this presumably is why he is mentioned here: MIKLOSICH-MÜLLER, IV, p. 133-134.

29. MIKLOSICH-MÜLLER, IV, p. 132-133.

30. MIKLOSICH-MÜLLER, IV, p. 126; cf. *infra*, Appendix, Case I.

31. This phenomenon appears in all documents from the 13th and 14th century which register dependent peasants (*paroikoi*) and their property, or record acts of sale and donation by peasants.

32. A. LAIOU, « The Role of Women in Byzantine Society », in *Gender, Society and Economic Life in Byzantium*, Variorum Reprints, London 1992, Study I, p. 240. Note, however, that J. Beaucamp finds scanty mention of dowry goods in the papyri as well: J. BEAUCAMP, « L'Égypte byzantine: biens des parents, biens du couple? », in *Eherecht und Familiengut in Antike und Mittelalter*, D. Simon ed., Munich 1992, p. 62. The practice would benefit the woman because she would have the right to sell or dispose of it at will; in such a case, it would never return to her natal family, though the dowry might do so.

33. *Bas.* XLV, 5, 2.

The scanty information we have from Thessaly lends some weight to the idea of an unofficial assimilation of dowry property to property in full ownership. There are a few acts of sale from a homogeneous population, peasants with some, although not much, property. They are all selling land to the founders of the monastery of Makrinitissa, pleading poverty. In one case, the woman is an only child and therefore an heiress, although she does not use the term; quite as expected, she owns land γονικόθεν, that is to say, in full hereditary succession.[34] But the same terminology is used by Anna, wife of Michael Martinos, who sells a small piece of vineyard (about 0.1 hectare), which she describes as γονικόν, even though the circumstances suggest strongly that it was dowry property: in her act of sale, in which are associated her husband and her daughters, it is Anna who is the principal; she explains her act as one of last resort – so that she and her husband could feed themselves and their young children – i.e., she invokes the only circumstances in which a dowry property may be sold. As to the property itself, it is contiguous to a vineyard of her brother's (of exactly the same size, also described as *gonikon*). So it is probably dowry property, and that is one reason for my suggestion that there is a confusion, or a presumption that the dowry property is very similar to hereditary property.[35]

The composition of the dowry

The data we have from the judicial decisions and opinions of Chomatianos and Apokaukos are more useful. For one thing, there is a good number of cases where dowry is at issue: thirty-one in the collection of Chomatianos' decisions. All of these cases concern disputes, and thus cannot be said to reflect normal practice. However, since they usually give a detailed history of the dispute, they are quite informative, both about the particulars of each case and about normal expectations. A few general observations may be made. First, as to the question of the kind of property women received from the patrimony, I still would rather not attempt a statistical approach, because the information is incomplete, so that an effort to try to correlate types of property transmission with social class, for example, would be impossible. I can only say that when women have property it is mostly as dowry that it appears in the source, except in a very few cases that have specific characteristics.[36] Secondly, I can say that the dowry appears overwhelmingly in the form of landed property, whether this was in vineyards or in arable land, or generally described as « immovable goods ». Thirdly, we can observe at least one case in which a woman did receive

34. Miklosich-Müller, IV, p. 393-396 (1271).

35. Miklosich-Müller, IV, p. 399-404; cf. p. 410-411.

36. None of this is meant to suggest that there were no women without dowry; there undoubtedly were very poor families where there were virtually no goods to go around. Such cases would normally be absent from our sources, since non-existent or minimal goods would not be objects of transactions, nor could they lead to judicial disputes.

immovable goods as dowry even when there was a brother, and even when the family belonged to the local aristocracy.[37] The documented cases of women with brothers who received land as dowry cannot be statistically correlated either with geography or with social class, because, among other things, the sample is too small and is not random. Of the few cases in this group of sources where a woman did not receive land as dowry, having been married with movable goods only, one has to do with a family that bears a Slavic name. The father had two daughters, and no sons; he married the daughters off with dowries consisting of movable goods only. His widow remarried, and had a daughter and a son, with the daughter receiving only movable goods as dowry, and the son receiving the paternal inheritance.[38]

There is clear evidence, then, that women received dowry property that included land. Their dowry could also include movable goods, and undoubtedly often did. This is sometimes explicitly mentioned, with the formulation that the woman's dowry consisted of « movable and immovable goods. »[39] The movable goods were the woman's trousseau, jewelry, and cash. As far as the trousseau is concerned, we get only the merest glimpse in the sources under discussion,[40] but we know from the few extant marriage contracts that it consisted of bedding, clothing, and household implements.[41] The sparse mention of movable goods in our sources is understandable in view of the fact that disputes mostly concerned the most important property, which was land. In one case, the dispute specifically mentions the money which the woman was given as dowry. It is an interesting case, concerning the dowry of a woman who belonged to the high levels of the provincial aristocracy, in Verroia. It is said that « among the various things that she brought in as dowry », there was a considerable sum of money in cash. There is mention, too, of « the other things that... made up her dowry ». She also received money as a gift from her father and grandfather (as did her husband), plus 121 gold coins from her sister by inheritance. Finally, she had, by hereditary right (γονικόθεν), a village.[42] The dispute, in this case, turns primarily around the cash, the « other things » being mentioned only vaguely, and one might reasonably assume that movable goods formed a very considerable portion of the woman's dowry. Does this mean that

37. CHOMATIANOS, no. 38 = no. 117.

38. CHOMATIANOS, no. 52.

39. CHOMATIANOS, no. 26 (a family from Verroia) ; no. 38 = no. 117 (an aristocratic family from Thessaloniki) ; no. 59 (a family from Skopje, perhaps local notables).

40. In one case, the daughter of the family seems to be dead, and one of her brothers mentions, as coming from her property, 10 gold coins, jewelry, clothing and cloth, all of which I assume to have been part of her dowry: CHOMATIANOS, no. 84, published by LAIOU, *op. cit.* (n. 8), p. 182. Cf. *supra*, p. 136.

41. The man also might bring such things into the marriage, especially if he was an *esogambros*: K. SATHAS, *Μεσαιωνικὴ Βιβλιοθήκη*, VI, Venice 1897, p. 608; GEDEON, *op. cit.* (n. 22), p. 114-115; A. LAIOU, « Ὁ θεσμὸς τῆς μνηστείας στὸν 13ο αἰῶνα », in *Ἀφιέρωμα στὸν Νίκο Σβορῶνο*, I, Rethymnon 1986, p. 288-294 (CHOMATIANOS, no. 19).

42. CHOMATIANOS, no. 25.

in the upper reaches of the aristocracy women received mostly cash and other movable goods upon marriage? We cannot affirm it, for there is another case clearly involving the aristocracy where the woman had both movable and immovable goods as dowry.[43] Nevertheless, the possibility cannot be excluded that among the aristocracy the dowry was in considerable part composed of movable goods.[44]

We retain, then, the fact that women did receive land as dowry, and the possibility that the dowry of aristocratic women may have included a sizable component in movable goods. How much of the patrimony did women get as dowry? Here things become complicated by a number of factors. First, to the degree that dowry functioned as pre-mortem inheritance, it can be argued that it followed the rules of succession. In case of intestate succession, all children of a marriage would have claims to equal shares of the property – equal partible inheritance; but it was possible to make testamentary dispositions or other arrangements that, while giving all of the children the legal minimum, could also treat them unequally. However, since, as has been argued by Dieter Simon,[45] the most important distribution of the family property took place not at the moment of the death of the parents, but rather at the point of the marriage of the children, through a marriage contract connected with a contract governing inheritance, it follows that the share of the property given each child at the moment of distribution may differ according to objective factors (changes in the family property; timing of each distribution) and subjective factors (the intent of the parents). Thus, marriage strategies come into play.

Marriage strategies

The marriage strategy seems to be dominated by the idea that the girls should be married, and that they should be married with a dowry – which may be a combination of the need to help set up a new household, and the need also to ensure that all of the children would be set up in life as well as possible. Sometimes we find in the documentation the echo of arrangements whereby the marriage of one child diminishes the expectations of the siblings. Thus, a man who lived in the countryside of Epiros (the theme of Vagenitia), and who

43. CHOMATIANOS, no. 38 = no. 117. In no. 102, discussed below, the people involved do not bear titles; they did, however, own very substantial property, half of which was given to their daughter as dowry. The other half was retained by her parents, and eventually passed to her brother. The girl's father was named Michael Syropoulos. A Theodore Syropoulos, from the same city of Verroia, was *grammatikos*, i.e., was a notable of the city: CHOMATIANOS, no. 99.

44. It should also be noted that the Slavic family whose daughters inherited *only* movable goods belonged to the aristocracy: CHOMATIANOS, no. 52.

45. D. SIMON, « Vertragliche Weitergabe des Familienvermögens in Byzanz », in *Hommes et Richesses dans l'Empire byzantin*, II: *VIIe-XVe siècle*, V. KRAVARI, J. LEFORT, and C. MORRISSON eds., Paris 1991, p. 182-195, and ID., « Erbvertrag und Testament », *Zbornik Radova Vizantološkog Instituta* 24-25, 1986, p. 291-306. For an exception, see the case of Karavas, *infra*, pp. 147-149.

was probably a peasant, married off all of his daughters with a dowry; he also married off one of his sons, the oldest one, giving him property.[46] At his death, the two younger brothers, who were still minors, were forced to emigrate. It appears that there was some parental property left over (the house with some land?), but that it was insufficient to provide for their needs. Eventually they returned, took over this piece of property which is described as deserted, returned it to production, and exploited it together. Forty years after the original distribution of the property, the grandson of one of the sisters who had been married off with a dowry, brought claims on the property held by the descendants of one of the younger brothers. What we have in this case is the unequal and preferential treatment of the daughters and the eldest son, which is probably a function of the timing of the distribution of the property. The younger brothers were certainly not excluded from the inheritance – but they came into a smaller share than the others.

In another case, the father seems to have intentionally practiced preferential treatment of some of his daughters at the time of their marriage. That is to say, he married off his first daughter with a dowry, and also the second daughter, perhaps with a dowry. He made no provision for his three sons; two left the household and emigrated to make a living, and these two were specifically excluded from the inheritance, by the testament of their father, except for his blessing and a tiny legacy. In the end, two offspring of the father survived: a woman, who ended up with the entire property on the father's and the mother's side, and one of the sons, who inherited nothing, and brought the case to court. This parental disposition had clearly been contrary to the law, and perhaps also to common practice; the son easily won his right to the legal minimum from the parental property.[47] The exclusion of younger sons may have been due to particular in-family problems in this case. But it was, I think, not a unique occurrence, partly because of the exigencies of making good matches for the daughters.

The difficulties of such preferential treatment are evident. For one thing, the rights of the other children, both legal and presumed, create tensions. Furthermore, decisions taken at one point in the family cycle affect decisions further down the line, so that the younger children may be in a detrimental position. A case illustrating the first point is the following: An *anagnostes* (an ecclesiastical official) was promised, on the occasion of his marriage, the following dowry: one third of the property of the girl's father, and one third of the property of her paternal grandfather. The property of the paternal grandfather, it would seem, was to be handed over after his death; but in the meantime, his sons protested that this would reduce their own inheritance, and therefore the grandfather tried to revoke his promise by making a testamentary disposition that would divide his property equally between his two sons, leaving nothing to the granddaughter. The court's opinion was that if the grandfather's

46. CHOMATIANOS, no. 37. On other aspects of the case, see *infra*, Appendix, Case VII.
47. CHOMATIANOS, no. 99.

property had been reduced between the time of the marriage contracts and the time of the testament, he might have been justified in making different testamentary dispositions. But since his property had remained intact, the testament was not valid; eventually a compromise was reached, but the case points out the problems created by preferential treatment, and it also illustrates the fact that, in their effort to make a good marriage for a daughter (in this case granddaughter), people might have to promise more than they were really willing to give.[48]

Preferential treatment of some children, because of the point in the family cycle or for other reasons, can take place at the time of marriage of these children, male or female. In the early thirteenth century, a man named Stefanos Mardaropoulos, from Ioannina, who seems to have been a man of some property, died « not constituting his daughters equal heiresses of his goods, as law and justice decree. » Rather, he left his wife executrix and warden of his estate and tutor of their three daughters, « *perhaps* with the intention that she should marry them off legally and divide the paternal estate equally among them ».[49] The widow's dowry arrangements eventually brought the matter before two courts, that of Georgios Vardanes, metropolitan of Corfu, and that of Ioannes Apokaukos, metropolitan of Naupaktos. The details are somewhat unclear, since the case was presented differently in the two courts. However, the basic facts are clear enough. The widow married off two of the daughters with handsome dowries, which exhausted her husband's property. The third and youngest daughter was also married off, to an army officer (Theodore Diavatenos, *primmikerios* of the Varangians of Ioannina), but with a very small dowry which, it would seem, came from the mother's own property. Here we have a case of unequal dowries for reasons that are unknown. Perhaps the mother meant to make better provision for her third daughter out of her own property, but, since she had remarried, her second husband may have objected. Diavatenos had been willing to take the bride anyway. It may have been a love-match, or it may be that the marriages of the first two daughters were to well-connected men, whose social position Diavatenos may have considered adequate compensation for the small dowry he received. However, later he decided that he had been cheated of his proper share, and sought redress from the court. Apokaukos' decision (as well as that of Vardanes) was that the three brothers-in-law should, indeed, divide equally the property of their father-in-law, as both law and justice require. The legal aspects of the case are not entirely clear, since the legal argument is based on intestacy, and it is not at all certain that Mardaropoulos had died intestate; besides, the same argument is applied to the disposition made by his widow, regarding her own property. As for

48. Chomatianos, no. 98; the case has been discussed by Simon, « Erbvertrag » (cit. n. 45), p. 292-294.

49. N. A. Bees, « Unedierte Schriftstücke aus der Kanzlei des Johannes Apokaukos », *Byzantinisch-neugriechische Jahrbücher* 21, 1976, no. 4; cf. A. Papadopoulos-Kerameus, « Kerkyraika », *Vizantijskij Vremennik* 13, 1907, p. 342, and *Ekklesiastikos Faros* 4, 1909, p. 63-67.

justice, I suppose that one should understand it as the social norm, or custom, and this seems to be the stronger of the arguments. Thus we see here not only the effects of preferential treatment of one or more heirs, depending on the family cycle, but also perhaps the complex nature of these arrangements, which transcend purely financial matters; and, finally, we may be seeing a normative corrective (whether that of laws or that of custom) that brings particular financial matrimonial arrangements closer to equality than individuals would have wished.[50]

It is neither possible nor necessary to detail all of the marriage strategies and marriage arrangements that one can find in this collection of sources. A major point that should be kept in mind is the fact that all of the evidence argues for partible inheritance among the children of a family, with the dowry functioning as a pre-mortem inheritance; in cases of dispute between siblings regarding inheritance, the issue turns around the question whether the daughters had received a dowry or not; if they had had the proper amount of dowry, they were thought to have no further claims on the inheritance, although the parents could certainly bequeath property to them if they so chose.[51] *Equal* partible inheritance may have been an ideal, but individual decisions varied with the specifics of each union, while the marriage of each child changed the configuration as far as the other children were concerned. This was the case not only with the dowry of female children but also with the marriage portions of married children, where again a set of different arrangements was possible: while sometimes we find the eldest son getting all of the family property into his possession, by exploiting his moral and emotional hold on younger siblings, at other times the older children might be married off and leave the household, with their marriage portions, while younger children could be promised their portion at the point of marriage, but not expect to receive it until after the father's death.[52] Death sometimes relieved the pressure on the family property, permitting its re-concentration in the hands of one or another of the siblings. All of this underlines the importance of timing in marriage arrangements: much depends on who is married first, on the point in the family cycle that the marriage takes place, and on whether the property actually changes hands at the time of the marriage.

50. But see CHOMATIANOS, no. 65. This is a case involving people in Corfu. A man and his wife divided, both by testamentary disposition, their property unequally between their two daughters. One of the sons-in-law tried to dispute the will. However, since apparently the legal minimum had been met, the validity of the testaments was upheld. The disposition made by Apokaukos was probably fairly disruptive: cf. *infra*, Appendix.

51. See CHOMATIANOS, no. 63; *infra*, Appendix, Case V, and the discussion in the Appendix.

52. For the first type of situation, see LAIOU, *op. cit.* (n. 8), p. 164-165. For the second, see CHOMATIANOS, no. 100.

Fragmentation?

The sum total of the information regarding dowry suggests that it did indeed result in fragmentation of the paternal holding. On the part of the woman's natal family, there was the possibility of giving as dowry movable property, which is something of a corrective, but not very useful in this social milieu, where much of the property consisted of or came from land. There is another corrective, when the dowry is promised but not delivered until later, by which time intervening events (for example, the death of the woman) might obviate the need to pay it; but this cannot have had much significance in the society as a whole.[53] The property may also have gone to the woman as inheritance, but this simply defers the time of the transfer.[54] From the point of view of the woman's natal family, the dowry was indeed a net outflow of resources, especially since neo-local or patri-virilocal marriage was prevalent; and the rules on close marriage, which, as far as we know, were followed, broadly speaking, except sometimes by the imperial aristocracy, made re-concentration of the property by endogamous marriage impossible.

Restructuring

We must, now, turn to the new family, the one created by the marriage. For the husband and wife, the dowry and the man's counter-gift formed the economic nucleus of their household, which could later be augmented by other acquisitions. The protected status of the dowry meant that the basic economic nucleus was, in theory, and less so in practice, stable for a while: the dowry could not be bought, sold or donated except in extreme conditions, and the husband was responsible for it, while the revenues derived from it had to be used for the needs of the family unit. From the point of view of the new family, there is the creation of a new economic unit as well as a new biological unit. Thus, the fragmentation of the property of the natal families is at the same time a restructuring of property, that of the new household. This is an obvious but important fact, which forces us to look at things not only from the point of view of the original property, but over time. Over time, then, the major point is that we have a dynamic development, since with each generation the patrimony is re-organised, the new patrimony consisting of pieces of the patrimony of the two natal families, along with new acquisitions. In times of demographic stability, the new households are not necessarily poorer than the original one, at least once the parents are dead. In times of demographic growth, of course, they are poorer in the beginning and remain so, unless they increase their

53. I do not include among the correctives the well-known custom of the *sogambroi*, that is, the uxorilocal or patri-uxorilocal residence of the husband of a sole heiress. The number of these cases must have been significant, but in this society they are not the result of choice. For an example of delayed payment of part of the dowry (in cash), see FERRARI DALLE SPADE, « Registro Vaticano » (cit. n. 25), no. XVI.

54. CHOMATIANOS, no. 37.

property through other means: demographic growth may, in some circumstances, lead to economic growth, both global and individual, through land-clearance, for example.[55] The original patrimony becomes very diffused; the most extreme case I know of is the case of a mill, in Asia Minor, on which fifteen people had rights.[56] Thus there is instability in landholdings, but the counterpart of instability is the creation of new households.

Where the new household is concerned, there are both connections and tensions with the natal families, especially with the woman's family. For the natal family, of course, does not sever links with the married daughter, sister or niece, nor does she sever her links with them. On the contrary, we find time and again a woman's kin (especially her male kin, since our sources deal with legal matters) acting as protectors of their married daughter, or sometimes of more remote female relatives, and bringing their cases to court when the occasion arises. The woman's natal family also has residual claims on her dowry, for example, if the woman dies without heirs, in which case the dowry returns to the family. At the same time, the new family, created by the marriage, acquires a certain degree of autonomy, and this may lead to a tendency to treat the dowry as though it were the common property of the new household, and to reduce or deny the claims of the woman's natal family. There are some indicators which suggest such a tendency. First, I recall the fact that in the registering of the property of dependent peasants, as well as in acts of sale or donation of land, it is quite uncommon for property to be differentiated between dowry and non-dowry property, and quite common to find the term *gonikon*, hereditary. Does this suggest a confusion of goods in practice, so that the family property is the family property, without much regard for its provenance?

Secondly, I mention a piece of information, brought to the attention of the Patriarchal tribunal of Constantinople in 1317, by the metropolitan of Attaleia. It was reported that

> some of the men of the region, when they marry women according to the laws, and the agreed-upon dowry is handed over to them, they force and oblige [the girl's family] to give some of the dowry goods to them in the form of a gift, and the rest to the woman in the form of dowry. So that, if the woman should predecease the husband, and the dowry is reclaimed [by her family], only the part that is registered as dowry would be returned to them, while the rest will remain with them [the husbands] without any claim, since it was given them as gift. This custom has become prevalent and it is practiced, unreasonably, so that these men refuse to marry otherwise, and hence those who have daughters cannot get them married in any other way, but are forced into this [practice].

55. According to one calculation, in a system of perfect partible inheritance, if a peasant had three sons surviving to adulthood, within four generations the original holding would be one fifth of its original size: A. LAIOU-THOMADAKIS, *Peasant Society in the Late Byzantine Empire: A Social and Demographic Study*, Princeton 1977, p. 196, after BERKNER and MENDELS, « Inheritance Systems ».

56. MIKLOSICH-MÜLLER, IV, p. 196-197.

> They suffer great damage, despite the provisions of the law, and lose their own property. So he [the metropolitan] asked for a decision on our part... Regarding these marriages and marriage arrangements, our mediocrity, along with the holy synod, concluded and stated that this unreasonable and wrong custom, when it occurs, is invalid and without [legal] force. If it should happen that the wife dies, and the dowry goods are reclaimed, the husband should return them in their entirety, according to the pious laws. He should keep nothing from these [goods], and profit nothing from them, pretending that he holds them as a gift, for such an action is entirely unreasonable and for this reason ought to be invalid from this day onward, and forever.[57]

From the legal point of view, « gifts » do not enter into the discussion of dowry, but in terms of the subject we are discussing this « custom » clearly takes part of the « marriage property » outside the control of the woman's natal family forever, and into the control of the daughter's husband.

Third, it is quite clear that the dowry and the countergift exist as the property of the new household and its children. But what happens to the dowry if the woman dies childless and predeceases her husband? By law, if there are no agreements to the contrary, and the woman dies intestate, the property returns to her natal family, except for a portion which goes to the husband.[58] It seems that generally, in the early thirteenth century, the portion was agreed upon at the time of the marriage contracts. But in a case where there were no nuptial agreements covering the case of the husband's gains upon the death of the wife, Chomatianos ruled that nevertheless the husband would keep one third of the property, as was the custom.[59] Finally, there are a few cases in the Chomatianos dossier which are very interesting indeed. While the legal aspects are rather complex, the question they raised may be reduced to the following: a woman dies, and her dowry is inherited by her child (or children); then they die too, and the husband contracts a second marriage; does the dowry property eventually revert to the woman's family of origin or has the property passed forever into the hands of the husband, and therefore to his successors? The point of interest for us is that the *local* court, in the small town of Verroia, that judged this case in the first instance, argued that the law that limited the rights of the man on his dead wife's dowry if he remarried had not been applied for a long time, and had therefore become moot. The court thus supported the rights of the new family, even when that had become truncated, on the dowry property, which means that the local « custom » was taking a big step toward

57. MIKLOSICH-MÜLLER, I, p. 77-78.

58. *Bas.* XXVIII, 8, 68; XXVIII, 8, 54; XLV, 3, 8; XXIX, 1, 119, 6; XXVIII, 14, 1; XXVIII, 14, 18; XLV, 5, 2; II, 12, 2; XXVIII, 12, 1; XXVIII, 12, 2. Cf. SIMON, « Erbvertrag » (cit. n. 45).

59. CHOMATIANOS, no. 56. There is some contradictory information here: in case 56, Chomatianos claims that most marriage contracts include clauses on what will happen to the goods in case of the death of the spouse; but in case 38 he says that marriage contracts had long ago stopped including provisions for the *casus liberorum non existentium.*

removing the dowry property from the control of the natal family, whatever the circumstances.[60]

All the points I have mentioned suggest a first answer to the question posed for this Colloquium. In the presence of prohibitions regarding close marriage, and given the system of diverging devolution of property, the patrimony of the natal family does become fragmented, and the dowry contributes to the fragmentation, even more than is made necessary by the laws. The patrimony of the natal family is diffused, and becomes the nucleus of the property of other families. But this is only a formal answer, and a first approximation. The other side of the coin is a further strengthening of the new family and of the new household created by the marriage. If dowry fragments the property of the natal family, it also is joined with the property of the husband to form the nucleus of a new property which, augmented by the joint efforts of the spouses, will devolve upon their children. This is a dynamic process. And to get a full picture, one must know what really happened to people and their property. That depends on many questions; demography is a factor, for things are different depending on the number of children and on issues such as contraception and infanticide; it also depends on the stability of the marriage, which is not necessarily a controllable factor, given the mortality rate.

Family and property cycle

The normal situation assumed a stable marriage, with children who survived to adulthood. In such a situation, tensions would be reduced, even when the marriage was dissolved at the death of one of the parents. A good example is given by a testament, which falls somewhat outside the period with which I am dealing. It is the testament of Theodore Karavas, inhabitant of Thessaloniki, a merchant who also owned rural property outside the city.[61] He was a careful man, who wrote everything down, and kept copies and receipts. His testament probably lists all of his property as it existed at the time of his death, and he also gives a history of his earlier dispositions. Among his urban properties, he lists six houses with an *aule* (courtyard) which was common to his property and that of his nephew, the son of his sister. Another two houses were in a complex with an *aule* held in common with his nephew and with the husband of his spiritual daughter. He had been married twice, receiving dowries from both wives. Among his rural properties, he had a piece of vineyard, from the dowry of his

60. CHOMATIANOS, nos. 26, 61, 38, 117, 62. The cases have been commented upon by D. SIMON, « Eine Juristenkontroverse über das Schicksal der Mitgift », *Byzantina* 13/1, 1985, p. 649-666, and A. LAIOU, « Contribution à l'étude de l'institution familiale en Épire au XIIIème siècle », in EAD., *op. cit.* (n. 32), Study V, p. 299-300.

61. L. PETIT and B. KORABLEV, « Actes de Chilandar », *Vizantijskij Vremennik* 17, 1910, supp. 1, no. 27 (1314).

first wife, which had been listed in his marriage contracts.[62] He had given this to his son, as he should have done. Indeed, all of the property of his first wife, which had been properly listed in the marriage contracts, he had given to the two children he had had of her (a son and a daughter), and he possessed written receipts for these transactions. This was clearly done at the time of their marriage, at which point he had also given them the part of his own property to which they were legally entitled; all of this was written down in their marriage contracts, and his son had also received other property, not so registered. Thus he had no further obligations to his one surviving child. The dowry of his second wife had also been registered in her marriage contract. It consisted of houses and vineyards (this was a man who produced wine for the market, and had very little arable land). That dowry had been liquidated; he ensures that his wife will have restitution for it, in vineyards from his own property. In his will, he left some property to his son and to his spiritual sons and daughters, and small legacies to his two grandchildren from his daughter, his nephews, to all his blood relatives, and to priests and churches. The bulk of his estate went to his second wife, who also became the executrix of his will. The family property changes in configuration: land is acquired by purchase, dowry property is sold, presumably to buy other land, and then is restored. The will is like the dissolution of a partnership: his partnership with his first wife is partly dissolved at the moment of her death and fully dissolved at the point of the marriage of their children, at which point the mother's dowry is distributed to the children, as is part of his own property. The partnership with his second wife is dissolved in part, but not entirely, by his death, for he leaves her a legacy with which to ensure his commemoration. With his children there is hardly any partnership; they get the property to which they are entitled, and form their own autonomous households. One must remember, however, that there was property which he held in common with his nephews.

It should also be added that at the moment of his death Karavas left a very sizable estate; the value of his investments in vineyards and urban real estate alone can be estimated at almost one thousand hyperpyra (977, to be exact). Having already fulfilled all his legal obligations to his children, he felt free to dispose of his property as he wished, the main beneficiary being his second wife. Legacies to priests and the church were exiguous.

The freedom exhibited by Karavas in his will, especially the somewhat surprising gifts of a house and/or vineyard to each of his godchildren, may well be the result of the fact that he was rather wealthy, and also that, by profession

62. For examples of dowry contracts, see Gedeon, *op. cit.* (n. 22), p. 114 ff (13th-14th c.); G. Ferrari dalle Spade, «Diritto matrimoniale secondo le Novelle di Leone il Filosofo», *Byzantinische Zeitschrift* 18, 1909, p. 168-169; J. and P. Zepos, *Jus Graecoromanum*, I, Athens 1931, p. xvii; G. Ferrari dalle Spade, *I documenti greci medioevali di diritto privato dell'Italia meridionale*, Leipzig 1910 (repr. Athens 1974), p. 100-105; Laiou, *op. cit.* (n. 41), p. 280-298; Chomatianos, no. 19; Ferrari dalle Spade, «Formulari» (cit. n. 25), nos. 1, 2, 3; K. Sathas, *op. cit.* (n. 41), p. 612, 615, 618-619, 631-632, 638-639.

and perhaps by the fact of his residence in Thessaloniki, he was well aware of the laws or had the benefit of legal advice. The fact remains that, in this man's case, the division of his property took place both at the time of the marriage of his children and at the time of his death. The first division was governed by legal requirements; the second far less so. The impression one gets is that the bulk of his estate was distributed at the second and final point.

Instability and stability: joint administration of property

The real corrective to the inter-generational instability of the patrimony comes not necessarily from formal marriage or succession contracts, but rather through informal but nevertheless very real arrangements within families and between related families.[63] They are arrangements which have to do with the administration and exploitation of the patrimony (which is what really counts where land is concerned) rather than with its ownership. Sometimes, these arrangements may indeed have been formally made. Such is the case of the marriage of Ioannes Pepagomenos, from Verroia, who, in the late twelfth century, married the daughter of Michael Syropoulos and Anna Paulopoulina. He received, by virtue of marriage contracts, a dowry, which must have been considerable. Included in the dowry was, along with other immovable goods, one half of two domains (ζευγηλατεῖον), which consisted of buildings, arable and vineyards; the girl's parents retained the other half, eventually to give it to their son. There was what the document calls a « division » (μερισμός) of these lands, in the presence of witnesses. The shares, however, of the domain situated in Vaniane were not made up of entire and separate parcels of land; rather, each strip was divided in half.[64] The exploitation of the entire property was in the hands of the son-in-law. Therefore, although the dowry goods were divided from the rest of the property, the division was such that it necessitated common exploitation, an intentional arrangement. The fact that the agreement eventually broke down, when the girl's brother tried to lay claims on the entirety of one of the two domains, is a different story.[65] The point is, that there was to be, from the beginning, joint exploitation of the entire property of the girl's natal family, despite the fact that half of it had been given as dowry. Joint exploitation, indeed, is encouraged by exogamy rules. For if a woman must marry someone not her kin, eventually this will take her out of the village, while

63. What follows is based on chapter V of my *Mariage, amour et parenté.*

64. CHOMATIANOS, no. 102. This is how I understand παρέλαβε δὲ ταῦτα καθ'ὁμάδα μὲν οὐκοῦν κατὰ ἄρουραν δέ, ἑκάστη δηλαδὴ ἰσομοιρία μεριζομένης, καὶ ἐξ ἡμισείας ἀποκαθισταμένης ἀνὰ μέρος ἑκατέροις... A similar division of lands is made in western Crete today: F. SAULNIER-TERCELIN, in *Familles et biens en Grèce et à Chypre*, C. Piault ed., Paris, 1985, p. 56. In the case discussed by Chomatianos, there was common exploitation of the property (no. 102, col. 436).

65. The case described in this document bears certain resemblances with Chomatianos no. 81, republished and commented in LAIOU, *op. cit.* (n. 8), chapter V. In both cases, the problems arise from the process of dowry, inheritance and indivision.

the land will remain there, which creates a problem. The problem can be solved either by an exchange of lands, or by the joint exploitation of her dowry lands by her brothers or other kin who stay in the village. It thus may be argued that, contrary to what one might expect from a formal reading of dowry arrangements, exogamous marriage and bilateral inheritance lead to joint exploitation of resources.

Arrangements which, in various ways, result in the exploitation of the patrimony as a whole, are highly visible in our sources.[66] We find eldest sons who, honestly or dishonestly, use their position of seniority to exploit the patrimony in which younger brothers have a share as if it were their own property, thus assuming, for a time, the role of a son in a system of primogeniture. We find brothers and brothers-in-law and kin exploiting undivided patrimonial property together. That is to say, neither dowry nor succession need necessarily lead to the fragmentation of the *exploitation* of the property. We find the reconstitution of parts of the original patrimony of a family through purchase by members of that family who already hold part of the original property, or through gifts. We find brothers and brothers-in-law buying property together, so that a kind of society is created, whereby the economic links between members of the original family become reinforced. At the same time, there is an evolution of the right of preemption so that kinship becomes the primary factor that gives rights of preemption on the purchase of a piece of property.[67] This is another informal but nevertheless institutional response to the diverging devolution of property.

Close economic relations, including the indivision and joint exploitation of property, involve not only the biological descendants of a family, but also the affines, the spouses of the biological children. They involve not only lineal descendants but also lateral ones. Close economic cooperation is observable through the fourth degree of kinship, and disappears thereafter. First cousins and the spouses of first cousins are kin with multiple links, which may include very close economic relations. Marriage between first cousins had been forbidden since 691-692 by the church, since 741 by the state; marriage of two brothers to two first cousins had been forbidden since 997, and henceforth the reconstruction of the patrimony that such marriages would entail had become impossible. A new system was in place, one of restructuring rather than reconstruction. But the first-cousin relationship continued to form a sort of boundary, within which there was close contact and much economic cooperation, including the joint exploitation of property.

66. On joint exploitation of land in medieval Italy and Catalonia see, respectively, the articles by J.-M. Martin and L. To Figueras, in this volume.

67. E. Papagianni, « Vorkaufsrecht und Verwandtschaft », in *Eherecht* (cit. n. 32), p. 147-160. A similar combination of autonomy of the new family/household and economic cooperation between households is observable today as well. See, for western Crete, Saulnier-Tercelin, *op. cit.* (n. 64), p. 54-62. Various articles in this volume are suggestive of the variety of arrangements in a situation where the ecclesiastical rules against endogamy are still in force and where the Greek Civil Code incorporates the principle of equal partible inheritance.

Conclusion

To conclude, I should like to stress a few points that I have already made in the text. First of all, and above all, it seems to me that it would be false to seek a simplistic connection between diverging devolution of property, the prohibition of close marriages and the fragmentation of property. Even before we get to the point of marriage strategies, we can easily understand that what inheritance and dowry divide, marriage unites. If the accent is placed on the new family, created by marriage, as surely it was by the participants, then we acquire a different perspective, which allows us to look at the dynamic process of the creation of a new patrimony that is augmented in the course of the marriage, to be redivided when the children marry, and restructured yet again. Indeed, a study of what happens to the property acquired by the couple in the course of the marriage has never been made, at least for Byzantium, and is sorely missing. As a subsidiary point, I repeat that timing is very important, both in the arrangements themselves and in our observation of them.[68] A second point is that marriage strategies are just as important, if not more so, as norms; through marriage strategies, the system becomes flexible, as each family tries to achieve the best possible arrangement for itself and for the new family. In this effort, it is not only the exchange of property that matters, since issues of social standing play an important role. Finally, I think it important to insist on the fact that the division of patrimonial property is sometimes a notional division; and in any case, one should study not only the formalities of property division but also the realities of joint exploitation of property. The multidimensional picture that results may be a jurist's nightmare, but it is reality as it is lived.

Appendix

Dowry and Inheritance: The Meaning of ἐξώπροικος

A recurring question regarding the dowry is whether it may be seen as an advance on inheritance, which would mean that at the point of death of the parents an estimation of their property would be made, including the dowries already given out, and the final division would take place, or whether it functioned as a replacement of inheritance, or pre-mortem inheritance, which would mean that the child married off with a dowry had no further rights on inheritance. A permutation of the second eventuality is that the offspring married off with a dowry were excluded from the inheritance, which is different from having no further rights on it. The question has usually been posed only with regard to women, but in Byzantium of the 13th and 14th centuries it relates to men also.

In the sources of this period we find the term ἐξώπροικος, referring to persons, a term which is to be distinguished from ἐξώπροικα, referring to goods. The meaning of the latter term is not in dispute: the ἐξώπροικα consist

68. For the importance of time, see Bourdieu, *op. cit.* (n. 2), p. 5.

of property which is given to the woman not as dowry but in full ownership. According to the Lexicon of (pseudo)-Zonaras it is equivalent to the term ἕδνα.[69] As for ἐξώπροικος, it has been taken to mean the children that have been married off with a dowry, and which are, therefore, excluded from inheriting part of their parents' property.[70] A closer examination of the sources allows us to refine our understanding of both the term and the practice to which it refers. Here, we will look briefly at the 13th – and 14th – century documents that use the term ἐξώπροικος, or refer to this practice, and try to draw some conclusions.

Case I. In his testament, a man named Theodore Gordatos, from Asia Minor, tries to guard against his sister's laying claim on property which Gordatos is leaving to his wife, « by reason of the one third which she (the sister) has here ». If the sister raises a claim, she should give up the land which she « has from Karvones, for she was ἐξώπροικος ». This case is the least clear of the dossier. Matses has interpreted it as meaning that the sister had received a dowry plus land from inheritance from her parents; if she should raise claims on one-third of the inheritance, she should relinquish the land she already had been given, as having no right on it because she was ἐξώπροικος.[71] It is not an unlikely interpretation. In the light of other documents, it is also possible that the land the sister had from Karvones was her dowry; if she raised a claim based on rights of inheritance, this land should be reckoned into the total of the inheritance, which would then be divided between the testator's heirs and his sister.[72] Because we do not know the details of the various arrangements, there is not much more that we can say.

Case II. This is a decision of the patriarchal court, dated 1401. Georgios Mamalis brought a suit against his brother, Andreas Doukas Mamalis, regarding a garden that had belonged to their parents. The plaintiff claimed that he owned 3/5 of the garden: one fifth he had bought from his brother Nicholas, another fifth he had received as payment of a debt owed him by his brother Constantine (now dead), and a fifth he had from inheritance. Andreas Doukas Mamalis argued that neither Georgios nor any of his siblings who had been married off by their parents had any claim on this garden. He said that the garden had remained in the possession of the parents, and upon her death their mother had left as heirs (κληρονόμοι) of all the remaining parental property himself

69. *Ecloga* II, 5, 1: the goods that a woman has brought into her husband's household, over and above the dowry; cf. D. SIMON, « Das Ehegüterrecht der Pira », *Fontes Minores* VII, Frankfurt am Main 1986, p. 223. Cf. also *Iohannis Zonarae Lexicon*, Leipzig 1808, I, *s.v.* ἕδνα: τὰ πρὸ τοῦ γάμου διδόμενα ταῖς νύμφαις δῶρα, ἅτινα καὶ ἐξώπροικα λέγονται. According to this Lexicon, the property is given by the girl's father (*s.v.* ἑδνωτής); according to Suida, by the future husband (*s.v.* ἕδνα).

70. N. P. MATSES, *Τὸ οἰκογενειακὸν δίκαιον κατὰ τὴν νομολογίαν τοῦ Πατριαρχείου Κωνσταντινουπόλεως τῶν ἐτῶν 1315-1401*, Athens 1962, p. 180-181.

71. MIKLOSICH-MÜLLER, IV, p. 126; MATSES, *op. cit.* (n. 70), p. 180 n. 3.

72. Cf. *infra*, our Cases III, VIII.

and his brother Nicholas, who were ὑπεξούσιοι. The others were ἐξώπροικοι, and had no rights on the garden or the rest of the property. Eventually, however, the mother's testament was found, and she had, indeed, divided the garden equally among her five children; the court honored the testamentary disposition.[73]

Case III. This is a decision of the patriarchal court (1394) regarding a case which had been referred to it by the metropolitan of Thessaloniki. The suit was between Georgios Prinkips and his sister. The plaintiff, Prinkips, claimed that his father had given the sister three dowries, for she had been married three times, and had agreed to give his son (Prinkips) a «dowry» of 300 hyperpyra and some other (movable) property. Prinkips had lived with his father for one year, until the father's death; he had received the movable goods, but had not pressed the father for the cash. At the father's death, the only remaining property was a vineyard, part of which the sister was claiming by right of inheritance. The court decided that, after various other claims on the vineyard had been settled, Prinkips should get from the value of the vineyard the 300 hyperpyra promised him by his father. If there was anything left over, he and his sister should divide it equally. Alternatively, if the sister preferred, both children should bring back into the valuation of the paternal property all that they had received as dowry (i.e., as marriage gifts), add the remaining paternal property, and divide the whole equally. It should be noted that the term ἐξώπροικος is not used for the sister, but the substance of the case is identical to that of other cases where the term is used.

Comments on Cases II and III. Both cases clearly establish the fact that children married off with a dowry were not *ipso facto* excluded from inheritance. Testamentary disposition (Case II) is of paramount importance in this regard: the parents may, by testament, leave property to children that have already received a dowry. In Case III the father has died intestate; the daughter who was married with a dowry is still considered to have rights of inheritance on the paternal estate, and she is also given the possibility of considering her dowry as an advance on the inheritance. However, one wonders whether the patriarchal court, in recognising the woman's rights, was not being deliberately unrealistic, giving her rights which were either meaningless or which she would surely not wish to exercise. There were so many claims on the vineyard that it seems unlikely that after they had all been met there would be anything left over for the two siblings to divide. Furthermore, according to the plaintiff, to whom the court was clearly sympathetic, his sister had received so much in dowry that it

73. Miklosich-Müller, II, p. 543-546. All of the cases discussed here include many other points of interest and various legal complications. We are not discussing the cases fully, but only with regard to the problem at hand. For Cases II and III, see also R. Macrides, «Dowry and Inheritance in the Late Period: some cases from the Patriarchal Register», in *Eherecht* (cit. n. 32), p. 96-97.

would be hardly in her interest to bring her dowries into the property for an equal division. The Patriarch's offer to the woman was virtual blackmail.

In both cases, explicitly in Case II, implicitly in Case III, a distinction is made (by the defendant and the plaintiff respectively) between children married off with a dowry and children who are regarded as heirs. The heirs (κληρονόμοι) are the children who remain in the parental household, either because they are still ὑπεξούσιοι and unmarried (Case II) or because they have been married but still live with their parents and take care of them (patrilocal residence). The expectation of the «heirs», certainly in Case II, is that they have full and exclusive rights on the remaining parental estate, even though the court does not recognise such rights, and the mother's testament does not either. We will encounter again the distinction between heirs and children that have been dowried.

Case IV. In the early 13th century, a man from Corfu, named Konstantas, brought to Chomatianos a complaint against his maternal uncle, Makronikolaos. Konstantas said that his maternal grandparents had married off his mother with a dowry which included, among other things, half their landed property. Makronikolaos was, at the time, resident in the parental household, although later he went away for many years, hiring himself out as a laborer. On his return, Makronikolaos held his half of the property for 22 years; he was now laying claim on the entire property, saying that Konstantas' mother had been «ἐξώπροικος», and for that reason none of the immovable goods were included in her dowry contract; Makronikolaos wanted the contract to be produced, so that it could be determined whether «her parents had also given her immovable goods» (ὥστε δῆλον ἐντεῦθεν γενέσθαι, εἰ καὶ ἀκίνητα οἱ γονεῖς ἐκείνῃ ἐκληροδότησαν). The dowry contract not having survived, Konstantas' paternal uncle, Kalos, gave sworn testimony supporting Konstantas' claims. Makronikolaos did not desist. Chomatianos rendered an opinion in favor of Konstantas, but his argumentation did not bear on the question of the rights of Konstantas' mother on the property. Rather, the opinion was based on the issues of long-term good-faith possession, and on the validity of sworn testimony.[74]

In terms of our topic, the following observations may be made. First of all, Konstantas' grandfather had given half of his immovable property to his daughter upon her marriage, while the other half was inherited by his son (τῆς ἁρμοζούσης αὐτῷ ἡμισείας ἐδράξατο...). Thus, dowry and inheritance each implicated one half of the landed property of the natal family. Makronikolaos' claim might, at first glance, be interpreted as meaning that an ἐξώπροικος woman had no right on *any* immovable property, even given as dowry. I think, however, that this was poor and inaccurate phraseology, or specious

74. CHOMATIANOS, no. 90. On CHOMATIANOS, nos. 90, 37, 152, cf. N. P. MATSES, *Νομικὰ ζητήματα ἐκ τῶν ἔργων τοῦ Δημητρίου Χωματιανοῦ*, Athens 1961, p. 73-79. He also comments briefly on CHOMATIANOS, nos. 45, 56, 63, 100: p. 73, n. 1.

argumentation, especially when one bears in mind that the argumentation is reported not by Makronikolaos himself but by his nephew, with whom he was engaged in litigation. I think that what Makronikolaos in fact laid claim to was the part of the parental land which was left over after the woman had received her dowry. In other words, I think he may have argued that the « other things » mentioned in the document had been her dowry, and that the lands in question were the residue, which constituted his inheritance. Such argumentation is given in the next two cases.

Case V. John, father of a priest from Skopje named Symeon, had had three daughters and two sons. The three daughters received dowries and « were sent off to their husbands' houses ». The two sons (Symeon and George, who had since died) were *together* constituted heirs (συγκληρονόμοι) of his house and his entire landed property (ὑπόστασις, the same term used in Case IV, and meaning, I think, the remaining property of the father). The problem was that one of Symeon's sisters wanted a share of this property by right of inheritance from their brother George, who had left descendants, on behalf of whom Symeon was acting. Chomatianos resolved the case against the sister, on the basis of the law that gives first right of inheritance to direct relatives, not to lateral ones. But for us what is of interest is a secondary argumentation on his part, which was that the sister had no rights of inheritance because « (her father) had sent her away from the paternal household with the dowry to which she was entitled. »[75]

While the term ἐξώπροικος is not used here, it is, I think, what Chomatianos had in mind, as may be seen from Case VI.

Case VI. This does not turn on the relationship between dowry and inheritance, but does, almost incidentally, give an interesting piece of information. A man named Vasileios had two daughters and, it would seem, no sons. The eldest daughter was married off, ἐκπροικισθεῖσα παρὰ τοῦ πατρὸς αὐτῆς, while the second was also married off and was constituted her father's heiress « κληρονόμος τῶν ἐκείνου ἀποκαταστᾶσα. »[76] I suggest that the participle ἐκπροικισθεῖσα has a meaning identical to the adjective ἐξώπροικος. I further suggest that Cases V and VI provide important clues as to the relationship between dowry and inheritance.

In both cases, the distinction is drawn between, on the one hand, those children who have been married off and left the parental household, along with their dowries, thus forming neo-local or virilocal households; and on the other hand, the child or children who are constituted heirs of their parents. The strong presumption is that these children co-reside with their parents, and inherit the residue of their property, i.e., what is left after the other children have received their dowries. In Case VI, the property dispositions are perfectly

75. Chomatianos, no. 63.
76. Chomatianos, no. 56.

clear. The man had no sons; one of his daughter left the household; the other became his heir, her husband would have been a *sogambros*, and the couple would have resided with the girl's parents until the parents died.

This would seem to be the functional distinction: between offspring who leave the household with their dowries, and offspring that stay and receive the residual parental property.

Case VII. This case introduces a variation on the same type of property arrangement. Theodore Glykys, from the theme of Vagenitia, sought a decision from Chomatianos, regarding a property claim in which his wife had an interest. The part of the case which is of interest to us here is as follows. The parents of his father-in-law (Nikolaos Kalognomos) had married off all their daughters with dowries and let them go off and live in their husbands' households (εἰς ἀνδρῶν ἀπελθεῖν ἀφῆκεν). One of their sons was also married off, ἐξοδίῳ γάμῳ. The last two sons were minors at the time of their father's death. They went off for many years, then returned and took over the parental house with, it is clear, some land. A dispute arose between the descendants of these siblings, since the grandson of one of the sisters who had been married off with a dowry now laid claim on part of the property of her brother Kalognomos, invoking her right of hereditary succession from her father. Glykys presented written testimony, confirmed by two bishops, that « only two brothers, Kalognomos and Manuel, were constituted heirs (κληρονόμοι) of the immovable goods in question, because the parents had provided in different ways for the other brothers and sisters. » Chomatianos agreed with the plaintiff that Kalognomos' sister had no claim on this property, « ... εἰς γάμον ἐκδοθείσῃ [sic] ἐξώπροικον. »[77] But his legal argumentation was based on the rights governing long-term *bona fide* possession, and the limitations on challenging a testament.

We have, in this case, the mention of a son who had been married ἐξοδίῳ γάμῳ. I understand this to mean that he had married and left the household, to be contrasted with offspring who were unmarried or who had married but had not left the household. The two younger sons, although they had left the household physically, had not left it formally; they were expected to return, and did so. The fact that they had been designated as sole heirs by their parents is a strong indication of a distinction being drawn between offspring, male and female, who marry and leave the parental household, and, on the other hand, the offspring who remain on the parental household, and who inherit all of the remaining property (unless, I think, there is testamentary disposition to the contrary).

Case VIII. It is a response by Chomatianos to the following question. A man had three daughters, one of whom he married off with a dowry, during his lifetime. His other two daughters were married after the father's death, receiving the rest

77. CHOMATIANOS, no. 37. For other details of this case, see *supra*, p. 140-141.

of his property in inheritance (εἰς κλῆρον). When their mother died intestate, the first daughter demanded an equal share of the maternal property as her legal right in an intestate succession. Her younger sisters thought that, since she had received an inordinately large part of the father's estate, it was not just that she would also receive a part of the mother's estate. They did offer her the possibility of bringing in, or collating, her dowry with the rest of their maternal and paternal property, so that they could then proceed to an equal division of the whole. The elder sister, of course, refused, and Chomatianos agreed that she had full rights on one third of the mother's estate. As for the paternal property, he upheld the father's right to unequal treatment of the children, as long as the legal provisions regarding the *falkidios* (the legal minimum which parents had to leave to their children) were observed.

The term ἐξώπροικος is not used here. For our purposes, four points are of interest in the document. First, there is, again, a distinction drawn between dowry (received by the eldest daughter) and inheritance (received by the two younger daughters). Secondly, the dowried daughter was certainly not excluded from inheriting from the *maternal* estate. Thirdly, there is a clear tension between the dowry dispositions of the father and the expectations of the least favored daughters for equality in the shares of the parental estate. And fourthly, Chomatianos did not consider that the eldest daughter was obliged to agree to the collation of her dowry for the reasons advanced by her sisters.

Conclusions

The following conclusions account for all of the evidence known to me.

As far as terminology is concerned, the term ἐξώπροικος must be connected with the verbs ἐκπροικίζω (Case VI) and ἐξωπροικίζω, attested in the 12th century. While these verbs may simply have a general meaning, equivalent to « to marry off with a dowry » or to « give into marriage » (ἐγγαμίζω),[78] there is a strong lexicographical connection between the dowry and the departure of the woman (and her dowry property) from the parental household. In the Lexicon of pseudo-Zonaras, the word προίξ is glossed as « she who is delivered up to the husband's household », « she who goes forward to the husband's household. »[79] This meaning is not at all obvious, and incorporates, I think, contemporary views and contemporary practice. Thus, there is both a general and a specific meaning of the verbs. Similarly, the adjective ἐξώπροικος means not simply the woman who is given to marriage with a dowry, but the woman who takes her dowry outside the parental household; a girl who marries a *sogambros* would

78. For ἐξωπροικίζω, see PTOCHOPRODROMOS, ed. H. Eideneier, *Ptochoprodromos*, Köln 1991, Poem I, l. 64-65: Τὰ γονικά σου πράγματα καὶ ἡ οἰκοσκευή σου· ἀρκοῦν τὰς θυγατέρας σου νὰ τὰς ἐξωπροικίσῃς. In that poem there is a distinction between dowry and paternal inheritance (κλῆρον): l. 62-63. For ἐξωπροικίζω = ἐγγαμίζω, see Eustathios of Thessaloniki, in KOUKOULES, *op. cit.* (n. 25), I, p. 480-481.

79. ZONARAS, *Lexicon*, *s.v.* προίξ: ἡ προδιδομένη εἰς τὸν τοῦ ἀνδρὸς οἶκον... ἡ προϊκνουμένη εἰς τὸν τοῦ ἀνδρὸς οἶκον.

not, I suppose, be described as ἐξώπροικος, nor is she so described in any of the documentation known to me.

As far as substance is concerned, what we see in the sources is the effort of the Byzantines to cope with competing legal and customary requirements. One strong presumption was that of partible equal inheritance, required in the case of intestate succession. The other was the legal requirement to give dowries and marriage portions to the male and female children at the time of marriage.[80] In reality, it was not easy to satisfy both of these requirements, because the timing and chronology of marriages and deaths interfered. If parents died leaving a testament, the situation would be resolved, for they could exercise their legal right to bequeath to their children unequal parts of their property. Children that had received a dowry were perfectly capable of also receiving a part of the parental property if the parents so stipulated by testamentary disposition (our Case II). Thus, children that had received a dowry were not necessarily excluded from inheritance, always assuming that the parents left a testament, in which they exercised their discretionary rights, and which also, in principle, would not necessitate a reassignment of the property already given as dowry.

The real problem existed in cases of intestate succession, which must surely have been in the majority. Here, the application of both legal principles could give rise to very uncomfortable, litigious and economically disruptive situations. If a woman (or, indeed, a man) had received a dowry years before the parents' death, and an equal division of parental property nevertheless were to be made, with the dowries called in to be counted as part of the parental property, the possible complications would be intolerable. What was one to do, for example, with land given as dowry but which had since been meliorated? In a case where the dowries had been unequal, would any dowry goods have to change hands? What about the rights of the children on their parents' dowries, as originally constituted? The list of possible problems may easily be extended.

There was at least one other consideration, not legal but social. The parents had to keep part of their property for their own sustenance; and they also had need of help in the cultivation of their land and generally in living out their old age. Thus the custom arose whereby there was a distinction between the children who married and left the household and the one or two children, male or female, who stayed on the parental household. Those who left, with their dowries, were the ἐξώπροικοι. Those who stayed were the heirs: in the case of girls, they were probably given in a patri-uxorilocal marriage. They inherited the residue of the parental estate, after the other children had received their dowries. By custom, though not by law, the out-marrying children had no claim on the residue of the estate (our Cases I, IV, V, VI, VII). This custom reduced friction, and allowed arrangements made at the time of the children's marriage to stand. Married children could, but customarily did not claim their right of equal inheritance. The wisdom of the custom was recognised (implicitly) by

80. Our Case VIII exemplifies this tension.

Chomatianos in his decisions; but he, being a man profoundly acquainted with the law, based no legal argumentation on this custom.

The one occasion in which the rights of children to equal inheritance from parents dying intestate were clearly recognised by a court occurs in our Case II. I have argued above that the court gave a polite acknowledgment of the law, with no expectation that the dowry would, in fact, be brought into the inheritance so that an equal division of the original parental property could be made.

In sum, the point is not that women who married with a dowry were by law or custom excluded from inheritance, even when there was no testament; but that by custom they (and men in an equivalent situation – see our Case VII) were thought to have no right on the inheritance. All of this is necessary in a society where marriage strategies played an important role. And this interpretation also helps to understand a piece of legislation which has usually been considered as problematic.

This is the Novel of an Emperor of Trebizond, John II or John IV Grand Comnenus.[81] The Emperor refers to a « law », which had been dormant for a long time but had recently been re-introduced by some people, « for their own profit. » The « law » permitted men and women, who had received a dowry or, in the case of men, some property from their parents, to collate it with the inheritance at the time of the parents' death, and presumably divide among themselves the entire property. Quite rightly the Emperor says that this had created major upheavals, and the « destruction of numerous and great houses » ; he had been requested to abrogate it. He then decrees the following. In the case where the parents made testamentary disposition, this will remain valid, for both male and female children, even when they had received a dowry; there is, thus, no exclusion of dowried daughters, if there is a testament. In case of intestate succession, the girls who received a dowry, or were promised one, would have no rights on the inheritance. In the first instance, the property of a father dying intestate would be inherited by his sons and daughters who were still under his *potestas* – I understand by this, children who were minor, or unmarried, and who lived in his household. Daughters were absolutely forbidden to collate their dowries and seek equal inheritance. Sons who were not under paternal *potestas* were not so forbidden. A « θυγάτηρ ἐξώπροικος » would thus be excluded from inheriting from a father dying intestate, *unless* there were no other sons or daughters under paternal *potestas*.

There is nothing curious about this law, nor are the different dispositions regarding sons and daughters the result of misogyny. Indeed, the law makes perfect sense if its object is to safeguard marriage arrangements and to minimise social disruption. The validity of testamentary arrangements is affirmed – because these would not, except in thoroughly abnormal circumstances, disrupt previous arrangements. The distinction drawn in the

81. Zepos, *op. cit.* (n. 62), p. 364-365.

imperial decree between ἐξώπροικοι daughters and heirs residing in the household is the same distinction that obtained by custom in Byzantine lands. The only apparent peculiarity is the fact that sons who were emancipated (I understand: married and living off the household) were permitted to collate their share of parental property into the whole, while daughters were not. But this, too, might make sense since the daughter's dowry left the control of the natal family, while at least part of the property the son received upon marriage (the *hypobolon*) was a promise and/or guarantee to his wife, and did not change hands as long as the marriage lasted.

Normally, then, the Byzantine dowry was not an advance on inheritance but the girl's major share of the parental property, unless there was different testamentary disposition. On Byzantine lands, the same seems to have obtained with sons who married and left the household. This was no small factor in preserving the stability of marriage arrangements, painstakingly concluded.

III

THE EVOLUTION OF THE STATUS OF WOMEN IN MARRIAGE AND FAMILY LAW

The organisers of this conference have presented me with a formidable task. The evolution of the status of women in marriage and family law over a period of perhaps one thousand years - the Byzantine period - is an immense topic, certainly incapable of being treated fully in a short time[1]. In the spirit of the Congress, it is primarily the influence of canon law on this process which is at issue. That, too, is a very large topic. The very fact of the Christianisation of marriage, a process that was greatly advanced by the tenth century, when the only recognised marriage became the one performed and blessed by the Church, created new parameters within which relations between the genders and the generations functioned[2]. Nor was the process ended in the tenth century, since the church continued to legislate on aspects of marriage and betrothal, especially but not only on the question of impediments created by blood relationship or by affinity, and the state followed suit. In order to make the topic more manageable, I shall focus on some aspects relating to the most important points in marriage and sexual activity: the establishment of the marriage bond and its effect on the status of women, divorce, especially for cause of adultery, and sexual relations outside of marriage.

There are several ways in which canon law exerted its influence on formal relations, on institutions and on society. The first is through the canons themselves. The Byzantine canonical system, certainly with regard to issues connected with the family, was somewhat fluid. Most of the important canonical statements are incorporated in the legislation of the fourth-century Fathers and that of the oecumenical councils, through the Council in Trullo. The rest are to be found in new legislation, which proceeded through the centuries. Given the relationship between civil and canon law in Byzantium, however[3], canonical statements did not really have the force of law until and unless they were incorporated in imperial legislation, either formally, or more informally, i.e., with a statement that a particular piece of legislation was ordered or accepted by the Emperor[4]. Cases in point abound: An obvi-

[1] For a discussion of some of the topics, see J. BEAUCAMP, La situation juridique de la femme à Byzance, in: Cahiers de Civilisation Médiévale 20 (1977) 145-76.

[2] See, for an overview, H. HUNGER, Christliches und Nichtchristliches im byzantinischen Eherecht, in: ÖAKR 18 (1967) 305-25.

[3] See, on this, S. TROIANOS, „Θεσπίζομεν τοίνυν, τάξιν νόμων ἐπέχειν τοὺς ἁγίους ἐκκλησιαστικοὺς κανόνας ... ", in: Δώρημα στόν Ι. Καραγιαννόπουλο, Thessaloniki 1985, 1193-1200. He speaks of two legal systems but a single authority. After 545, civil and canon law followed the same rules of applicability and interpretation, which increased the power of the Emperor.

[4] The decree of the Patriarch Sisinnios on prohited degrees of relationship is a case in point.

ous one is the prohibition of fourth marriages. Already in the fourth century, St. Basil of Caesarea had voiced opposition to any marriage after the first, and called the fourth marriage „fornication"[5], but it was not until the Tome of Union (920) that this opposition became general law. The same is true with the virtual equation of betrothal to marriage, legislated by the Emperor Leo VI, who made specific reference to canon 98 of the Council in Trullo[6]. A third example concerns the extension of marriage impediments to lateral relatives and affines, where the law code of the Isaurians, the Ecloga, adopted almost all the prohibitions of the Council in Trullo[7]. This is direct influence of canon law on the institution of marriage and on family life.

A second sort of influence is indirect. It is influence on mores, ideology and modes of thought and action which eventually become legislation or common practice. This influence may be exercised through canon law, or through Christian tenets and statements which are voiced by ecclesiastics and become normative at some point. An example may be seen in the mandatory involvement of the church into what had been a civil contract, i.e., marriage and even betrothal. Already in the Ecloga, a church ceremony is sufficient (though not necessary) substitute for a marriage with written contracts. By the mid-ninth century, it was presented as a *sine qua non* of marriage by Byzantine missionaries active in Bulgaria[8]. Leo VI made marriage with benediction into the law of the land, but it probably had been by far the commonest sort of marriage before its formalisation through imperial legislation.

A third category has to do with statements of the canonists and theologians which did not have direct effect on legislation but influenced the mind-set and the practice to some extent at least, although they themselves may already reflect a certain social preference. Such is St. Basil's statement concerning inheritance. He thought that children should inherit equally, just as they were equally given life by their parents[9]. Civil law always allowed the possibility of differential treatment of children once the legal minimum had been met. But Leo VI issued a Novel on some aspects of unequal inheritance, making it more difficult, and delivering a general statement on the justice of partible inheritance. He used a variant of the words of St. Basil, stressing that as the parents equally gave birth to their children

[5] Canons 4, 12: G. RALLES, M. POTLES, Syntagma ton theion kai hieron kanonon 4, Athens 1854.

[6] P. NOAILLES, A. DAIN, Les Novelles de Léon VI le Sage, Paris 1944, no. 74.

[7] Ecloga: Das Gesetzbuch Leons III. und Konstantinos V. (ed. L. BURGMANN, Frankfurt 1983) 2,2, and canon 54 of the Council in Trullo (RALLES-POTLES, 2, 432-3).

[8] A.E. LAIOU, Consensus facit nuptias-et non, in: Rechtshistorisches Journal 4 (1985) 189-201.

[9] Homilia VIII in Hexaemeron, J.-P. MIGNE, Patrologia Graeca, 29, 177-80, and cf. Novel 19 of Leo VI. A later canonical text, the Pedalion, glossing this statement, threatens with „epitimia" those parents, especially on the islands, who practiced primogeniture giving all their inheritance to the first son or the first daughter: Cf. K.E. ZACHARIAE VON LINGENTHAL, Geschischte des Griechisch-Römischen Rechts, 3rd edition, Berlin 1892, 204, note 660.

so they should give them property. Equal partible inheritance exercised a powerful influence on the system of succession of the Byzantines. It also made a great difference to women, for a preferential system of inheritance, in a society which also practices divergent devolution of property (bilateral inheritance) benefits men much more than women. The divergent devolution of property, coupled with at least a strong inclination toward equal inheritance, made women carriers of property, and thus allowed them some power within the home, as well as permitting them the possibility, at least, of an economic role connected with the disposition and management of their property. Of course, in cases such as this, it is very difficult to disentangle the specific role of statements like that of St. Basil from the many other factors which result in the formation of such practices and institutions-for example, the desire of parents to ensure that both male and female children retain or improve their condition in life, and thus reproduce the position of the family or the lineage[10]. A more visible connection may exist between patristic thinking on divorce and legal practice, as will be discussed later.

The functioning of ecclesiastical courts is another way in which canon law influenced life in general, and the life of women in particular. This was especially so after the Emperor Alexios I gave ecclesiastical courts the right to judge cases regarding matrimony[11].

A final category is more subtle. It is that of subtexts, that is, canonical statements or canonical exegesis that are very strongly influenced by societal attitudes toward women, and in turn place a powerful stamp of approval upon them.

Let us turn to the substance of our topic. I would argue that one of the most interesting aspects of the influence of canon law and canonical thinking on legislation is connected with a certain sense of equality, between genders as between social classes.

This may be seen, for one thing, in the legislation concerning marriage. The Ecloga, the law-code of the Isaurians, published in 741, was imbued with religious ideas, as is obvious both in the Prooimion and in the text itself. As far as marriage law is concerned, it incorporated a good deal of canonical vocabulary and legislation. The Ecloga stressed the validity of a marriage performed without written contracts, that is to say, without dowry contracts, specifying that this affects persons who are of poor or humble condition. In such cases, marriage may be performed with the consent of the contracting parties and their parents, and validated either by church benediction or by public announcement (announcement to their „friends")[12]. The non-requirement of dotal contracts for people of humble condition was already established by Novel 117 of Justinian I (542), after the Emperor

---

[10] See A. LAIOU, Marriage Prohibitions, Marriage Strategies and the Dowry in Thirteenth-century Byzantium, in: J. BEAUCAMP, G. DAGRON (edd.), La transmission du patrimoine, Paris 1998, 129-60, esp. p. 130.

[11] Novel 27.4 in: J. and P. ZEPOS, Jus Graecoromanum I, Athens 1931.

[12] Ecloga 2.6. See also CJ ,5,17, 11 (533), N. 22, 18 (535), N. 117.5

had vascillated considerably on the issue of „unwritten marriage"; here, too, there may have been ecclesiastical influence[13]. But the Ecloga makes the matter clear[14]. The importance of the consent of the contracting parties, a concept of Roman law, is brought to the fore, even though in the Byzantine Empire the consent of the parents was always necessary (except for men after the age of 25)[15]. The consent of the contracting parties was never in itself sufficient to establish a valid marriage, as it eventually became in western Europe, where the *verba de praesenti* (exchange of present consent) created a valid mariage[16]. In the Ecloga, consent needs to be validated by the consent of the parents and public notification. Interestingly, the social status of those who may contract unwritten marriages is not precisely specified, as it would be in the Macedonian law codes which followed Justinianic legislation. The eventual development of this was the emergence of benediction as a necessary condition for a valid marriage, made into law by Leo VI. As far as the Ecloga goes, there is the attenuation of social distinction as a factor in a valid marriage, with probably differentially beneficial effects on women. Slaves are still excluded from this equalisation, until the late 11th century. Social distinction as an important factor in contracting a marriage reappears in the 12th century.

Also beneficial was the recognition of what in English law would be called a common law marriage. The Ecloga describes it from the point of view of the woman: „Whoever has brought into his house a free woman, and entrusted her with running his household and has had carnal relations with her, is held to have contracted an unwritten marriage with her". If he puts her aside for any reason other than the recognised causes of divorce, and if she has had no chidren, he gives her one fourth of his property, that is, exactly what is given to a propertyless („*aporos*") woman as *casus liberorum non existentium,* when her husband dies intestate. This harks back to Justinian's legislation (Novel 74.5, 538), which mentions the complaints of women who, after men take them home, swearing on the Gospels or in church to treat them as wives, live with them for many years, perhaps have children, and then are thrown out; such women, he says, are to be considered legitimate, and so are the children. The passage on unwritten marriages in the Ecloga is a combination of Codex 5, 17, 11, an Novel 74.5. But in the Ecloga, the position of the woman who cohabits with a man for a long time is entirely equated to that of wife. Some scholars have understood this clause to be connected with concubi-

---

[13] N. 117. 4-6 (by affection alone). Cf. J. A. BRUNDAGE, Law, Sex, and Christian Society in Medieval Europe, Chicago-London, 1987, 114.

[14] Possible influence from the fourth-century Fathers, who were against the importance played on contracts and dowries in his period, and asks for a return to earlier, simpler customs: MIGNE, Patrologia Graeca, 54, 441 and 489, quoted by G.S. MARIDAKES, To astikon dikaion en tais Nearais ton Vyzantinon Autokratoron, Athens 1922, 41.

[15] On women losing that right, see BEAUCAMP, op.cit., 171-2.

[16] BRUNDAGE, op.cit., 334, 588.

nage, whereas others have objected[17]. While from the strictly juridical viewpoint the objection is valid, it seems to me that from the point of view of real life and society, we are seeing the transformation of concubinage into Christian marriage. In effect, concubinage is tacitly abolished by being considered as marriage without the necessity of any further action on the part of the man; this obviously raises the status and increases the property rights of the woman[18]. The arrangement follows the tendency in Justinianic law which, however, had simply allowed the legitimisation of the children born in concubinage after a subsequent marriage.

Neither in this passage of the Ecloga, nor in Justinian's legislation is there specific reference to canon law. But one may suppose the influence of canons, such as that of Gregory of Nyssa and St Basil (4, 59), which state that there is only one legal cohabitation (meaning marriage) and everything else is illegal, and seem to include concubinage under porneia (*stuprum*), while canon 17 of the Apostles likens the effect of concubinage on members of the clergy to the effects of bigamy. These are probably the „divine precepts, proper to Christians", to which Leo VI referred in his Novel (91) that abolished concubinage and the old law that governed it[19]. So the provision in the Ecloga is within the spirit of the purpose of the Church to bring all sexual relations under the umbrella of marriage. It also furthers social equalisation insofar as women are concerned. In Roman society, concubinage was contracted primarily with women of low status. The Ecloga removes the detrimental effects of class from the women involved. Earlier, Justinian had spoken of „philanthropy toward women" in a Novel regarding a free woman who lives with a man and subsequently marries him[20].

As far as I know, this legislation, which I consider progressive, is unique to the Ecloga. It was not repeated in the legislation of the Macedonians[21], and it did not overnight turn concubinage into valid marriage. The evolution is as follows. Concubinage was abolished by Novel 91 of Leo VI, specifically in order to bring civil law in concordance with ecclesiastical law. In some ways, this measure may be considered the opposite of the legislation in the Ecloga, unless we imagine that its effect was indeed to extirpate concubinage and turn all long-term unions into marriage, not automatically as in the Ecloga, but because the other choice was

[17] MARIDAKES, op.cit., 43, 77, contra J. ZHISHMAN, Das Eherecht der orientalischen Kirche, Vienna, 1863, and ZACHARIAE VON LINGENTHAL. The Ecloga, 6, 7 mentions concubines („pallake").

[18] CJ. 5, 27, 8, N. 18, 11, N. 19, N. 89, 3. Cf. A.E. LAIOU, Contributionà l'étude de l'institution familiale en Épire au XIIIème siècle, in EADEM, Gender, Society and Economic Life in Byzantium, Variorum Reprints, Hampshire, 1992, Study V, 284.The arrangement in the Ecloga is more beneficial than the Justinianic legislation, which does also recognise property rights to a concubine and her children, in case there are no legal descendants: MARIDAKES, op. cit., 76, with reference to CJ. 5, 27, 8.

[19] The law is „De concubinatu", CJ. 6,57,5, D. 25,7, N. 18,11.

[20] N. 18.11 (534).

[21] Cf. Procheiros Nomos 4,14 and 4,26, in: ZEPOS, Jus, 2, Athens 1931; Eisagoge 16,1, 16,11, 16,27 and scholia (in: ZEPOS, ibid).

removed. Indeed, this is the attitude that may be perceived in a decision of the thirteenth-century archbishop and jurist Demetrios Chomatianos. There was a case involving a long-term cohabitation between a man and a woman. The woman wished for the relationship to be legalised through marriage, „adducing as arguments the length of cohabitation, a little over five years, and the fact that two years earlier she had given birth to his child. For this reason, she desired to live with him in perpetuity, and to receive the customary benediction". Chomatianos tried to persuade the man to accede to the woman's request. He refused, although, by arrangement, he gave her an ox and part of the year's crop[22]. The custom of concubinage continued, as we see in Epiros in the thirteenthth century. In the case of monogamous unions, and in the eyes of some of the people involved, it appears to have been equivalent to marriage *solo consensu*, which is why Demetrios Chomatianos used in his decisions Novels 89 of Leo VI and 24 of Alexios I, which stated that the only legally accepted marriage was that performed with benediction, and he distinguished it from the marriage *solo consensu*.

The ecclesiastical court of Chomatianos provides the greatest part of the information we have regarding concubinage as it existed in practice. The learned archbishop tried to introduce some order in the situation that had resulted from the existence of this institution despite its formal abolition, but, interestingly, he did not refer to Novel 91 of Leo VI. He tended to recognise some rights to children born in concubinage, although his main concern was with the rights of the children of the first marriage, concubinage often being a substitute for second and third marriages. The rights of women, as established by the Ecloga, appear to be greatly attenuated[23].

Thus, in this matter, the canonical concerns and legislation followed two different directions. Before benediction became mandatory for a valid marriage, a common-law marriage, beneficial to women, was possible; its existence was even, I think, facilitated by the insistence of the church that marriage was the only legal form of cohabitation. But once the position of the church on valid marriage had been made into law, any marriage not blessed by the church was considered illegitimate, and the old disadvantages of concubinage returned, although some people voiced divergent opinions[24]. The status of lower-class women was improved by the Ecloga, but greatly reduced by the abolition of concubinage through the influence of the church. Only by applying the pre-Ecloga civil law could a „concubine" receive some property, and that depended on the disposition of the judge.

In the matter of divorce, also, the influence of eclesiastical law was multiple and varied. The indissolubility of marriage stems from Mat.19,9, which also pro-

---

[22] Chomatianos, in J.-B. PITRA, Analecta sacra et classica spicilegio Solesmensi parata, 6, Paris-Rome 1891, no. 135; Cf. LAIOU, Contribution 284-300.

[23] LAIOU, Contribution, 284 ff.

[24] Cf. the divergent opinions on the disposition of propery by testament to children born of concubinage, in Chomatianos, no. 21; cf. LAIOU, Contribution, 290-91.

vides the only acceptable cause for divorce: „Whosoever shall put away his wife, *except it be for fornication*, and shall marry another, committeth adultery; and who so marrieth her which is put away doth commit adultery". The only cause for divorce is the adultery of the *woman*. This differential treatment of adultery with regard to the dissolution of marriage is also present in Roman law, which, in the case of unilateral divorce, recognises the adultery of the woman as valid cause, but is much more lenient toward the sexual misdeeds of a married man[25]. We recall, of course, that in the Roman Empire, and until the time of Justinian, it was perfectly possible to have a divorce communi consensu. Adultery as grounds for divorce is only important in the case of a non-consensual, unilateral dissolution of the marriage. It is also to be remembered that Justinian, in abolishing the consensual divorce, separated the valid grounds for divorce into two categories: the grounds on which a woman may divorce her husband and those on which a husband may divorce his wife[26]. Adultery is *ipso facto* grounds for divorce only when committed by a woman; the equivalent for a man is the prolonged, frequent and blatant promiscuity of the man who introduces other women into his house or lives with another woman in another house, in the same city, and thus brings dishonor („*hybris*") to his wife's position and status. The woman's adultery, however, is pollution according to the church fathers[27]; it sullies the marriage bed, and, according to St Basil, the man who stays with an adulteress is „senseless and impious". In the Ecloga, a divorce is possible on very few grounds: only one, adultery, is specific to the woman, and only one, impotence for three years, is specific to the man (2.9.2-3); the pertinent legislation makes clear reference to the New Testament.

The early canonical pronouncements, and subsequent ones, such as canon 87 of the Council in Trullo, were somewhat embarassed and ambivalent on the different treatment of male and female adultery, as were the 12th-century canonists. St. Basil says, disapprovingly, but accepting the fact, that the spirit of divine law condemns equally the man and the woman who have sexual relations outside mariage. But „custom" orders that the woman be punished as adulteress and divorced, while the man may not be divorced from his wife on the grounds of adultery (canon 9). He is guilty not of adultery but of fornication (canon 21), and his wife must stay with him. „The reason", says St. Basil, „is not easy to understand; but this is the prevailing custom". The Synod in Trullo labels „adulterer" the man who leaves his wife and takes another, which created exegetical problems to the twelfth- century canonists, called upon to reconcile the canons of St. Basil and Trullo. They found

---

[25] S. TREGGIARI, Roman Marriage, New York-Oxford 1993, 462-3.

[26] N. 117, 8-9. Note that the husband may take back the adulteress within two years (cf. Balsamon's commentary to canon 87 of the Council in Trullo, in: RALLES-POTLES, 2, Athens, 1852, 505 ff), an arrangement which may also be due to the influence of the Church that wanted to preseve marriage. Such a thing was not possible in Roman law: cf. A. ROUSSELLE, Porneia; on Desire and the Body in Antiquity, Oxford-New York 1988, 101, on similar pronouncements in the 2nd century in western Europe .

[27] St. Basil, canon 21.

the answer in the distinction between the man who commits fornication while in a married state, and the one who has abandoned his wife and taken another[28]. The uneasiness, however, persisted, for Ioannes Apokaukos, in the first part of the thirteenth century, voiced again the statement regarding the irrationality of the differential treatment. Perhaps the strictest and most detrimental canonical legislation pertaining to women is the one relative to the woman who is abandoned by her husband and marries another: she is deemed an adulteress, after Matthew 5, 32: „whosoever shall put away his wife, save for the cause of fornication, causeth her to commit adultery“[29]. She is an adulteress even though the fault is not her own; her husband, on the other hand, „is responsible“ for her sin, but his own sin is not clearly spelled out. From the viewpoint of the church, it would have been more rational to punish equally the adultery of man and woman. Indeed, the embarassment expressed by the canonists on the treatment of adultery stems, I think, from the fact that the church was faced with a sin which knows no gender in the abstract, but which was, indeed, differentiated by gender in a society where sexual pollution was gender-specific.

A study of the extant decisions of ecclesiastical courts of the thirteenth and fourteenth centuries reveals that some of this unease, as well as the difficulties of imposing intransigent legislation upon a living society, influenced the decisions of the courts in ways that reduced the severity of both civil and ecclesiastical legislation. For one thing, Balsamon interpreted canon 48 of St. Basil to mean that the husband who abandons his wife is responsible not, to be sure, of adultery, but of having divorced without cause which, according to Justinian's legislation, is punished with the loss of the property of the guilty party and the entry into a monastery. Thus the one-sidedness of the canon was attenuated, since the man was also punished. Similarly, Zonaras glossed canon 87 of the Council of Trullo, regarding the punishment of a woman who leaves her husband „without cause“ as meaning that if she leaves him *with* cause, i.e., because he beats her, or makes her suffer greatly, or for other such reasons, even if she marries another[30], she is not guilty. This, it should be said, goes against the usual canonical tradition, starting with St. John of Damascus and continuing through Balsamon's gloss on the same canon, which does not recognise the mistreatment of a wife as valid cause for divorce or for leaving her husband. Zonaras' interpretation shows a concern with the lack of recourse for a woman who is mistreated by her husband.

As for the practice of divorce, we have fairly extensive documentation, from the ecclesiastical courts of Chomatianos and Apokaukos in the thirteenth century, the Patiarchal court of Constantinople in the fourteenth century, and sporadic deci-

[28] Commentary of Zonaras and Balsamon to canon 87 of the Council in Trullo. In fact, the canons are perfectly reconcilable, and the problem of the canonists must be that they felt uneasy about the whole issue.

[29] Canon 48 of St Basil.

[30] This last clause is not found in all manuscripts.

sions of other courts or Patriarchs. The bulk of the information comes from the thirteenth and fourteenth centuries, and originates in areas widely different from each other, Epiros, Greece and western Macedonia on the one hand, and Constantinople on the other. The local customs visible in the sources were, of course, specific to various areas. But given that both Chomatianos and Apokaukos were learned men in the canonical tradition of Constantinople, there is a certain comparability as far as we are concerned.

The plight of the abandoned woman is addressed primarily by Apokaukos. According to the civil law, a woman whose husband has disappeared cannot remarry except on well-grounded presumption of his death, which, if there is no secure information, may be made after an absence of five years[31]. Canon law follows and reaffirms this legislation, St. Basil saying that the woman who marries another without proof of her husband's death commits adultery[32]. This is reaffirmed by Canon 93 of the synod in Trullo, the 12th-century canonists, and Patriarch Manuel II. However, when Apokaukos was faced with specific cases of men who had abandoned their wives and whose whereabouts were known, he granted the woman a divorce, even though he was perfectly aware of the fact that abandonment was not a recognised reason for divorce, and said so. In one case, the decision was made somewhat easier by the fact that the man's most recent absence had lasted for five years, which retains a memory of the lapse of time necessary under civil law for presumption of death. Here, however, there was no presumption of death; the man was thought to be alive. In part, the court was swayed by the fact that the woman was young and not unsightly, and chose to rescue her from the sin of adultery. Economic factors, too, played a role in this case as in the other case of abandonment judged in the same court. That this was probably not an idiosyncratic judgment, stemming out of the instabilities of the lower economic strata of a provincial population, is suggested by a decision of the Patriarchal Court of Constantinople, in the early fourteenth century, which again granted a divorce because of the abandonment of the wife[33]. We are, I suggest, witnessing something of an equalising of the odds in a marriage. Whereas a husband could divorce his wife for moral reasons (if she frequented the baths or banquets with men, if she stayed outside the house without his permission, if she committed adultery)[34], a wife could also divorce her husband basically for not fulfilling the normal expectations one had of a husband.

The ecclesiastical courts also parted company with the law on the matter of what should happen when a marriage irretrievably breaks down. Both civil and

---

[31] Bas. 28, 7, 3-4; N. 22, ch. 5,6,7.

[32] Canon 31.

[33] F. MIKLOSICH, J. MÜLLER, Acta et diplomata Graeca medii aevi, 1, Vienna 1860, 53 ff; N. MATSES, To oikogeneiakon dikaion kata ten nomologian tou Patriarcheiou Konstantinoupoleos ton eton 1315-1401, Athens 1962, 165-6.

[34] Justinian, N. 117.

ecclesiastical law adopt an attitude of „grin and bear it" in this matter which, significantly, they see mostly as affecting women: that is, the question is mostly what a *woman* should do in the case of a marriage that has gone wrong, not what a man should do. In the old days, before Christianity made itself felt, there was the divorce *communi consensu.* Under the influence of church and canons, that had been abrogated. In its place, we find the emergence, in ecclesiastical courts, of a divorce „for implacable hatred". It is pleaded that one of the partners has developed implacable hatred for the other, and therefore a divorce is necessary, to avoid a greater evil, murder, suicide or adultery. It is not necessarily argued that the fault lies with one or the other of the partners; this kind of divorce has old antecedents, and the hatred was sometimes ascribed to demonic interference[35]. The interesting thing is that, in most cases, independently of who brings the case to court, the partner who pleads implacable hatred is the woman[36]. This was partly due to the way in which marriages were arranged, since girls were betrothed at a very young age, and sometimes, when they reached puberty, either they or their parents had changed their minds. It may also have been due to an underlying idea that women were more prone than men to demonic influence. It was, finally, at least in some cases, used as an alternative to divorce for cause of adultery on the part of the woman, perhaps because the court was unwilling to issue such a divorce, with its disrupting effects on the woman, her family, and her property[37].

The civil courts may not have had the flexibility of ecclesiastical courts in this matter. The dossier of the eleventh-century judge Eustathios Romaios does not contain divorces granted for implacable hatred. It does contain cases of consensual divorce, described in a way which suggests that, despite the law, such divorces were not rare. However, once they were challenged in court by one of the parties, or their relatives, the judge had little discretion: he was forced to declare the divorce invalid although, interestingly enough, he preserved the property dispositions made at the time of the divorce agreement[38].

Let us return to adultery, wherein , as we know, lay the most important distinguishing factor between men and women as far as divorce is concerned, the factor that made divorce most expensive for women. Strikingly, in the civil court of Eustathios Romaios divorce for adultery is mentioned in connection with women only incidentally, and in an interesting fashion: he explains why the dowry of a woman divorced for adultery does not go to her husband if she enters a monastery, despite the legislation of Leo VI, while it does if the woman repeatedly

---

[35] See LAIOU, Contribution, 308 ff, for fuller discussion and interpretation of the sources.

[36] Thus in Chomatianos and Apokaukos. Not so in MIKLOSICH and MÜLLER, 1, 28 ff: both partners developed hatred.

[37] Chomatianos in PITRA, op.cit., col. 556, S. PETRIDES, Jean Apokaukos, lettres et autres documents inédits, in: Izvestija Russkago Arckheologicheskago Instituta v Konstantinopolje 14 (1889), no 16, and MIKLOSICH-MÜLLER, 1, 28 ff.

[38] Eustathios Romaios, Peira, in ZEPOS, Jus, 4, 25.41, 25.44, 25.62, 25.37, 68.62.

feasts or bathes together with other men[39]. The reason for this apparent paradox is explained as a protection for women against the machinations of the husband who might even introduce a male friend into the house to support a false accusation of adultery. More interesting than this entertaining decision is the fact that the few real cases of adultery mentioned are those of men. In one case, a husband is divorced by his wife, with his agreement, for having affairs with other women; the legal justification of such a divorce is not given, nor is the word „adultery" uttered. Interestingly, it was the woman's sister who eventually brought a charge of adultery against the divorced woman, presumably on the grounds, well known to canon law but not to civil law, that a divorce granted for reasons other than the woman's adultery is invalid, and the woman, if she remarries, is an adulteress[40]. It would not be the first time that individuals tried to use the stricter ecclesiastical laws to get their way; the phenomenon was common in the eleventh century, especially with incest legislation. Possibly as an additional rumination on the topic, the next item in the Peira is a general statement on the man who has slept with other women, and has not contested a divorce „because he was the cause of it"[41]. It is necessary to note this treatment of male adultery in a civil court before we turn to the information gleaned from ecclesiastical courts.

Here we can summarise the situation in the thirteenth century as follows. Divorce for adultery *is* mentioned, but it does not necessarily entail all the punishments the law requires. On the contrary, Chomatianos was prone to not punish the adulterous woman. In one case, he even found that the woman was not, properly speaking, guilty of adultery, since her husband had been impotent for three years. It is a nice point, buttressed by quotations from St. Paul: „To avoid fornication let every man have his own wife, and let evey woman have her own husband"; „Defraud ye not one the other, except it be with consent..."[42]. But it can hardly be suspected that St Paul meant that in the contrary case adultery was justified. What we have here is an approach toward adultery that is more lenient to women than civil or ecclesiastical law allowed. It is a leniency rare in canonical texts, although occasionally we find it there also: in canon 34, St. Basil counsels against making public the sin of the repentant adulteress, since this might cause her death. The twelfth-century canonical glosses on this suggest that the husband, enraged, might kill her. Balsamon further states that men who are confessed adulterers need not be treated so mercifully because they do not run the same dangers, thus providing a graphic detail of the different risks run by men and women in the matter of adultery. It may be that the ecclesiastical courts were eager to minimize such problems.

Having imposed the quasi-indissolubility of marriage through the abolition of the divorce *communi consensu* and the diminution of grounds for divorce, the

---

[39] Peira 25.23 and cf. Bas. 28,7,1, and Novel 32 of Leo VI.

[40] Peira 25.41.

[41] Peira 25.42

[42] 1 Cor. 7.2; 7.5

church maintained, in its legislation, a strict position on this issue. However, both in the exegetical literature and, much more clearly and to the point, in the decisions of ecclesiastical courts, churchmen took a much more lenient position, one which brought the reasons for which a woman may divorce her husband closer to equality with those for which a man may divorce his wife. They also substituted the divorce „for implacable hatred" to both the divorce *communi consensu* and the divorce occasioned by the woman's adultery. This attenuated the severity of the civil law, which itself had been due to the influence of the church. Nor is there anything surprising in this. The church wished to become the arbiter of marriage (as did the state, of course), and to increase its control over the institution. Once its control was in place, it could offer itself the luxury of further control through the exercise of leniency, *„oikonomia"*.

It may be noted, almost parenthetically, and in order to avoid giving the impression that leniency was always practiced in ecclesiastical courts, that it was perfectly possible for an ecclesiastical court to take a decision that was very strict, even outside the limits of legality, and detrimental to women. Such was a case judged by the Synodal court of Constantinople in 1023, which dissolved the marriage of a woman on the grounds of incest, even though the degrees of relationship did not prohibit the marriage according to existing law, and even ordered the woman to enter a monastery and become a nun. On the contrary, the civil court of Eustathios Romaios, judging the same case, presumably on appeal, somewhat later (between 1025 and 1030) pronounced the marriage legitimate[43]. This serves to remind us that much depended on political circumstances and interests, as well as on the disposition of the particular judges, and that ecclesiastical courts did not necessarily prove more flexible toward women, especially at times when law on specific issues was still evolving.

The influence of the Church, of canonical statements and of canon law on the life, and even the status, of women is also visible in the legislation concerning sexual crimes, outside of adultery - I am speaking of fornication (*„porneia"*, *„fthora"*, *stuprum*) and abduction. The important legislation here is the Ecloga where, as I have already indicated, the influence of ecclesiastical law was heavy. For one thing, there were changes in the way in which categories were established and punishment was meted out. In Roman law, the categorisation of such crimes more or less followed the priciples that social class was pertinent, and that women's crimes hurt the male of the family. Thus, the important factors were the social status of the woman - whether she was free or slave, of ill repute and low social status or a *mater familias*, and her marital status: whether she was married or

---

[43] RALLES-POTLES, 5, 57; Peira 49,34; K. G. PITSAKES, To koluyma gamou logo suggeneias ebdomou vathmou ex aimatos sto Vyzantino dikaio, Athens-Komotene 1985, 60 ff; LAIOU, Mariage, 119.

a concubine, or unattached[44]. In Byzantine law, starting with the Ecloga, social status seems less important (although the differentiation between free and slave remains), the age of the woman becomes more important, and the marital status of the man also plays a role. Thus, the man who is unmarried and is found guilty of fornication is beaten with six lashes, whereas the married man suffers double the punishment, „be he rich or poor“[45]. This must be influenced by canon law, which certainly differentiates between sins of the flesh committed by married man and those committed by unmarried men. Thus, canon 21 of St. Basil explicitly states that „If a man who is living with a woman is not content with marriage but falls into fornication, he is a fornicator, and he will suffer longer ecclesiastical punishment“. It is true that he does not specify how much longer, but the spirit is clear. In canons 58-59, he punishes the fornicator with seven years of „*epitimia*“, and the adulterer with fifteen years. The doubling of the punishment of the married man who is guilty of fornication in the Ecloga may be an indication that, although the legislators certainly did not revoke the distinction between adultery and fornication as far as their effect on the man were concerned, they were, in practice, creating a certain degree of equality between men and women in this respect. The same may be true of the punishment given to the adulterous woman and to the man guilty of adultery, that is, of sexual relations with a married woman: they both have their nose slit, even though the man is not divorced from his wife[46]. Perhaps similar is the tenor of the legislation which affects the punishment of a man who has sexual relations with the fiancée of another. Under the clear influence of canon 98 of the Council in Trullo, the Ecloga punishes the man as if he had committed adultery, i.e., with the slitting of the nose[47]; but the woman remains unpunished.

The Isaurian legislation, which was retained in the law codes of the Macedonians, including the Basilics, is an important example of the influence of ecclesiastical law, both toward an equalisation of punishments and toward a redefinition of sexual crimes that become sins of the flesh, into which both men and women fall equally. Subsequent jurisprudence sometimes followed the spirit, although not the letter, of this approach. Chomatianos, in the case of the deflowering of a virgin by a married man, punishes the man with a fine, more or less following Ecloga 17.29, but applies only the normal, seven-year „*epitimia*“ to the man; in another case, he does not punish the man at all; while Eustathios Romaios, again in the case of the deflowering of a (willing) virgin, eschews corporal punishment but makes the man pay a much heavier fine for his crime than was required by the pertinent law[48].

---

[44] A.E. LAIOU , Sex, Consent and Coercion in Byzantium, in: EADEM, Consent and Coercion to Sex and Marriage in Ancient and Medieval Societies, Washington, D.C. 1993, 115-6.

[45] Ecloga 17.19; 17,20.

[46] Ecloga 17.27. All of this is repeated in Procheiros Nomos (ch. 39) and Eisagoge (ch. 40); Bas 60, 37, 71 ff.

[47] Ecloga 17.32; a sort of precedent in D. 48.5.14.3.

[48] Chomatianos, nos. 74, 136; Peira 49.4.

The other way in which ecclesiastical legislation and the philosophy of the Christian religion influenced the position of women within the context of family law is its attitude toward consent. Consent was important in Roman law in all manner of things, from business contracts to marriage contracts. It becomes very important in the Ecloga in establishing the category of sexual crimes and the punishment of the man. That is so because of the general principle that the internal forum of conscience is important in Christianity. It is so specifically in family law, because the consent of a woman to a sexual act (fornication or abduction) makes it possible to find a remedy, namely, marriage, which is the state in which the church wanted to enclose all sexual activity[49]. Thus, fornication with a woman, with her consent, first of all is taken as meaning that the girl has also consented to marriage, and secondly is remedied by marriage[50]. The ecclesiastical precedent may be canon 38 of St. Basil, which states that, if a girl follows her lover and subsequently her parents agree to the marriage, the situation may be remedied in that way. The deflowering of a girl under thirteen, however, is the equivalent of statutory rape, since her age makes her incapable of consent[51].

Eventually, even abduction, which had received the harshest penalties in Roman law, became capable of being remedied by canon law, following the canons of St. Basil which walk a fine line between true abduction, presumably without the consent of the woman (canon 22) and elopement, carried out with the consent of the woman, although for various reasons the couple may make it look like true abduction (canons 30, 38). There is a certain incoherence in canon law, since canons 27 of Chalcedon and 92 of Trullo strike with anathema anyone who is guilty of abduction. The incoherence continues in the canonical exegesis, with the two great twelfth- century canonists pronouncing conflicting opinions. Zonaras allows the couple to marry if the act is truly elopement, and has the woman's consent, while Balsamon allows it in some cases and not in others[52]. The woman's consent, then, for at least one major canonist, can remedy even abduction. Zonaras introduces a social component into his exegesis: he thinks that women pretend to be abducted because the man is low-born, and they are ashamed to give themselves to him openly. This was undoubtedly a common enough reason for elopement, and the canonist accepted that the fact that it was disguised as abduction should not obscure its true nature. I have studied elsewhere the realities of abduction in the middle and late Byzantine period, and concluded that civil law and the courts also followed this path, differentiating between abduction with the use of force, and

[49] Cf. BEAUCAMP, op.cit., 168 ff.

[50] Ecloga 17.29

[51] Ecloga 17.31, the man has his nose slit and gives her half his property.

[52] Commentary of Zonaras to canon 30 of St. Basil, and Balsamon's responsum to Mark of Alexandria (RALLES-POTLES, op.cit., 4, 169-71 and 495-96). Cf. LAIOU, Sex, Consent,133 ff.

elopement with the girl's consent[53]. In all cases, sexual intercourse attendant upon abduction/elopement aggravated the crime, for it was a sin.

What does this mean for the position of women? First of all, the acceptance of elopement allowed a way out of the stringent Roman and Byzantine requirement of the consent of the parents or guardians to marriage; this has been the role of elopement through the centuries. To that extent, it allows a woman greater freedom to make her own marriage. But it is an extreme measure, and I do not think it was often taken in reality. Secondly, it points up the importance of woman's consent in all that has to do with sexual relations. I should like to insist on this, because what is normally stressed is the fact that women suffered very strict controls of their marriage and their sexuality[54]. There is no question that church, state and family were all insistent on controlling marriage alliances, something which affected both men and women, certainly women more than men. But at the same time, there is a strand of the acceptance of equality: the idea that both man and woman have a right to the pleasures of marriage, including the pleasures of sex, received both a theoretical expression in statements by laymen as well as ecclesiastics, and practical application in court; the malaise voiced by the fourth-century fathers about the unequal treatment of adultery also found applications in real life, as we have seen. And the idea that marriage is based on consent, both a Roman and a Christian ideal, was given expression in the development of legislation and practice in the case of abduction; and even in divorce, when the absence of continuing consent made a marriage unbearable.

It is not to be forgotten, however, that there were also underlying ideas, of sex as pollution and of women as the incarnation of temptation and pollution. These ideas had wide diffusion, certainly lie behind the continuing differential treatment of adultery, and sometimes emerge in canon law and canonical exegesis; they also are undoubtedly at the base of the harsher treatment of elopement when it is attended by sexual intercourse. Furthermore, the insistence on women's consent sometimes hurt women. It most certainly did so in real life, since it suggested that women bore increased responsibility for sexual crimes committed against them. This was even, sometimes, expressed in the law: witness the Novel of Athanasios I (1305-6) which punished with shameful exposure the woman who consents to her own seduction.

The influence of canon law on the position of women was not universally negative, nor was it universally beneficial. Through its own legislation and its impact on civil law, the church certainly strengthened the institution of marriage and the position of women in it. Eventually, women who found themselves outside the boundaries of marriage saw their position deteriorate. The emphasis of canon law on consent, and the practicality of ecclesiastical courts, introduced a certain

---

[53] LAIOU, Sex, Consent, 157 ff; Peira 63.5.

[54] For example, BEAUCAMP, op.cit.

flexibility in the application of the law, since ecclesiastical courts had greater latitude than civil ones in the exercise of „*oikonomia*". Of course, much depends on chronology: the influence of canon law was more beneficial to women in the eighth century, at least insofar as inscribing them into the institution of marriage was concerned. And much, in the Byzantine Empire, depended on the court and the judge, and therefore not only on the circumstances of the moment but also on broader social assumptions which, under the influence of ecclesiastical, although usually not canonical, writings, may have seen in women a sexual force hard to contain and therefore dangerous. The perception of moral weakness in women had a powerful impact in a society based on honor and shame.

IV

Women in the Marketplace of Constantinople (10th–14th Centuries)

[p. 261] The artisan, the street hawker, the shopkeeper, the investor, the moneylender – all of the female persuasion. What role did they play in the marketplace and the commercial economy of Constantinople? Was it a minimal, marginal one, as our sources would suggest at first glance? Was it specific in any respect? Did women in the marketplace overcome the barriers of a restrictive ideology, or did they work within the ideological parameters of the society? These are the questions addressed in the following pages.

First, let us revisit briefly the part of the terrain that is already well exploited. The evidence for women's presence in the marketplace, as manufacturers and sellers of cloth, starts with St John Chrysostom, who had nothing complimentary to say about the women who sold their wares in the market. It was a sordid thing, he wrote, to have women in the marketplace, engaging in trade, but less sordid than for women to be *subintroductae*.[1] After the late antique period, as far as I know, there is very little to no evidence of women in the marketplace of Constantinople, until the time of the publication of the *Book of the Eparch*; but then, we know little of the personnel of the marketplace generally in the late seventh, eighth and ninth centuries.

It is in the tenth century that we begin to have usable evidence of women's presence in the marketplace and the economy of Constantinople – evidence that is sporadic, and qualitatively and quantitatively different in different periods. Thus for the tenth and eleventh centuries it is sparse but with weighty implications; in the late fourteenth century it is more extensive, because of the survival of the Registry of the Patriarchate of Constantinople, and the fact that this ecclesiastical body dealt with issues of civil and even commercial law in this period. It is hard to say whether the increase in the documentation **[p. 262]** signals an increase in the economic activity of the women of Constantinople. Certainly, it need not necessarily be the case.

The evidence for the tenth and eleventh centuries, limited though it is, has a certain weight. If I read the *Book of the Eparch* correctly, women dressers of raw silk (*katartarioi*) were members of the guild of *katartarioi*, and they also

---

1 *PG* 47, 520.

participated in the lower levels of the silk trade.[2] Now, admittedly, the *katartarioi* were the poorer of the artisans engaged in silk trade, and the silk merchants in question seem not to have been members of a guild. Nevertheless, the formal participation of women in the treatment of silk is established. Nor would the presence of women in guilds be a unique phenomenon in the European Middle Ages. According to David Herlihy, women workers in wool in western Europe were members of guilds, although in the thirteenth century their position became subsidiary, and after 1350 they were excluded from the guilds.[3]

For the eleventh century, the most interesting text is the little treatise of Psellos on the female festival of "Agathe," describing a procession of women cloth-workers – spinners, weavers and wool carders – which took place in Constantinople on 12 May; it undoubtedly formed part of the celebrations, festivities, and dancing that attended the celebration of the founding of Constantinople, on 11 May. Psellos provides a vivid description of the procession, led by older women who were experts in the craft. It ended at a church, where decorations illustrated the art of cloth-making, and where the women made votive offerings. After the ceremony at the church, the women danced, accompanied by a rhythmical song. Psellos, in a typical manner, presents this with his usual condescension toward artisans. But the condescension is primarily a social one, and not directed particularly to women, although certainly the subject lends itself to pithy remarks about the inappropriateness of women in the streets, in the marketplace, celebrating the art of cloth-making. For this was, I believe, a festival of professionals, not one celebrated by women who engaged in the ideologically safe pursuit of making cloth at home for the needs of the household. Rather, the treatise refers to a guild-like group **[p. 263]** with ceremonial and ritual activities which took place in the streets.[4]

The social condescension of the sources merits a little reflection. The women who are visible in the marketplace before the fourteenth century are presented as poor women, and undoubtedly many were: these were the hawkers of vegetables and pickled cabbage, the tavern keepers and innkeepers

---

2 Koder, *Eparchenbuch*, VII.2. Cf. A. Laiou, "The Festival of 'Agathe': Comments on the Life of Constantinopolitan Women," in *Byzantium: Tribute to Andreas N. Stratos*, I (Athens, 1986), 118–20.

3 D. Herlihy, *Opera muliebria: Women and Work in Medieval Europe* (Philadelphia, 1990), 95–7, 147–8, 185–91.

4 Cf. Laiou, "Festival of 'Agathe'," 111–22.

(a disreputable occupation in the twelfth century as it was earlier), the butchers' wives and cooks made famous by Ptochoprodromos, the lower strata of those engaged in the treatment and sale of silk. Undoubtedly, women of an urban middle class also showed up in the market: witness the example of St Thomais of Lesbos, an early tenth-century saint whose *vita* was probably written later in that century. Her husband is described as being "of the middle sort"; she herself made cloth and sold it in the marketplace, with which she was so familiar that she even frequented it at night, looking for the poor on whom to lavish her alms.[5] But anyone with aristocratic pretensions would not be seen dead in the marketplace.

In the eleventh century we observe a double ideological bias: an "aristocratic" contempt for the marketplace, and a theoretically gender-based bias against women's activities outside the home which, however, on closer examination seems to affect primarily women of the aristocracy or the aspiring aristocracy.

For one thing, the marketplace is, and was recognized as, the very antithesis of the house, the most public of public places. It was also seen as the place where temptation in various forms was encountered. Well brought up women would not go near the marketplace, nor did they wish to know what went on there, or so their male relatives would have us believe. Psellos' mother, her proud son tells us, "wanted to know nothing, not what was happening in the marketplace, nor in the palace."[6] The conservative aristocrat, Kekaumenos, would not have dreamed of seeing his womenfolk in the marketplace, nor would he have told us if he did. At an earlier time, the sainted Theodora of Thessalonike used to cross the marketplace when she went shopping for the monastery, but sometimes people met her who knew who she was, and they would ask her, "Why do you thus demean **[p. 264]** your good birth?"[7] This was certainly not a place for well-born women – and our Thomais of Lesbos was not a well-born woman.

The marketplace was also ideologically tainted in other ways, for the activities that went on there were considered to be problematic, at least during some periods of Byzantine history. According to some ideologues, the merchant, in order to carry out his trade, was forced to lie, cheat, and run all

---

5 A. Laiou, " Ἡ ἱστορία ἑνὸς γάμου: Ὁ Βῖος τῆς ἁγίας Θωμαΐδος τῆς Λεσβΐας," in *Πρακτικά τού Α΄Διεθνούς Συμποσίου ΗΚΑΘΗΜΕΡΙΝΗ ΖΩΗ ΣΤΟ ΒΥΖΑΝΤΙΟ* (Athens, 1989), 237–51.

6 K.N. Sathas, *Μεσαιωνική Βιβλιοθήκη*, V (Venice-Paris, 1876), 5, 24.

7 Arsenii, *Zhitije i podrigi sv. Feodory Solunskoi* (St Petersburg, 1899), 14.

sorts of risks; indeed, these were inherent aspects of his profession.[8] The idea has a venerable antiquity, going back to classical Greece, where, as has been demonstrated by a relatively recent study, the retail merchant in particular is someone who lies, who perjures himself, who shouts like a barbarian or an animal, whose very looks are wild, who is the opposite of the orderly, civilized citizen.[9] These very negative views of the merchant and his activities, coming out of the Greek civic world, and overlaid with Christian morality, did not, I believe, last after the sixth century. They did resurface, however, at least to some extent, with the restructuring of urban society and the aristocratization of society, in the eleventh century. The marketplace, then, was considered a low-class place, populated by low-class people. Women in the marketplace were in a triple jeopardy: the two I have already mentioned, and the third is connected with stereotypes about woman's nature and behavior.

For women, the marketplace was seen as particularly inappropriate because of a set of factors that have to do with the fact that the tenor of the activities that went on there conflicts with age-old ideas regarding the proper behavior of women. An ancient prejudice against the loud haggling and calling out of wares and prices was brought home to the inhabitants of Constantinople by the presence, in the Forum of Constantine, of a statue of a pig "which signified the noise of the fair," and a naked stele "which signifies the shamelessness of those who buy and sell."[10] But we know that one of the most commonplace pieces of wisdom regarding women in Byzantium, as in Antiquity, was that "silence is an ornament to a woman." The marketplace certainly was not a place where this female virtue could be exercised. No wonder, then, that the women in Ptochoprodromos' **[p. 265]** poems, most of whom, including his own fictitious wife, had some connection with the marketplace, appear as irrepressibly garrulous individuals, loud, coarse, vulgar in word and deed.

The gender-based ideological position regarding the presence of women in the marketplace was, to my mind, anchored on firm socio-economic foundations. There was high value placed on women's work, especially moral value. But of course the work was to be at home, and for the needs of the household. This has venerable precedents: the good woman of

---

[8] *PG* 64, 436.

[9] L. Soverini, "Parole, voce, gesti del commerciante nella Grecia classica," *Annali della scuola normale superiore di Pisa, Classe di lettere e filosofia*, ser. III, vol. 22/3 (Pisa, 1992), 811–33.

[10] Preger, *Scriptores*, II, 206. The *Patria*, as this compilation is known, probably dates from the 10th century: ibid., p. ix.

Proverbs 31.22, who makes for her husband double-weave cloaks and for herself garments of fine linen, has a Greek counterpart in Xenophon's good housewife, who works all day long and supervises her servants so that she can manage a self-sufficient household internally, as her husband manages it externally. We find these ideas repeated throughout Byzantine history, even as late as the fourteenth century; Solomon's good woman, and Xenophon's too, had a very long life.[11]

In the ideological universe, it was a poor, sad, miserable woman who had to hire herself out on wages – and a very poor husband or father who had to allow this to happen. Why was this so? Undoubtedly it was connected with the preservation of the honor of the lady, but this I will leave out of consideration. More prosaically, it was so because women in Byzantium were carriers of property. In this sense, the Byzantine attitude to labor outside the home is unexceptional, for we can encounter it in many other societies.

Anthropologists have taught us that societies in which women marry with a dowry, i.e. where property of one form or another goes from the woman's family to her husband, are distinguished from societies where marriage is made with the payment of a bride-price or bride-wealth, i.e. where there is transfer of property from the husband to the woman's natal family. In societies where the dowry system predominates, as among the upper castes in North India for example, the husband has a clear obligation to support the wife and children. Of course, anthropologists also note that this does not apply to the poorer strata of society, where women do engage in agricultural and craft activities.[12] In Byzantium, too, a woman who had to **[p. 266]** work after her marriage, in work other than the sanctioned work for the household, who had in some way to provide for herself, was a woman who had made a failed marriage. There is dishonor for her natal family, which did not arrange matters well for her, and dishonor for her husband, who could not carry out the promise of caring for her.

A woman, therefore, should not work for an economic purpose, if I may put it this way, for her family has already endowed her with the means not to do so. It is, one readily understands, an ideological construct which cannot in reality affect the majority of women, for the households were few that could provide a sufficient dowry (and man's marriage portion) to conform to it. In

---

11 See, for example, Psellos in Sathas, *Μεσαιωνικὴ Βιβλιοθήκη*, V, 9–10; E. Miller, ed., *Manuelis Philae Carmina*, II (Paris, 1857), no. 131: Ἐπιτάφιοι εἰς γυναῖκα σώφρονα.

12 S. J. Tambiah, "*Bridewealth and Dowry* Revisited: The Position of Women in Sub-Saharan Africa and North India," *Current Anthropology* 30 (1989), 416 ff. and 416 n. 4.

practice, the implementation of this ideal was directly related to the social class and economic condition of the individual woman.

Interestingly, in this ideological construct, the external economic relations of women included an important component of expenditure outside the marketplace. Money should be given away in charitable gifts. The most powerful example from Constantinople is the story of St Thomais of Lesbos, our artisan saint, who spent her own money, and, according to her husband, the household resources as well, on charity. I have the strong impression that charity, a virtue for everyone, was a specific virtue for women. One can see that most clearly in saints' lives, especially of the tenth century and after; harsh asceticism being available to only a few women as an avenue to sainthood, charity takes pride of place. We can also see it in the ideal of the good woman propounded by Psellos and others in the eleventh and twelfth centuries. Here, too, charity is the primary virtue in social and economic relations. Thus, women were carriers of the Christian ideological burden of investing in ventures which brought rewards in heaven rather than on earth.

Women were also carriers of the ideological burden of self-sufficiency, as we have seen already. Here, the dowry system played an important role. Landed possessions given in dowry could not, in theory, be alienated, except in times of intense hardship for the household. Movable goods could be alienated, but had to be restored; even in the first years of the fifteenth century the principle was affirmed that dowry goods had to be invested in risk-free enterprises.[13] Thus, one **[p. 267]** might suppose that investment of dowry goods in trade was generally limited at normal times – a statement that must be mitigated by the fact that dowry goods were, despite the prohibitions, invested, a fact that we know from several periods, specifically the eleventh, thirteenth and fourteenth centuries; and also by the fact that dowry property could and did include shops, and that women also owned other types of property, free of encumbrances. It is possible, for example, that the shop sold by Eudokia Hetairiotissa in the tenth century was not dowry property.[14] To the extent that the law was followed, the dowry is the institutional expression of the search for self-sufficiency: women's property is the stable part of the household property, and thus women's ideological role is firmly rooted in the economic behavior of women's property.

As always, ideology was only partly reflected in reality. The ideal of self-sufficiency was often expressed, but rarely achieved, and the profit motive,

---

[13] MM II, 550 (November 1401).

[14] N. Oikonomides, "Quelques boutiques de Constantinople au Xe s.: prix, loyers, imposition (*cod. Patmiacus* 171)," *DOP* 26 (1972), 345.

although ideologically less soothing, was strong indeed, probably at all times, certainly in the tenth century and after.

The interplay of various ideological positions and realities suggests the following observation. Women of the lower and middle economic and social strata and their capital functioned in the marketplace as owners/operators of small retail shops, or as traders in retail trade. As is the case with the men of the same class, their presence in the sources is limited and incidental. Women of the aristocracy might own commercial property; as managers of the household, they probably knew a great deal about the operation of the market, but they were not physically present in the marketplace.

An interesting question would be that of women as consumers. To my knowledge, it has not been posed. But women were the household managers, and they had a certain degree of liquidity; there is some evidence that they shopped in the marketplace. The *Book of the Eparch* shows them also in the marketplace, offering to sell to the *argyropratai* gold or silver objects, pearls or precious stones. Was this for the purposes of consumption (that is, the result of hardship), or because they invested relatively liquid capital? The question is impossible to answer in the current state of knowledge, but the whole issue begs to be investigated. **[p. 268]**

Is an evolution discernible in the role of women in the marketplace or in the urban economy of Constantinople? Our limited information forces us to say that it is discernible only extremely dimly, and for the most part with regard to textiles. We have seen that our documentation shows a certain participation of women in organized textile production in the tenth and eleventh centuries. For the twelfth century, I have no knowledge of any relevant information outside Thebes. It is possible that in the late Middle Ages the general decline in the Byzantine silk industry, where we have seen women in a market environment, also affected adversely female labor in that industry. The manufacturing of woolen cloth was always a household production, and women's role in it may have been unaffected. As for the participation of women in the commerce of Constantinople, again there is little we can say about its evolution. Women are certainly more evident in the eleventh and twelfth centuries, at a time when there was more commercial activity generally, as well as a certain détente in mores. At the same time, one must entertain seriously the idea that rising wealth among the trading population in the eleventh century also took a number of women out of circulation: had she lived in the tenth century, Psellos' mother might well have sold cloth in the marketplace she shunned in the eleventh century.

The involvement of women in the marketplace of Constantinople becomes much more visible at the end of the fourteenth century, when the well known hardships, combined with trading opportunities, released a certain amount of female capital and female economic energy. We then find women as shopkeepers, sometimes with partners, and as investors in the long-distance trade. Thus, we arrive at the question of women's credit and its particularities.

It has been remarked for western Europe that, unlike other economic activities where, in the Middle Ages, there was gender differentiation, both men and women participated in credit operations.[15] The role of women can be specified to some extent. They participated very actively in pawning and small, short-term loans which carried a high interest rate. It is important to note the existence of female networks, with women borrowing from women. The female creditors were not professional moneylenders, but tradespeople – alewives or other tradeswomen who also accepted pawns, including articles of female apparel. **[p. 269]**

As far as productive loans are concerned, still in western Europe, there are some gender specificities. Widows appear frequently as moneylenders, but some married women also loaned money. Depending on the society in which they lived, they made their investments in different activities. In England, with its agrarian economy, women invested mostly in agricultural production and mortgages, and it seems that they were heavy investors: that is, more of their assets were engaged in loans than was the case with men. In the maritime cities of Italy, on the other hand, women invested both in trade ventures, that is, in risky activities, and in the public debt, which promised a lower but surer return on their capital.

In the Byzantine Empire, as is well known, interest-bearing loans did not bring upon the creditor the same kind of opprobrium as in western Europe, for interest was legal. So whatever particularities depended on the legal difficulties of giving credit were non-existent in Byzantium. The question is, whether women had available capital, the right and the opportunity to use it, and whether they had a risk-taking mentality. Here, as in so many other matters, we suffer from a paucity of sources, except for specific periods, distant from each other in time and locality.

Outside of Constantinople, in fourth and fifth-century Egypt, and again in Venetian Crete of the fourteenth century, for which we have sources, the

---

15 W.C. Jordan, *Women and Credit in Pre-industrial and Developing Societies* (Philadelphia, 1993).

small, consumer loan patterns of western Europe hold very well. For the middle Byzantine period, we have no sources regarding consumer loans made by women; indeed, we possess very little evidence of the realities of consumer loans generally. We do have evidence for the late fourteenth century, and we find, again, in Constantinople this time, some confirmation of the patterns observed in parts of western Europe. We find female networks which extend to family members. Thus, there is the example of a consumer loan in 1365, at a time of crisis, when a woman pawns a sword to a female relative, perhaps in order to help her husband or her family while the husband is at war.[16]

Productive loans are more evident. In the tenth century, Byzantine law registers anew a provision of sixth-century legislation, that if a woman appoints a ship captain – that is, if she invests in a ship – she bears responsibility for his transactions. The same applies to the **[p. 270]** transactions of a shop in which she has appointed a supervisor. Both cases constitute an exception to the general principle that a woman cannot in law be responsible for the transactions of a third party; these transactions are deemed to be her own, not those of another.[17] What this suggests is that women were investing in sea-borne trade and in trade in shops, and they took the risk of the transactions. How frequently they did that in the period before the fourteenth century is not known, as I have already indicated.

We find some interesting cases in late fourteenth-century Constantinople. Women own, invest in and operate workshops: a perfume shop, a dairy shop, taverns, etc. A woman operates a clothier's shop in partnership with her children.

The following examples exhibit what may well be more general patterns. A widow owns a dairy shop. She takes in her orphaned god-children and creates a partnership (*syntrophia*) with her god-son: she contributes the capital, he the labor, at a half share of the profits. Did the woman inherit her husband's shop? Possibly, but not necessarily. In any case, she continues to invest and makes shrewd deals. Her partner is not an outsider, but someone with whom she has family connections.[18]

A woman lends her son 36 *hyperpyra* to invest in trade. When he loses the money and has to sell a house he had inherited, she buys the house from him and forgives him part of the loan. It is clear that the woman had disposable

---

16 J. Sakkélion, "Συνοδικαὶ διαγνώσεις τῆς ιδ' ἑκατονταετηρίδος," *Δελτίον τῆς ἱστ. καὶ ἐθν. ἑταιρείας τῆς Ἑλλάδος* 3 (1889), 274.

17 *Bas.* 53.185 = *Cod. Just.* IV.25.4.

18 MM II, 474–5 (*sine anno*).

capital and invested it in a risky enterprise; the family connection is apparent in this case as well.[19]

Around the year 1400, when Constantinople was blockaded by the Ottomans, which is to say in very hard times, women seem to come into their own. A member of the aristocracy, a widow named Theodora Palaiologina, had invested in commerce and loans. She had also invested her daughter's future dowry in these enterprises. She offered to provide for the spouses for one year and then to deliver the dowry. The story then becomes very interesting: this lady and her daughter's mother-in-law, another Theodora (Trichadaina), had together borrowed money, mortgaging the dowry of Palaiologina's daughter in order to loan to – that is, to invest with – John Goudeles, a relative by marriage of Trichadaina, who was to use the money **[p. 271]** in his trading ventures. Then, the two women fell out. First they fought about whether the profit from the venture should go to Palaiologina or the young spouses; then, after the venture had proved to be a loss, they quarrelled about who would shoulder the risk.[20]

As in western Europe, widows were particularly active in such transactions. In the last-mentioned case, they have the administration of the property of their children and feel free to invest it. The dowry here functions as a form of liquid capital: it can be invested, and the two mothers agree that it must be invested. The dowry goods are pawned. The money thus acquired is given out at risk, although in theory it should not be. The two mothers combine forces, for they both agree to the investment. The investment is made within the family. Legally, the dowry is protected property, so even after the loss as much of the original property must be reconstituted as possible.

We note here that in fourteenth-century Constantinople women invested even dowry goods in trade. In a rural environment, as in thirteenth-century Epiros, for which we also have some information, most such investments would be in land. In Constantinople, too, women took their cases to court themselves, not through a male relative, as was done in thirteenth-century Epiros, which is another indication of a certain autonomy of action.[21]

In this particular period and place, widows are very much in evidence. The reasons are obvious. Upon the death of the husband, the widow receives the administration of dowry and marriage goods, which during the marriage were in theory administered by the husband. The widow then can do all sorts of things with the property. Many aristocratic women have liquidity and

19 MM II, 386–7 (May 1400).

20 MM II, 399–400, 511, 550 (June 1400–November 1401).

21 E.g., MM II, 386–7, 367–8, 368–9, etc.

assets, including land and shares in shops. They lend money within the family for productive use, whether trade or manufacturing. Family networks are important. Widows may also have the administration of dowry and marriage portions of unmarried minor children, and sometimes of married ones as well, and act in their name. Because of hardship, there is pressure on available capital, and they lend – even though dowry goods are protected. Because they are protected they receive precedence over all other debts; therefore, women are in a privileged position as creditors. The borrower is in an unfavorable position when he or she borrows dowry goods. To the extent that dowry **[p. 272]** goods are protected, even in these harsh times, the profit of the enterpise of the debtor is reduced, for the capital is borrowed under some institutional constraints.

The protection of dowry property can mean that the goods may be recycled, that is, they may be invested several times over. Dowry property can be lent out, but it has precedence over other debts or is under protection,which means that part or all of it is returned to the creditor even when other capital is not,[22] and can then be lent out again.

One may suggest that women's capital becomes more important in adverse circumstances or when there is increased demand for capital. Women were quite wily and shrewd in the administration of property and the loans they made. At the same time, family connections seem paramount, which would indicate that women more than men played their role of investor or lender within the framework of the extended or the narrow family.

We thus return to the family, and the role of the woman in it. Ideology, as well as family pressures, may have played some role in keeping part at least of female investment within the family. One also has to assume an underlying network of associations that was important in economic transactions and which, for women, was closely bound with the family.

What can we conclude about women in the marketplace of Constantinople? We have seen them, at different times, as street hawkers, bakers, owners of shops, tavern keepers, textile workers, investors, rentier landlords;[23] we have surmised them as consumers. So they were there, throughout the period under examination, active in the marketplace, ideological constraints notwithstanding. Most evident in our sources are the poorer women, and that is entirely understandable, for it was mostly they who had to be in the marketplace. The aristocratic woman who invested in its activities without

---

22 E.g., MM I, 279 ff.

23 Like the *sklavinikarion ergasterion* bought by Sophia, *patrikia*, for 6.5 lbs of gold: Oikonomides, "Boutiques," 346.

being physically present is dimly visible, though the dimness lifts at the end of the fourteenth century. We find a close connection between women's activities in the marketplace and the institution of the family, at least in some operations and in some ways: in the fact that shops owned by women were sometimes dowry property, but also in the fact that **[p. 273]** shops were manned by family members, that loans and investments were made within the family network, and that networks among women tended to be among relatives as well. In this *highly* nuanced sense, the family and the home were very much at the center of women's economic activities, even when these activities took place in or in connection with the marketplace of Constantinople.

V

FAMILY STRUCTURE AND THE TRANSMISSION OF PROPERTY

THE PARAMETERS OF THE ISSUES

That family and the transmission of property are among the most important structuring elements of a society is a statement that needs little elaboration. The family, in the Byzantine empire and in most other medieval societies, is both a social and a biological unit based on consanguinity and marital affinity. It is a unit of reproduction of human resources, but also the framework in which the societization of children and the maintenance of the elderly took place. David Herlihy has added a new dimension, by describing the family as a moral unit and a moral universe, within which human relations are very different from those outside it.[1] The role of the family extends to production. In non-slave societies, the family, whether nuclear or extended, was at the base of the household, which was the unit of production of the majority of the population, that is, the peasantry. This is evident even in northwestern Europe, where over the medieval period there was a tendency for economic exploitation to be carried out through tenant household production rather than through the cultivation of a large domanial reserve. In the southern European lands, the household, based on the family, has a clearer diachronic role in agrarian production.[2] This feature is perhaps most pronounced in the Byzantine lands, where the peasant household was the unit of production even at times when large estates were the prevalent form of organization.[3] It is also the case that part of the artisanal production took place within the household, and that workshops along with the trades they served were transmitted through the generations. Certainly, there were large units of production, of silk, for example, or ceramics, but small family workshops were also common.

[1] Laiou-Thomadakis 1977: 72–3, with bibliography; Herlihy 1991: 1.

[2] Toubert 2004: 95ff; Contamine et al. 1993: 157ff, 225ff, 361ff.

[3] Lefort 2002; Laiou 2002.

That family links are closely connected with the transmission of property in most societies is also an unsurprising statement. Certainly this was the case both in the Roman empire and in the Byzantine empire, heir to much of the Roman legal system. In fact, issues having to do with inheritance extend to kinship groups that are much larger than the immediate family, since in the Roman and Byzantine systems relatives up to and including the seventh degree of consanguinity (son or daughter of second cousins) could be called into the inheritance. The question of rights of inheritance was settled by jurists of the Roman and early Byzantine periods. Subsequently, the main interest focused on the definition of family and kinship as it affected marriage impediments.[4] But the two were closely linked, so that the transmission of property has much to do with the notion of kinship and effective kinship (affinity, that is, relationship created by marriage, spiritual kinship, etc.), which can be and was manipulated to facilitate or impede the formation of marriage alliances and the concentration of property. The church was the first to take action in extending the rules regarding close marriages, but the state followed suit. Because of this fact, the development of practices concerning the transmission of property should be studied together with the effects of normative action taken by the state or the church in order to regulate marriage alliances. To some extent, and with the passage of time, norms were internalized. The transmission of property was in any case of interest to the state, which intervened in a number of ways, and which was even the residual heir of those who died childless, without identifiable heirs, and intestate.

Thus, the two most important normative powers, the state and the church, played a role that at particular times became very significant in the transmission of property. Family property consists not only of material goods but also of symbolic capital, such as social status and networks.[5] In a society like the Byzantine one, in which state office was a source of revenue as well as the main marker of status, the transmission of goods becomes a complex and subtle matter, since material and symbolic capital may both complement and compensate for each other in the upper reaches of society.

Family structure makes a difference to forms of property transmission, and the reverse is also true. A patriarchal and patrilineal family will certainly privilege the male line, affecting both the way property is transmitted and the role and position of women. A society in which bilateral succession (inheritance by both male and female offspring) and partibility, that is, inheritance by all of the children, prevail would coincide with a prevalence of nuclear households and high nuptiality. Whether the household consists of nuclear or extended families, therefore, will depend in part on the mode of transmission of the parental property.

What is involved here is the present and future of productive resources, a matter of equal interest to peasant and aristocrat, although it remains to be seen whether the strategies adopted by different social and economic groups were similar or dif-

[4] Pitsakis 2006.

[5] Cheynet 1998.

ferent. In any case, the vital importance of the issues involved brought to the fore conflicting interests and purposes. Conflicting imperatives, too, are evident in Byzantine society, while for Byzantinists the interpretation of some of the issues has been fraught with controversy.

Conflicting imperatives regarding the transmission of property were created by the interests of the families involved, sometimes in opposition to each other, and by the differences between what the normative powers proclaimed and what was optimum or at least feasible in social and economic terms. Here are some of the conflicting imperatives.

Parents wanted to provide for their children, especially when these married and left the household. The Byzantine system of succession, based on partible inheritance, meant that all of the children inherited. This desire is in possible conflict with the needs of the older generation, for whom provision has to be made. Furthermore, and especially in times of demographic growth, providing for the children has the inherent danger of so diminishing the property that it becomes non-viable or economically weakened.

There was also a conflict between some normative rules and social needs. Roman law demanded partibility and, since the sixth century, exhibited a marked preference for equal inheritance.[6] Thus, in the absence of a testament, all children, male and female, were to inherit equal portions of the parental property. It may be that Christianity played a role in the equal treatment of children. In the fourth century, St Basil of Caesarea preached that all children should inherit equally. Arguing by analogy, he spoke of the eagle, which has two offspring but raises only one, throwing the other out of the nest. And he continued: "Such are the parents who, claiming poverty, expose their babies, or those who treat their offspring most unequally in the distribution of property. It is just, however, that, as they gave each one life equally, so they should also provide them equally with the resources necessary for living."[7] St. Basil's is a fine principle, and indeed it was broadly practiced in Byzantine society, albeit with significant modifications. However, if it were to be compulsory rather than admonitory, it would become problematic. For one thing, it would not work well with another tenet of Roman law, namely, the freedom of action on which a testament is theoretically based. Furthermore, it would make impossible any discretionary action concerning property arrangements at the time of marriage. But Byzantine matrimonial alliances, as we shall see, were a matter of strategy that sometimes necessitated unequal distribution.

Finally, there is a potential conflict between the needs of the children, or of others who had an interest in the property, namely, in some cases, the imperial treasury, and the needs of the individual, who might want to safeguard his or her salvation through donations to the church.[8] That too was capable of solution, and a solution was found.

[6] Beaucamp 1985: 199–200.

[7] Homilia VIII in Hexaemeron, *MPG* 29, 177–80.

[8] Dagron 1998.

The disagreements among Byzantinists are to some degree the result of uneven source survival, specifically, the distribution of legal sources and narrative sources or private acts that show how things worked out in practice. For the period down to the seventh century, the survival of Greek papyri in Egypt allows us to study some aspects of social practice, which may then be compared to the abundant legislative sources of the sixth century.[9] But Greek papyri peter out after the conquest of Egypt by the Arabs in 642. After that, and for more than 250 years, we have legislative sources for the subject at hand, but extremely limited information otherwise. Narratives, judicial decisions, and acts of practice survive starting with the early eleventh century, while for the late thirteenth to the fifteenth century we even have sources that are capable of statistical treatment and quantitative analysis, at least for some parts of the Byzantine empire. As a result of this state of the documentation, one of the topics discussed here, namely, the transmission of property, has been, in the first instance, the purview of jurists or legal historians. They make excellent use of the normative sources, and in the past they used to privilege normative rules. In the last few decades, however, the study of documents has increased, and these often give evidence for deviation from the rules. An ongoing discussion has to do with a possible disjunction between Roman legal norms and Greek or Hellenistic custom, on matters affecting the family and the transmission of property. The debate goes back to the late nineteenth century, when powerful statements were made about the existence of a substratum of ancient customs under the Roman law edifice. It goes on today, less as an overarching theory of law and custom and more as a disagreement on specific points and specific periods.[10] Social circumstances or social needs were rarely taken into account in past scholarship. In recent years, historians as well as legal historians with an understanding of the importance of practice have done some interesting and important work.[11] These studies tend to be concentrated in the two periods for which extra-normative sources are extant, that is, the period through the seventh century and the period from the eleventh century onward. Unfortunately, there remains a considerable gap, covering the period which in many respects holds a profound interest for the social historian. For it was in the seventh through the tenth century that Byzantine society was transformed from a late Antique one to a medieval one, and it was in this same period that important social transformations took place that made this society first a relatively flat one with unusual equality, while by the end of the tenth century the ruling élite underwent a sea-change, as the aristocracy collectively increased its power and changed its structure, from a clan structure to a family structure. The gap, unfortunately, cannot be easily filled.

[9] Beaucamp 1985.

[10] On the debate, see Beaucamp 1998: 10–17; Dagron 1998: 82. Joëlle Beaucamp is among the historians who are critical of the view that there is a clash between Roman law and Greek custom – ibid. Dieter Simon (Simon 1986) is among the most eminent modern historians who speak of a conflict between two basic ideas, one a Greek and Hellenistic concept that privileges family decisions and remains strong in customary law, and the other a Roman one, that privileges individual decisions.

[11] See, for example, the work of D. Simon and the articles in Beaucamp and Dagron 1998.

The more recent generations of social historians and social legal historians, if I may so put it, have different interests from legal historians of the past.[12] But they do not agree among themselves on all points. There is a fairly sharp controversy regarding the important question of whether the dowry is a final arrangement or a temporary one, to be revisited and revised at the moment of death of the girl's parents.[13] There has also been some considerable debate regarding the question of the rights of political and ecclesiastical powers over the inheritance of people dying without heirs and without a testament, and over the question, arising from the same early-fourteenth century source, whether different rules obtained for dependent peasants on the one hand and everyone else on the other.[14] This is a matter of some significance, since it directly impinges not only on the question of variant practices among people of different status, but also upon the issue of whether, in the late Byzantine period, the state ruled on the matter of the transmission of property differently depending on the status of the affected individuals.

Family arrangements, family strategies, and modes of transmission of property tend to change slowly, especially in pre-industrial societies. That must be understood and taken into account, since these institutions are connected to other, equally conservative, social and economic arrangements: modes of cultivation and exploitation, mentalities and social constructs. Change there is, however. In the Byzantine empire, the precipitating factors of change were the state and the church, with their various and changing interests, and with the weight of normative force behind them. The state, for example, legislated differently when its intent was to preserve small peasant ownership, and differently when its primary concern was to curtail the economic and political power of the aristocracy.[15] The church became involved primarily through the extension of marriage impediments between people already related by consanguinity or linked by affinity, issues which affected the transmission of property as well.[16] The élites may be a factor for change, as they sought to manipulate or bypass the legislation thus in turn giving rise to further normative action. And the peasantry developed some strategies that differed from legal norms. This was also an agent of change, not so much in the normative universe as in the material one.

In this chapter I will focus on the period after the seventh century, with a few glances backward. Much of the discussion will of necessity be focused on the period from the eleventh century onward, given the state of the sources. But this is by the way. The main articulating principle of this chapter is the fact that issues regarding family structure and the transmission of property are never static. They are dynamic,

[12] It is regrettable that the ranks of those interested in Byzantine family history are being augmented by younger scholars only in a limited way. Gender history seems to have largely replaced family history in the work of young scholars. While both have merit, it would be a pity if one were to continue being privileged over the other.

[13] Beaucamp 1998; Cheynet 1998; Laiou 1998; Lefort 1998; see *infra* pp. 64–7.

[14] See, for example, Karpozilos 1979; Nakos 1988; Tourtoglou 2000; Laiou 2000: 114–20.

[15] See *infra*, pp. 63, 70–1.

[16] Pitsakis 1985 and 2006.

and must be examined as such. Time is of the essence, both in the structure of the family and in the transmission of property. A family looks very different when it is at the initial stages and when it matures and children start to get married.[17] Moreover, whatever the norms, all families, whether aristocratic or peasant, develop strategies in order to try to achieve the optimum for their family and their property, and this too is a dynamic process.[18] The norms simply limit the degrees of freedom.

Finally, it must be stressed that we are very unequally informed about regional variation in the Byzantine empire. Moreover, the size of the state fluctuated very considerably between the 7th and the 15th centuries. It may be taken on faith that regional variations there were, just as there are in modern Greece, for example, even though its geographical extent is considerably smaller than that of the Byzantine empire through most of its history.[19] Of course, modern Greece emerged with a Civil Code after at least four centuries of Ottoman occupation, during which time local customs flourished and diverged. Whether the diversion by area was less or greater in the Middle Ages we are unable to tell.

THE BYZANTINE FAMILY

It appears that the family as a social structure was strengthened between the fourth and the eighth centuries, through the combined action of church and state and perhaps because of the spontaneous action of individuals, although this latter point can be disputed. The strengthening came about through the support given to the institution of marriage and the legislation controlling it. The church, after an initial stance that favored virginity and asceticism, preached the importance of the marriage bond, the legitimate outlet for sexual needs and the means of having legitimate children. In the fourth-century canonical legislation, especially the canons of St. Basil of Caesarea, marriage even became a remedy for certain sexual crimes, heavily punished in Roman law, such as fornication and abduction.[20] The state, too, promoted marriage by making it available to everyone except slaves, and by progressively improving the status of lower-class women who cohabited with men, as well as that of concubines. This culminated in a provision of the law code that was seminal for family law, the *Ecloga* issued by the emperors Leo III and Constantine V (in 741), by which if a man introduced a woman into his house, had carnal relations with her, and entrusted her with the management of his household, he was considered to have contracted marriage with her.[21]

17 For the impact of time, see Bourdieu 1994: 5.

18 On the peasantry, see Kaplan 1992: 488.

19 Bresson 2006: 19, and see also various articles in Piault 1985.

20 Laiou 1993: 130 ff.

21 *Ecloga* (Burgmann 1983): 2.6.

According to Evelyne Patlagean, the tightening of family bonds in the fourth through the seventh centuries coincides with the decline of the city and the ruralization of the empire, which led to social involution. This theory is based on the evidence for first-cousin marriages and uncle–niece marriages which, however, it must be noted, had been legal in the Roman empire, the first until 741 and the second until 342. The evidence is found in rural contexts and in far-away provinces such as Osroene and Mesopotamia, and thus it is difficult to see the connection of these practices with the decline of cities. However, the more general point made by Patlagean, that is, the suggestion that the importance accorded to the family meant the spreading of small groups of individuals that produced, shared, and distributed resources, remains valid.[22]

As for the structure of the family, there is continuity in the fact that the family never seems to have been patriarchal or patrilineal in the Byzantine empire. That is, the father did not have the extensive rights of a Roman *pater familias* over the members of his household, nor was status or property transmitted only through the male line. It is certainly true that there existed diachronic ideological norms that made of the man the head of household, and also the person whose will should be respected by his wife and their children. In family life, it has been noted, the point of view projected by the sources is that of the man: thus, for example, the prescription regarding abstinence from sex before communion is addressed to the man, who should abstain from his wife, not to women.[23] Scholars have placed greater or lesser weight on these aspects of the question, and stressed variously the subordinate position of women within the family, or the possibilities that they had partly to bypass the norms.[24] It is also true that, in normal times, the man had the management of all family property, including his wife's dowry; only in case of grave mismanagement, carrying risk for the survival or well-being of family members, could the wife take over the administration of the family property. However, it was accepted in law and it occurred in practice that women could and did become heads of household when widowed, even in the presence of adult offspring in the household.[25] The *Ecloga* established extensive rights for the mother in terms of property ownership and the upbringing of children: she acquired the right to manage the entire family property on her own, with the obligation to bring up and marry off her children, with the appropriate marriage gifts.[26] As for patrilineality, it has already been indicated that Byzantine succession law and, I may add, practice, was based on bilateral succession, so that property traveled along both the male and the female line.

Unfortunately, while the legislation can be followed through the centuries, the material that pertains to practice becomes abundant only with the eleventh century and into the fifteenth. Changes doubtless took place between what may be

[22] Patlagean 1977: 113–55.

[23] Beaucamp 2000a and 2000b; Laiou 1981.

[24] For an optimistic view see, for example, Laiou 1981; for a more pessimistic view, Herrin 1983 and Beaucamp 2000b.

[25] Laiou-Thomadakis 1977: 90–4.

[26] *Ecloga* 2.5.1.

considered two end-points, the eighth century and the fourteenth. The general statement, that the family was not patriarchal, I think remains true. But one may dimly discern some differences, due both to social class and to chronology. It would seem, for example, that, while the legal framework was more or less the same in the eighth and the eleventh centuries, élite women played a less important role before the late tenth century than they did later. It has been shown that women of the imperial family (but also some of the men, it is true) were discouraged from marriage by being cloistered.[27] A Novel of the Emperor Leo VI sought to regulate the transmission of property to women. An earlier law (Bas XI, 1, 76=C II, 3,15) had allowed parents to rescind their promise, made in marriage contracts, that the daughter who was getting married would receive, upon the father's death and by his testament, a part of the parental property equal to that of other children. In Novel 19, Leo VI (886–912) abrogated this law, arguing that one should not give a child a smaller portion than was stipulated in the marriage contracts, and indeed stressing the virtues of equal partible inheritance; he seems to be arguing that all paternal property should, upon his death, be equally distributed among his offspring.[28] While the Novel makes no distinction regarding the gender of the offspring in question, it is possible that the proximate cause of the legislation was connected to women's dowries or that the legislator was extending the category of offspring to whom the law applied to include both sons and daughters.[29] Some scholars think that the situation redressed by Leo VI would have left girls with less of a share in the parental property than had their brothers.[30] If this were so, then one might argue that among the élite, who would be in the first instance on the mind of the legislator, men had been favored in the transmission of property, although the emperor himself claims that the earlier law had not been followed in practice. All this is terribly vague and uncertain, but the general statement that aristocratic women were disadvantaged before the late 10th century may stand. In the centuries between the seventh and the early eleventh century, the Byzantine élite was for the most part a military one, with the exception of the officialdom of the central administration, housed in the Palace. Many of them had their estates in Asia Minor, where the frontier zones expanded and contracted until the mid-ninth century, and then expanded consistently, in the onward march of the Byzantine armies. Military values were prevalent, which almost certainly privileged the male offspring both in terms of prestige and in terms of inheritance. It is telling that we rarely learn the names of the female members of the great families.

27 Patlagean 1984.

28 The emperor presented legal arguments for this new disposition, but the most forceful argumentation was based on St. Basil's simile of the eagle: see *supra* p. 53. On the Novel, see Michaélidès-Nouaros 1937: 135 ff., who argues that it did not have much influence.

29 It is noteworthy that a decision by the early eleventh-century judge Eustathios Romaios, surviving as a gloss to Bas. XI,1,76, and making reference to Novel 19, is concerned exclusively with the inheritance rights of men. Furthermore, unlike the Novel, the case judged by Eustathios concerned not the entire property of the father but, rather, that part of it which remained after the marriage of one of the sons, and after the marriage gifts given to this son: Scholion 3 to Bas. XI, 1, 76.

30 Beaucamp 1998: 16.

At some point, changes occurred in the strategies and the structure of the élite. Aristocratic families became closely linked to each other through multiple marriages,[31] and matrimonial strategy became a fine art in the eleventh and twelfth centuries, by which time vast networks of aristocratic families had been created.[32] Some genealogical excursions of the Byzantines themselves are useful in this connection. The genealogy of Basil I (867–886), created by his grandson Constantine VII, traces his parental ancestry to the ancient Arsacids through two Armenian princes, whose nobility is stressed without reference to any females. Later, in the late eighth century, one of their descendants married the daughter of Leo, an Armenian official resident in Constantinople, and their son, the father of Basil I, married a girl descended through her mother from both Alexander the Great and the first Christian emperor, Constantine I![33] In this constructed genealogy a nameless woman, Basil's mother, is introduced to legitimate the peasant who eventually became an emperor; but her genealogy is clearly fictitious. In the genealogy of one of the half dozen most important aristocrats of the late tenth century, Michael Maleinos, women have more of a place, since their status is such that with their marriage to the males of the family they introduce imperial blood and connections.[34] In the twelfth century, the genealogies of members of the high, imperial aristocracy, both female and male, trace both lineages and give equal weight to the male and female ancestors. Indeed, at the very basis of the Komnenian dynasty lies the marriage of two offspring of the most powerful families of the day, Alexios (I) Komnenos (1081–1118) and Irene Doukaina. After that, the family was known by the combined name Komnenodoukai. In brief, certainly in the aristocracy from the eleventh century onward and until the end of the empire, women were transmitters of both lineage and property, and the Byzantine family of at least this segment of society was equal in terms of gender.

We know next to nothing about similar developments in the majority of the population, that is, the peasantry. When information becomes abundant, starting with the late thirteenth century, we do find, here too, that the family is not patriarchal.[35] It is true that the censor, because the information is contained in population censuses, starts with the head of household, statistically a male, and then

[31] For example, the great aristocrat Michael Maleinos was an uncle of the emperor Nikephoros II Phokas (963–969); the mother of the emperor John I Tzimiskes (969–976) was a sister of Nikephoros Phokas, while Tzimiskes' first wife was sister to another great magnate, Bardas Skleros.

[32] Laiou 1992: chap. 1.

[33] Theophanes Continuatus, ed. Im. Bekker, Bonn, 1838, 212–16.

[34] Gounaridis 2006: 273–4; Petit 1902: 550–1. Maleinos' mother had imperial blood, of sorts, being related to Romanos I Lekapenos (920–944) who himself had been of peasant stock. Maleinos' sister married Bardas, father of the future emperor Nikephoros II.

[35] Here I must correct some earlier statements of mine (Laiou-Thomadakis 1977: 78) that affirmed just the opposite. I had taken as indices of patriarchy the fact that marriages were mostly patrivirilocal or virilocal (in fact, neolocal, I now believe), that relationships and names were usually traced through the male line. I had, however, noted that while such was usually the case, descent through females did occur, and there were female heads of household. This latter fact is significant, while the indices I had used do not establish the existence of patriarchy properly speaking.

registers his wife, children, chattels etc., with the ignoble designation "(he) has," but on the other hand a considerable proportion of the households (around 20%) is headed by widows, even though some of these households have resident adult males.[36] In this period we also have secure information that allows us to observe the structure of the household. The majority, over half and, in some areas, around 70 percent, consists of nuclear families, although it is important to notice that there are also vertically extended families, consisting of two nuclear families, parents and married child. That type of extended family, of course, is connected to the family cycle, since when the older generation dies the family becomes nuclear once again. Laterally extended households, which include two or more fraternal nuclear families, are significant in certain areas, especially those with a large admixture of people with Slavic names.[37] The importance of this will be discussed in connection with the transmission of family property. We retain, in any case, the prevalence of the nuclear family, which therefore is not at all tied to modernization or indeed to the "western" model of the family as has been argued by some demographers.[38] We admit also the role of the time factor, since the family is a live organism that becomes constantly reconfigured as children are born, get married, and older people die.

It is unfortunate that we do not have equally clear indications for the structure of the family and household in earlier periods. Nonetheless, some information, though anecdotal and sporadic for the most part, is available. Michel Kaplan has argued that the nuclear family predominated in the rural world between the fourth and the seventh centuries, being occasionally augmented by brothers and sisters; he finds virtually no co-resident uncles and aunts.[39] He notes that this nuclear family structure corresponds to the function of the family/household unit as a unit of production.[40] One may suppose that if that was indeed the case, there was some connection with demographic factors and with the land/labor ratio: for much of this period land was abundant compared to labor. Certainly, in the late 6th and 7th century there was a steep population decline and the demographic curve did not begin its upward trend until some time in the mid-eighth century.[41] But even after that there was an abundance of land. In such conditions, it might not be necessary for families to pool resources. In times of demographic expansion, when too many children might threaten the well-being of the household, some children were encouraged to leave the village and the hearth to create their own plots (and households, presumably nuclear ones), on outlying lands that belonged to their family.

[36] Laiou-Thomadakis 1977: 89ff.

[37] Laiou-Thomadakis 1977: 78ff.

[38] Of course Peter Laslett (1969) long ago disproved the idea that the nuclear family is a modern phenomenon; but the "western" model, which does not include the Byzantine empire, remains.

[39] In the real population, however, there must have been some households that were vertically extended, comprising members of two or more generations.

[40] Kaplan 1992: 483–88.

[41] Laiou and Morrisson 2007: ch. III.

This is precisely what an important document, the *Fiscal Treatise*, describes vividly.[42]

In the period before the eleventh century, the prevalent form of social and economic organization in the countryside was the village, a fiscal unit to be sure but also, in most cases, equivalent to what we know as a village. Here, there was a considerable degree of economic and fiscal cooperation, and peasants owned arable land, which was no longer the case (exceptions aside) in the documents we have for the late thirteenth century and after. Perhaps it was unnecessary to resort to the additional intrafamily pooling of resources that extended families serve.

It is also unfortunate that the only information we have on the structure of the household, late though it is, comes only from the peasant milieu and we know nothing about the aristocracy or the urban classes more generally. I am certain, however, that this ignorance can be remedied to some degree by a systematic search into narrative and hagiographic sources.

THE TRANSMISSION OF PROPERTY

The law decreed and individuals normally desired that part at least of the patrimonial property devolve to the children: a minimum of $^1/_3$ or $^1/_2$ of the material property was by law reserved to the children. And according to the law, in the absence of a testament, all children, male and female, should receive an equal share of the family property. These simple-sounding rules had many permutations, and were applied differently depending on chronology and perhaps social class. The matter is greatly complicated by the fact that there are actually two points at which the family property is divided: at the marriage of each child, and at the moment of death of the parent(s).[43] It has been argued that the most important stage in the division of patrimony is the first one, and that the testament is the last act, that confirms or upsets the earlier arrangements. At first glance, this would seem to affirm the discretionary power of the parent(s) at every strategic moment; however, each action decreases their degrees of freedom, since it must take into account all previous actions. It looks as if marriage contracts, incorporating the various acts of transmission, acquired greater importance with the passage of time.[44] If that is reality and not an accident of the survival of sources, then the patrimony was divided earlier in the family cycle and there was less of an effort to preserve the patrimony intact for the longest time possible, than if the major act of transmission had been effectuated in one's last will and testament. It also means that, since the children had already received their portion through their marriage contracts, the

[42] Dölger 1927: 115.The generally accepted date of this text is tenth century; N. Oikonomidès has redated it to the twelfth: Oikonomidès 1996: 44–5.

[43] Simon 1986; Dagron 1998.

[44] Dagron 1998.

parent(s) had greater freedom in the disposition of the residual, which they could then use to provide for the salvation of their souls, or to create pious foundations etc.[45] Most importantly, it means that the distribution of property, where property there was, can best be seen as a set of strategic decisions, aimed at preserving or increasing the wealth and power of the family, especially the offspring, while preserving part of the patrimony for oneself. Therefore, the transmission of property and matrimonial strategies become intimately connected. That statement probably applies to many societies. It certainly applies to western medieval Europe; but where primogeniture obtained, matrimonial strategies affected the fate of the patrimony less than in societies with bilateral inheritance, where both males and females inherit.

These arguments, however, must not be taken to extremes nor be assumed to have been universal. One of the most interesting testaments of the Byzantine period is that of a man from Thessaloniki, named Theodore Karavas.[46] He was perhaps a merchant, and he had, at the moment he composed his will, rather significant property consisting of vineyards and urban real estate, to the tune of 977 gold coins. Karavas had fulfilled all his legal obligations to his children at the time of their marriage, and he had carefully kept account of their marriage contracts, and registered those dispositions in his will. Having done so, he was quite free to distribute the rest of his property in his testament: there were exiguous legacies to the church and to priests, some property to his son, quite considerable property to his godchildren, small legacies to two grandchildren as well as to nephews and blood legacies, with the bulk of his assets going to his second wife. It is quite clear that a considerable part of his estate was distributed by testament, at a time when, having met his legal obligations to his children, he was free to dispose of his property at his will, and did so.

In the Byzantine empire, the transmission of property at the point of marriage led in the first instance to fragmentation. Marriage itself might offer a remedy, if the marriage of close relatives to each other were permitted or encouraged, as it was in ancient Greece and Rome. Under the influence of Christianity, however, close marriages were forbidden, and between the late seventh and the twelfth centuries the prohibitions became extended to consanguinous relatives into the seventh degree and to some affines to the sixth degree. Thus, this particular remedy became increasingly difficult, indeed virtually impossible, to apply.

The aristocracy

In the absence of the simple solution of primogeniture, which to the Byzantines would have seemed unjust in the extreme, complex strategies were developed. Let

[45] Dagron 1998: 98–9.

[46] Živojinović et al. 1998: no. 30 (1314).

us first take the case of the aristocracy. Again, it is not easy to find information for the period of the black hole. Informed guesswork is therefore necessary. In the eighth, ninth, part of the tenth centuries, there are few stable, well-established aristocratic families extending over many generations.[47] The ruling class depended greatly on state office for its revenues and its social status. Therefore, social capital was quite as important as, if not more important than, material capital. Social capital was not strictly speaking inherited, since office was not inherited, except for the imperial office which, however, was very unstable in that period. Still, access to social capital was doubtless easier for already established families. Given how significant and lucrative office was, it is possible that keeping the patrimony intact in the hands of a single individual was less important than one might imagine. Besides, it was still possible to keep the patrimony within the larger family since it was still permitted, for example, to two brothers or sisters to marry two first cousins.

A turning point came with a patriarchal decision, the *Tomos* of Sisinnios in 997. The decree forbade the marriage of two brothers (or sisters) to two first cousins, and that of uncle and nephew with two sisters and its mirror-image, that of an aunt and her niece with two brothers. It was issued at the urging of the emperor, Basil II, and the impulse came from a specific marriage alliance that was contemplated or had already been made. The decree came just after the time when Basil had been bitterly contested by members of the great aristocratic families of Asia Minor, linked among themselves with family ties. There is no question in my mind that the emperor was aiming to put obstacles to the economic and political consolidation of such families, even though the Patriarch used different arguments in his decree. The decree, and its long evolution, has been discussed extensively with regard to marriage impediments, but it is equally important for the transmission of property. The desirability of the kind of close marriage forbidden by the Patriarch is proven by the fact that such marriages did occur within the imperial family in the late eleventh century, despite the prohibition. Nevertheless, after the decree, they could not be commonly practiced.

Jean-Claude Cheynet has studied the transmission of the patrimony in the aristocratic milieu in the period after the restriction of close marriages, that is, in the period from the eleventh to the thirteenth century. He finds that in this class, as in the society as a whole, property was transmitted to all of the children. When the great Asia Minor aristocrat, Michael Maleinos, died, his property was divided equally between his two sons, but it was reconstituted because the younger brother bought the share of the eldest. Maleinos' married daughter is not mentioned, but it is certain that she had received a dowry.[48] Aristocratic women could and did inherit land, but there is no way to tell whether they were favored or disfavored in relation to their brothers, or whether all the children received virtually equal

[47] On this period, see the interesting article by Brousselle 1999.

[48] Cheynet 1998: 64–5.

portions.[49] Of course, in this class testaments were usual, so there was a good deal of discretionary power on the part of the parents. Cheynet thinks it possible that aristocratic women received a large portion of their dowry in cash, jewels, and other movable goods. As he acknowledges, however, this is conjecture. The decisions of the judge Eustathios Romaios, in the early eleventh century, which are incorporated in the *Peira* and which arise from an urban milieu consisting of aristocrats, usually not of the highest order, and a wealthy urban population, make it clear that in this milieu also property was transmitted to both men and women, although the details and strategies do not emerge clearly. Simply, the principle of bilateral inheritance is confirmed.[50]

Another, and major, remedy to the dispersion of property and therefore to the impoverishment of the family down the generations is obvious but rarely enters the discussion. It has to do with marriage strategies. With every marriage there is certainly transmission of property both to the bride and to the groom, and there is, thus, a restructuring of some of the property of two families in the creation of the third. The corollary of the inheritance system is that the patrimony is fluid, and in order to follow its fate we have to look at it through three families across time. Here is where matrimonial strategies come in. A judicious marriage can ensure an excellent future for the offspring, as two families exchange material and social capital. A case in point, although the marriage never took place, is that of the eleventh-century savant and politician, Michael Psellos, who had promised his future son-in-law, as part of the dowry of Psellos' daughter, an imperial title that would yield an annual revenue, but most notably would ensure the groom's social position.[51] A good marriage, indeed, itself becomes social capital, as it allows siblings to make better marriages with less expenditure in terms of marriage gifts. All of which suggests that pre-mortem inheritance, that is, the division of material goods among children while the parents were alive, was unequal among members of this class. This is observably the case among the lesser, provincial aristocracy in the Despotate of Epiros in the early thirteenth century.[52] As different arrangements are made for various children of the same family, the process of property transmission becomes dynamic and flexible, much more so than a simple look at the laws would lead us to believe. There is consolidation of property and social capital in the new household, offsetting the fragmentation of the paternal landed property.

In the same connection, it seems to me that for members of this class the distribution of property at the time of marriage was final, unless, of course, the marriage was dissolved by divorce. Each matrimonial union required subtle strategies and negotiations, and complex arrangements, making renegotiation at a later point very

[49] A clear case of a woman owning non-dowry property is that of Maria Tzousmene, daughter of John II Komnenos, in the twelfth century: Acts of Zographou (Regel et al. 1907): no 5; cf. Acts of Xeropotamou (Bompaire 1964): no. 8 (ca. 1200).

[50] Beaucamp 1985.

[51] Sathas 1876: 205.

[52] Laiou 1998.

delicate indeed, and a factor of instability. There is considerable dispute among Byzantinists precisely on the point I have just made. The dispute, in summary, is as follows: whether indeed the disposition of property at the point of marriage was final, or whether it was an interim arrangement, to be revisited at the time of death of the parent(s), under the principle of equal distribution of property among all the children of a family. The burden of the law seems to be that the dowered children should "return" (collate) their dowry at that point, place it in the family pot, as it were, so that redistribution could take place. Some scholars think that this law was applied, certainly at various points in Byzantine history, and probably throughout.[53] Other scholars have argued strenuously that such was not the case: that the woman, specifically, either did not collate her dowry or was not allowed to do so, that is, was excluded from the succession. This has been described as a custom, sometimes a Greek custom, which prevailed over Roman law, a view espoused mostly by scholars of earlier generations.[54] Whether it is a Greek custom or not is a question I will not address in this discussion. The evidentiary material supporting one or another of the two positions, however, is of interest. The older position, perhaps because it is older, does not find much favor with most scholars today.[55] Yet one is hard put to find evidence for the "return" of the dowry. In the early period, that is, before the mid-seventh century, Joëlle Beaucamp, despite her profound knowledge of Egyptian papyri, finds no direct evidence, but nevertheless deduces that the dowry was, indeed, returned to become part of redistribution.[56] As far as the Constantinopolitan aristocracy in the period between the eleventh and thirteenth centuries is concerned, there is, similarly, no evidence either way, and J.-Cl. Cheynet wisely draws the conclusion that the question cannot be answered.[57]

For a later period, some conclusions may be drawn from documents of the thirteenth and fourteenth centuries: judicial decisions or opinions from the Patriarchal court in Constantinople, which judged cases of family law, and from the chancery of the Archbishop of Ochrid, Demetrios Chomatianos (he was archbishop from 1216/17 until his death, ca. 1236). The relevant cases implicate not the highest aristocracy but individuals from a range of social strata: members of the aristocracy from Constantinople, provincial aristocrats from Thessaloniki and Corfu, and people from the Despotate of Epiros whose status is unknown but was not particularly high.[58] Each case has its own peculiarities, but general conclusions may be reached. These suggest that in practice people had developed strategies for the distribution of property that were wise, aimed at serving the interests of different members of the family, and also at minimizing instability in the family and social

53 Beaucamp 1998.

54 On the earlier bibliography, see Beaucamp 1998:11–17.

55 For the peasantry, see Lefort 1998: 176–7.

56 Similarly, there is no evidence for the aristocracy in the period between the eleventh and thirteenth centuries.

57 Cheynet 1998: 61–2.

58 Laiou 1998: see the cases in the Appendix; cf. Matses, 1961b: 73–8. On the Constantinopolitan aristocracy in the 14th c., see Macrides 1998: 184–5.

environment. It is clear that the dowry was not necessarily an equal part of the patrimonial property: it could be less or more, and the dowries of girls of the same family could also be unequal. The laws that mandated the possibility of the return of the dowry to the family for redistribution were known and acknowledged. Dowered women, therefore, were not excluded from the inheritance, and could press their claims. However, the legal and actual custom seems to have been for all children who had received marriage gifts, men and women alike, and had left the parental household (*exoproikoi*) to be considered as having no claim on the residual of parental property. That was to be distributed among the "heirs," those who had not left the household along with their marriage gifts. The courts more or less recognized this custom when claims were brought by married children, and rendered decisions that either upheld it on grounds other than the ones recognized by the law, or made the application of the law very expensive for those who sought to have it applied. The customary disposition preserved for the parents a part of the property, so that they would not be destitute in their old age. It provided for the distribution of a portion of the property while the parents were alive, and the rest of it after their death, to be distributed among the "heirs." And it avoided the huge disruption that redistribution of the property many years after the original arrangements would entail: a disruption that would affect marriages, would give rise to great disputes about the value of the original dowry and any increase in its value, and force a reevaluation of the parental property. Thus, social arrangements prevailed over legal norms, without the law having been abrogated.[59]

As for the higher aristocracy, the only information we have regarding this issue comes from an area that was, at the time, outside the Byzantine empire, the Empire of Trebizond. There is a Novel of John II (1280–1297) or John IV (1429–1459/60) Grand Komnenos that regulates the matter of the property of out-marrying children. According to the emperor, an old, dormant law had recently been re-introduced, that provided for the collation of the property given to out-marrying children with the property available at the time of the parents' death, the whole to be redistributed. With acuity, the emperor signals the social disruption thus created: the "destruction of numerous and great houses." The dispositions of the new piece of legislation are a little complicated to describe in detail. In essence, what the emperor orders is that when a testament exists, its dispositions must be observed – the sanctity of the testament is affirmed. If there is no testament, the property will in principle be divided among the children still living in the parental household. Out-marrying daughters are absolutely forbidden to collate their dowry, but out-marrying sons are not excluded from collating their marriage gifts. This last provision is not as disruptive as the collation of the dowry would have been, since the man's marriage gifts are more of a guarantee to his wife, and do not change hands while he is alive and the marriage lasts. The legislation in question obviously had local application only. But it seems simply to make into law what I think were informal arrangements, on the margins of the law, in the Byzantine territories. It is

[59] Laiou 1998.

not a piece of legislation that privileges men over women; it simply preserves the stability of property arrangements.[60]

One other type of property distribution must be mentioned, although it probably is not within the spirit of a book on social history, but rather a matter related to political ideology and foreign relations. It concerns the dowry of members of the imperial family married abroad. In the days when the Byzantine empire was powerful, an imperial princess married abroad did not receive lands as her dowry, at least not extensive lands. Thus, when Manuel I married off his niece, Theodora, to Baldwin III, king of Jerusalem, he gave her a significant dowry, which consisted only of moveable goods and cash, and did not include land.[61] This cannot be taken to mean that Byzantine aristocratic women did not receive land as part of their dowry, a thought that can only be entertained if one does not consider the consequences of giving Byzantine lands as dowry to a foreign prince. If all went well in the marriage, the offspring would inherit these lands, which would therefore pass into foreign hands; in the case of Theodora and Baldwin III, if the first son became king of Jerusalem, the Byzantine lands would become part of the territory of his kingdom. Whatever inroads western feudal thinking may have made into the Byzantine empire in the twelfth century,[62] it had not led the Byzantines anywhere near even dreaming of the situation that obtained in France and England, for example, where the Plantagenet kings of England held large parts of France as fiefs from the kings of France. It must have been unthinkable for Manuel I to give lands as dowry to the bride of the king of Jerusalem. The same emperor gave to Renier of Montferrat, upon the latter's marriage to Manuel's daughter Maria, what western sources call a "feudum" or "honor" or even "regnum Salonichi," but which in all probability would have been the revenues of the city and its environs, or, at most, the revenues of the theme of Thessaloniki.[63] In any case, Renier and Maria were expected to live in the Byzantine empire; little danger of alienation of property there. On the contrary, in the late thirteenth century, when the Byzantine empire was vulnerable on any number of fronts, the emperor Andronikos II (1282–1328) ceded to his new son-in-law, Stephen Urosh II Milyutin of Serbia, large parts of Macedonia as the dowry of the imperial princess Simonis who was given at a very young age to the middle-aged Serbian king as his bride (1299).[64] In essence, this was an official cession of lands that had been conquered by Milyutin. It is a comment on the Byzantine concept of the state in this late period that state lands could be given away as a dowry, as though they were private, patrimonial lands of the emperor. But here we are in the domain of foreign relations and acts under duress, which do not necessarily have explanatory power as to the normal system of property devolution.

60 Novel in Zepos and Zepos 1931: I, 364–5.

61 Hendy 1985: 270, after William of Tyre.

62 On this, see Magdalino 1993: esp. 176–7, 248–9.

63 For the sources, see Magdalino 1993: 100.

64 Laiou 1972: 98–9.

The peasantry

We do not have a very clear view of the family structure or the transmission of property among the peasantry for the period before the eleventh century. As far as the structure of the family is concerned, the little that is known or can be reasonably proposed, has already been discussed. As for the transmission of property, it has been rightly observed that peasants in the eleventh century exhibited ingenuity in manipulating inheritance arrangements so as to achieve optimum conditions for the exploitation of family holdings.[65] For the rest, one has to work backward from our knowledge of affairs in the thirteenth to the fifteenth centuries. It is a process that historians would rather not undertake, for it has the inherent danger of privileging elements of continuity as opposed to elements of change which, after all, are what distinguishes various historical periods. Here, the medievalist can take solace from the reflections of Alain Bresson on Greek kinship: he argues that kinship in Greek societies is a palindrome, and that problems can be solved if we approach them both from the start and from the end, both from ancient and from modern Greek society. This is not so because social forms remain unchanged, but because at a deeper level a logic may be at work which creates similar forms at different times.[66] I think that this approach, cautiously used, can indeed give us a realistic idea of the situation before the sources become rich, as well as allow us to pinpoint certain plausible points of change.

Let us, then, look at the situation as it appears in the thirteenth through the first half of the fifteenth century. For the first part of that period, much of our information comes from the records of the monastery of Lembiotissa in Asia Minor, with their numerous acts of sale or donation that involve peasant families.[67] Acts of sale and donation may also be found, though in very significantly lower quantity, in Thessaly. Information of a different kind, relevant to questions of inheritance disputes that became so severe as to reach the court, is available for Epiros in the early thirteenth century, down to the 1230s. At the end of the thirteenth century we begin to get large sets of data, mostly from Macedonia, from the archives of the monasteries of Mt. Athos. These are richest for the period up to the early 1340s, and reappear in the early fifteenth century. The data they contain are so rich that they have been subjected to statistical analysis.[68]

What follows is a summary of the picture as it emerges primarily from the Mt. Athos documentation. To a surprising degree, some important features of property transmission are similar in both the peasant milieu and the aristocratic one. There is no primogeniture among Byzantine peasants; although some examples can be adduced of preferential treatment of the elder brother, such may also be found among the aristocracy. The impact of state forms and the legal system upon the

65 Kaplan 1992: 487–8.

66 Bresson 2006: 22.

67 Miklosich and Müller (1860–90): IV.

68 Laiou-Thomadakis 1977 and Laiou 2002.

system of inheritance is observable in what happened in the Principality of Achaia, under western control after 1205. Here, Greek feudatories were allowed to practice partible inheritance, since, clearly, that had been their custom, based on law, before the Latin conquest. Western feudatories, on the contrary, practiced primogeniture. It seems that Greek serfs also held to the Byzantine way of partible inheritance among their heirs; but the *Assizes of Romania*, the feudal law code of Frankish Greece, tried to superimpose a western law that would make it impossible for more than one person to succeed to the holding. Whether that was successfully imposed or not is hard to discern. But we have here a clear indication of how political powers tried to intervene in the rules and customs of succession.

In Byzantine lands, dependent peasants, the class of peasantry for whom we have by far the most information, were more affected than other classes by the negative corollaries of equal partible inheritance to which they were certainly bound by law, since the incidence of testaments, which permitted discretionary disposition of part of the property, must have been exceedingly small. At the same time, as we have seen, the ownership of arable land among the dependent peasants of Mt. Athos was exiguous: they were tenants of monastic lands. So there was little arable land to be inherited and subdivided. There was, however, other immobile property: houses, vineyards, which were a very important resource, fruit trees and the land on which they stood, gardens, olive trees and groves. A study of the property composition of peasant households in Macedonian villages shows variegated patterns of property transmission. The underlying pattern, of which the others are deviations, is equal partible inheritance, with the girls receiving their portion primarily in the form of dowry.[69] The vagaries of the life-cycle, the death of siblings, for example, or even matrimonial strategies, make perfect equal partibility impossible, but it seems to have been the desideratum and to some considerable extent the practice. Deviations from equal access to the parental resources include occasional efforts to preserve the property, in its totality or for the greatest part, in the hands of a single individual. Preferential partible inheritance results in the concentration of most of the holding in the hands of one offspring, male or female. In very rare cases, one person inherits the entire holding, and the parents live with him or her until they die, and this continues through the generations. This type of inheritance, which has been called the stem family, was not common in Byzantium.[70] On the whole, then, among

[69] I cannot agree with Lefort 1998, who thinks that a few (three) cases indicate that women collated their dotal property with the parental one at the time of the parents' death, for redistribution of the total among all the heirs. None of these cases makes the point. The only one that on the surface seems to do so is *Lavra* II (Lemerle et al. 1970–82): no. 109, l. 521–523. On closer inspection, however, it turns out that it is unclear whether the marriage of Demetrios and Siligno took place before or after the death of her parents, which makes any conclusion as to the fate of the dowry uncertain.

[70] On the above, see Laiou-Thomadakis 1977: 197–203. For very similar patterns in modern Greece, with similar deviations from the (mandated) pattern of partible inheritance, see Friedl 1963: chap. 4; also, Saulnier-Thiercelin 1985: 54–60. Research published over the last 40 years has established that the stem family was also uncommon among peasants in western Europe, despite earlier opinions to the contrary. See, for example, Anderson 1995: 9–20.

Byzantine peasants, at least in the period for which information is available, equal or quasi-equal distribution of property was the norm, with some deviations. Officially, there was not here, as there was not among the aristocracy, any formal right attached to primogeniture. There are, however, situations in which an elder son has clearly received preferential treatment, having been better educated than his brothers and being in charge of the entire parental property, although he did so illegally, and probably by force of character and status.[71]

In both the peasantry and the aristocracy, the inheritance system was concomitant with a high degree of nuptiality, as anthropological theory would predict. Since resources were divided among all the children, and new households were started with a certain amount of property, it was possible for all the children of a family, or a large number of them, to contemplate marriage, something far less easy in societies where one heir acquires the bulk of the property. Among the peasantry, the existence of lands that could be cleared and cultivated further increased the possibilities available to new households, at least until a Malthusian impasse was reached, always a possibility in pre-industrial societies.[72]

The most important way in which the fragmentation of holdings was held at bay was the ownership and exploitation of holdings by people who had their own households and who were related to each other. That phenomenon is certainly observable among the Macedonian peasantry in the fourteenth century.[73] The documentation from the Despotate of Epiros and Asia Minor, in the early thirteenth century, shows that similar arrangements existed also among the aristocracy and the peasantry in those regions. Indeed, one can trace the custom much earlier, to the eleventh century if not the tenth. An extraordinary document, whose date is unfortunately quite insecure, but which I believe to date to the eleventh century, throws light on several aspects of this phenomenon. It is a commentary on the Novel of Romanos I Lekapenos on preemption (traditional date: 922; alternative and probably better date: 928). The emperor, trying to stop the accumulation of land into the hands of powerful people through the purchase of land from the peasants, had established several degrees of preemption, that is, first rights, on the land that was to be sold. The first right of preemption goes to the *anamix sygkeimenoi syggeneis*, which I translate as "the relatives who are mixed in and whose property is intermingled," i.e., those who are holding lands that are interspersed into each other. The second right goes to the partners who are similarly interconnected.[74] In interpreting the Novel, the commentary both changes it and provides an illustrative example of what the emperor had in mind when he used the term *anamix sygkeimenoi syggeneis*.[75] Here is an excerpt:

71 Papadopoulos-Kerameus 1909, no. 11.

72 A Malthusian impasse was reached in the very late 13th c.: Laiou and Morrisson 2007: chap. V.

73 Laiou-Thomadakis 1977: 200ff and 80.

74 Svoronos 1994: 62–3.

75 The most important change comes in the second degree of preemption, where the commentator subsitutes "similarly interconnected *relatives*" instead of partners. For the most recent edition and translation of the commentary, see Laiou 1992: 178–81, 150–1.

> When someone sells immobile property . . . he must first offer it to the relatives who are mixed in and whose property is intermingled. . . . For example, my father and your father were brothers. Their own father died without a testament, and our parents did not divide their patrimonial goods [between them]. We, too, retained the holding undivided and intermingled, and we hold it in common. . . . And sometimes I cultivated one of the fields and you the other one; sometimes I cultivated the field you had cultivated the year before, while you worked on the one in which I had labored the previous year; or else, we cultivated the field together. . . . When one of us, holding this land in this way, wishes to sell his part of the undivided field, the other is preferred to all other buyers . . .[76]

This intriguing text clearly refers to peasants – since it mentions the cultivation of the land. It establishes the relationship of first cousin, not brother, as the point at which the ancestral holding is still held and exploited without being divided, but also as the point at which the common exploitation might give out. Both the Novel and, much more clearly, the interpretation given by the commentary, aim at keeping the holding intact over three generations, and to facilitate its exploitation by a single individual subsequently. The legislation of Romanos I was not class-blind: it was issued for the benefit of the peasants, and it favored the common exploitation of peasant land.

What about practice? Documents from all the periods in which documentation exists make it perfectly clear that joint exploitation of property generally, but land more specifically, with benefits especially in terms of the more rational and efficient division of labor, existed both among the provincial aristocracy and among the peasantry in the thirteenth and fourteenth centuries. It is noteworthy that the boundaries of common exploitation and common ownership are placed at the level of first cousin. One is tempted to recall the Patriarchal decree of Sisinnios on marriage impediments, which had forbidden the marriage of two brothers to two first cousins, and therefore impeded, at the practical level, the pooling of resources or the economic cooperation between two groups that were already in close economic contact. I suggest, therefore, that we have two instances of powerful intervention of the state, albeit in oblique ways, into the strategies of the transmission of goods. For the peasants, the Novel of Romanos I Lekapenos made it easier to retain their holdings or part of their holdings undivided over three or possibly more generations. For the aristocracy, Basil II, through the Patriarch, sought to make the accumulation of economic power harder. Interestingly, however, in this matter too legislation could only go so far, and customary practices surfaced easily, giving the family bond greater claim on patrimonial land than any law prescribed. Already in the eleventh century kinship was affirmed as creating a more powerful claim to land than did any other kind of connection. And in the thirteenth century, a learned and wise jurist, Chomatianos, made it clear that in his court a family had the right to reconstruct its patrimonial lands, despite the fact that others might have a higher

[76] Svoronos 1994; Laiou 1992: 149–50.

claim according to the law on preemption.[77] Patrimonial property was the tangible form of the family bond.

CONCLUSION

Family structure and the transmission of property in the Byzantine empire follow a pattern whose principal traits are very similar to those described by David Herlihy for western Europe after the year 1000, and by anthropologists like Stanley Tambiah for North India.[78] The constitutive act, marriage, creates a family that is monogamous, is created by the consent of both parties, and has a property element consisting, commonly, of the bride's dowry and the bridegroom's marriage gift to her. These become the property of the new household, although the natal family of both bride and groom have residual claims on them. Descent is cognatic, and the family property is transmitted through bilateral inheritance, with a strong preference in law for equal inheritance, and a complex system of strategies developed on the ground in order to lend flexibility – and inequality – to the system. The effects of bilateral inheritance on the fragmentation of holdings cannot easily be given the remedy of re-concentration through close marriage, since that became increasingly difficult; common exploitation of patrimonial lands did provide a remedy. The nuclear family predominated for the entire period, as far as one can see, and is connected to the form of agricultural exploitation, which was based on the peasant family and household.

The values that flow from such a system are also common to similar situations in other parts of the world: the married woman is protected, and, having contributed a dowry, she is not expected to work outside the household; an ideological posture which cannot be practiced except among the wealthy.

The Byzantine case also has important specificities. These stem from the fact that there were not one but two normative powers trying to manipulate the transmission of property and therefore everything that results from it: the church and the state. The continuing survival of important tenets of Roman law, too, meant that there was a framework within which decisions, both those of the state and those of individuals, had to be formulated. The law changed, of course, but in whatever form it added its own complexities to the development of family and property relations over time. So there were many players, with their own interests and limitations, the conjunction of which gives fluidity and flexibility to what at first glance looks like a fairly stable system.

77 Chomatianos 2006: no. 71. On this, see Papagianni 1992.

78 Herlihy 1985: chap. 4; Tambiah 1989.

BIBLIOGRAPHY

Anderson, M. (1995) *Approaches to the History of the Western Family, 1500–1914*. Cambridge.

Beaucamp, J. (1985) "Au XIe siècle, Byzance: le jeu des normes et des comportements," in Piault 1985: 197–210.

Beaucamp, J. (1998) "Les filles et la transmission du patrimoine à Byzance: dot et part successorale," in Beaucamp and Dagron 1998: 11–34.

Beaucamp, J. (2000a) "Les femmes et l'église: droit canonique, idéologie et pratiques sociales à Byzance," in *Mutter, Nonne, Diakonin: Frauenbilder im Recht der Ostkirchen, Kanon*, XVI. Egling, 87–112.

Beaucamp, J. (2000b) "Exclues et aliénées: les femmes dans la tradition canonique byzantine," in D. C. Smythe, ed., *The Byzantine Outsider*. Aldershot, 87–103.

Beaucamp, J., and G. Dagron (1998) *La transmission du patrimoine; Byzance et l'aire méditerranéenne*. Paris.

Bompaire, J. (1964) *Actes de Xéropotamou*. Paris.

Bourdieu, P. (1994) "Stratégies de reproduction et modes de domination," *Actes de la recherche en sciences sociales* 105, 3–12.

Bresson, A. (2006) "La parenté grecque en palindrome," in A. Bresson, M.-P. Masson, S. Perentidis, and J. Wilgaux, *Parenté et société dans le monde grec de l'Antiquité à l'âge moderne*. Paris, 11–23.

Brousselle, I. (1999) "Les stratégies matrimoniales de l'aristocratie byzantine aux IXe et Xe siècles," in S. Lebecq, A. Dierkens, R. Le Jan, and J.-M. Sansterre, eds., *Femmes et pouvoirs des femmes à Byzance et en Occident (VIe–XIe siècles)*. Villeneuve d'Ascq, 51–64.

Burgmann, L. (1983) *Ecloga. Das Gesetzbuch Leons III. und Konstaninos' V*. Frankfurt am Main.

Cheynet, J.- Cl. (1998) "Aristocratie et héritage (XIe–XIIIe siècle)," in Beaucamp and Dagron 1998: 53–80.

Chomatianos (2006) = G. Prinzing, ed., *Demetrii Chomateni Ponemata Diaphora*. Berlin.

Contamine, Ph., M. Bompaire, St. Lebecq, and J.-L. Sarrazin (1993) *L'économie médiévale*. Paris.

Dagron, G. (1998) "Hériter de soi-même," in Beaucamp and Dagron, 1998: 81–99.

Dölger, F. (1927) *Beiträge zur Geschichte der byzantinischen Finanzverwaltung, besonders des 10. und 11. Jahrhunderts*. Leipzig.

Friedl, E. (1963) *Vasilika, A Village in Modern Greece*. New York.

Gounaridis, P. (2006) "Constitution d'une généalogie à Byzance," in A. Bresson, M.-P. Masson, S. Perentidis, and J. Wilgaux, *Parenté et société dans le monde grec de l'Antiquité à l'âge moderne*. Paris, 271–80.

Hendy, M. (1985) *Studies in the Byzantine Monetary Economy c. 300–1450*. Cambridge/New York.

Herlihy, D. (1985) *Medieval Households*. Cambridge, MA/London.

Herlihy, D. (1991) "Family," *American Historical Review* 96, 1–16.

Herrin, J. (1983) "In search of Byzantine women: three avenues of approach," in A. Cameron and A. Kuhrt, eds., *Images of Women in Antiquity*. London, 167–89.

Kaplan, M. (1992) *Les hommes et la terre à Byzance du VIe au XIe siècle*. Paris.

Karpozilos, A. (1979) "Αβιωτίκιον," *Dodone* 8, 73–80.

Kazhdan, A. P., and G. Constable (1982) *People and Power in Byzantium*. Dumbarton Oaks, Washington, DC.

Laiou, A., and C. Morrisson (2007) *The Byzantine Economy*. Cambridge.

Laiou, A. E. (1972) *Constantinople and the Latins; The Foreign Policy of Andronicus II (1282–1328)*. Cambridge, MA.

Laiou, A. E. (1981) "The role of women in Byzantine society," *Jahrbuch der Österreichischen Byzantinistk* 31, 233–60.

Laiou, A. E. (1992) *Mariage, amour et parenté à Byzance aux XIe–XIIIe siècles*. Paris.

Laiou, A. E. (1993) "Sex, consent and coercion in Byzantium," in *Consent and Coercion to Sex and Marriage in Ancient and Medieval Societies*. Dumbarton Oaks, Washington, DC, 109–221.

Laiou, A. E. (1998) "Marriage prohibitions, marriage strategies, and the dowry in thirteenth-century Byzantium," in Beaucamp and Dagron 1998: 129–60.

Laiou, A. E. (2000) "Le débat sur les droits du fisc et les droits régaliens au début du 14e siècle," *Revue des études byzantines* 58, 97–122.

Laiou, A. E. (2002) "The agrarian economy, thirteenth–fifteenth centuries," in A. E. Laiou, ed., *The Economic History of Byzantium from the Seventh Through the Fifteenth Century*. Dumbarton Oaks, Washington, DC, 311–75.

Laiou-Thomadakis, A. E. (1977) *Peasant Society in the Late Byzantine Empire. A Social and Demographic Study*. Princeton.

Laslett, P. (1969) "Size and structure of the household in England over three centuries," *Population Studies* 23, 199–223.

Lefort, J. (1998) "La transmission des biens en milieu paysan dans la première moitié du XIVe siècle en Macédoine," in Beaucamp and Dagron 1998: 161–77.

Lefort, J. (2002) "The rural economy, seventh–twelfth centuries," in A. E. Laiou, ed., *The Economic History of Byzantium from the Seventh Through the Fifteenth Century*. Dumbarton Oaks, Washington, DC, 231–310.

Lemerle, P. et al. (1970–82) *Actes de Lavra*. 4 vols. Paris.

Macrides, R. (1998) "The transmission of property in the Patriarchal Register," in Beaucamp and Dagron 1998: 179–88.

Magdalino, P. (1993) *The Empire of Manuel I Komnenos, 1143–1180*. Cambridge.

Matses, N. P. (1961a) *Τὸ οἰκογενιακὸν δίκαιον κατὰ τὴν νομολογίαν τοῦ Πατριαρχείου Κωνσταντινουπόλεως τῶν ἐτῶν* 1315–1401. Athens.

Matses, N. P. (1961b) *Νομικὰ ζητήματα ἐκ τῶν ἔργων τοῦ Δημητρίου χωματιανοῦ*. Athens.

Michaélidès-Nouaros, G. (1937) *Contribution à l'étude des pactes successoraux en droit byzantin (Justinien et post-Justinien)*. Paris.

Miklosich, F., and J. Müller (1860–90) *Acta et diplomata graeca medii aevi sacra et profana*. 6 vols., Vienna.

Nakos, G. P. (1988) *Προβλήματα του Βυζαντινού κληρονομικού δικαίου επί Παλαιολόγων – η ισχύς της Νεαράς* 26 *Ανδρονίκου* Β' *Παλαιολόγου*. Thessaloniki.

Oikonomidès, N. (1996) *Fiscalité et exemption fiscale à Byzance, IXe–XIe s*. Athens.

Papadopoulos-Kerameus, A. P. (1909) "Synodika grammata Ioannou tou Apokaukou, Metropolitou Naupaktou," *Vyzantis* 1.

Papagianni, E. (1992) "Vorkaufsrecht und Verwandtschaft," in D. Simon, ed., *Eherecht und Familiengut in Antike und Mittelalter*. Munich, 147–60.

Patlagean, E. (1977) *Pauvreté économique et pauvreté sociale à Byzance 4e–7e siècles*. La Haye-Paris.

Patlagean, E. (1984) "Les débuts d'une aristocratie byzantine et le témoignage de l'historiographie: Système des noms et liens de parenté aux IXe–Xe siècles," in M. Angold, ed., *The Byzantine Aristocracy IX to XIII Centuries*. BAR International Series 221. Oxford.

Petit, L. (1902) "Vie de Saint Michel Maleinos," *Revue de l'Orient Chrétien* 7, 543–94.

Piault, C., ed. (1985) *Familles et biens en Grèce et à Chypre*. Paris.

Pitsakis, C. G. (1985) *Το κώλυμα γάμου λόγω συγγενείας εβδόμου βαθμού εξ αίματος στο βυζαντινό δίκαιο*. Athens-Komotini.

Pitsakis, C. G. (2006) "Parentés en dehors de la parenté: formes de parenté d'origine extra-législative en droit byzantin et post-byzantin," in A. Bresson, M.-P. Masson, S. Perentidis, and J. Wilgaux, *Parenté et société dans le monde grec de l'Antiquité à l'age moderne*. Paris, 297–325.

Regel, W., E. Kurtz, and B. Korablev (1907) "Actes de Zographou," *VV* 13.

Sathas, K. (1876) Μεσαιωνική Βιβλιοθήκη. Venice.

Saulnier-Thiercelin, F. (1985) "Principes et pratiques du partage des biens. L'exemple crétois," in Piault 1985: 47–64.

Simon, D. (1986) "Erbvertrag und Testament," *ZRVI* 24–5, 291–306.

Simon, D., ed. (1992) *Eherecht und Familiengut in Antike und Mittelalter*. Munich.

Svoronos, N. (1994) *Les novelles des empereurs macédoniens concernant la terre et les stratiotes*. Athens.

Tambiah, S. J. (1989) "Bridewealth and dowry revisited: the position of women in sub-Saharan Africa and North India," *Current Anthropology* 30, 413–35.

Toubert, P. (2004) "La part du grand domaine dans le décollage économique de l'Occident (VIIIe–Xe siècles)," in idem, *L'Europe dans sa première croissance: de Charlemagne à l'an mil*. Paris.

Tourtoglou, M. (1978) "*Τὸ ἀβιωτίκιον. Συμβολὴ εἰς τὸ Βυζαντινὸν κληρονομικὸν δίκαιον*," *Ξένιον. Festschrift für P. J. Zepos*, I. Athens/Freiburg/Cologne, 633–46.

Tourtoglou, M. (2000) "*Παρατηρήσεις ἐπὶ τῆς φερομένης ὡς* 'Νεαρὰς 26' *τοῦ* 'Ανδρονίκου Β' Παλαιολόγου," in idem, Μελετήματα *ἱστορίας ἑλληνικοῦ δικαίου*, III. Athens, 9–31.

Zepos, J., and P. Zepos, eds. (1931) *Jus Graecoromanum*. 8 vols. Athens.

Živojinović, M., V. Kravari, and Ch. Giros (1998) *Actes de Chilandar*, I. Paris.

VI

Law, Justice, and the Byzantine Historians: Ninth to Twelfth Centuries

The Just King

"He was strict about justice, so that all evil men feared him and all good men admired him, for the ones saw him as a just man and hater of evil, while the others saw that he was severe and strict. He himself was not entirely clean of all evil, for, although he kept the faith in God and His most chaste Mother, he also embraced the ancestral heresy of Iconoclasm. . . . Holding fast to justice, and also to his faith in the Mother of God, he would, each week, proceed on horseback . . . towards the holy church of Vlachernai. . . . He made himself available to everyone, but most especially to those unjustly treated, so that they could relate freely the injustices done to them, without being hindered by evil men who feared retribution. Also, by going through the marketplace, he wanted to observe the state of the market, and so he asked about the price of commodities, very insistently, and not of every single commodity but those which are most necessary to life, whether things to eat, drink or wear. . . . Thus did he show great attention and diligence toward public matters, both in the courts of justice (ἐν κριτηρίοις) and, as we have said, on his weekly rides."[1] Such is the beginning of the portrait of the emperor Theophilos, as given by the anonymous Continuator of Theophanes and repeated by John Skylitzes. The emperor's justice in action is illustrated by the following example. The

[1] *Theophanes Continuatus,* Bonn ed. (1838), 86–88 (hereafter *Th Cont*), repeated with variations by John Skylitzes, ed. I. Thurn (Berlin-New York, 1973), 50–51. (Not in Genesios: see 75 ff.) On this kind of imperial portrait, new since the sixth century, see R. Jenkins, "The Classical Background of the *Scriptores post Theophanem,*" *DOP* 8 (1954), 17.

widow of a soldier accused a *strategos* of having confiscated her husband's horse, and thus of having been responsible for her husband's subsequent death in battle. The emperor called in the *strategos,* who claimed that the horse was his own; but when the woman, hidden behind a curtain, came out, the *strategos* was shocked into admitting his actions. He was relieved of his command and exiled, and his property was given to the widow. "Thus all could see the justice of his decisions, and his abhorrence for those who seized the goods of others."[2]

This tenth-century image of justice on horseback, and the stories attendant on it, presents several points of interest. To be noted, first of all, is the surprisingly positive presentation of an iconoclastic emperor by the Continuator of Theophanes. Whereas Theophanes the Confessor did not have one good word to say about Leo III and Constantine V, the Continuator counterbalances the unfortunate iconoclasm of both Leo V and Theophilos with their concern for justice. In the case of Leo V, the judgment is much more ambivalent than it is for Theophilos, but nevertheless the Continuator goes into the trouble of relating approvingly an incident where Leo V gave justice to a man whose wife had been abducted by a rich and powerful gentleman.[3] For the chronicler, in

[2] *Th Cont,* 92–94; Skylitzes, 54–55. On the author of this part of *Th Cont,* see A. P. Kazhdan, "Iz istorii vizantijskoj hronografii X v.," *VizVrem* 19–20 (1961), 77–96. A further example of Theophilos' sense of justice is given by other chroniclers: it concerns the case of the widow who accused Petronas, Theophilos' brother and *droungarios tes vigles,* of having built tall buildings that surrounded and darkened her little house. The emperor sent the quiestor and the census-takers to check on the story. They found the story to be true, and the actions of Petronas unjust. Petronas was beaten in public, and his buildings were razed to the ground: Symeon Magister, 627–28, Georgius Monachus, 793–94.

[3] *Th Cont,* 30–31, 40; Skylitzes, 17–18. Genesios (17–18) gives the incident in greater and interesting detail. He stresses that Leo V, although impious, was most profoundly concerned with the good management of public affairs and was justly severe toward those who wronged others. A man appeared before the emperor and lodged an accusation against a man of senatorial rank who had abducted his wife and was holding her for a long time, without fear. The plaintiff said that he had appealed to the prefect of the city, but to no avail. The emperor ordered the accused man and the prefect to be brought before him, in the palace, at once. He then had the plaintiff repeat the accusations. The defendant admitted the crime, since it was undeniable, and the prefect, too, had to admit that the plaintiff had brought the complaint to him. The emperor immediately relieved the prefect of his duties, since he had proved himself to be negligent in the exercise of justice, and punished "according to the laws the man who had been caught in adultery." The *Scriptor incertus de Leone Armenio,* Bonn ed. (1842), neither

the case of both emperors, the good management of public (civil) affairs is expressed through the administration of justice and the correction of injustice, a virtue sufficiently great to be weighed against the impiety of iconoclasm. Second, the judgments involve the punishment of high officials—a *strategos,* the eparch of Constantinople (in the case of Leo V), the *droungarios tes vigles.* Third, it is evident and important that what we see here is personal justice. Theophilos, and Leo V, take it upon themselves to correct injustice and judge particular cases; justice is available to all, at least in the city of Constantinople or wherever the emperor might find himself. The rules of evidence are those appropriate to such a way of doing business: there is on-the-spot investigation of the facts, the confrontation of witnesses, the confession of the culprit.[4] The chronicler's view of personal justice is nuanced: in the case of Theophilos he is entirely positive, but Leo V is accused of taking over the administration of justice and judging cases on his own.

It is also interesting that laws are hardly mentioned. In the case of abduction judged by Leo V, it is true, the culprit was punished according to the law: τὸν . . . μοιχὸν νόμῳ ἐκδοθῆναι προστέταχεν; mention of the law is already a departure from previous historiography.[5] But as far as Theophilos is concerned, there is no mention that he followed the law in his judgments. Furthermore, Theophilos, the Just Emperor, is not also Theophilos, the Law-Giver.

---

mentions the incident nor praises Leo V for his sense of justice or, indeed, for anything else.

[4] In the case judged by Leo V, Skylitzes mentions that the culprit was forced to confess because there was irrefutable proof of his evildoing, but this is absent in *Th Cont,* and is undoubtedly editorial comment. Skylitzes' account derives from the longer text of Genesios.

[5] Note that the abductor is called an adulterer, which, according to the law of the *Ecloga,* would carry a more certain punishment than would the abduction of a married woman, which the *Ecloga* does not mention. See A. Laiou, "Sex, Consent, and Coercion in Byzantium," in *Consent and Coercion to Sex and Marriage in Ancient and Medieval Societies,* ed. A. Laiou (Washington, D.C., 1993), 113–32. *Th Cont* also mentions the punishment that was prescribed by law and was meted out to Euphemios, who, in Sicily, following the bad example set by the emperor Michael II, abducted a nun to marry her. Michael the Amorian ordered Euphemios to be punished by the slitting of the nose, "according to the letter of the law"; "κελεύει τῷ στρατηγῷ . . . τὴν ῥῖνα τοῦ τετολμηκότος Εὐφημίου ἀποτέμειν κατὰ τὴν τοῦ νόμου ἀκρίβειαν" (*Th Cont,* 81–82). The law invoked is *Ecloga* 17.24.

Now, it appears to be the case that he did not, in fact, legislate much, and the few pieces of legislation that the chroniclers mention as originating from him are somewhat strange.[6] So we cannot make much of the statement that he does not appear in the sources as a Law-Giver, except to note that legislating is not, in this case, an essential part of being a Just King.

There were, however, other emperors of the late ninth and tenth centuries who did legislate quite a lot, and who also codified laws. Among them are Basil I, who issued two law codes, the *Procheiros Nomos* and the *Eisagoge,* and Leo VI, under whose reign the codification of the *Basilics* was completed, and who issued in his own name a large number (113) of Novels. Let us see how the tenth-century historians present Basil I. The main source is the *Vita Basilii,* since Pseudo-Symeon Magister and the Continuator of George the Monk, that is, Symeon the Logothete, say nothing about Basil's legislative activities.[7] In an exceptionally long passage, the author speaks of Basil's unceasing efforts to reform the empire and rule in a way that would be beneficial to all. Basil starts by appointing the best officials; they would have to be uncorrupted, take no bribes, and above all honor justice and equity (ἰσότητα), through the protection of the poor from the exactions of the rich (τῶν πλουτούντων). After a longish discussion of the protection of the poor, "so that each could rest under the shadow of the patrimonial olive tree and fig tree,"[8] and the rescinding of all unjust taxes and exactions, we move to justice. The most detailed discussion concerns the mechanisms of ensuring the proper administration of justice: the appointment of fair and uncorrupt judges, the creation of a court in Chalke, and the distribution of a *per diem* to poor litigants, so that they

[6] On Theophilos' legislation, see below, 161–62.

[7] Indeed, Georgios Monachos is hostile to Basil I: pp. 828, 836 ff; cf. F. Tinnefeld, *Kategorien der Kaiserkritik in der byzantinischen Historiographie* (Munich, 1971), 103–4. On the image of Basil I, see P. A. Agapetos, "῾Η εἰκόνα τοῦ Αὐτοκράτορα Βασιλείου Α᾽ στὴ φιλομακεδονικὴ γραμματεία (867–959)," ῾Ελληνικά 40 (1989), 285–322.

[8] *Th Cont,* 258: Καὶ τὴν ἐλαίαν καὶ τὴν συκῆν τὴν πατρῴαν μηδένα εἶναι τὸν τολμῶντα ὑπὸ τὴν ἑαυτοῦ ποιεῖσθαι ἐξουσίαν, ἀλλ᾽ ἕκαστον ἐν τῇ συνήθει καὶ πατρῴα τούτων σκιᾷ ἀναπαύεσθαι. Cf. Mic. 4:4: But they shall sit every man under his vine and under his fig tree, and none shall make them afraid. Καὶ ἀναπαύσεται ἕκαστος ὑποκάτω ἀμπέλου αὐτοῦ, καὶ ἕκαστος ὑποκάτω συκῆς αὐτοῦ, καὶ οὐκ ἔσται ὁ ἐκφοβῶν, διότι τὸ στόμα Κυρίου παντοκράτορος ἐλάλησε ταῦτα. Note the addition πατρῴα by Theophanes Continuatus.

would not be forced by indigence to leave the city before their cases had been adjudicated. The emperor himself judged cases, primarily dealing with tax collection; in the same spirit, he is said to have undertaken another reform, namely, the simplification of the tax registers, so that all sums were written out in full, not in an abbreviated form, and could thus be read by everyone, including the peasants. We then get to the church, with a discussion of the replacement of Photios by Ignatios, and finally to Basil's legislative work. The statement is terse: he found the civil laws in great confusion, since good and bad laws, currently valid and long disused legislation, were mixed together in the books. He removed the invalid laws and purified the others, making sure that they were divided into chapters, almost like a summary, for easy reference. This statement corresponds most clearly to the *prooimion* of the *Procheiros Nomos,* and must therefore refer to it. Skylitzes adds that Basil I "did not have time to carry out his work, being overtaken by death, so that it was subsequently completed by his son, Leo."[9] The interest of the author of the *Vita Basilii* is clear: justice and equity are of the greatest importance for the well-being of the state and its population (as well as being a cardinal imperial virtue which Basil must be shown to have had).[10] Justice is served by proper administration; the protection of the poor, orphans, and widows; impartial judges; and reform of the law codes. Theophanes Continuatus is a particularly interesting source, since the first five books, including the portrait of Theophilos and the *Vita Basilii,* were either commissioned or written by Constantine VII, and they encapsulate the normative, tenth-century view of justice.[11] That is why I have taken this text as a point of departure in our investigation.

Genesios shows much less of a concern with Basil I's efforts to ensure justice. He mentions Basil's beneficent actions, his alms to the poor, his erection of hospitals and houses for the old and the poor, and his rebuilding of churches. As for justice itself, Genesios gives the curious information that during Lent Basil would go to the *sekreton* after the senators had left the palace

[9] *Th Cont,* 259–63, cf. 346–48; Skylitzes, 133–34. The passage of *Th Cont* is a very succinct and accurate rendering of the spirit of the *prooimia* to the *Epanagoge, Procheiros Nomos,* and *Basilics.* It is not a summary of any of these, but comes closest to the *Procheiros Nomos.*

[10] Jenkins, "Classical," 28.

[11] I. Ševčenko, "Storia letteraria," in *La Civiltà bizantina dal IX al XI secolo* (Bari, 1978), 95 ff, especially 97.

and resolve the controversies, presumably on tax questions. Again, we have here a personal, imperial intervention in the process of (fiscal) justice.[12]

The concern with justice that we find in the *Vita Basilii* and the kind of personal justice I have described is present, to a greater or lesser degree, in all Byzantine historians, at least of the tenth century and later. It is also a more generally medieval idea of justice, which one can find in the description of St. Louis by Joinville, for example. Its presence in the Macedonian period may owe something to Greek and Roman models.[13] The concern with justice is, of course, also something of a commonplace, since justice and equity are cardinal virtues to be expected of all good Byzantine emperors.[14] Indeed, it is no accident that the figure of Theophilos, despite the man's regrettable theological position, came down through the centuries as the personification of the Just King, for the portrait drawn by Theophanes Continuatus is a compelling one.[15] What is interesting to the historian is the content given to the concept of justice and the changes it undergoes over time; but that is only a secondary focus of our inquiry here. Of greater importance to us is the degree to which the concept of justice embraces, or is dependent upon, law in its various aspects: lawgiving, knowledge and application of the law, judging according to formal law as opposed to a general concern for justice. In other words, to what extent are the

[12] Genesios, 126, 128. On Genesios, see C. de Boor, "Zu Genesios," *BZ* 10 (1901), 62–65, who argues that Constantine VII asked Genesios, *patrikios* and *epi tou kanikleiou,* to write a continuation of Theophanes, and *ODB,* where it is stressed that Genesios is not a source of Theophanes Continuatus, but that, on the contrary, he borrowed extensively, especially from the *Vita Basilii.*

[13] Jenkins, "Classical," 25 ff, for Constantine VII's models, which include Isocrates.

[14] A. Kazhdan, "The Social Views of Michael Attaleiates," in A. Kazhdan and S. Franklin, *Studies on Byzantine Literature of the Eleventh and Twelfth Centuries* (Paris, 1984), 24 ff, and M.-T. Fögen, "Gesetz und Gesetzgebung in Byzanz: Versuch einer Funktionsanalyse," *Jus Commune* 14 (1987), 137–58, especially 150 ff.

[15] In the *Timarion,* he appears as one of the three judges of the underworld, along with the eminent figures of Ajax and Minos: P. Magdalino and R. Macrides, "The Fourth Kingdom and the Rhetoric of Hellenism," in *The Perception of the Past in Twelfth Century Europe,* ed. P. Magdalino (London-Rio Grande, 1992), 152–53. I thank the authors for allowing me to consult this article in proof. *Timarione,* ed. R. Romano (Naples, 1974), 76: οἶσθα δὲ ἀκηκοὼς ἐκ τῶν ἱστορουμένων περὶ ἐκείνου, ὡς λίαν δικαιότατος ἦν. Cf. pp. 78–79, reporting that Theophilos was a simple man, but renowned for his fairness, justice, and other virtues.

law and laws instrumental for the concept of justice? The answer to these questions may help interpret the place of law in Byzantine society.

Law and the Laws in the Ninth Century

If we go back to the ninth-century historians, especially Theophanes, we discover an interesting and curious phenomenon.[16] I should make it clear that what follows cannot be an examination of the attitude of Theophanes himself, since much of the *Chronicle* is a compilation from other sources, only some of which are extant. To disengage his own attitude is a different task. The concern here is, rather, an examination of the treatment of law in this important source. With this caveat in mind, the following observations are pertinent. First, there is very little mention of law and legislative activity, and much of what is there is presented in a negative light. The immense legislative activity of Justinian I and his jurists is misunderstood and telescoped: the emperor "renewed all of the ancient laws, making a single book, which he called 'the Novels,' in which he forbade all the governors to buy land, build a house, or inherit from anyone other than their own relatives in the province which they govern."[17] The confusion may be due to a conflation of Malalas' statement regarding the recodification of the ancient laws and the publication of the Novels.[18] The only other "laws" mentioned are those against homosexuals, and the measures against the pagans.[19] Clearly there is no knowledge of the Justinianic corpus, and for the rest, what is of interest to the author is the question of the probity of governors and the salacious business of the persecution of homosex-

[16] The "Short History" of Nikephoros is not very useful for our purposes. See the new edition by C. Mango, *Nikephoros Patriarch of Constantinople, Short History* (Washington, D.C., 1990). Nor is Georgios Hamartolos useful for us.

[17] Theophanes, Bonn ed. (1839–41), 272 (ed. de Boor, I [Leipzig, 1883], 177). The citations will be given in the Bonn edition first, with the de Boor edition in parentheses.

[18] *The Chronicle of John Malalas,* trans. E. Jeffreys, M. Jeffreys, and R. Scott (Melbourne, 1986), 262. The *Chronicon Paschale* (Bonn ed. [1832], 619, 633) is much more accurate than Theophanes, mentioning both the Codex and the Novels.

[19] Theophanes, 272 and 276 (177, 180). Cf. Malalas, Bonn ed. (1831), 436, 449; Prokopios, *Anecdota,* ed. and trans. H. B. Dewing, VI (Cambridge, Mass., 1935), 140 and 194–96. Cf. Leo Grammaticus, Bonn ed. (1842), 128–29, but he does not mention the legislation of Justinian.

uals, reported in greater detail by other sources. It is, perhaps, not irrelevant to note at this point that Justinian I did not fare well in subsequent centuries either. Zonaras, writing in the twelfth century, did not even mention Justinian's legislative work, not because he did not know it, since the twelfth-century intellectuals, and the canonists like Zonaras, were much exercised about juridical science, but presumably because he did not want to temper his criticism of that emperor.[20]

If Justinian's legislative work is treated in a cavalier fashion, that of Leo III and Constantine V is treated not at all: there is no mention of the *Ecloga,* although it would have been possible to mention it in a negative manner. I think that here it is not suppression of a fact that might shed positive light on the iconoclast emperors, but rather a complete lack of interest in the matter.

There are, however, specific pieces of legislation that appear in the *Chronographia.* I should, perhaps, explain here that I have not included in this category various decrees, such as those of the Isaurians on icons, but have limited myself to those pieces of legislation that are called *nomos,* or where the verb *nomothetein* is used. This in itself is a debatable position, since it begs the question of what, in the eyes of the Byzantines, constituted legislation. I have decided, however, since we all have our limitations, that on this matter we must await enlightenment from legal historians. To return to Theophanes, he mentions some pieces of legislation that, in the tenor of the *Chronicle,* are positively viewed. These are the laws issued in support of Christianity or Orthodoxy, such as those of Jovian (363–364) and Theodosius I (379–395).[21] In one case a law is mentioned in what seems like a neutral voice: Theodosius II passed a law forbidding eunuchs to become patricians; although this was occasioned by the case of a particular individual, laws issued in response to specific circumstances are not uncommon, and the reporting of them as such does not necessarily carry a negative implication.[22] Other laws are either plainly illegal or seem peculiar to us today and must have seemed peculiar then: thus, the emperor Valentinian I (364–378), a Western emperor, is credited

[20] On the twelfth century in this regard, see P. Magdalino, "Die Jurisprudenz als Komponente der byzantinischen Gelehrtenkultur des 12. Jahrhunderts," *Cupido Legum,* ed. L. Burgmann, M. Th. Fögen, and A. Schminck (Frankfurt a. M., 1985), 173. On the image of Justinian I in Byzantium, see G. Prinzing, "Das Bild Justinians I in der Überlieferung der Byzantiner vom 7. bis 15. Jahrhundert," *Fontes Minores* 7 (1986), 1–99.

[21] Theophanes, 83, 106 (53–54, 68).

[22] Ibid., 148 (96); cf. Malalas, 361.

with "an illegal law," permitting a man to take two wives, and issued because he wanted to marry again even though his first wife was still living.[23] As for irrational or strange laws, we can list the following, all issued by non-Byzantines: the Persian king Kavadh I (488–496, 498–531) ordered that "women be held in common." During the reign of Tiberius I (578–582), the Persian king Chosroes I (531–578/9), smarting under a defeat, passed a law that no Persian king should ever go to battle again; and under the reign of Anastasios, Priskos, on an embassy to the Chagan of the Avars, told him the cautionary tale of Sesostris, king of Egypt, who had forced defeated kings to draw a chariot but who, on being reminded of the wheel of fortune, "legislated" that never again would kings be forced to draw a chariot.[24] Theophanes, of course, did not always understand his sources quite accurately. Thus, Prokopios[25] writes that Kavadh issued a law ordering Persians to have communal intercourse with their women (ἐπὶ κοινὰ ταῖς γυναιξὶ μίγνυσθαι), which has a somewhat different flavor from Theophanes' κοινὰς τὰς γυναῖκας ἐνομοθέτησεν ἔχειν. Theophanes' report that "no Persian king should ever go into battle again" is different from Evagrios' statement that Chosroes ordered that "no king of the Persians should henceforth lead an army *against the Romans*,"[26] and very different from Theophylact Simocatta's report that the law was that "never again should a Persian king trade with the monies earmarked for war."[27] Finally, for what it is worth, it might be noted here that in the *Chronicle* of Theophanes the terms "law" or "legislating" are used mostly for the period through the reign of Justinian, and almost never thereafter.

On the other hand, the term "paranomia," strictly translated as "illegality," is quite frequent. Its meaning is not, in most cases, "breaking the law of the land," that is, the civil law. What *paranomia* means in the *Chronicle* is either deviation from whatever the orthodox doctrine might be, or irregularities in one's private life, or the imposition of excessive taxation.[28] In the case of the

[23] Theophanes, 88 (56).

[24] Ibid., 190, 386, 422 (123, 251, 273–74).

[25] Prokopios, *De Bello Persico* 1.5. On Kavadh I's heresy regarding communal access to women, an anti-noble measure, see P. Crone, "Kavad's Heresy and Mazdak's Revolt," *Iran* 29 (1991), 21–42. I owe this reference to Victoria Erhart.

[26] Evagrios, *Historia Ecclesiastica* V, 15.

[27] *Theophylacti Simocattae Historiarum libri octo,* Bonn ed. (1834), 134, 145.

[28] Theophanes, 167 (108: Valentinian's adultery); 248 (161: Anastasios' monophysitism); 626 (406), 634 (412), 636 (413), 680 (440) (Leo III and Constantine V, for obvious reasons); 742 ff, 745, 750 (478 ff, 480, 483) (Nikephoros I's deposition of

Isaurians, the emphasis is on their religious "illegality"; but the insistence, sometimes so tendentious as to be irrational, on their unjust taxation shows that the concept of illegality here has two aspects, religion and fiscality.[29]

The case of the emperor Nikephoros I is, of course, well known. Theophanes labels him "paranomotatos" and calls him the worst of all previous emperors by reason of his greed, licentiousness, and barbaric savagery, even though the chronicler declines to give details.[30] This is the opposite of a Mirror of Princes, and the most detailed denunciation comes in the recital of the emperor's ten misdeeds, which, it will be remembered, are mostly economic and fiscal measures. True, Theophanes does not use the term "law" or "legislation," and so I should perhaps not count these misdeeds as pieces of legislation. But the verb "he ordered" suggests that Theophanes did consider these edicts to be the equivalent of law. In any case, Nikephoros is also accused of having created an "unjust court" in Magnaura, again in connection with fiscal measures.[31] My purpose here is not to discuss the probity or otherwise of these measures, but rather to insist on two points: first, that the term *paranomia* in the *Chronographia* very rarely has the meaning of breaking a specific law and means more generally an unjust polity or one which goes against church doctrine; and second, that when laws or lawgiving appear in the *Chronographia,* the context is most frequently negative.

It may be objected that the *Chronicle* of Theophanes is a particular kind of source. Theophanes wrote in a genre that would not require him to discuss legislation, in positive terms or otherwise. With regard to recent events, in particular, his purpose had more to do with religion than with anything else. That

Irene, his sexual life, and his efforts to collect revenues). There is a useful commentary on the iconoclastic period in I. Rochow, *Byzanz im 8. Jahrhundert in der Sicht des Theophanes* (Berlin, 1991).

[29] Theophanes, 631, 634–35, 685 (410, 412, 443). In another ninth-century source, Georgios Hamartolos, "νόμος" is divine law, broken by Leo III's attack on icons. "Παρανομία" in the case of the iconoclastic emperors refers to their religious position: C. de Boor, *Georgius Monachus Chronicon,* II (Leipzig, 1904 and 1978), 748, 750, 755, 777, 789.

[30] Theophanes, 745, 765 (480, 491–92).

[31] Ibid., 742 ff, 755 (478, 486 ff): he heard personally the complaints of the poor against the rich. W. Treadgold, *The Byzantine Revival* (Stanford, 1988), 130–31, assumes that the courts must have heard complaints against rich tax evaders, whose poorer neighbors had to pay their taxes. Cf. Tinnefeld, *Kaiserkritik,* 74–75.

is true. It is also true that ninth-century historiography, as a genre, is primarily concerned with politics, wars, and marvelous occurrences; the law being none of these, its place in such sources is limited.[32] Investigation of other historians will show that some of the attitudes found in Theophanes are not specific to him, or to the ninth century, but have a more general tenor.

Attitude Toward Legislation

Strikingly, a negative reporting of legislation continues in the historians and chroniclers of the tenth century, even though the genre changes and becomes that of biography, where both justice and legislation might have been treated. In these sources the mention of specific laws is relatively rare; it is, therefore, all the more surprising to encounter here pieces of legislation that are either laws of which the author disapproves, or laws which are, on the face of it, unimportant, strange, or ridiculous. This is to be set against the fact that, as we shall see, laws which in our own eyes, at least, were much more important, receive only scant mention, and against the further fact, already established, that major efforts of codification or legislation are mentioned almost in passing. As examples of this treatment of lawgiving one may take the case of Theo-

[32] For comparison with other contemporary sources, one may turn to the patriarch Nikephoros. The only two passages in his *Short History* that are even remotely connected with legal matters are the following, for neither of which is there a known source. The first refers to the death and funeral procession of the empress Eudokia, Heraclius' wife. While the procession was going through the city, a barbarian servant girl carelessly spat from a window, and the saliva fell on the empress' corpse. The people seized the girl and burned her, "in the manner of barbarians" (βαρβαρικῷ νόμῳ χρησάμενοι), and tried to inflict the same punishment on her mistress who, wisely, fled. The other reference is, perhaps, more interesting. It concerns a widow who had a land dispute with a rich man named Boutelinos or Bizoulinos; as the dispute became more violent, Bizoulinos' slaves killed one of the widow's sons. She then came to Constantinople and confronted Heraclius, demanding justice. He ordered her to go away and seek justice at a time of his choosing (ἐπεξιέναι . . . τὰ τῆς δίκης ὁπηνίκα ἄν αὐτῷ δεδογμένα εἴη). She left, lamenting that she did not receive justice (μὴ δίκης τυχόν). But a while later, Heraclius saw Bizoulinos in the Hippodrome. He had the man arrested, summoned the woman, made a closer investigation of the murder, and ordered that Bizoulinos be killed by his slaves, and that the slaves also be killed. Here, once again, we have a personal rendering of justice by the emperor, with no visible appeal to the law, no courts and no judges: Mango, *Nikephoros,* 40, 42.

philos' reported legislation. This paragon of justice produced two identifiable pieces of legislation according to the chronicles: one is the visibly strange law forbidding all Romans to wear their hair long. The Continuator of Theophanes is clearly sarcastic about this measure: he attributes it to Theophilos' own sparse hair and claims that, according to the new law, if anyone were found to have long hair, he would be forced, by the use of the whip, "to return to the virtue of the Roman ancestors."[33] The other piece of legislation, the order that the "Persians" (Khurramites) who had come over to Byzantium in 834 should marry Byzantine women, is not discussed in a visibly negative light, although the entire episode is presented in an ambivalent way.[34]

One is further struck by the fact that historians could choose, out of an entire body of legislative activity, to single out those pieces of legislation of which they disapproved. A case in point is Leo VI. He had, in the course of his reign, completed the codification of the *Basilics,* and issued a large body of "new" legislation. This may have been ineffective, as has been argued, and even the *Basilics* was perhaps too unwieldy a code; nevertheless, it remains noteworthy that of all this vast outpouring of ink, very few traces remain in the historians. At the end of the eleventh century, Michael Attaleiates mentioned a Novel of Leo VI on the subject of the dissolution of a marriage when one of the partners becomes demented (Novel 111), but he mentioned it only to point out that it had fallen into oblivion until it was revived by Nikephoros Botaneiates. Otherwise, the historians closer to Leo VI's time, that is, the Continuator of Theophanes (Pseudo-Symeon) and Skylitzes after him, saw fit to mention only one piece of legislation, the πονηρὸς νόμος, which the emperor contemplated, and which would have permitted a fourth marriage.[35] This negative reporting of legislation suggests a number of things. First, it does make one realize that law and lawgiving were not regarded by the chroniclers and historians, at least of the ninth and tenth centuries, as the paramount avenues through which justice could be exercised. Second, is it possible that we have here an

[33] *Th Cont,* 107.

[34] Ibid., 111–12. Genesios, 55 ff, does not mention this edict, although he does mention the marriages. On the Khurramites (mostly Kurds), see Treadgold, *Byzantine Revival*, 282 ff.

[35] *Th Cont,* 371; Symeon Magister, 709; cf. Skylitzes, 185, who adds that the emperor was hindered by the patriarch Euthymios from carrying this out. Cf. Georgios Monachos, 866; N. Oikonomides, "Leo VI's Legislation of 907 Forbidding Fourth Marriages," *DOP* 30 (1976), 177.

even more negative perception of the law, at least of new legislation (as opposed to codification), as an expression of imperial meddling, of the exercise of imperial authoritarianism or arbitrariness, as a way of disturbing rather than regulating society? This is particularly striking in the case of laws regarding economic and fiscal measures—the most frequently reported and most often criticized.

In this vein, but in a somewhat different tone, it can come as no surprise that bad legislation, or rather, legislation the chronicler considers bad, becomes an element of *Kaiserkritik.* Thus, Skylitzes' general dislike and condemnation of Nikephoros Phokas is expressed, in part, through his condemnation of that emperor's legislation. His source for this reign (Source A) has been recognized as one hostile to Phokas and particularly favorable to the church, with which Phokas had his problems.[36] One of the broad criticisms levied against Phokas is his stinginess, and indeed his many fiscal exactions, through which he financed his wars; all of this is contrasted with the generosity of John Tzimiskes. Within that general critical assessment comes the list of bad laws issued by Phokas: his Novel placing limits on church property, "because," he said, "the bishops spent badly the money of the rich and thus impoverished the soldiers"; a law according to which no bishop could be appointed or promoted without the emperor's consent; a law regarding the goods of a bishop who dies; his scheme to pass a law making martyrs out of the soldiers who died in battle; a law making his own coinage worth more than that of other emperors.[37] The two outstanding elements of criticism concern fiscal exactions and an arbitrary tampering with the privileges of the church, through the means of legislation. Interestingly, there is also an element of criticism regarding arbitrary attitude toward existing laws: thus, in the matter of the coins, Nikephoros' action went against earlier laws, which had given equal value to all coin issues bearing the imperial portrait, *unless they were of different weight.* Similarly, Skylitzes

[36] Kazhdan, "Iz istorii vizantijskoj," 126–28.

[37] Skylitzes, 274–75; Zonaras, Bonn ed. (1897), III, 504–7, is much more detailed on the matters concerning the church and on the fiscal exactions, particularly as regards the properties of the soldiers. Cf. F. Dölger and P. Wirth, *Regesten der Kaiserurkunden des oströmischen Reiches* (Munich-Berlin, 1924–), no. 699 and 702: Zepos, *Jus,* I, 299 ff. The justification mentioned in Skylitzes is absent in the Novel. Cf. M. Hendy, *Studies in the Byzantine Monetary Economy, c. 300–1450* (London, 1985), 507–8. On the criticisms levied against Nikephoros Phokas, see Tinnefeld, *Kaiserkritik,* 108–21, especially 111.

(presumably following his source) says that Nikephoros proposed the invalidation of the law forbidding the marriage of people connected with the bond of God-parenthood, "since this was a law of Copronymus, and should not be observed."[38] Leo the Deacon, on the other hand, with a much more positive attitude toward Phokas, says that he "judged according to the laws and legislated soundly" (ἐννομώτατα δικάζων καὶ νομοθετῶν ἀσφαλῶς); a favorable assessment, to be sure, and relatively unusual in passing positive judgment through a mention of legislation, yet, interestingly, a general assessment, which does not mention specific laws.[39]

That is not to say that all mention of legislation is negative; on the contrary, we have already seen that Basil I's legislative activity was positively viewed. This activity, however, was presented in a general way, not by reference to specific pieces of legislation, of which, it is true, Basil did not issue very many. And, it will be remembered, what was praised was Basil's reform of the laws, to make them easier to use and more appropriate to changed conditions. Justice, therefore, was served through good administrative and fiscal practice, which means through good personnel. The reform of the laws is a good, general, and time-honored attribute of the emperor as well. It was left to the biographer of Constantine VII to become more specific. The first reference to specific laws enacted by an emperor, and used by the historian as an integral and positive part of his assessment of the reign, comes in the account of the reign of Constantine VII.

"And He Even Issued A Law"

The interplay between justice, a virtue much prized in Byzantium and considered essential for the survival of the state, and law and legislation is a rather complex business. Considering what has been said up to now in connection with the scant mention of legislation by the ninth- and tenth-century sources, one is led to the conclusion that Leo VI, for example, was very much a man of his times when he enacted the kind of legislation that Fögen has called highly

[38] Skylitzes, 261; the law is *Ecloga,* 2.2. Cf. *Bas,* 28.5.15; *Proc.Nom,* 7.28; *Epan.,* 7.28.

[39] Leo the Deacon, Bonn ed. (1828), 89. He may have been using a chronicle of the Phokas family. (See *ODB,* s.v. Leo the Deacon.)

symbolic.[40] For the tenth-century historians, justice was paramount and law did not seem nearly as important. Certainly, the emperor cannot have shared this attitude consciously, otherwise his promulgation of all that legislation would have been the action of a paranoid man, but if his legislation seems less a body of decrees to be followed exactly and more a codification of general precepts, then in this he was in tune with the times.

For modern economic and social historians, the Macedonian period is marked by the intensive legislation that surrounds the question of landed property, particularly the right of preemption and the relative rights of poor and powerful on the land and within the village communities. Here, at least, it looks very much as though the emperors, starting with Romanos Lekapenos, exercised a concerted effort to influence economic and social developments through the means of legislation; in the process, they invoked the principles of justice and redressing injustice. I quote from the most eloquent of these texts, the great Novel of Basil II of 996: "What we say below will make it clear that Our Majesty does not overturn the prescription of time either aimlessly or carelessly, but because Our Majesty is merciful to the poor, and it looks after the public (good), that it be properly constituted, and it embraces what is just and it seeks to correct the terrible ill of greed. . . . For we have seen with our own eyes the greed and injustice done daily to the poor. . . . How, then, can we not seek to hinder them (the powerful), and how can we not give back to the poor what is just in regard to the things which were wrongly and for greed taken away from them?"[41] The Macedonian emperors, then, invoked principles of justice to explain and justify their legislation, through which they hoped to change specific practices. The way this legislation is reported by the historians would be a good test case of the relative weight given by them to law and justice.

We have already seen that the *Vita Basilii* discusses at some length and in most laudatory tones that emperor's concern for the poor, especially the poor of the countryside, and his administrative reforms designed to have open tax collection, openly arrived at. The question here is not whether our sources find the principles invoked by the Macedonian emperors laudable, but rather how

[40] Marie Theres Fögen has argued that the legislation of Leo VI has as a primary function the projection of certain ideas of peace, justice, God, love, unity—that it is, in fact, an example of symbolic legislation: "Gesetz und Gesetzgebung," 150 ff.

[41] Zepos, *Jus*, I, 263–64.

they deal with the laws on preemption (*protimesis*). As might be expected from what has already been said, the reporting is rather minimal. One of the most important pieces of legislation, we know, was the Novel of 934 of Romanos Lekapenos, issued as a result of developments attendant on the great famine of 927–928.[42] Theophanes Continuatus (Pseudo-Symeon) mentions the great famine as having been much more severe than any that had occurred before; he does tell of measures taken by Romanos Lekapenos to alleviate the effects of the famine, "measures worthy of his . . . charitable nature." All the measures he details, however, are just that: charity, shown to the poor (πτωχοί, πένητες) and the monks of Constantinople; there is no word on the Novel and the structural ills it sought to address in the countryside.[43]

The measures taken by Constantine VII on behalf of the poor are, however, reported more fully, and with some attention to the legislation. There are two passages in Theophanes Continuatus (this is the part possibly written by Theodore Daphnopates) that discuss the emperor's measures.[44] Both passages praise, in different ways, Constantine's concern for justice. The first and somewhat longer passage starts with praise of the emperor's beneficial measures toward the *penetes,* who "had suffered many injustices and losses during the reign of his father-in-law, Romanos, at the hands of *strategoi,* and protonotaries, and soldiers and cavalry men." The measures reported involve the appointment of virtuous administrators. There was, in other words, according to this text, a change in administrative personnel, not in procedures and, in this passage, not in legislation. These virtuous men were sent to the Asia Minor themes with the task of lightening (κουφίσαι) the burden of the unjustified fiscal exactions that had been levied on the poor. Whether the term κουφίζω is here used in a technical or a general sense, the point is that, once again, according to this passage, reform and the redress of justice passes through the appointment of

[42] P. Lemerle, *The Agrarian History of Byzantium from the Origins to the Twelfth Century* (Galway, 1979), 94 ff.

[43] *Th Cont,* 417–18; Symeon Magister, 743–44; Georgios Monachos, 909–10. Skylitzes, 225, has a much shorter mention of the emperor's good works, with no specific mention of the poor. Only Skylitzes makes a passing mention to Romanos' legislation (340).

[44] Theodore Daphnopates was a jurist, at least if we can judge from his curriculum vitae, which includes the offices of *protasekretis* and prefect of Constantinople. Cf. J. Darrouzès and L. G. Westerink, *Théodore Daphnopatès, Correspondance* (Paris, 1978), 1–4.

just administrators.[45] It may be noted specifically that even Constantine VII's measures to reform judicial procedure and stop the venality of provincial judges are not mentioned.

The other pertinent passage is, in a way, related to the one just mentioned, and does refer to a specific law. Before looking at it, let us see the context in its entirety. We are at the beginning of Constantine VII's independent reign, and the chronicler is relating a number of measures and virtues of the emperor. In sequence, these are the appointment of Basil the Parakoimomenos (Basil Lekapenos), an exchange of prisoners between Byzantines and Arabs, the passage about relief to the poor discussed above, the appointment of Theophilos, "a learned man, with knowledge of the civil laws," as quaistor and his replacement as eparch of Constantinople by Constantine the *protospatharios,* the appointment of Polyeuktos as patriarch, the appointment of Joseph (Bringas) as *sakellarios* and then *droungarios* of the fleet. We then move to the emperor's cultural achievements, which, says the narrator, he will only mention briefly. We start with a discussion of his interest in educational reform, which in a short while "enriched and embellished the Roman state with wisdom." We proceed to his restoration of imperial vestments and the beautification of Boukoleon, as well as the freeing of prisoners. Then comes the pertinent passage: "He honored virtue and knowledge more than had any other emperor, ever; whenever he found anyone who was knowledgeable and had a natural bent and talent for the laws, he promoted him. . . . And one could see lawfulness and fair justice (δικαιοδοσίαν καὶ εὐνομίαν) in all things, for the emperor himself . . . embraced it. *The emperor even issued a law* (καὶ νόμον ὁ αὐτοκράτωρ ἐξέθετο)." There follows a summary of the Novel of 947, in which the emphasis is on the injustices done to the poor by the greed of the powerful who seized or bought or acquired through donation the lands of the poor. The emperor is

[45] *Th Cont,* 443–44. Dölger (*Regesten,* no. 656), thinks that the passage refers to the implementation of the Novel of 947, but there is no reason to think so. This is a measure against greedy administrators. It should be noted that Skylitzes, in a very negative passage, accuses Constantine VII of making civil and military appointments not with regard to merit, but indiscriminately and even venially; thus, says Skylitzes, many vulgar people (πάντα τινὰ χυδαῖον) reached high civil office, which may be the real complaint of Skylitzes' source: Skylitzes 237, 13–20. Tinnefeld considers that the virtue most praised here is *philanthropia* (*Kaiserkritik,* 106–7, and cf. 95).

praised for the punishment inflicted on the greedy powerful.[46] The summary is, in fact, quite accurate, although it insists on the greed of the powerful, and gives a *very* brief and necessarily incomplete account of the conditions under which property illegally acquired would return to the poor. The accuracy suggests that the author was well acquainted with the text. The law, here, certainly is one of the avenues through which justice is attained. Readers of the *Peira* will also recognize the spirit of the phrase "and he also published—issued—a law," a phrase similar to those which the compiler uses when he comes to Eustathios' legal arguments after having presented his rhetorical ones.[47] The conclusion must be the same for both cases: the law is only one, and perhaps not the most important element either in the effort to promote justice or in a court of law.

The passage of Theophanes Continuatus (or Daphnopates) discussed above continues with a description of Constantine's courts, to return to the principle of personal justice, exercised by the emperor in court. He himself, it is said, sat along with the judges and, having a sharp mind, he could see things that others could not; he could distinguish falsehood from a smidgen of truth contained in an argument, and he could detect false documents. Thus, he opposed the deceitful arguments of the lawyers of the defendants; as a result, the defendants learned to be fearful, and "to judge themselves in the case of those whom they had wronged."[48]

Of the other Macedonian social legislation, we have seen that Skylitzes' source mentions the measures of Nikephoros II against the expansion of church property, and the rescinding of that law by Tzimiskes.[49] The only other

[46] *Th Cont,* 447–48. Dölger, Regesten , no. 656. Zepos, *Jus,* I, 214–17. Skylitzes, 340. The chronicle included in Vatic. Gr. 163, also of the second half of the tenth century, and not dependent on Theophanes Continuatus, mentions the Novel of Constantine VII without qualifying it as "law," merely introducing it by the word προσέταξε: A. Markopoulos, "Le témoignage du Vaticanus Gr. 163 pour la période entre 945 et 963," Σύμμεικτα 3 (1979), 93.

[47] καὶ ἐποίησεν ὑπόμνημα πάγκαλόν τι καὶ χάριεν, βάθος ἔχον νοημάτων καὶ χάριν λόγων ἡδέων καὶ σχημάτων, καὶ ἑρμηνείας νόμων οὐκ ὀλίγων. Cf. D. Simon, Ἡ εὕρεση τοῦ δικαίου στὸ ἀνώτατο βυζαντινὸ δικαστήριο, trans. I. M. Konidaris (Athens, 1982), 15–16.

[48] *Th Cont,* 448. It is to be noted that in the court of Constantine VII the accused were assumed to have been guilty.

[49] Dölger, *Regesten,* 699; Cf. Lemerle, *Agrarian History,* 109–10 note 2.

clear mention of imperial legislation in this connection is the mention of the Novel of Basil II on *protimesis* by Skylitzes, which I mention here for the sake of completeness, although it takes us out of the tenth century. It is a short item, coming right after a discussion of the confiscation of the property of Eustathios Maleinos: "The emperor also wrote a law, forbidding the powerful to increase (their properties) in the village community. This had also been done by Constantine Porphyrogennetos, the emperor's grandfather, and by Romanos, Constantine's father-in-law."[50] Skylitzes is also the first source to mention Basil's *allelengyon,* which he describes as an "irrational burden," eventually rescinded by Romanos Argyros.[51]

If one were to summarize the basic points about the law as it appears in the historians of the tenth century, one would observe the following. Interest in justice is paramount; justice means, among other things, equitable treatment and support for the poor against the rich; it also is very closely connected with fiscality: the imposition of new or heavy taxes is unjust, the rescinding of taxes is an act of justice. The chroniclers are interested in the administration of justice, and that is both an institutional matter and a matter of personnel. The idea of personal justice, exercised by the emperor himself, is reflected also in the fact that the appointment of good, incorruptible judges, and good, uncorrupted administrators of the fiscal system is given great importance in the sources. Justice is served less visibly by legislation. Here we can observe a difference between Theophanes and the tenth-century historians. In the tenth century, mention of specific laws, and knowledge of them, is more frequent than is the case with Theophanes. There is a surprisingly frequent reporting of "bad" laws, which, as I have argued, may suggest a certain suspicion of legislative activity, which in these cases appears as serving specific and not very laudable interests of the lawgiver. The case of the laws on *protimesis* bears out a number of these conclusions. The Continuator of Theophanes knew the legislation, at least as is evident by the relatively accurate summaries of those laws which are mentioned, that is, the Novel of Constantine VII and the law of Nikephoros II on church property. At the same time, that some of these laws are mentioned

[50] Skylitzes, 340. Cf. Lemerle, *Agrarian History,* 103 note 2.

[51] Skylitzes, 347; cf. 365, 375. Zonaras, III, 561 says, with regard to the *allelengyon,* that Basil II wanted his own will to prevail, and not to follow the laws made by the legislators (νομοθέται). Thus, his criticism of the *allelengyon* is part of his general criticism of imperial authoritarianism.

at all seems to me to owe a good deal to the fact that they spoke to the very things the Byzantines held dear, that is, justice and the punishment of greed. It is noteworthy that the passage on Constantine VII lays great stress both on the administration of justice and on appointing people learned in the law. It is exactly the same thing that the *Vita Basilii* tells us about Basil I's polity.

So, in the tenth-century view, legislation and the laws are not really instrumental for the concept of justice. Why is this so? It is so partly because of the genre. The tenth-century sources are either annalistic (Continuator of George the Monk) or historical biographies and *enkomia* (Theophanes Continuatus, *Vita Basilii,* Leo the Deacon). The historical biographies are by definition interested in the personal attributes of emperors, and beholden to antique models. They are, further, beholden to Menander Rhetor, whose model for an imperial encomium mandates that one show the emperor appointing good officials and uncorrupt judges. One must also show the emperor's interest in just and light taxation: ἐρεῖς ἔτι καὶ περὶ τῶν φόρων οὓς ἐπιτάττει. The emperor, too, must be shown to be a just lawgiver: ἐρεῖς τι καὶ περὶ νομοθεσίας, ὅτι νομοθετεῖ τὰ δίκαια, καὶ τοὺς μὲν ἀδίκους τῶν νόμων διαγράφει, δικαίους δὲ αὐτὸς θεσπίζει.[52] The *Vita Basilii* follows this model almost exactly. Yet there are degrees of freedom permitted by the canon. "You must say something about legislation," says Menander, but that allows, even in his model, a discussion of specific laws. If our tenth-century sources refuse to discuss laws at any length, that is a choice they make. So one must turn to explanations that transcend the question of genre. One is the general (Roman) principle incorporated in legislation, that justice is the constant desire to give everyone that to which he is entitled: Δικαιοσύνη ἐστὶ σταθηρὰ καὶ διηνεκὴς βούλησις ἑκάστῳ τὸ ἴδιον ἀπονέμουσα δίκαιον.[53] It would follow that the administration of justice, and especially fiscal justice, is of the first order of importance. Hence, the interest of our sources in good administration is realistic. This makes sense in a tax-gathering society, where the relationship of the state to its subjects is heavily mediated through fiscality. It is also realistic in a state where a great deal of judicial authority, as well as legislative authority, is ultimately vested

[52] Menander Rhetor, Περὶ ᾽Επιδεικτικῶν, in D. A. Russell and N. G. Wilson, *Menander Rhetor* (Oxford, 1981), 84 ff, especially 88–90.

[53] *Bas* II.1.10 = D.I.1.10. On this, see D. Simon, "Princeps legibus solutus," in *Gedächtnisschrift für Wolfgang Kunkel,* ed. D. Nörr and D. Simon (Frankfurt a. M., 1984), 456.

in the emperor; what remains in the end, what is important from the beginning, is less *what* he legislates, since that can be altered, and more *how* he administers justice and the state. Thus, administration and fiscal administration in particular may indeed have had more to do with justice that did the laws. The historical sources of the tenth century project the realities of that particular society: establishing the principles of good government, justice, and polity is important; particular pieces of legislation are less so.

Two further points should be made here. The stress on personal justice is, perhaps, fully to be expected in a society in which the emperor is God's vicar on earth, and where he functions as "nomos empsychos." Within such an ideology, a connection between justice and specific laws does not arise, for the emperor is the source of both. As for the connection between fiscality and justice, Dieter Simon has suggested that the emphasis on fiscal justice may indicate that the state played a rather limited administrative role so that state power became particularly visible on the issue of taxation, in which we do know that the state had a pervading interest. In such a case, the emphasis on fiscal justice would occur precisely because fiscality was the one institution through which imperial intervention in society took place, and where, therefore, the emperor's justice (or lack of it) could be put into practice. This intriguing suggestion runs contrary to our usual view of the Byzantine state. It is noteworthy that a recent study has shown precisely such an absence of state regulation of society, in a specific context, and surprisingly, in the tenth century.[54] The matter will certainly profit from further investigation.

Finally, one should stress the fact of a significant interdependence between the sources that formulate tenth-century ideas about justice and the law. The portrait of Theophilos gives an image whose elements are repeated in other sources. The portrait of Basil I seems to have codified something of a canon as far as justice is concerned. Theodore Daphnopates patterned his own discussion of Constantine VII on the *Vita Basilii,* so much so that one wonders whether the discussion of the Novel of 947 is introduced to provide a parallel to Constantine's mention of Basil I's codification of the laws. Daphnopates returns to the model, as best he can, in his portrait of Romanos II, during whose

[54] G. Dagron, "'Ainsi rien n'échappera à la réglementation': État, Église, corporations, confréries: à propos des inhumations à Constantinople (IVe–Xe siècle)," in *Hommes et richesses dans l'Empire byzantin,* ed. V. Kravari, J. Lefort, and C. Morrisson, vol. 2 (VIIIe-XVe siècle) (Paris, 1991), 155–82, especially 171, 182.

reign he wrote and who had appointed him prefect of Constantinople. The first reported measures of Romanos II were connected with the appointment of good officers. Among them was Sissinios, appointed prefect just before Daphnopates. Sissinios, says the historian, "was an eminent prefect through equity and justice, and he adorned the holy palace."[55] The next sentence—about Sisinios judging cases and opposing the deceitful arguments of the defendants and their lawyers, so that everyone "judged themselves in the case of those whom they had wronged"—almost exactly repeats the passage about Constantine VII, except that the text does not make sense in the case of Sissinios because some words were omitted.[56]

Thus, there are intimate interconnections between the first, anonymous Continuator of Theophanes (portrait of Theophilos), and, much more so, between the *Vita Basilii* and the last part of the Continuation of Theophanes. Is this mere coincidence, the imitation of a successful model, or the imprint of an individual? The emperor Constantine VII is known to have commissioned the first four books of Theophanes Continuatus (including the portrait of Theophilos). Until recently, it was thought that he himself wrote the *Vita Basilii.*[57] If that were the case, one could argue for a Constantinian influence on the discussion of justice and the concept of justice and the laws dominating the tenth-century historiography. The model would have been Constantine's *Vita Basilii;* the ideas expressed in it would have been incorporated in the portrait of Theophilos, and explicitly followed in the portraits of Constantine VII and Romanos II. Ihor Ševčenko has argued that Constantine VII did not, in fact, write the *Vita Basilii* .[58] His argumentation, however, does not seem to preclude the possibility that the author's words expressed the emperor's ideas, in which case Constantine's influence would remain significant. What is, in any case, incontrovertible, is the close dependence of Daphnopates (assuming that he was the author of Book VI, and thus of the lives of Constantine VII and Romanos II) on the *Vita Basilii.*

[55] *Th Cont,* 470: Cf. *exactly* the same phrase to describe Constantine VII's prefect, Constantine the protospatharios: *ibid.,* 444. The connection between these passages has not been noticed by Ja. N. Ljubarskij, *Prodalzatelj Feofana* (St. Petersburg, 1992).

[56] *Th Cont* 470, and 448.

[57] P. Lemerle, *Byzantine Humanism: The First Phase* (Canberra, 1986), 318.

[58] I. Ševčenko, "Re-Reading Constantine Porphyrogenitus," in J. Shephard and S. Franklin, *Byzantine Diplomacy* (London, 1992), 167–95.

The Eleventh and Twelfth Centuries

The historians of the eleventh and twelfth centuries present a particular interest to us for many reasons, one of which is immediately evident. A considerable number of them were jurists or had a close connection with the law. Of the major historians who lived in this period, Michael Psellos, John Skylitzes, Michael Attaleiates, John Zonaras, and Niketas Choniates all share this trait, while John Kinnamos, as imperial secretary, must at least have had firsthand knowledge of the legislation. The first three also wrote juridical treatises, which presupposes a greater or lesser degree of familiarity with the body of written law. Only Anna Komnene, her husband, Nikephoros Bryennios, and Constantine Manasses fall outside this category. This prosopographical fact must be kept in mind when we look at their historical works.

Their interest in the law and their attitude to it could almost be plotted along a continuum which does not, interestingly enough, necessarily coincide with their presumed knowledge of the law. At one extreme I would place Michael Psellos, at the other, Michael Attaleiates.

Michael Psellos is a curious case. Here I will deal exclusively with the *Chronographia,* since other papers in this volume discuss his other writings, equally curious, as far as I can see. Although, as is well known, Psellos had been a judge, although he wrote a synopsis of the laws in verse for his pupil, Michael VII, in his historical work he is singularly uninterested in the laws or in legislation. It is, of course, true that the emperors whose reigns he discusses, with the exception of Basil II, did not issue many or memorable pieces of legislation; the period is rather sleepy as far as legislative activity is concerned.[59] Nevertheless, it is striking that of all past and present legislation, Psellos should mention only the law on trigamy.[60] More striking is the cavalier attitude he has toward the importance—or rather the unimportance—of being acquainted with the laws. His portrait of Michael VII, the most sympathetic portrait of them all, mentions a number of virtues, which do not quite form the regulation imperial portrait: his generosity, leniency, wisdom, love of books and learning; his virtue in things sexual; his physical aspect, which had something of the old man in it (a hagiographic trait); his modesty; his love for his

[59] For exceptions, see Dölger, *Regesten,* 863 (the reestablishment of a law school in Constantinople by Constantine IX), 944 (Isaac Komnenos), 1004, 1047 (Michael VII).

[60] M. Psellos, *Chronographie,* trans. E. Renauld (Paris, 1967), I, 127, 143; II, 46.

wife and brothers; and the fact (fictitious) that he arrested the decline of the empire.[61] A sense of justice does not find its way into this roster of virtues, except by the back door: "He had not studied the laws very deeply, but in judging he could list many of them, not in the letter but in the spirit (or, not from the books but by heart").[62] This is not so bad, considering other emperors. Basil II, according to Psellos, always governed by the unwritten laws in his soul; Michael IV was ignorant of the laws and canons, but when a decision depended on logical reasoning, he could outargue the lawyers because of his native intelligence.[63] The moral is clear: one does not need to know the laws to pronounce judgment wisely. Occasionally, a lawyer's pride raises its professional head: Isaac I also was ignorant of the laws; he wisely let the judges decide on the merits of a case and write up the text of the decision, so that he would not commit errors of terminology; but he then pretended the decision was his own, and always added or subtracted something in the final decision—here Psellos is somewhat ironic.[64] The one emperor who, according to Psellos, took an interest in the law was Constantine X. During his reign, we are told, the laws returned once more to the palace, and unjust decisions were torn up, and all that he decided either had the force of law or was more just than the law. He judged without prejudice as to persons but only according to their deeds. Not only that, but in order to test his son Michael's talent for being emperor he had him judge a case, and when he saw that Michael judged "according to the laws" (ἐννόμως), he crowned him emperor.[65] But then, Psellos' view of the law is not that of a modern lawyer: what matters is less jurisprudence and more rhetoric, that is, the ability to embellish legal texts.[66]

Perhaps all of this is in the same general tenor as what we have already seen: the general attitude that law is less important than justice, and that justice does not necessarily depend on laws. It is less expected, coming from the pen of a lawyer. Furthermore, his idea of justice does not come through with anything like the clarity it has in the tenth-century historians. It is true that when

[61] Psellos, II, 172–78.

[62] Ibid., II, 175.

[63] Ibid., I, 18, 56 ff.

[64] Ibid., II, 113.

[65] Ibid., II, 146, 148. Nikephoros Bryennios accepts and copies this positive assessment: *Nicéphore Bryennios, Histoire,* ed. and trans. P. Gautier (Brussels, 1975), 83–84.

[66] Psellos, II, 58–59 on Constantine Leichoudes.

he discusses Constantine X he uses traditional terms: the emperor's first concern was to establish equity and justice, and to punish greed. He heard cases with equanimity and fairness, so that injustice was exposed. And this is followed by the statement that the rural population could now profit from his *philanthropia*.[67] These are all very proper and traditional sentiments. In a way, it is also proper and traditional for Psellos to castigate Romanos III for "breaking the law" in his vast expenditures for his church—although the lawbreaking is less obvious than the idea that he was guilty of "injustice."[68]

However, these pious sentiments are not as persuasive as others, less conventional but more deeply felt. Thus, the condemnation of Constantine IX for having managed improperly the two things that assure Byzantine hegemony, namely, dignities and money, is an eloquent condemnation not of an unjust or inequitable distribution of these resources, but rather of the fact that they were becoming available to the wrong social class.[69] Furthermore, there is an extraordinary and ambiguous passage about what passed for justice in Constantine IX's time. Psellos praises Constantine's generosity and sympathetic attitude toward the plight of others, and illustrates it by the following case. A rich man owed taxes to the fisc, which was being inexorable. He implored the emperor to hear his case personally, rather than submit to the normal tribunal. The emperor agreed, there was a trial, and the man begged that he be held responsible only to the extent of his own property, not that of his children. The emperor took pity on him and his exalted family, and promised him the remission of two-thirds of his debt. As the man thanked him profusely, Constantine added, "and I remit the other third as well."[70] One would like to think that this is a spoof, and a silent condemnation of Constantine's concept of justice. It is, however, rather disturbing that this is the most vivid judicial episode reported by Psellos, and that it is the exact opposite of the sort of justice lauded by the various authors of Theophanes Continuatus, or other tenth-century historians, such as Leo the Deacon.

[67] Ibid., II, 139, 146. Cf. II, 50–51, on the historian as a judge who must give everyone his due, with equanimity and with no regard for personal likes and dislikes.

[68] Ibid., I, 42–43; cf. I, 25 ff, on Constantine VIII, who was generous but unjustly so, giving more to those closest to him.

[69] Ibid., I, 132; cf. P. Lemerle, *Cinq études sur le onzième siècle byzantin* (Paris, 1977), 289–90.

[70] Psellos, II, 55–56.

Michael Attaleiates, writing late in the twelfth century, is at the other end of the continuum from Psellos. His history, remarkable in many ways, is interesting for us in two respects.[71] First, because for him justice and following the laws was a measure of the probity of various emperors, something which it really was not for Psellos, or, indeed, for the twelfth-century historians, with the possible exception of Zonaras. Second, because in his relation of the reign of his hero, Nikephoros III Botaneiates, he gave a detailed account of some at least of that emperor's legislation, a feat remarkable in itself since the legislation was not earthshaking—although, it must be admitted, more considerable in quantity than that of his immediate predecessors.

Let us take briefly the first point. "Eunomia," good order and justice, is a prime virtue in an emperor, and for Attaleiates it means taking care of the weak, giving justice to those unjustly treated, and giving justice according to the laws. Thus, the description of the reign of Michael V Kalaphates begins with a statement about that emperor's love of justice and good order, expressed by the fact that he brought people (Dalassenos, Maniakes) back from exile and relieved his many relatives from office.[72] Justice and fiscality go together in Attaleiates, as they have done since the ninth century, even though here they have a more specific social context, identified by Kazhdan as the protection of private property as opposed to that of the state.[73] But Attaleiates strongly implies an additional, and very important, point: justice must be given according to the laws, and when it is not, that is unjust. He is, thus, arguing for proper court procedure and for proper regard for the laws, so that the idea of personal justice is tempered, although it does not entirely disappear, as we shall see. His condemnation of some eleventh-century emperors centers around these points. Monomachos, about whose extravagance Psellos had something to say, collected taxes harshly and unexpectedly, especially from those who were well-off; and he judged unfairly in the process. Constantine X came to the throne promising truth and justice and indeed, says Attaleiates, he devoted himself to increasing the public revenues and judging the cases of individuals, while neglecting military affairs.[74] But his polity was not good. Not only did he, like

[71] *Michaelis Attaliotae Historia,* Bonn ed. (1853). See, on him, A. Kazhdan, "The Social Views of Michael Attaleiates," in Kazhdan–Franklin, *Studies*, 23–86.

[72] Attaleiates, 11–12.

[73] Kazhdan-Franklin, *Studies,* 41–43.

[74] There may be an echo of Menander's injunction to the encomiast to say that the emperor raised taxes for the army: Menander Rhetor, 89–90.

Monomachos, exact a lot of taxes, but, and here Attaleiates waxes eloquent, he judged in an authoritarian way (κατ' ἐξουσίαν). His courts were busy, among other things, with fiscal cases; the arguments of the accusers were full of sophistry, the decisions were not consistent with the laws (οὐ νομικῶς), many people were judged unjustly. It is a grave indictment, to be contrasted with Psellos' pronouncement about law residing in the palace under Constantine X.[75]

It may be of interest to note here that in his evaluation of various emperors, Attaleiates often employs a language and style reminiscent of a judge. In the case of Constantine X, he mentions both his good and his bad qualities, and concludes "but the bad part won by many votes." About Isaac Komnenos, he reports different assessments of his actions by different people: "I accept both opinions . . . and do not decide against either of them as being inferior."[76]

The point at issue, in the case of Isaac Komnenos, has to do with his confiscation of the property of individuals, despite the fact that they held them in full ownership by imperial chrysobull and, primarily, with the large-scale confiscation of monastic lands. Attaleiates suggests that this was both illegal and an act of impiety. However, and this is interesting, he argues that it had two beneficial results: it forced the monks to return to their primary occupation, and it was a great relief to the ἀγρογείτονες of the monks who had suffered from the monasteries' greed. He also tells how the monasteries had increased their properties: the monks would bring their neighbors to court and, because of their wealth, would be able to prevail and take over the property of the poor.[77] This is undoubtedly an oblique reference to the application (or

[75] Attaleiates, 50–51, 70–71, and especially 76–77; Psellos, II, 139. Skylitzes attributes the decline of the Roman state to the profligacy and pretentiousness of Monomachos (ed. Thurn, 476). Skylitzes Continuatus shares the negative assessment of Constantine X, adding that he judged cases himself, and not equitably, but rather according to the status of the individual, being particularly harsh toward the *dynatoi:* Eu. Tsolakes, Ἡ συνέχεια τῆς χρονογραφίας τοῦ Ἰωάννου Σκυλίτση (Ioannes Skylitses Continuatus) (Thessaloniki, 1968), 112. Note that judging cases oneself, often a positive attribute, is a negative one here. Cf. also this chronicler's indictment of Nikephoritzes, on similar grounds: 156.

[76] Attaleiates, 76, 70.

[77] Ibid., 61–62. Cf. Skylitzes Continuatus, 104. I'm afraid I cannot agree with Kazhdan's statement that there is a difference, even a subtle one, between the assessment of Isaac's reign by Skylitzes Continuatus and Attaleiates. I find Attaleiates much less critical of Isaac's policy than does Kazhdan, and I find no difference in the two accounts except for those imposed by the brevity of the text of Skylitzes Continuatus,

nonapplication) of the laws on *protimesis,* and a candid assessment of what went on in provincial courts. It is interesting that Attaleiates, while recognizing the illegality of Isaac's measures, considers that they redress a greater injustice.

Justice, then, remains a major virtue in an emperor and a great benefit to the state. Indeed, for Attaleiates more than for any other historian, the visible decline of the empire in the late eleventh century, just before the accession of Botaneiates, was due to injustice and lack of piety, which led to injustice. Greed, no regard for the law, the illegality of the actions of rulers, the oppression of the subjects brought forth divine wrath. God's anger is expressed through the victories of the pagans, "for it is said that the pagans honor justice and keep their ancestral customs unchanged."[78] If fiscality and justice go together here as in earlier chronicles, the role of justice and injustice is highlighted.[79]

In the assessment of the reign of Nikephoros Botaneiates, justice and regard for the law play a major role, and one quite different from anything we have seen up to this point. Botaneiates' generosity is praised in commonplace terms, to be sure: he gave justice to widows and orphans (as Alexios I was to do according to his daughter, Anna)—a shorthand expression for the traditional *philanthropia* of the emperor.[80] But it was far more than commonplace, since Botaneiates was indeed exceedingly generous, distributing largess, lands, and offices with a free hand.[81] He also judged cases himself—another attribute

and one phrase, in which Skylitzes Continuatus says, "It would have been a good thing if this had been achieved not only with regard to monastic property but also for all ecclesiastical property" (Kazhdan-Franklin, *Studies*, 33–34). Nor do I see that Skylitzes Continuatus "completely reverses A.'s judgment of Isaac's confiscations." The judgment seems to me to be exactly the same (see Attaleiates 61, 69–70, and Sk. Cont. 109–10). Kazhdan's argument about Attaleiates' overwhelming concern with private property is weakened if my interpretation is correct. Another favorable assessment of Isaac's policy may be found in Psellos, II, 119–21.

[78] Attaleiates, 194–97, 211–12. The second passage is particularly connected with Michael VII's lack of charity toward the population of Constantinople in the face of famine and severe cold weather.

[79] See P. Magdalino, "Aspects of Twelfth-Century Kaiserkritik," 331–32, and "Jurisprudenz," 176, in idem, *Tradition and Transformation in Medieval Byzantium* (London, 1991).

[80] Attaleiates, 312; cf. *Annae Comnenae Porphyrogenitae Alexias,* ed. A. Reifferscheid, II (Leipzig, 1884), 255.

[81] On Attaleiates, see the references in Kazhdan-Franklin, *Studies,* 29–30; cf. Sk. Cont. 179.

which, we have seen, has had a positive value since the tenth century, illustrating as it does the imperial concern for justice.[82] But, and here is the difference from other historians, Attaleiates also insists not only on the emperor's general concern for justice but on a concern for justice that passes through the laws. Botaneiates, who had come to the throne as a result of rebellion, and whose third marriage to Maria of Alania was branded by contemporaries (but not by Attaleiates) as trigamy and adultery, according to his historian studied the law books day and night (possibly a dig at Michael VII).[83] And he addressed himself to legislation, reforming those laws that needed reform and thus ending the confusion created by poor laws. This is the most important difference between Attaleiates' view of justice and that of his predecessors. For him, legislation is an important means of ordering society, and justice is achieved not only by a personally good emperor, not only by the reform of the courts, but also by the reform of the laws.

He then proceeds to list some of Botaneiates' laws: he reformed "in a more majestic and just manner" Novel 111 of Leo VI on divorce in case of madness of one of the spouses, a law which had fallen into disuse. Apparently, his reforms had to do with the length of time the sane spouse had to wait before obtaining a divorce.[84]

Attaleiates mentions a law, passed by the emperor and approved by the senate and the people, which sought to mitigate some of the problems brought about by the frequent change of emperors. Namely, Attaleiates says (and so does the Novel) that each time there was a change of emperor the imperial servants, that is, those officials closest to the emperor, saw their properties confiscated and often also found themselves exiled. Attaleiates (and the Novel) suggest that this would be acceptable only after an examination of the officials' polity, to see whether it was lawful; and that otherwise their properties and persons should remain inviolate. I suspect that this law had a particular object: the emperor might well be concerned about the eventual fate of two of his favorite servants, Borilos and Germanos, who were hated by the senate. But he gave his concern the force of a general law, much praised by the senate, ac-

[82] Attaleiates, 312.

[83] On his marriage, see A. Laiou, "Imperial Marriages and their Critics in the Eleventh Century: The Case of Skylitzes," *DOP* 46 (1992), 173–75.

[84] Attaleiates, 312. The Novel is not extant, but it is mentioned by Balsamon in Rhalles-Potles, Σύνταγμα τῶν θείων καὶ ἱερῶν κανόνων, I (Athens, 1852), who says that it simply repeated the Novel of Leo VI.

cording to Attaleiates, because its members could see that this measure could be generally beneficial (to themselves as well, one suspects).[85]

The law that Attaleiates seems to be most proud of is one mandating a 30-day delay between an imperial decision to inflict capital punishment (either death or mutilation) and its execution. This is, again, not a new law but a restoration of a law of Theodosius I.[86] The description by Attaleiates has many points of interest: the circumstances of the promulgation of the law of Theodosius are detailed (as they are not in the Novel itself); Botaneiates' *philanthropia* is praised several times, as it is in the text of the Novel; a justification of the delay is given, which looks like a summary of the lengthy and semiphilosophical justification given in the text of the Novel.[87] But by far the most important statement, for our purposes, is Attaleiates' statement regarding the emperor's purpose, to wit, that the emperor did not want simply to exercise his personal *philanthropia* "making it a private, not a public virtue, for his own glorification," but rather he wanted all subsequent emperors to observe this law so that all would profit from it; and that is why he issued a Novel. It seems to me that the law was occasioned by the shocking blinding and near-execution of Romanos Diogenes; but this is the first and probably the only time in the Byzantine historiography from the ninth to the twelfth centuries that we see so clearly expressed a view about what the laws can do that justice cannot. Attaleiates is as interested as anyone in praising the personal *philanthropia* and justice of his hero; but he is the only one who transcends the praise of a private kind of justice and argues that legislation transforms a man's sense of justice into mandated behavior, which then becomes independent of the quirks of individual emperors.[88] But then, Attaleiates also has a unique concept of the source

[85] Attaleiates, 316–18. Cf. Sk. Cont., 185, and Zepos, *Jus,* I, 285–87. Attaleiates also says that Botaneiates restored the property of many and recalled them from exile. A general effort toward reconciliation?

[86] *CTh* IX.40.13.

[87] Attaleiates, 313–15, and Zepos, *Jus,* I, 283–85. The description of this Novel and the one regarding imperial officials is such as to suggest that they were drafted by Attaleiates himself. On this Novel, see L. Burgmann, "A Law for Emperors: Observations on a Chrysobull of Nikephoros III Botaneiates," to be published in the *Acts of the 26th Byzantine Symposium,* St. Andrews. On Attaleiates' high regard for the law, see Magdalino, "Jurisprudenz," 176.

[88] Of the rest of Botaneiates' legislation, Attaleiates does not mention his Novel on betrothal, or his injunction that every four months the patriarch remind the emperor of the exiles: Zepos, *Jus,* I, 288–90, 287–88.

of legislative authority. In his discussion of two of Botaneiates' laws, he says that the law was read to the senate (and, in one case, to the townspeople as well); in the first case, the senate "found the law much to its liking and assented to it" (καὶ σύμψηφον ἔσχεν αὐτὴν καὶ λίαν εὐάρεστον).[89] In the other case, the citizens (οἱ τῆς πολιτείας) agreed and approved the law (δεξάμενοι καὶ ἀποδεξάμενοι).[90] The Novels themselves, which are extant, do not mention the senate's assent or approval, indeed, in one case it is the patriarch and the synod who act together with the emperor;[91] nevertheless, what is important here is the historian's assumption that legislative authority, while vested in the emperor, is also shared by the senate. I leave aside the practical consideration that Botaneiates had come to the throne because of the actions of the senate, the synod, and the people (παρὰ πάσης τῆς συγκλήτου βουλῆς καὶ τῆς συνόδου καὶ τῶν δημοτικῶν), and insist instead on the theoretical issue inherent in Attaleiates' statements.[92]

Having started with the portrait of Theophilos, the Just King, by the anonymous Continuator of Theophanes, it is, perhaps, appropriate to end with the portrait of Nikephoros Botaneiates, the Just Lawgiver, by Michael Attaleiates: personal justice as contrasted with legal justice. This is the closest we will get to the lawgiver, and it is the most positive statement made by a Byzantine historian about the importance of law for society. The twelfth-century historians include, as I have already indicated, a number of jurists who were, however, not terribly interested in preserving the legislative work of the emperors for posterity, nor in truth did they necessarily believe in the great power of the laws. They were all concerned about justice—and Choniates is very bitter about the lack of probity and competence of judges and the disregard for the law among his contemporaries.[93] But from the considerable legislative activity of the Komnenian emperors, he chooses to preserve at great length only a Novel of Andronikos I on shipwreck and salvage, arguing, interestingly enough, that this piece of legislation would have been sufficient to preserve the good memory of that emperor.[94] For the rest, his *History* is full of complaints

[89] Attaleiates, 314.

[90] Ibid., 318.

[91] Zepos, *Jus,* I, 287. On this, see J. Gouillard, "Un chrysobulle de Nicéphore Botaneiatès à souscription synodale," *Byzantion* 29–30 (1959–60), 29–41.

[92] Attaleiates, 298.

[93] See, for example, Choniates, ed. J. L. van Dieten (Berlin-New York, 1975), 438 ff, 334–37, 456.

[94] Ibid., 326–29.

about the ἀνομία, the lawlessness of the age.[95] True, Choniates is a historian of the decline. But Anna Komnene, while praising her father's *comme-il-faut* concern for justice to widows and orphans, and the proper administration and government of her grandmother, Anna Dalassene, when she was acting as regent, has nothing to say about Alexios' laws or about laws, period.[96] Kinnamos, on the other hand, does present an evaluation of Manuel I, which includes some of his legislative work, specifically, a law freeing men unjustly reduced to servitude and legislation regulating procedural questions about the functioning of the courts during holy days. Kinnamos includes among these pieces of legislation the privilege granted by Manuel to the clergy of Constantinople.[97] This is not, in my view, legislation properly speaking; but it is utterly appropriate that, in the twelfth century, when government by chrysobull was becoming common, Kinnamos should consider privileges on the same footing as legislation.

One other point is worth raising in this connection. The period of the Komnenoi was one in which emperors, patriarchs, jurists, and canonists had a great interest in the law, and when considerable legislation was issued. However, I have the strong impression that for the administration of justice the laws were less important than imperial privileges or the imposition of imperial will. Part of the process is reflected in the historians already in the eleventh century and in the first half of the twelfth. In the tenth century, the historians had stressed imperial impartiality (real or fictitious) in the administration of justice. In the eleventh century, leniency acquires much greater weight. Psellos mentioned it as a virtue in Monomachos with his tongue in his cheek. But even Attaleiates saw leniency—that is, the nonapplication of the laws, or even of judicial decisions—as a great virtue, and its absence as a shortcoming.[98] Alex-

[95] Ibid., 494–95, under Alexios III.

[96] *Alexias* iii.6–7 (vol. I, 108–113).

[97] Kinnamos, Bonn ed. (1836), 275–77; Dölger, *Regesten,* nos. 1476, 1466, 1419. Zepos, *Jus,* I, 397–402, 381–85 and N. Svoronos, "Les privilèges de l'église à l'époque des Comnènes: un rescrit inédit de Manuel ler Comnène," *TM* 1 (1965), 375–76.

[98] Attaleiates, 206–7: Roussel de Bailleul is convicted and sentenced to death, but his sentence is commuted. On pp. 152–53, Romanos IV is severely castigated for punishing with nose-slitting (instead of a monetary fine) a soldier who stole the donkey of a Turk. The Farmer's Law (II.6) punishes the thief of an ox or a donkey with whipping, the restoration of the fruits of the animal's work, and a fine of double the value of the animal. For an example of the tenth-century attitude, see Leo the Deacon on Nikephoros Phokas: some complained that Phokas was too strict a man, who expected

ios I made a career of overturning the sentences of rich or powerful individuals, according to the admiring Anna Komnene and Nikephoros Bryennios.[99] I do not wish to demean the importance of leniency: I simply wish to point out that it is a short step from leniency, especially toward people in high places, to government and justice outside the law, despite all the legislation of the Komnenian period.

In our examination of the historical sources of the ninth through eleventh centuries, we have seen a number of developments. One element that remains constant, although with different meanings over time, is the connection between fiscality and justice. The element where we see the greatest differentiation is the concept of law as a constituent element of justice, justice being a routine virtue, highly and visibly prized at least since the tenth century. We have seen in the ninth century a very nebulous concept of civil law. In the tenth century, justice emerges as a major concern: it means impartiality, good government, protection of the poor, and, to some extent—and it is a limited extent—good laws as well. Personal justice is the paramount good, but governing according to law is also given its day in court, despite a lingering suspicion of new legislation. Significantly, the laws that are specifically and positively mentioned are those that show the emperor's concern for his subjects, especially for those who are weak; Leo VI, not concerned with them, gets short shrift. In the eleventh century, the story becomes more complex. If for Psellos the law is of secondary importance, for Attaleiates it becomes a means of ordering society. There is, undoubtedly, an element of professionalism here: this jurist thinks that justice can be guaranteed by good laws. There is also a reflection of eleventh-century realities. If in the relatively undifferentiated society of the tenth century contemporaries could suggest that society could be mediated with principles of justice, fair dealing, equity, and support for the poor and the weak, in the eleventh century much had changed. Paul Lemerle has shown the emergence of a more differentiated society, and one where different social groups were claiming their due. The aristocracy had emerged as a powerful class with self-awareness, and the urban population was coming into its own, even in political terms.[100] Such a society could, I think, no longer be mediated

---

everyone to be virtuous and who was very strict about the letter of the law. He thus was implacable in his punishment; but for Leo the Deacon this was a virtue: 89–90.

[99] See, for example, P. Gautier, *Nicéphore Bryennios, Histoire* (Brussels, 1975), 193 ff; *Alexias,* I, 50 ff, 191 ff; II, 160–65, 236–37, 300–303.

[100] Lemerle, *Cinq Etudes,* 272 ff.

by principles of justice alone; the institutionalization of justice through the laws—predictable, binding, repeatable, limiting imperial authoritarianism—would have been more consonant with the needs of that society. Hence the air of modernity around some of Attaleiates' ideas, especially his confidence in the laws as guarantors of justice. The modernity in his concept of the relationship between law and justice is connected with, or stems from, his idea that legislative authority is shared between the emperor and the senate. If this interpretation of his thinking is correct, then we have a profound modification of the Byzantine view of the emperor as "nomos empsychos." The professionalism of the jurist, also an element in Attaleiates, goes hand in hand with these developments, which, if pursued, would have meant both a different system of government and a different, and quite modern, attitude toward the law.[101] But the development was cut short by the feudal authoritarianism of the twelfth century and by the principle of governing by privilege couched as law.

This study must end on a note of caution. What has been presented here is only an analysis of more or less explicit notions regarding law and justice, and that is quite inadequate, although I hope not misleading. In fact, all of the historians I have discussed, some more than others, are of a complexity far greater than can be uncovered by an investigation such as the one undertaken here. There is much hidden below the surface, and considerable knowledge of the laws lurks in the pages of Skylitzes, Attaleiates, Zonaras, and even Psellos. They all discuss tense, ambivalent, or difficult situations with legal overtones, and it is the close study of their treatment of such situations that is the most rewarding, for only then can one see how much our historians really knew about the law and how much they really cared.[102] In other words, what the

[101] I consider the eleventh century to constitute an exception to the statements made by Marie Theres Fögen in "Legislation in Byzantium: A Political and a Bureaucratic Technique" (in this volume), since I think that in this period, while there was no political revolution, there were changes of sufficient magnitude to bring about a different attitude toward law and lawgiving. In another study, I have tried to show that in the historical sources of the eleventh century there is an implicit criticism of the idea that the emperors were above the laws (Laiou, "Imperial Marriages," 175–76). Thus, we seem to be dealing with a general, if half-formed, eleventh-century phenomenon and not with a peculiarity of Attaleiates, although his statements are by far the most conscious and the most interesting.

[102] One case in point is problematic marriages, which many of our historians treat. See, for example, Theophanes, 523–24, 686, 718. On some of these, see Laiou, "Impe-

historians wanted to tell us about law and justice is interesting and important; what is hidden in indirect statements, in the manner of reporting unlawful or illegal actions, is just as important. There, in my opinion, it is possible to establish a much greater differentiation between the various historians. This is potentially a very rich field, well worth cultivating.

rial Marriages," and *Mariage, amour et parenté à Byzance aux XIe—XIIIe siècles* (Paris, 1992), chap. 1.

VII

Peasant Rebellion:
Notes on its Vocabulary and Typology

In the history of the Byzantine Empire, rebellions, power contests, unrests and uprisings are far from unusual. Jean Claude Cheynet has studied the profile of rebellions and rebels for the period 963–1204, identifying 223 uprisings, and discussing their traits.[1] These were, however, rebellions of the aristocracy or the army. The typology and vocabulary of peasant rebellion remains to be established.

Not that the phenomenon is widespread. Full-fledged peasant rebellions are few, indeed barely visible before the 1260's. Some earlier rebellions may have commanded peasant support, but, as Cheynet has observed, they were under the leadership or to the benefit of the aristocracy; or they were movements primarily of the army. Peasant uprisings did occur, in a circumscribed area (Asia Minor) and a brief period of time, the late 13th century. These also are few in number, but they do permit the possibility of establishing a typology and a portrait of the peasant rebel. Several questions may be posed. What were the circumstances of peasant uprisings? Were they uprisings or mere acts of opposition, and what is the dynamic between the two? Who were the leaders, the followers of peasant uprisings? What was the course of uprisings? What was the vocabulary used by the sources, all of them external? And, finally, why the concentration in the late medieval period?

Let me start with a description of what is probably the best-documented act of peasant opposition to the central government.[2] This is the rebellion of the inhabitants of Trikokkia, to the south-east of Nicaea, shortly after the blinding of the legitimate emperor, John IV Laskaris, by

[1] Jean-Claude Cheynet, *Pouvoir et contestations à Byzance (963–1210)* (Paris, 1990), esp. 13–14.

[2] G. Georgiadis-Arnakis, Οἱ πρῶτοι Ὀθωμανοί (Athens, 1947), 39–45; I. Sykoutris, "Περὶ τὸ σχίσμα τῶν Ἀρσενιατῶν", *Hellenika*, II, 1929, 291, 293–4; H. Ahrweiler, "L'histoire et la géographie de la région de Smyrne entre les deux occupations turques (1081–1317) particulièrement au XIIIe siècle", *Travaux et Mémoires* 1 (1965), 9; cf. M. Bartusis, *The Late Byzantine Army; Arms and Society 1204–1453* (Philadelphia, 1992), 54ff.

the co-Emperor Michael VIII Palaiologos in December 1261. The rebellion began in 1262 as an act of support for the child-emperor; there was a pretender although, according to our major source, he was manufactured by the rebels themselves: a blind child was found and proclaimed to be John IV; he was dressed in appropriate clothing, and proclaimed emperor. The rebels swore loyalty to him, in consequence of oaths sworn to his "father" (the Emperor Theodore II), and they also claimed to be avenging a victim of injustice.[3] Michael VIII, fearing that the rebellion would spread, "collected his entire army, and sent it to fight this civil war."[4] At this point, the rebels proclaimed the rebellion openly, swearing "to be victorious or for all of them to die."

There follows a detailed description of the war, which "lasted a long time" (263). The rebels were armed with bows and arrows, while their opponents had swords and clubs. The rebels also had the advantage of a mountainous terrain which they knew well. They moved to fortified places and high rocks, where, hiding among the trees, they shot arrows at the soldiers who could not see them to fight back. The wives and children of the rebels were sent deep into the interior of this mountainous area, and were surrounded by a circle made of wagons and palissades which kept the soldiers out. Only sometimes were the soldiers victorious against isolated groups of rebels. Seeing that they could not win in the field, even though they were "many against a few and townsmen against country bumpkins," "πλειόνων ὀλίγοι καὶ ἄγροικοι ἀστικῶν",[5] the leaders of the imperial forces took other measures. Pachymeres says that the rebels could not agree to peace, because they remained firm in their oaths; they also were suspicious of each other, and feared death if they surrendered. The army leaders made promises to some of the rebels: they tried to persuade them that the young boy was a false pretender, offering to take them to the real John's prison; they promised amnesty and money, indeed sent money to some. Eventually, "the majority" of the rebels were won over, "especially the notables" (καὶ μᾶλλον τοὺς ἐπιδήλους: 265). Some preferred death by battle to "the punishment they would receive if they were to submit and be betrayed" (265). It must have been they who made an incoherent argument to each other.

[3] Pachymeres, *Georges Pachymérès Relations Historiques,* A. FAILLER, ed. (Paris, 1984), I: 259ff. Cf. *MPG* 140, 956 (effort to implicate the Patriarch Arsenios).

[4] Pachymeres (Failler), I: 261: ἅπαν τὸ στρατιωτικὸν ἐν ταὐτῷ συλλέξας ἀπέστελλε πολέμους πολεμήσοντας ἐμφυλίους.

[5] Pachymeres (Failler), I: 261; cf. 263: ὀλίγοι . . . πρὸς πλείους, . . . καὶ ἀγρόται.

It's incoherent both because Pachymeres, having said that the majority of the rebels had made secret pacts, now says that those who argued against abandoning the young rebel had the upper hand. It is also incoherent in its argumentation. Those who did not want to abandon the pretender argued that if, after having put their lives on the line, they were to abandon him, they would not be able to respond convincingly to accusations of betrayal (against the pretender): they could counter neither that they acted under duress, nor that they suffered without having chosen to, nor that they were taken in by a false pretender. Who knows, they said, whether he is false, and whether we would not be shown another, not John IV himself, but a real fake? In the end, according to Pachymeres, they decided not to give up the "stranger" ("ξένος"), who "would be slaughtered for trusting in them" (267). A compromise with the imperial forces allowed the youth to flee to the Turks. The imperial army then made peace with those with whom they had secret agreements, "while towards the others they behaved cruelly and imposed insupportable exactions, more than they could bear (προσετίμων ζημίαις οὐ φορηταῖς)" (267). But the Emperor stopped short of banishment, for fear of emptying the defences of the eastern frontiers against the Turks.

The punishment was fiscal: the inhabitants of the entire areas of Bucellarii, Maryandinon and Paphlagonia, i.e. the areas to the east of Trikokkia, were subjected to heavy and frequent taxes. These were peasant landholders, as is proven by Pachymeres' statement that they got the necessary things from farming; they had no cash, since the taxes, collected in cash, left them with nothing for themselves. Nor were they good soldiers. They responded by fleeing to the Turks, so that the area was abandoned by its inhabitants and soon was conquered. Later, Michael VIII put the blame on bad and greedy commanders and on the Unionist (and Arsenite?) clergy, mentioning in particular poor and vagabond monks.[6]

Some salient traits of this uprising can be discerned, as can the bias of the sources. First of all, there is no stated leader. But it may be deduced that the "notables", among the first to abandon the cause, were also among the leaders, as is common in medieval uprisings. The identity or even the social status of the notables is quite unknown. Had they belonged to the aristocracy, one assumes that they would have been

[6] Pachymeres (Failler), I: 291–3, 405, 633–5.

named. They probably were the richer and more important peasants.[7] The Patriarch Arsenios was accused of complicity, and while he denied it, complicity is probable. He was accused of *lèse majesté*, and Pachymeres obliquely suggests that he may have helped the rebels.[8] It is also undoubtedly true that the rulers in Constantinople needed to have a highly-placed leader, namely Arsenios, to blame.

The presence of a pretender is a typical trait as well, to be repeated soon thereafter. Atypical is the statement that the rebel leaders *consciously* created a pretender. The statement is suspect although, surprisingly, a manufactured pretender will be tolerated by the government later in the 13th century. The statement is also subverted by other points of Pachymeres' narrative: the offer of the army leaders to take rebels to visit the true Emperor, to check out the impersonation; and the rebels' argument that even seeing a boy presented to them as John Laskaris would not prove the pretender was a fake. The point to retain is the absence of an identifiable leader, and so the absence of an identifiable villain: proof of the grass-roots support for the rebellion, or an unwillingness of the source to name the leaders of such an uprising?

At the same time, the figure of the blind boy of humble origins is haunting, especially given the concern the rebels showed for him even at the moment of defeat. Was he, perhaps, rather than a mere pretender, a symbolic figure such as popular rebellions sometimes have – someone with the charisma of youth, innocence, poverty, who by these very traits is expected to lead to victory?

This possibility gains force when one considers the ostensible reasons for the rebellion. The rebels were peasants who were skilled in the art of war with certain weapons, especially the bow: these were the peasant-soldiers of Asia Minor, cultivated by the Laskarids, especially Theodore II. Significantly, Pachymeres stresses the oath they had taken to Theodore, not to his son, the blinded John IV. They rebelled for a reason which is somewhat counterintuitive in the case of peasants: an oath to a dead Emperor, to support his son. The entire affair is ringed with oaths and with the fear of anathema if the oaths are broken; thus the rebels' loyalty to the dead monarch and his young son acquires an aspect and a sanction which, though not apocalyptic, are certainly heavily tinged with religion and a religious vocabulary.

[7] Cf. the term εὐϋποληπτότεροι τῶν παροίκων: F. Miklosich-J. Müller, *Acta et Diplomata Graeca Medii Aevi*, VI (Athens, 1871), 42.

[8] *MPG* 140, 956; Pachymeres (Failler), I: 295.

The role of oaths is of primary importance in this rebellion. Probably in fact, and certainly in the way it is presented by Pachymeres, the "rebels" were carrying out a duty imposed on them by oath. The rise to power of Michael VIII is surrounded by a multitude of oaths, breach of oaths, and innovation in the oath sworn. Theodore II Laskaris had composed a testament by which he exacted φρικώδεις ὁρκωμοσίας, terrible oaths of loyalty to his young son and to the regent, George Mouzalon. The oaths were sworn by all, great and small, twice: once when the testament was made, and once after Theodore's death. According to the Patriarch Arsenios, the oath was to John IV, and was sworn by all: the clergy, the senate, and the entire army and people (καὶ ἅπας στρατὸς καὶ ἅπας δῆμος).[9] Later, Mouzalon exacted even more terrible oaths from the aristocracy and the army (τοῦ δήμου τοῦ στρατιωτικοῦ), by which they invoked curses upon themselves and their families if they broke their loyalty.[10] Still later, after Mouzalon's assassination, and at the moment of the coronation of Michael VIII and John IV as co-Emperors (1258), numerous oaths were exchanged: the aristocracy promised loyalty and submission (δουλεύσοντες) to both; and they promised further to aid the co-Emperor against whom the other might conspire; there were reciprocal oaths of the two Emperors; and there was an extraordinary oath, taken by all the inhabitants, that they would rise (ὁρμᾶν) against whichever Emperor conspired against the other.[11] In his testament, the Patriarch Arsenios mentions a plethora of oaths, and quotes the details of this last oath, sworn by Michael

[9] Nicephorus Gregoras, *Nicephori Gregorae Byzantina Historia*, L. Schopen, ed. (Bonn, 1829), I, 63; George Akropolites, *Georgii Acropolitae Opera*, ed. A. Heisenberg, new ed. by P. Wirth, I (1903, 1978), 154; *MPG* 140, 949. Cf. O. Lampsides, *'Εφραὶμ τοῦ Αἰνίου χρονογραφία* (Athens, 1985), II: 300: πρόσθεν (before Theodore II's death) προβάντων ὁρκίων φρικαλέων ὑπηκόοις ἅπασι καὶ τοῖς ἐν τέλει ...

[10] Gregoras, I, 64–65.

[11] Pachymeres (Failler), I: 130–37, especially 135.23–137.5: Τάττεται δὲ καὶ τοὺς ὁπουδήποτε τῆς Ῥωμαΐδος ὀμνύειν ἐπ'ἀμφοτέροις ὅρκον δουλείας κατὰ τὸ σύνηθες. Πλὴν προσέκειντο τοῖς συντεθειμένοις, ἐπ'ἀσφαλείᾳ καὶ ἀμφοτέρων μείζονι, ἦ μὴν ἕτοιμον εἶναι τὸ ὑπήκοον ἐπ'ἐκεῖνον ὁρμᾶν φονώσῃ χειρὶ ὃς ἂν ἐπιβουλεύσοι θατέρῳ· ὡρκωμότουν γὰρ μετὰ τῶν ἄλλων καὶ τοῦτο, κατὰ φόβον, οἶμαι, ἢ χρείαν ἀληθινήν· εἰ δ'οὖν, ἀλλ'οὐδὲν ἂν καταγνοίη τις μεῖζον τῶν ταῦτα πραττόντων ἢ τὸ ἐμφυλίους πολέμους τῷ κοινῷ προξενεῖν, εἴ ποτε τοῦτο συμβαίη. Ὅμως ἐδόκει ταῦτα, καὶ εἰς ἔργον τὰ βουλευόμενα προὔβαινον. Χεῖρα τοιγαροῦν ἐτίθουν, καὶ ἐπὶ τῶν ἁγίων εὐαγγελίων ὤμνυον ἦ μὴν καὶ ἀμφοτέροις δουλεύειν καὶ ταῦτ'ἐκτελεῖν. Cf. Cantacuzenus, I, 396; N. Svoronos, "Le serment de fidélité à l'empereur byzantin et sa signification constitutionnelle", idem, *Études sur l'organisation intérieure, la société et l'économie de l'empire byzantin* (London, Variorum Reprints, 1973), study VI, 111–12, 129, 139.

Palaiologos and binding all the people; as Patriarch, he was the guarantor of the oath:

> Σὺν τούτῳ τῷ ὅρκῳ καὶ ἕτερος γέγονεν ὅρκος πρὸς ἅπαντα τὸν λαόν, ἀρχιερεῖς, ἱερεῖς, μεγιστᾶνας, στρατευομένους καὶ ἰδιώτας· ὅντινα ἀπὸ τῶν δύο βασιλέων ἴδοι ὁ λαὸς ἐκκλίναντα εἰς ἐπιβουλὴν τοῦ ἑτέρου, εἰ μὲν φονεύσει τὸν ἐπιβουλευθέντα ὁ ἐπίβουλος, ἵνα σωρεύονται ἅπαντες, καὶ φονεύωσι καὶ τοῦτον· ἀναγορεύωσι δὲ ἐκ τῆς συγκλήτου βασιλέα ὃν καὶ θέλουσιν· εἰ δὲ ματαία φανῇ ἡ ἐπιβουλή, ἵνα κρατῇ ὁ λαὸς τὸν φανέντα ἐπίβουλον, καὶ φονεύῃ τοῦτον, καὶ ἔχῃ καὶ τὸν ἐπιβουλευθέντα βασιλέα· *εἰ δὲ οὐ ποιήσει οὕτως ὁ λαός, ἵνα ὦσι καὶ αὐτοὶ ἀφωρισμένοι καὶ ἀνατεθεματισμένοι.* Τούτοις τοῖς ὅρκοις συνδεσμήσας αὐτὸς ἑαυτόν, καὶ πάντα τὸν λαόν.[12]

> "Along with this oath [i.e., the one sworn by Michael Palaiologos to the Patriarch and the prelates], he [Michael] swore another oath to the entire people, the prelates, the priests, the magnates, the soldiers and the civilians, that should the people see one of the two emperors incline toward a conspiracy against the other one, if the conspirator killed the one conspired against, they [i.e., the people] should all come together and kill him. And then they should proclaim emperor whomever they wished, among the [members of] the Senate. But if the conspiracy was unsuccessful, then the people should arrest the [emperor] who was patently conspiring and kill him, and have as emperor the one conspired against. *And if the people do not do this, they should be anathematized and excommunicated.* With such oaths he [Michael] bound himself *and the entire people.*"

This is no less than a duty imposed upon the people, on pain of excommunication, to rise up in arms against one of the Emperors, if he successfully or unsuccessfully tried to unseat the other. What this meant to the Byzantines of this period was a duty to rebel, to oppose a crowned emperor, ruling in the capital, if he took a certain action. This is a novel definition of the subjects' duty toward the emperor, which in the past had meant support of the emperor ruling in Constantinople against rebels.[13] Now the duty of rebellion is imposed on the population under certain circumstances, that is to say, the people are the guarantors of the political order, and mere success does not guarantee an Emperor's right to rule.

The inhabitants of Trikokkia referred not to this oath but to that sworn to Theodore II (or so Pachymeres would have us believe). It is clear, in any case, that they were carrying out a duty undertaken by oath; and Pachymeres saw it as such, but presented it in his usual oblique and convoluted way. Only his vocabulary shows the connection:

[12] *MPG* 140, 952 (my Italics).

[13] See, for example, G. G. Litavrin, *Sovety i rasskazy Kekavmena* (Moscow, 1972), 248, 252, 268.

the people of Trikokkia rushed to John IV's aid: ὑπὲρ αὐτοῦ κινδυνεύειν ὥρμων – note that they had taken an oath to ὁρμᾶν.[14] He calls the rebellion a civil war; and when discussing the last oath he writes, with hindsight, that this was a mistake, for it would surely lead to civil war.

This was, then, in political terms, a loyalist rebellion. Its course is interesting. Our major source may exaggerate the Emperor's fear and the collection of a vast army; but the subsequent fiscal measures suggest that the rebellion, although based on the mountainous region of Trikokkia, may have spread or had sympathizers in the adjacent territories, and thus constituted a real threat. The reality of the threat is pointed out by the eventual outcome, and the escape of the pretender. The compromise of the "notables" is easy to understand. Less easily understandable is the fact that a number of the rebels held out: an act of dynastic loyalty, or a desperate act on the part of some people?

As for the vocabulary of the rebellion, the Patriarch Arsenios calls the act itself ἐπανάστασις (revolution), while Pachymeres calls it *apostasia* (rebellion), and the rebels are called *apostatai, afistamenoi*: it is a true rebellion against the Emperor.[15] The fight is called an *emphylios polemos* (civil war), the ultimate result of a rebellion.[16] The participants are called χωρῖται, ἀγρόται, γεωργίας προσέχοντες (peasants, farmers: 259) – all neutral terms; but also ἀγροῖκοι (rustic, boorish people: 261), a less neutral term, opposed to ἀστικοί ("urban", but also "civilised"), here used to suggest that the urban populations were more war-like. Surely this kind of juxtaposition of town and country is meaningless. The true juxtaposition must be between peasants and the imperial (Constantinopolitan) army – but the terms in which it is presented suggest forcefully the underlying assumption that peasants were not expected to fight and win, and that the inhabitants of cities were superior to those of the countryside. Finally, the statement that the rebels were "few",

[14] Pachymeres (Failler), I: 261, and cf. I: 135.

[15] See the terminology in J. and P. Zepos, *Jus Graecoromanum* I (Athens, 1931), 273–4.

[16] See, for comparison, the definition of the rebellion of Thomas the Slav: ἐμφύλιος πόλεμος, κίνησις, στάσις, ἀνταρσία, ἀποστάτης, ἐμφύλιοι στάσεις. Theophanes Continuatus (Bonn, 1838), 49, 52, 53, 58, 62-63. Georgius Monachus, *MPG* 109.2: 844, 949: ἀντάρτης, ἐκίνησεν, ἐμφύλιος πόλεμος. Genesios (Bonn, 1834), 32, 34, 35, 36, 37, 38, 39, 40, 41 , 42, 43, 44, 45: νεωτερισμός, ἐνεωτερίσατο, στασιώτης, μουλτίων, ἀποστάτης, στασιάρχης, τύραννος, στασιῶται, τυραννικὴ νόσος. The vocabulary of urban rebellion incorporates some of these terms: see the description by Michael Psellos of the uprising of 1042: νεώτερον, φορὰν καὶ συγκίνησιν, τυραννεύσας, καινοτομία, πολιτικὸς πόλεμος, στασιάσας δῆμος: Michel Psellos, *Chronographie*, ed. E. Renauld (Paris, 1926), I, 95, 101, 102, 103, 104, 106.

contrasts with other statements in the same narrative: it is, more than anything else, an indictment of the imperial army, which allowed "a few" to overwhelm its forces. This is another pointer to an interpretation of the episode: Pachymeres is actually presenting it in a favorable light, first by dignifying it with a long description and a reported oration, and secondly by the literary ploy of contradictions as well as of the attribution of the most unrealistically altruistic motives to those who held out.

In the course of the late thirteenth century, that is, for over a generation after 1262, the possibility of uprisings of the rural population of Asia Minor remained vivid, both in fact and in the memory of the imperial authorities. At one extreme, there is popular (peasant) support of a traditional rebellion by a member of the aristocracy. Such was the case with the rebellion of Alexios Philanthropenos, in 1295. Not only was he a member of the aristocracy, he was a nephew of the Emperor; he was also closely connected with members of the upper class who were allied to the Arsenite cause, and so appealed to the pro-Laskarid sentiments of the population of Asia Minor.[17] The rebellion of Philanthropenos is mentioned here for two reasons only: first, that when his army incited him to rebellion, they mentioned, among the reasons that they thought the rebellion would be successful, the fact that "the people, burdened with exactions and taxes, was ready to rebel" (τὸν λαὸν πάντα ζημίαις βαρούμενον καὶ συνδόσεσιν εἰς ἀποστασίαν ἕτοιμον εἶναι),[18] a reference to the peasant population of Asia Minor and its discontent with fiscal exactions, which was thought sufficient to move it to rebellion.[19] Secondly, the vocabulary of that rebellion is quite typical of the generic vocabulary; but the use of certain terms connects it both to the rebellion of 1262 and to subsequent peasant unrests of various kinds. The most frequent term is ἀποστασία and its derivatives, quite correctly for what was a true rebellion against the Emperor.[20]

The term ἐμφύλιος πόλεμος, also common, was used for 1262 as well.[21] Other terms, καινοτομία, κάκωσις, ἐγχείρησις, ταραχή, ἀποστροφή (from

[17] On this, see A. Laiou, "Some Observations on Alexios Philanthropenos and Maximos Planoudes", *Byzantine and Modern Greek Studies* 4 (1978), 89–99; Pachymeres, (Bonn, 1835), II, 210–32; Gregoras, I, 195–97.

[18] Pachymeres (Bonn), II, 215.

[19] On taxes, fiscal exactions, and the excesses of tax-collectors both in Thrace-Macedonia and in Asia Minor, see *Maximi monachi Planudis epistulae*, ed. P. A. M. Leone (Amsterdam, 1991), letters 3 , 4, 11, 12 to Phakrases, and 5 to Leon Vardales.

[20] Pachymeres (Bonn), II, 210, 216, 224, 226, 229, 231.

[21] Pachymeres (Bonn), II, 223. Note also the use of the word πλῆθος to describe Philanthropenos' followers: ibid., 224.

the emperor), while perfectly appropriate for an aristocratic rebellion, are also terms that may be found in descriptions of peasant opposition to various kinds of authority.[22] Noteworthy is also the fact that the major factor in the collapse of Philanthropenos' rebellion was the bribes and the amnesty offered to the best troops in his command, the Cretans, who had been the ones to incite the rebellion. Pachymeres reports a discussion among them, weighing the wisdom of staying with Philanthropenos or changing sides, which has some resonances with the reported arguments of the rebels of 1262.[23]

If in 1262 we have a rebellion in which peasants (though armed and probably well-off) were the main force or potential/active participants, there are, in the late 13th century, other movements where peasants rise to arms, in actions which the government considers potentially rebellious. These are important to consider in a study of the typology and vocabulary of rebellion. Two movements , close to each other, one in 1294 and one sometime before 1302, should be considered. They are the affairs of Pseudo-Lachanas and John Choirovoskos. Briefly, here are the stories. In 1294, as the situation in Asia Minor deteriorated, a Bulgarian appeared in Constantinople, claiming to be Lachanas (the "kitchen-gardener", in fact a shepherd), who had led a rebellion against Michael VIII and his Bulgarian protégé, Konstantin Tish in 1277, and had been killed.[24] He sought the permission of the Emperor, Andronikos II, to perform wondrous deeds against the enemies, presumably the Turks. The Emperor at first was afraid; then he investigated, by means of a recognition scene with his niece Maria, the true Lachanas' widow. She stated that the man was not her husband, indeed did not even look like him. But people believed that he was; he professed great piety, and people had high hopes of him. The Emperor imprisoned him, but could not cut off people's hopes for, says Pachymeres, when people are ill they often have faith in unreasonable medicine, especially when it is strange and unusual (ξένα καὶ μὴ συνήθη).[25] The "people" here mentioned seem to have been refugees from Asia Minor. Furthermore, the Turks also feared "the barbarian," for they had some sort of oracle that was applied to him. Thus, the Emperor himself freed him and sent him off to Asia Minor, to the Sangarios front. There, large numbers of people, unarmed peasants according to Pachymeres, joined him, spreading like fire or like

[22] Pachymeres (Bonn), II, 214, and cf. Theophanes Continuatus, 53.
[23] Pachymeres (Bonn), II, 224–5.
[24] Gregoras, I, 130–31.
[25] Pachymeres (Bonn), II, 188–92; 189.

rivers. At this point, the Emperor became afraid that the people would suffer, but also that, if they were victorious, they would rebel. He therefore recalled pseudo-Lachanas home, stripped him of his command, and the "ignorant multitudes" (τὸ δ'ἀμαθὲς ἐκεῖνο πλῆθος καὶ ἄλογον) who followed him disbanded.

Sometime before 1302, another Bulgarian, called John Choirovoskos because he had been a swine-herd, collected 300 men armed with bows and clubs, and aimed to join Michael IX in Asia Minor to fight the Turks. Once again, we are told that the Emperor was afraid that these people, unused to war and boorish (peasants) (λαὸς ἀγροῖκός τε καὶ ἀπόλεμος) would be slaughtered, so he imprisoned the leader for nine months.[26] He escaped, found asylum in a church and then escaped again; he collected a mob (ξύγκλυδα λαόν) made up of refugees who "wanted either to recover their lands or to die gloriously (in battle)". Thus a large army (στρατός) was collected, under his leadership. Pachymeres uses the term for an army leader, a general ("στρατηγοῦντι"), perhaps sarcastically, perhaps to establish a connection with the pseudo-Lachanas episode. This was an "army" of infantry–although the word army again is probably used sarcastically. At first, their large numbers allowed them some victories over the Turks, but eventually they were defeated. Choirovoskos was taken captive; some said that he was killed because his ransom was not paid. The most common opinion was that he escaped once again, became "sebastos" of the Bulgarians (an official position), and with one thousand men attacked the Turks, but also looted (κακῶς ἔδρα) in the area around Thessaloniki.[27]

The two episodes have a good deal in common, so that one might think that Pachymeres was to some extent patterning his description of the second episode on the first, which is presented in a more structured way. Among the points of similarity are the origins and actions of the leaders. In both cases they were Bulgarians, and of lowly origins. Choirovoskos is said to have actually been a swineherd, while the origins of pseudo-Lachanas cannot have been very glorious. Both begin their careers by offering their services to the Emperor against the Turks. In both cases

[26] Pachymeres (Bonn), II, 442. As a curiosity, I mention that Thomas the Slav is also described as a man of poor and inglorious birth, and of Slavic extraction: Theophanes Continuatus, 50.

[27] Pachymeres (Bonn), II, 442–4; A. E. Laiou, *Constantinople and the Latins: the Foreign Policy of Andronicus II, 1282–1328* (Cambridge, MA, 1972), 191–2. On Choirovoskos, see also V. S. Georgiadou, "Η ιστοριογραφία των πρώτων Παλαιολόγων απέναντι στο πρόβλημα της τουρκικής επέλασης", *Ελληνική Ιστορική Εταιρεία, ΙΔ΄ Πανελλήνιο Ιστορικό Συνέδριο, Πρακτικά* (Thessaloniki, 1994), 112–115.

they are initially imprisoned; pseudo-Lachanas is freed and sent to Asia Minor with an imperial command, while Choirovoskos escapes on his own. Unlike Choirovoskos, pseudo-Lachanas is also an impostor: indeed, the two adjectives used to describe him are "barbarian and impostor" (πλάνος). The curiosity here is that, unlike most impostors who impersonate a glorious personage, pseudo-Lachanas was impersonating an unsuccessful rebel, himself a former swineherd. The facts themselves suggest strongly that both men were charismatic; but the source of charisma is not clear, unless a clue may be found in the reported prophesies the Turks had. Possibly, a poor and low-born leader was thought to be successful where aristocratic generals and organized armies were not; it is useful to recall in this connection the blind pseudo-John Laskaris. Pachymeres gives such an explanation for the support the pretender pseudo-Lachanas gathered among the refugees from Asia Minor: desperate people, he said, are willing to try all sorts of medicine, especially if it is "strange and unusual" (ξένα καὶ μὴ συνήθη – p. 189). A further trait of pseudo-Lachanas was his piety; it is an interesting trait to mention, since peasant uprisings in the middle ages often had a religious aspect. Perhaps something similar can be said of Choirovoskos, who found asylum in a church when he escaped from a Byzantine prison.

Both pseudo-Lachanas, officially, and Choirovoskos unofficially, began their activities in Asia Minor in the service of the Emperor: pseudo-Lachanas was actually made a general, while Choirovoskos was not, but ostensibly he was fighting the Emperor's cause. Furthermore, according to the prevailing theory about his fate, he became σεβαστὸς τῶν Βουλγάρων, that is, he was given imperial office after his defeat.[28]

The followers of both men were, in the first instance, refugees from Asia Minor. Once they had crossed into Asia Minor themselves, their following consisted of peasants, as Pachymeres says unequivocally. As with the armed peasants of the Trikokkia rebellion, but with more justification, we are told that these were men ignorant of war. Pachymeres' description of pseudo-Lachanas' following is virtually a stock phrase: they were men who "knew nothing more than agricultural work, and the spade, and how to prod oxen; they were shepherds and boorish" (γεωργικῶν ἔργων καὶ σκαπάνας καὶ τοῦ κεντρίσαι τὸν βοῦν καὶ ποιμένες θρεμμάτων καὶ ἄγροικοι). And again: ἄγροικοι, βουκαῖοι, βοωτοί (rustic, cowherds, ploughmen). They were armed with sticks and shepherds'

[28] See H. Ahrweiler, "Le sébaste, chef de groupes ethniques", *Polychronion – Festschrift für F. Dölger* (Munich, 1966), 34–38, especially p. 35.

crooks, forming an unarmed army (ὁπλῖται ἄοπλοι). Choirovoskos' men were "a boorish and unwarlike group" (λαὸς ἀγροῖκός τε καὶ ἀπόλεμος).[29]

In both cases, the followers are described in terms suggesting a multitude that is essentially a mob (ξύγκλυδα λαόν: II, 442 and ἄπειρον πλῆθος συγκλύδων – 191); a large group, unorganised, (συντάξεις ἀσύντακτοι – 191); an irrational and ignorant mob (192), easy to collect and easy to disperse. There is a deep Constantinopolitan fear of large groups of people, essentially out of the control of the government.[30]

In both cases, although most clearly in pseudo-Lachanas' rebellion (that of Choirovoskos in any case looks like a replay or a coda) it is the large numbers of followers that is stressed. The word "ὁρμή" is often used. Similies to fire and rushing streams suggest both large numbers and the possibility of geographic spread.[31] It is this that gets a reaction from the Emperor. Significantly, the numbers themselves bring up fear of rebellion, despite the fact that the people are said to be incapable of fighting a proper battle, and are poorly armed. Here the similarities with and perhaps the memory of the rebellion in Trikokkia are evident. Thus there is fear of rebellion (μή τι νεωτερισθείη), although in fact there was no rebellion. The word rebellion (ἀποστασία) is not used, although images recalling rebellion *are* used, as when Pachymeres, in speaking of the large and immediate following collected by pseudo-Lachanas, says that it resembled nothing so much as the dislocation of the entire earth : οὐδὲν ἦν εἰκάζειν εἰ μὴ ταὐτῆς οἰκουμένης καὶ γῆς μετακίνησιν.[32]

A note is necessary on the use of the word λαός. In this period, it had the general meaning "people", that is, the totality of the subjects of the Empire. It is so used by the Patriarch Arsenios in his testament.[33] Pachymeres' use in some passages can also be understood in this general sense: Andronikos II was afraid for the λαός, that it might suffer from

[29] Pachymeres (Bonn), II, 191–92.

[30] For a similar vocabulary, see Gregoras' description of the peasants who joined the army of Michael IX to combat a Turkish force in Thrace, in 1311: ὅσοι . . . ἀγροῦ καὶ δικέλλης ἀπόζουσιν . . . τὸν ἀγοραῖον . . . καὶ ἀγρότην ὄχλον, καὶ ὅσοι σκαπάνης καὶ δικέλλης ἀπόζουσιν . . . ὁ συρφετώδης ἐκεῖνος καὶ ἀγρότης ὄχλος: Gregoras, I, 256–7.

[31] Pachymeres (Bonn), II: 192: δίκην ῥυάκων ἐπιρρεόντων τῶν ἀγροίκων ἐκείνων . . . Cf. Theophanes Continuatus, 53, for a parallel statement: οἱ ἐμφύλιοι . . . πόλεμοι . . . οἷόν τινες Νειλῷοι καταρράκται ἀνοιγόμενοι, οὐχ ὕδατι ἀλλ'αἵματι τὴν γῆν κατεπότιζον. Psellos uses the fire simile for the rebellion of 1042: ὡς εἰς πυρκαϊὰν ὁ σπινθὴρ ἀνεφλέχθη καὶ δεῖ πολλῶν ποταμῶν καὶ ἐπιφόρου τοῦ ῥεύματος ὥστε ἀποσβεσθῆναι: *Chronographie* I, 103.

[32] Pachymeres (Bonn), II, 191.

[33] *MPG* 140, 952: γέγονεν ὅρκος πρὸς ἅπαντα τὸν λαόν, ἀρχιερεῖς, ἱερεῖς, μεγιστᾶνας, στρατευμένους καὶ ἰδιώτας.

the Turks.[34] But the term is also connected with ignorance, disorganisation (ἀσύντακτος), boorishness, lack of experience in war; thus, as the equivalent of "mob". In the episode of the monk Ilarion, who collected a group of people to attack the Turks around the monastery of Elegmoi in Bithynia, the term "λαός" must refer to peasants.[35] In other passages, it seems to describe the tax-payers, typically, the peasants.[36] We have, therefore, an interesting configuration, where the people are the peasants, and they are disorganised, but dangerous, almost a force of nature and as such uncontrollable: better to disband them before they rebel, i.e., before they overturn the existing structure of power. Is it necessary to recall the fact that, to the contrary, in the middle Byzantine period λαός had the specific meaning of "army"?[37]

The events, uprisings and near-uprisings, we have been describing all belong to the late thirteenth century – a period which also saw the beginnings of social unrest in western Europe.[38] Social unrest in Byzantium remained very much alive in the 14th century, finding its

[34] For the general meaning "people", see also, e.g., Pachymeres (Bonn), II, 598.

[35] Pachymeres (Bonn), II, 596–7. An interesting episode; the Patriarch wanted to bring to bear on Ilarion the full *epitimia* of the canonical legislation against members of the clergy bearing arms; he was dissuaded by Andronikos II. Same meaning of λαός in Miklosich-Müller, *Acta*, IV, 154, where the purchaser of a disputed piece of land enters it μετὰ λαοῦ ἱκανοῦ καὶ ἔσπειρον αὐτὸ ἀνάρχως.

[36] Pachymeres (Bonn), II, 618 and possibly 596. The same meaning, "taxpayer", may be found in Manuel Philes' poem about Patrikiotes: Ὡς πῦρ κατὰ σοῦ τοὺς λαοὺς φασι βρέμειν τῶν στασιαστῶν ταῖς πνοαῖς ἐπηρμένους: *Manuelis Philae Carmina*, I, 205, quoted in K.-P. Matschke, *Fortschritt und Reaktion in Byzanz im 14. Jahrhundert* (Berlin, 1971), 239.

[37] The complexities in the use of λαός, with the interplay of old, general (and biblical) meaning of "people" and the specific meanings attached to it in particular periods are demonstrated by a passage in the *Vita* of St. Elias the Young, brought to my attention by A. P. Kazhdan. The commander of the Byzantine fleet in Italy is admonished to "purify his people", which could be understood to mean his army; but the reference is to Exodus 19,11, where the "people" is meant. However, when the commander then issues an order παντὶ τῷ λαῷ τοῦ στρατεύματος, the meaning comes much closer to "army": G. Rossi Taibbi, *Vita di Sant'Elia il Giovane* (Palermo, 1962), 64.876, 66.888. For the meaning "army" in the 11th century, cf. Kekaumenos in Litavrin, *Soviety i Rasskazy*, 252; probably in the generic sense, pp. 256, 260, 262, 264. For an opposition between a proper army (i.e., soldiers) and peasants, see Choniates (van Dieten), 245: ἀχρείους στρατολογήσαντι γεωργοὺς καὶ μοῖραν συνεπαγομένῳ Παφλαγόνων στρατιωτῶν. In Psellos' description of urban rebellion the word πλῆθος is used, sometimes qualified by the adjective "δημοτικόν"; also the words δῆμος and ὄχλος. See, for example, *Chronographie*, I, 100, 103, 104, 105. In the description of the rebellion of the "Macedonians", πλῆθος is opposed to the ἐν τέλει and the στρατιῶται (II, 18, 20); στρατηγικὴ ἀφέλεια is contrasted to πολιτικὴ βωμολοχία (II, 22), and the term ἀγυρτικὸς ὄχλος is used (II, 24).

[38] M. Mollat and P. Wolff, *Ongles bleus, Jacques et Ciompi: Les révolutions populaires en Europe aux XIV*ᵉ *et XV*ᵉ *siècles* (Paris, 1970).

most acute expression in the second civil war, in the middle of the century. That, of course, took place in Europe, since Asia Minor was just about lost, and it was primarily a struggle centered in the cities. To what extent can we attempt a synthesis about the typology of peasant unrest and about the vocabulary of peasant rebellion for the late thirteenth century?

The rebellion of the inhabitants of Trikokkia is the only one that Pachymeres has dignified by the term "apostasia", a term also used for a more usual type of aristocratic rebellion, that of Philanthropenos.That is quite right: it was the only peasant uprising which actually (not potentially) was against the political order and challenged the reigning emperor. If the typology is strange, in the fact that there was no acknowledged leader, ultimate loyalty being given to a dead emperor and possibly a Patriarch, that may be a *damnatio memoriae*, or, much more likely, a reflection of the fact that the leaders were not aristocrats, and the war was fought in the cause of legitimacy. The participants were peasants, but they were armed peasants, and possibly fairly well off. This was no "révolte de misère."[39] On the contrary, Michael VIII's remedy, to destroy the wealth of the peasantry so they would not rebel again, argues for the idea that we have here a revolution of rising expectations. Here are Michael's thoughts: "being suspicious of his subjects because of the events, he thought it useful to burden the people (τὸν λαόν) with taxes, so that they would not be able to rebel by virtue of being wealthy." They are echoed much more forcefully by Froissart writing on 1381: "Pour la grande aise et abondance de biens en quoi le menu peuple était alors et vivait, s'émut et éleva cette rébellion."[40] No *révolte de misère* – but certainly one of opposition to the established state, for reasons that may have been fiscal and social, but that appeared as primarily legitimist.

Opposition to fiscality by the peasant population of Asia Minor is clearly attested. The Patriarch Arsenios demanded that Michael VIII reduce the taxes and *kommerkia* before he would lift the excommunication imposed on the Emperor for blinding John IV.[41] It is difficult not to connect this demand (which was not honored) with the rebellion of Trikokkia. Fiscal motives are clearly stated in the case of Philanthropenos' rebellion – and Pachymeres is explicit in the condemnation of

[39] Mollat-Wolff, 276.

[40] *Ibid.*, 277, quoting Froissart, for 1381. Cf. Pachymeres (Failler), I: 293.

[41] *MPG* 140, 956.

excessive taxes that, among other things, are credited as having occasioned flight to the Turks. To that extent, what we have here is opposition to a tax-gathering state rather than to an emerging seigneurial régime. At the same time, it is unquestionable that there was peasant opposition to the progressive subjection of the peasantry to lay or ecclesiastical landlords. While this opposition is mostly episodic, and unsurprisingly hard to develop into a general uprising, some of the vocabulary is interesting. In one case, both aristocratic and non-aristocratic neighbors of the monastery of Lemviotissa are accused of ἁρπαγή (seizure) and καινοτομία (innovation, *res novae*), the latter being a term properly applicable to rebellion as well.[42] In another case the inhabitants of Neochorion are said to have gone to a disputed field and cultivated it ἀνάρχως ("lawlessly"); the term suggests the anarchy that characterises the description of peasant movements.[43] So does the term ἐπανέστησαν ("they rose up") in another case of opposition to the monastery.[44] Similarly, when the inhabitants of the village Vari in Asia Minor did not pay their taxes, the words "παίδευσιν" (punishment), ἀναγκάζειν . . . ὑποκεῖσθαι (force the peasants to subject themselves to the monks and pay the regular dues) is the vocabulary of disobedience and forcible obedience.[45] There was, here, actual opposition to seigneurial relations, and perhaps potentially a widespread opposition. We can see that in 1340, when the lands of the great aristocrat, John Cantacuzenus, were distributed to the peasants "and fishermen" who had spoken up against him. The words used here include the term "συγκλύδων" (mob, rabble), which we know from the descriptions of the various peasant movements of the late 13th century.[46] This is just before the great civil war that started in 1342, a war which included hostile action by the peasantry against the great aristocratic landlords of Cantacuzenus' party.[47] However, there was no

[42] Miklosich-Müller, *Acta*, IV, 257; cf. pp. 257–263 for other acts of opposition by peasants toward the monks of Lemviotissa.

[43] Miklosich-Müller, *Acta*, IV, 231 (1293). In other cases, the peasants belonging to a pronoia-holder did the same thing, at his instigation: p. 154. For another example of violence connected with the peasants' unlawful cultivation of the land of, in this instance, a lay landlord, see the decision of John Apokaukos in S. Pétridès, "Jean Apokaukos, lettres et autres documents inédits", *Izvestija Russkago Arheologičeskago Instituta v Konstantinopolje*, XIV (1909), 19–20.

[44] Miklosich-Müller, *Acta*, IV, 247–8.

[45] *Ibid.*, IV, 255–56.

[46] Gregoras (Bonn), II, 609–10.

[47] See, for example, the hostile activities of the people who lived outside Didymoteichon, presumably peasants: Cantacuzenus II, 288, and in Vera (Thrace), Cantacuzenus II, 196–97.

large-scale cooperation with the anti-aristocratic forces in the cities; and in fact urban concerns thwarted or failed to include those of the peasantry, so that whatever grievances the peasants had against their lords failed to become generalised.

Fiscal opposition (a common cause of rural unrest and rebellion in western Europe of the 14th century), opposition to the established political régime, and opposition to seigneurial exactions were not the only cause of peasant unrest. The two cases of peasant armed activity in the late 13th century illustrate other aspects of the general phenomenon. They illustrate, in fact, three points. One, that the rapid advance of the Turks, and therefore the loss of their lands, moved people's opposition into channels created by political factors rather than socio-economic ones. Secondly, that their relation to the state was one of high ambivalence: we do not find a powerful belief in the state, or in any individual emperor, although the leaders preserve a loyalty that makes them wish to act in the name of the Emperor; we do find belief in strange and strangely charismatic leaders who themselves were of lowly, possibly peasant stock. And thirdly, that the inchoate nature of these movements was in itself a threat to a régime that must have felt itself very unstable.

The state's reaction to the first of these movements, the rebellion of 1262, is the only reaction we know at all well: it was fiscal but harsh, very much the opposite of what had happened in the early 9th century, when an uprising that seems to have involved a considerable part of the population of Asia Minor resulted in the reduction by fifty percent of the fiscal exactions on the population.[48] Once again, what we are witnessing in the late thirteenth century is the considerable alienation of the state from the peasantry.

As for the perceptions that the ruling class had of these movements, a few points stand out. One is the fear of contagion, especially evident in the rebellion of Trikokkia. Until the end of his life, Michael VIII, faced with the devastation of Asia Minor, repeated that he had left the province to its fate because of his fears and suspicions of "apostasia".[49] A second, and much less obvious one, is that there were those who were sympathetic to these movements and to the reasons behind them. This group undoubtedly included members of the aristocracy who had their own political motivations. But it includes also our major source, Pachymeres. His frequent castigations of poor administrators, and especially

[48] P. Lemerle, "Thomas le Slave", *Travaux et Mémoires* I (1965), 296.

[49] Pachymeres (Failler, 407). For "contagion" with regard to the revolutions of the 1340's, see Cantacuzenus II, 178–180.

of greedy tax-collectors, who burdened the population of Asia Minor with unbearable burdens, is clear evidence of such an attitude. So is the fact that the peasant unrest he describes is attended by an exodus of the population toward the Turks. Given Pachymeres' deep concern for Asia Minor and its fate, these are condemnations not of the rebels but of those against whom they rebelled.

The last general point I wish to make stems from the dichotomy between soldier and peasant, and the very negative, indeed sarcastic, description of peasant "armies". This is a dichotomy which reappears, in the middle of the great civil war of the 1340's, in a well-known passage of Demetrios Kydones, writing for the aristocratic faction. He talks of a true revolution, i.e., of the overturning of the proper order of things, saying: Ἐνταῦθα δοῦλος μὲν τὸν δεσπότην ὤθει· τὸν δὲ πριάμενον τὸ ἀνδράποδον· τὸν δὲ στρατηγὸν ὁ ἀγροῖκος· καὶ τὸν στρατιώτην, ὁ γεωργός.[50] Such a dichotomy, with the peasant appearing as ignorant of arms, incapable of discipline, an object of mockery when he goes to war, is relatively new in Byzantium.[51] For comparison, note what the continuator of Theophanes has to say about the upheaval occasioned by the rebellion of Thomas the Slav: "They armed a murderous hand, servants against their lords; the soldier against the sergeant; the captain against the general"; no opposition of peasant and soldier

[50] *MPG* 109, 648. "At this point, servant was pushing master, the slave his purchaser, the peasant the general, and the farmer the soldier": J. Barker, "The 'Monody' of Demetrios Kydones on the Zealot Rising of 1345 in Thessaloniki", *Essays in Memory of Basil Laourdas* (Thessaloniki, 1975), 297. Cf. *MPG* 109, 646: Ἐγυμνοῦτο μὲν τῶν ὅπλων ὁ στρατιώτης· εἵλκετο δὲ ὑπὸ τῶν τυχόντων ὁ πολλὰ δὴ πολλοῖς εἰωθὼς ἐπιτάττειν. In Barker's translation, "and while the soldier was stripped of his arms, the man who was wont to exercise great and far-reaching authority over others was dragged off by people encountered entirely by chance": p. 295. This last statement contradicts I. Ševčenko's view that "stratiotes" is used in this text as a technical term, meaning pronoia-holder. Cf. I. Ševčenko, "An Important Contribution to the Social History of Late Byzantium", *Annals of the Ukrainian Academy of Arts and Sciences in the United States* 2 (1952), 456.

[51] I do not, of course, claim to have suddenly discovered the well-known fact that in the late Byzantine Empire the "soldier" is, for the most part, a member of the ruling class. One must also acknowledge, on the other hand, that even in the middle period there was, sometimes, a contrast made between the soldier and the peasants. To the texts which show peasants and soldiers as being of the same class, and almost interchangeable (P. Lemerle, *The Agrarian History of Byzantium* [Galway, 1979], 98–99, 126), one may contrast the Taktikon of "Nikephoros Ouranos", which says that if the soldiers do not exercise or go on annual campaigns they will be reduced to the ranks "of merchants and common farmers": G. T. Dennis, *Three Byzantine Military Treatises* (Washington, D.C., 1985), 318: 14–15: εἰς ἐμπόρων καὶ ἀγελαίων γεωργῶν τάξιν αὐτοὺς κατάγει.

here.[52] It has been said that the middle Byzantine period, until 1204, had no experience of peasant rebellions, that all rebellions were led by the aristocracy, or were to its benefit.[53] That is, indeed, so; or at least, so it looks in the sources. Of course, most rebellions, until the late 10th century, were supported by the thematic armies, which were composed of soldier-farmers. It is not unreasonable to suggest that the grievances the rural population of a region might have had would have been expressed through the actions of the thematic army. The lack of visible peasant unrest was the result neither of general contentment nor of misery so deep that it had no way of finding expression. It was, rather, the result of a political-military system where peasant unrest was subsumed in the actions of an army of peasant-soldiers. With the change in the structure of the army, which now (i.e., in the 13th and 14th centuries), was made up of aristocrats large and small, or of mercenaries, the distinction between soldier and peasant is drawn more clearly, with a more strident contempt for the latter. There arises also the possibility of a new and fearful kind of rebellion, presented as a sort of cosmological event, the overthrow of the social order.[54] Or at least so thought the opponents.

What the followers of such movements thought is, as always, not easily recoverable, but there are some suggestions in the vocabulary as in the actions. For one, it is perfectly clear, and normal, that the rebels thought of themselves as restoring rather than upsetting the real order of things. This was undoubtedly reinforced, in the rebellion of 1262, by the oaths administered and guaranteed by the Patriarch. It is also clear that the rebels, in all of the instances we have seen here, were, in various degrees, acting in defence of "la patrie en danger". This modern formulation does not necessarily describe modern as opposed to medieval situations. Certainly, the idea of self-defence, with appeal to imperial government, the traditional guarantor of defence, is a throwback to the tenth century, and opposes more recent developments. Yet, if the interpretation presented here is correct, the rebellion of 1262 incorporates truly innovative elements along with traditional ones: the primary innovation being lodged in the idea that subjects have a duty to

[52] Theophanes Continuatus, 53: Ἐντεῦθεν καὶ δοῦλοι κατὰ δεσποτῶν καὶ στρατιώτης κατὰ ταξεώτου καὶ λοχαγὸς κατὰ στρατηγέτου τὴν χεῖρα φονῶσαν καθώπλιζεν.

[53] Cheynet, *Pouvoir et contestations*, 13.

[54] Revolutions often occasion statements about the reversal of the proper order of things: cf. Psellos, *Chronographie*, I, 101, 102, 103 (rebellion of the people of Constantinople in 1042).

rebel. Even if that duty derives from an oath, with all its religious foundations and implications, its constitutional implication is that the sovereign is explicitly bound to a certain behavior, and the subjects are explicitly bound to hold him to it. This is vastly different from the usual Byzantine concept, where the Emperor had to have virtues (e.g., justice, philanthropy, bravery) and to exercise certain functions (e.g., to defend his subjects), but was not responsible to anyone except God and perhaps the church. Thus we have, in the late thirteenth century, an intriguingly complex situation, where traditional values and new and conflicting realities meet for a moment, with revolutionary implications. But this was in the countryside, and the conflict between province and capital is a given. Also given is the fact that after all, we are in the Mediterranean, where power is concentrated in the cities, whose population had developed a contempt and hostility, reciprocated by the peasants, that made peasant rebellion or unrest incapable of success; all the more so in this period, when urban and rural rebel very rarely met.

VIII

THE EMPEROR'S WORD: CHRYSOBULLS, OATHS AND SYNALLAGMATIC RELATIONS IN BYZANTIUM (11th-12th C.)

The development of links of political or social solidarity in the Byzantine Empire is an issue of abiding interest. Links of solidarity between social groups, whether the aristocracy or the middle class or the peasantry, did not remain stable over time. Similarly, relations between the emperor and his subjects were based on principles that differed from period to period. Bilateral, synallagmatic relations, which linked the emperor and his subjects, or a subset of them, upon a basis of mutual obligations, have been connected to the rise of quasi-feudal relations in the Byzantine Empire. The matter is relatively clear insofar as the Palaiologan period is concerned.[1] For the earlier period, the existence of bilateral, synallagmatic, arrangements has been admitted for the Treaty of Devol, between Alexios I and Bohemond (1108), while it was also posited by certain western Medieval sources for the arrangements between Alexios I and the participants of the First Crusade, an issue that remains debatable.[2]

1. N. Svoronos, "Le serment de fidélité à l'empereur byzantin et sa signification constitutionnelle", *REB* 9, 1951, pp. 129-42; M.-Th. Foegen, "Das politische Denken der Byzantiner", in *Pipers Handbuch der politischen Ideen*, II, I. Fetscher, H. Muenkler, eds., Munich-Zurich 1993, pp. 73ff.

2. At least two western sources report a bilateral feudal contract between Alexios I and the crusaders: Fulcher of Chartres and the *Gesta Francorum*. See Fulcher Carnotensis, *Historia Hierosolymitana (1095-1127)*, ed. H. Hagenmeyer, Heidelberg 1913, p. 332; *Gesta Francorum et aliorum Hierosolymitanorum*, in *Recueil des Historiens des Croisades, Occ.* III, Paris 1866, p. 125. On the oaths of the First Crusade, see, among others, F. Ganshof, "Recherches sur le lien juridique qui unissait les chefs de la première croisade à l'empereur byzantin", in *Mélanges offerts à M. Paul E. Martin*, Geneva

It is certainly easier to trace this matter in relations between Byzantium and foreign powers than in the relations between the emperor and his own subjects. However, it is useful and productive to examine the two aspects together, beginning with the second half of the eleventh century. Oaths confirming agreements, and agreements subsumed in the "pure donation" document that the chrysobull officially was, can throw some light on this issue, important for the political and constitutional development of the Byzantine Empire.

In August 1074, after negotiations had taken place, Michael Psellos drafted a chrysobull that was to cement the marriage alliance between the son of Michael VII Doukas and the daughter of the Norman leader Robert Guiscard.[3] This is a truly bilateral arrangement, with an exchange of promises, gifts in exchange for peace and military cooperation, and a marriage alliance, by its nature bilateral. Both matrimonial alliances and gifts and offices in exchange for an alliance were commonplace phenomena in Byzantine diplomacy. However, the chrysobull itself is a highly unusual document, in phraseology as in substance.[4]

The text starts with the statement that the word of the Emperor is equivalent to a chrysobull, and is irrevocable for all time. If to the imperial word is added a true and awful oath, confirming the convention (τὰ συμπεφωνημένα, συμφωνία), the link becomes truly unbreakable. The emperor has made an agreement, guaranteed by his word, to wed Robert's daughter to his own son Constantine. According to the laws governing marriage, the two parties give to each other (ἀντιδιδόναι ἀλλήλοις) whatever they have agreed upon.

The terms upon which Michael VII and Robert have agreed are as follows. Robert has promised not to attack the Empire, but rather to protect it and fight on its behalf, to which agreement he has added that he will consider the emperor's enemies as his enemies, and the Emperor's friends as his own friends (τοὺς μὲν ἀπεχθανομένους ἡμῖν ἐχθροὺς ἄντικρυς ἡγεῖσθαι καὶ τῆς σῆς ἀπωθεῖσθαι φιλίας καὶ

1961, pp. 49-63, and J. FERLUGA, "La ligesse dans l'empire byzantin", *ZRVI* 7, 1961, pp. 97-113. For a discussion of the issue, and bibliography, see J. H. PRYOR, "The Oaths of the Leaders of the First Crusade to Emperor Alexius I Comnenus; Fealty, Homage=*pistis, Douleia*", *Parergon*, n.s., 2, 1984, pp. 111-42 and n. 1. On the treaty of Devol, see SVORONOS, "Le serment" (n. 1), pp. 137-38.

3. MICHAEL PSELLOS, *Scripta minora,* ed. E. Kurtz, F. Drexl, I, Milan 1936, pp. 329-34; on this, see H. BIBICOU, "Une page d'histoire diplomatique de Byzance au XIe siècle; Michel VII Doukas, Robert Guiscard et la pension des dignitaires", *Byz.* 29/30, 1959/60, pp. 43-75. *Skylitzes Continuatus* (E. Th. TSOLAKIS, *Ἡ συνέχεια τῆς χρονογραφίας τοῦ Ἰωάννη Σκυλίτση (Ioannes Skylitzes Continuatus),* Thessaloniki 1968), pp. 167, 170 mentions that Michael VII sent to "Longobardia" Straboromanos, and got Robert's daughter Helen as bride for his son Constantine. He adds that Michael feared the Turks, and thought it necessary to make an alliance (σπείσασθαι) with Robert to get help against the Turks. Hence he made a marriage arrangement (κῆδος) with Robert, for Helen to marry Constantine. Anna Komnene speaks of βαρβαρικὸν κῆδος: ANNE COMNÈNE, *Alexiade*, I.x.2, ed. B. Leib, I, Paris 1937, p. 78.

4. F. DÖLGER, P. WIRTH, *Regesten der Kaiserurkunden des oströmischen Reiches*, II, no. 1003. Originally, Dölger had found the document suspicious, but eventually accepted it as genuine. BIBICOU, "Une page" (n. 3), rightly says it was meant to be an unusual chrysobull. D. I. POLEMIS, *The Doukai, A contribution to Byzantine prosopography,* London 1968, no. 23, accepts it as genuine. On the chrysobull, see also N. OIKONOMIDÈS, "Le serment de l'impératrice Eudocie (1067): Un épisode de l' histoire dynastique de Byzance," *REB* 21, 1963, pp. 116-18, reprinted in ID., *Documents et études sur les institutions de Byzance (VIIe-XVe s.),* London 1976, no. 3.

ἀντιλήψεως, τοὺς δὲ οἰκείως καὶ εὐμενῶς ἔχοντας οἰκειοῦν σεαυτῷ καὶ πάσης ἀξιοῦν εὐμενείας καὶ συγκροτήσεως). All of this, Robert has confirmed with oaths in the name of God and upon sacred objects (relics?). This is Robert's advance offer (προεισφορά).

The emperor's countergift (ἀντίδοσις) consists, first of all, of the marriage itself and the granting of imperial acclamations to the bride. Secondly, the emperor offers various dignities, with the attendant salaries, to one of Robert's sons and to some of his followers; the office of *novelissimos* to Robert himself; and a number of silk *pallia*.

There follows the emperor's oath that guarantees the agreement, and a statement repeating the fact that the emperor's word, especially when written down and sealed with a golden seal, as well as the oath in the name of God, make the agreement firm and unassailable.

Finally, the emperor wishes this agreement not to be limited to Robert's lifetime, or his own. For this reason, he expects a written document to be added to Robert's response, which should be drafted on the model of the imperial letter. The addition would give assurances as to the adherence of Robert's heirs to the treaty, and would be confirmed by Robert's oath.

The chrysobull is signed by Michael VII Doukas, his brothers and co-emperors Andronikos and Konstantios, and by the Patriarch. The signature of the Patriarch is unique in Byzantine chrysobulls up to this point. Its presence must serve as confirmation not of the chrysobull, but of the oath, a practice which has antecedents in Byzantine history.[5]

The chrysobull is unusual in a number of ways. It is a convention (συμφωνία, συνθήκη), that is, a bilateral agreement, in the form of a chrysobull, something very unusual in itself, since chrysobulls were, in theory, unilateral imperial donations. It is, in the first instance, a marriage contract – perhaps facilitating Psellos' task of incorporating a convention, a bilateral agreement, into a chrysobull. The bilateral aspect is clear from the word ἀντιδιδόναι; and the reference is to marriage contracts where, "by law", "the two parties give to each other what they have agreed on."

This is a central document in the development of the oath as sealing a binding bilateral agreement between the Emperor and someone else. It is also an important document as far as the creation of bilateral links through oaths is concerned. Robert's oath was probably an oath of fidelity, for he promised ὑποταγήν (submission) and εὔνοιαν (favor, devotion, fidelity)[6]. The phraseology is important here.

5. For an earlier example of imperial oaths guaranteed by others, see the oath of Nikephoros I to Vardanes Tourkos, promising not to harm him. The oath was co-signed by the Patriarch and all the *patrikioi*, and its breach horrified them all: THEOPHANES, *Chronographia*, ed. C. De BOOR, I, Leipzig 1883, pp. 479-80. For a later example, see Isaakios II's agreement with Frederick Barbarossa, guaranteed by the Patriarch, the aristocrats, and representatives of the people of Constantinople: see, in the last instance, A. E. LAIOU, "Byzantine Trade with Christians and Muslims and the Crusade", in *The Crusades from the Perspective of Byzantium and the Muslims World*, A. E. Laiou and R. P. Mottahedeh, eds., Washington, D.C. 2001, pp. 175-77.

6. Εὔνοια is translatable as both devotion/benevolence and as faithfulness/loyalty. P. HERRMANN, *Der römische Kaisereid. Untersuchungen zur seiner Herkunft und Entwicklung*, Goettingen 1969, pp. 49-50, n. 99, says it should be translated as loyalty, not as benevolence. In the texts of the 11th-12th

The term εὔνοια has a long pre-history. It appears in the oath given to Justinian I by office-holders, who promise to serve μετ' εὐνοίας ἀδόλως,[7] but it goes further back, at least to the time of the oath of the inhabitants of Phazimon, in Paphlagonia, to the Emperor Augustus (3 B.C.).[8] The term ὑποταγή, in the variant form δουλεία, also goes back to the time of Justinian I. Both terms, in a slightly different form, can be found in the treaty of Devol, in which Bohemond promised to Alexius I πίστιν καὶ δουλείαν καὶ εὔνοιαν ... πίστιν ἀκραιφνεστάτην καὶ εὔνοιαν καθαράν.[9] By this treaty, Bohemond became Alexios' ἄνθρωπος πιστός, his δοῦλος and λίζιος ὑποχείριος. In 1319, the inhabitants of Ioannina were to promise Andronikos II μετ' εὐνοίας ἀκραιφνῶς ὑποταγήν[10]. Robert also promised not to attack the emperor's lands; to protect them against enemies; to be a friend of Michael VII's friends and enemy of his enemies – and to swear on all this by the most awful oaths. The formula promising hostility to the other's enemies and friendship to his friends also has ancient antecedents; it is incorporated in the oath of the inhabitants of Phazimon and in the oath of the inhabitants of Aritium to Germanicus (37 A.D.) However, it is also noteworthy that the substance as well as the phrasing used in the chrysobull is very close to the *convenientia* of a chevalier soldé, published by Bonassie: *et faciat guerram per illos et teneat pacem illis hominibus quibus ipsi voluerint... et amet amantibus illos et voleat malum... ad illos inimicos*.[11] We cannot know if the formula, which Robert must have incorporated into his own oath, was suggested to him by the emperor or if, on the contrary, it was suggested by Robert himself. I suspect the former, which would indicate that the Byzantines were already familiar with terms of oaths which were common in the West as well. In any case, as far as I know this is the first time after antiquity that the formula was used in the Byzantine Empire; it reappears in the Treaty of Devol, and then, after a long gap, in the late thirteenth century, during troubled times.[12]

As far as the emperor is concerned, what is extraordinary here is that he took "an awful oath" in order to give the fullest possible guarantee of his promise. Until the second half of the eleventh century, emperors took oaths to individuals very rarely, and in special circumstances, usually in order to give guarantees to unsuccessful rebels. Michael's oath must have been administered by the Patriarch, who otherwise had no reason to cosign the document.

---

centuries, the meaning seems to be equivalent to πίστις. However, in the chrysobull of 1126 to Venice, the term is rendered as *benevolentia*: G. M. TAFEL, J. THOMAS, *Urkunden zur älteren Handels-und Staatsgeschichte der Republik Venedig*, I, Venice 1856, p. 96.

7. *Nov*. 8, Iusiurandum; cf. *Bas*. VI, 3, 50.

8. HERRMANN, *Kaisereid* (n. 6), pp. 123-24.

9. ANNE COMNÈNE, *Alexiade* XIII.xii.19 ed. Leib, III, Paris 1945, p. 134.

10. MM V, p. 79; cf. *infra*, pp. 360-361.

11. P. BONNASSIE,"Les conventions féodales dans la Catalogne du XIème siècle", *Annales du Midi* 80, 1968, p. 550 (1052-1071).

12. See the oath of the sebastokrator of Thessaly John Doukas to Andronikos II: S. EUSTRATIADES, "Γρηγορίου τοῦ Κυπρίου Οἰκουμενικοῦ Πατριάρχου ἐπιστολαὶ καὶ μῦθοι", *Ekklesiastikos Pharos* 4, 1909, no. 131, pp. 7-8.

Undoubtedly the Emperor, or rather Michael Psellos who drafted the chrysobull, was fully aware of the novelty of the situation. Hence the embarrassed *prooimion*, and the statements that the word of the Emperor, especially the written word, and most especially the chrysobull, was in itself sufficient guarantee of anything.[13] Indeed, in the discussions that preceded the drafting of this chrysobull, although the terms of the agreement were similar, not a word had been said about reciprocal oaths, which must have been a requirement inserted into the final Byzantine text of the treaty at the insistence of Robert Guiscard.[14] The chrysobull, then, bears the imprint of a particular situation, implicating a westerner, and in the form in which we have it is quite unique for the eleventh century. However, the very fact that an Emperor would agree to take "awful oaths" to a private individual to confirm a treaty may be connected to the currency that oaths and sworn associations had received in the second half of the 11th century, and the legitimacy or quasi-legitimacy they had acquired.

All in all this is an extraordinary document – a mixture between a chrysobull, which in theory depends on the will of the Emperor alone, and a formal and written bilateral oath.[15] The chrysobull form, with the inherent idea that this is a free donation on the Emperor's part, preserves the emperor's dignity – only just. But this was a true synallagmatic agreement, sealed with an oath; if the offices and their salaries may be taken as the equivalent of a money-fief, we have here the earlier known such arrangement in Byzantium.

The fact that the text in question was issued to a foreign prince might lead to the conclusion that the novelty was imported, in other words that it was not congruent with contemporary developments in Byzantium. Such a conclusion, I believe, would be largely erroneous. While Robert Guiscard may have insisted on the inclusion of some elements, the eleventh century, especially its second half, was a period in which sworn

13. In the period before the late eleventh century, chrysobulls functioned as a well-attested alternative to formal oaths, mostly promising immunity or rewards to rebels and potential rebels. See, for example, Romanos Lekapenos, who issued chrysobulls in the name of Constantine VII, basically promising immunity to followers of the rebel Leo Phokas: *Theophanes Continuatus*, Bonn 1838, p. 395. To my knowledge, only one piece of evidence, somewhat literary in nature, the *Vita Euthymii*, mentions oaths incorporated in a chrysobull – a unique case before the late eleventh century. See P. Karlin-Hayter, *Vita Euthymii Patriarchae CP*, Brussels 1970, pp. 24-25: Leo VI asks the rebel Andronikos Doukas to return to the Empire, διά τε χρυσοβούλλων γραμματείων καὶ φρικτῶν ὅρκων ἐν αὐτοῖς ἐγγεγραμμένων, οὐ μὴν δὲ ἀλλὰ καὶ αὐτῶν τῶν τοῦ βασιλέως φυλακτῶν. Cf. *Theophanes Continuatus*, pp. 373-74.

14. Michael Psellos, Ἱστορικοὶ Λόγοι, Ἐπιστολαὶ καὶ ἄλλα ἀνέκδοτα in K. N. Sathas, *Μεσαιωνικὴ Βιβλιοθήκη*, V, Venice 1876, pp. 385-87, 388-92.

15. It was certainly not unique in Byzantine history. When Andronikos II tried to make agreements with Roger de Flor, in order to persuade the latter to cross into Asia Minor, he promised dignities, money, offices and so on. Roger wanted the guarantee to be confirmed by an oath, which was taken by the Emperor's envoy; Andronikos then sent Roger the insignia of Caesar, 30,000 gold coins and τὰς χρυσοβουλλείους πίστεις: Georges Pachymérès, *Relations historiques* XII.18, ed. A. Failler, IV, Paris 1999, CFHB 24/4, p. 557. In the Palaiologan period, we find imperial oaths in chrysobulls, especially in those issued to foreign powers, in which the reciprocity of arrangements is no longer hidden; see, as one example among many, the chrysobull issued by Andronikos II in favor of Venice in 1324: MM III, pp. 100-105.

associations and oaths were becoming usual in the Byzantine Empire, between members of the aristocracy as well as between the Emperor and his aristocratic subjects.

The period, as is well known, was marked by political and dynastic instability and social restructuring. The great aristocratic clans of the 10th century had been largely destroyed; a much greater number of smaller aristocratic families fought for supremacy and eventually for the throne. The ties among aristocrats were still fluid in the eleventh century. This was a time when links of solidarity were sought, both by the emerging important families and by lesser people, including bureaucrats or what has been called the civil aristocracy, that is, the officeholders of Constantinople. The most frequent and, as it happened, the most successful in the end, was the link created by marriage and family connections. Aristocratic marriages in the eleventh century were very carefully arranged, and this became a fine art in the 12th century. The political alliances created by marriage were quite solid after 1081; but earlier they appear as one, the most frequent, but not the sole mechanism of creating alliances and associations. The links between these members of the aristocracy were not yet solid in the mid-11th c., and many mechanisms were used to create them. Artificial kinship (adoption, god-parenthood, ritual kinship or artificial brotherhood-*adelphothesia*) and ties made by sworn associations were two such mechanisms. The first of these will not be discussed here.

Oaths and sworn associations, formed in order to forge links of solidarity between members of the aristocracy, appear with some frequency in the 11th century. For the most part, they are connected with conspiracies for the throne.[16] The rebellions of the 11th century were attended by oaths, both on the part of conspirators and on the part of the reigning emperor who might try to bind part of the aristocracy with "terrible oaths and awful curses" (ὅρκοις φρικτοῖς καὶ ἀραῖς παλαιμναιοτάταις) to remain faithful to him.[17] The sworn conspiracies of the eleventh century, especially its second half, are marked by the fact that they involved fairly large groups of aristocrats, that often the relationships thus created were long-term rather than limited to a single act of rebellion, and that the oaths and sworn agreements were clearly meant to supplement, or were sometimes replaced by, in any case were interchangeable with other forms of links of solidarity (mostly real or artificial kinship arrangements).

The salient example of a sworn association of political import is that which preceded the rebellion of Isaakios I Komnenos against the Emperor Michael VI, in 1057. A rebellion of the great aristocratic and military families of the East, it found support among members of the urban aristocracy as well. In terms of its effects on the aristocracy, it was the most important rebellion of the eleventh century. The rebels were bound together by common interests; some of them were related to each other, and Isaakios Komnenos surrounded himself with his relatives. The rebels were also bound together by oaths, contracted with the utmost solemnity, in the

16. On which see J.-Cl. CHEYNET, *Pouvoir et contestations à Byzance (963-1210)*, Byzantina Sorbonensia 9, Paris 1990.

17. IOANNES SKYLITZES, *Synopsis Historiarum*, ed. I. Thurn, Berlin 1983, CFHB 5, pp. 497-98, on Michael VI.

Great Church of St Sophia no less, with the agreement, it appears, of the Patriarch Michael Keroularios, who was sympathetic to the rebellion from the beginning.[18] The oaths are called "ὅρκοι φρικωδέστατοι", meaning that they were solemn, sworn on religious objects or in the name of God, and binding.[19] They were meant to bind and guarantee the agreement of the would-be rebels, who proclaimed Isaakios Komnenos emperor soon thereafter; the conspirators also bound themselves never to accept the ruling emperor.

The oath of the conspirators, in this fluid period of the solidification of political links between members of the aristocracy, acquired almost constitutional significance: the oath was very solemn and public in its venue; the assembled aristocrats by their oath agreed to depose and replace an Emperor. Their oaths superseded loyalty to the ruling Emperor, and at least one of the rebels of 1057, Katakalon Kekaumenos, argued that it would have been perjury (ἐπιορκία) to still allow the old emperor to rule.[20] The narrative that describes these events as well as the counter-oaths to Michael VI is full of biting irony – a suggestion, perhaps, of the novelty of these developments.

The links created among the rebels in 1057 were lasting ones. The ties among the rebels and their families continued and multiplied in the course of the eleventh century. With the single exception of Romanos IV Diogenes, members of this sworn conspiracy or their descendants, who eventually forged among themselves powerful links through marriage, ruled the Empire from 1057 until the end of the Komnenian period. Is it a coincidence, or were oaths in this period becoming a way through which members of the aristocracy were creating links that became more long lasting than the conspiracy of the moment? I would argue that sworn associations – because that is what we are talking about – were indeed in this period an important means of forging solidarity, but that their importance was transitory, since they were soon replaced by the stronger ties of family; secondly, that links of solidarity created by oaths began as form of aristocratic opposition to the state and were transformed into a form used occasionally or frequently by the state to bind people to itself.

Alexios I (1081-1118), the ultimate successful aristocrat, was fully conscious of the value of sworn associations, and of the links thus created. As he was preparing for his own rebellion against Votaneiates, he had the support of his numerous family members. But with outsiders, he made sworn agreements. This was the case with two key generals, both of them of foreign, i.e. non-Byzantine, origins: Gregorios Pakourianos and Oumbertopoulos. The more important of the two was Pakourianos, a Georgian or Armenian (from Taiq) of noble family and exceptional valor. Just before the rebellion, at a very delicate point, before Alexios had secured the support of the Doukai and their allies, he asked for Pakourianos' help: they exchanged oaths, Pakourianos promising to help Alexios, and Alexios promising to promote him to the

18. SKYLITZES, ed. Thurn, pp. 486-87; cf. MICHAEL ATTALIOTA, Bonn 1853, pp. 56-57, who claims that Keroularios had perhaps acted under duress.

19. SKYLITZES, ed. Thurn, p. 497.

20. *Ibid.*, p. 497.

dignity of domestic after the success of the rebellion. This was, therefore, a bilateral agreement, sealed by oath, which was, as it happened, kept on both sides. Pakourianos remained faithful, and Alexios rewarded him with high office and very considerable land-holdings.[21]

The frequent rebellions elicited responses on the part of Emperors who had to give securities, guarantees or promises to rebels and would-be rebels.[22] These often took the form of chrysobulls, or other, less formal but just as powerful, symbols that guaranteed the Emperor's word. Such guarantees were not new; in the past, too, in the 9th and 10th centuries, similar guarantees had been given. But in the 11th century, the mention of guarantees becomes more frequent. The phenomenon might be interpreted simply as a function of the number of rebellions. That, however, is not all. There is a change of real political significance, the counterpart of the sworn associations. The Emperor's word, and even his most formal written document, the chrysobull, were no longer necessarily sufficient to guarantee his position; as his subjects formed sworn associations among themselves, so he too cemented his relationship to some among them with oaths and with a public display of his intent. For example, Michael VI tried to ensure the εὔνοιαν and πίστιν of the people (πολῖται, πλῆθος) of Constantinople, and, in order to secure, in an unbreakable way, the εὔνοια of the aristocracy, he demanded that the members of the Senate swear terrible oaths that they would not follow Isaakios Komnenos.[23] Later, Anna Dalassene, a formidable lady, grandmother of Anna Komnene, sought refuge in the Great Church, in the most solemn of environments. And when she was promised by the emperor Nikephoros Votaneiates safe-conduct, she demanded *his oath* and "as guarantee of my safety, the Emperor's cross… and not a small cross, but a large one". Her historian grand-daughter glosses this by saying that the purpose was for the Emperor's sworn promise to become visible to all; for if the promise were made with (or upon) a small cross, it would not be clearly known to the people.[24]

The Emperor, that is to say, was forced to contract bilateral agreements with his aristocratic subjects, in which visible signs, including the oath and symbols of his engagement (perhaps the very cross upon which the oath was taken) were a condition of the arrangement.

This development, quite new in its intensity, forms the background of the chrysobull to Robert Guiscard. Domestic and foreign relations must be seen in juxtaposition to each other, in this matter as well as in later developments.

In the early Komnenian period, significant changes occurred both in foreign affairs and in the relationship between the emperor and his subjects. The changes are quite evident in foreign affairs.

21. On Pakourianos, see A. E. LAIOU, "L'étranger de passage et l'étranger privilégié à Byzance, XIe–XIIe siècles", in *Identité et droit de l'Autre,* L. Mayali, ed., Berkeley 1994, pp. 69-88.

22. Adoption or the promise thereof was one response: see Michael VI's offer to Isaakios Komnenos to adopt him thus making him effectively his heir (SKYLITZES, ed. Thurn, pp. 496-500) and Votaneiates' similar offer to the rebel Nikephoros Vryennios: NICÉPHORE BRYENNIOS, *Histoire*, ed. P. Gautier, Brussels 1975, CFHB 9, pp. 263-65.

23. SKYLITZES, ed. Thurn, pp. 497-98.

24. ANNE COMNÈNE, *Alexiade*, II.v.5-6, ed. Leib, I, p. 78.

The oath became an important means of making binding treaties and arrangements with foreign powers. Ostensibly, it was always a unilateral oath, sworn by the foreign prince, king, nobleman or Italian republic in question. This is true of treaties with Christians and non-Christians; it is true of Alexios' arrangement with the crusaders – a subject which has engendered considerable discussion, especially among western medievalists, who have argued at great length the question whether the crusaders, in their own view, had simply sworn oaths of fealty or performed homage to Alexios I.[25] While this issue will not be discussed here, it is important to note that none of the Byzantine sources ever refer to oaths given by the Byzantine Emperor to give force to the agreements with the participants of the First Crusade.

In the early part of his reign, Alexios expected an oath from the Holy Roman Emperor, Henry IV, but it was a unilateral oath, not a reciprocal one – or at least so Anna Komnene says.[26] It was to be a most solemn oath, the form of which had been exactly described to Henry's ambassadors and would be further explained. Presumably, it would be an oath on the Gospels and on the Cross, taken by the German Emperor in person, and then included in an ὁρκωμοτικὸν ἔγγραφον, a written statement secured by the oath and also guaranteeing the oath-taking.[27] What Alexios promised in return is very similar to the promises of Michael VII to Robert Guiscard: cash, silks, imperial offices and the marriage of Henry IV's daughter to a son of the sebastokrator Isaakios, Alexios's eldest brother, since the Emperor himself had no children yet. But the Emperor did not guarantee his promises by an oath; his word, or a chrysobull, was deemed sufficient.[28]

The treaty of Devol (1108), between Alexios I and Bohemond, is the first feudal contract preserved in a Byzantine source. Anna Komnene's text presents Bohemond's part of the agreement, and only indirectly that of Alexios. According to the text, Alexios had given Bohemond possession of Antioch and its region as a donation (δωρεά). In return (ἀντίδοσις), Bohemond swore fidelity (ἄνθρωπος πιστός) to the emperor and his son; he also swore that he would fight the Emperor's enemies.[29] He swore liege homage, and also swore, by a most solemn oath, in the presence of witnesses, and in writing, to keep the agreements. Alexios' donation was in the form of a chrysobull, which is termed reciprocal (ἀμοιβαῖος), the reciprocity presumably being that of donation in return for fidelity and loyalty.[30] The text we

25. See *supra*, n. 2 and LAIOU, "L'étranger privilégié" (n. 21), pp. 84 -88.

26. ANNE COMNÈNE, *Alexiade* III.iii.10-III.x.8, ed. Leib, I, pp. 133-136. See DÖLGER-WIRTH, *Regesten*, I, no. 1077 (ca.1082).

27. Similar to Bohemond's oath, and to the oaths taken by heads of Italian city states: A. LAIOU, "The Foreigner and the Stranger in 12th-century Byzantium: Means of Propitiation and Acculturation," in *Fremde der Gesellschaft*, M.-Th. Fögen, ed., Frankfurt 1991, pp. 88-89.

28. For an excellent analysis of Alexios's letters to Henry IV, as reported by Anna Komnene, see O. KRESTEN, "Die Auslandsschreiben der byzantinischen Kaiser der Komnenenzeit: die literarische Überlieferung bei Anna Komnene und Ioannes Kinnamos. Mit einem Exkurs: Zur Chronologie der Auslandsschreiben Dölger-Wirth, Reg. 1068, 1077, 1080 und 1114," *Römische Historische Mitteilungen* 39, 1996, pp. 25-37 and 44-59.

29. ANNE COMNÈNE, *Alexiade*, XIII.xii.3, XIII.xii.18, and XIII.xii.27, ed. Leib, III, pp. 126, 133, 138.

30. The entire text of the treaty of Devol (or, rather, of Bohemond's agreement), is in ANNE COMNÈNE, *Alexiade*, XIII.xii.12, ed. Leib, III, pp. 125-138. On Devol, see Ja. N. LJUBARSKIJ,

have indicates that the chrysobull did not contain an imperial oath.[31] Antioch was given to Bohemond on condition of his utmost fidelity and clear loyalty: πίστιν ἀκραιφνεστάτην καὶ εὔνοιαν καθαράν.[32]

The treaty of Devol was a perfectly bilateral agreement in substance. However, in form it consisted of two separate documents: Bohemond's oath of fidelity and homage on the one hand, and, on the other, the imperial chrysobull containing the details of what was given him on condition of his loyalty. But the chrysobull that would have granted Bohemond his possessions is not extant; one wonders whether the preamble would have been, as in most Byzantine chrysobulls, that of a pure act of donation to a faithful subject, or whether it would have alluded to the bilaterality of the agreement or to any oaths taken by Alexios, oaths that are reported by Fulcher of Chartres but by no Byzantine source. The fact that Bohemond's part of the agreement speaks of a "donation" and makes no mention of an imperial oath indicates that the chrysobull would have been in the usual form of a unilateral, free imperial donation.[33]

It is worth noting that some of the same terms recur in Michael VII's chrysobull to Robert Guiscard and in the treaty of Devol: εὔνοια, ἀντίδοσις, two forms of the term for submission (ὑποταγή, δουλεία), as well as the statement regarding the Emperor's friends and enemies.

Similar points may be made with regard to the privileges granted by the Komnenian emperors to the Italian city-states. The agreements are bilateral in substance. In the chrysobulls to Venice in 1082 and 1126, to Genoa in 1169, it is stated that the chrysobull (with trade privileges) is granted in reward for their loyalty and services *(fidei et pure servitudinis premia... in remuneratione... ipsorum servitiorum*[34]; *eorum benevolentia et fide*, which is the equivalent of εὔνοια and πίστις[35]); or for their submission and loyalty (δουλείαν καὶ εὔνοιαν).[36] The last document mentions that the Emperor granted it in the first instance because of the benevolence (ἀγαθὸν θέλημα) which he bore toward Genoa. However, in none of these documents is it stated that the chrysobull had as a precondition faith and loyalty, nor that there were preconditions for the loyalty of the Italian city. Alexios I's chrysobull to Pisa is somewhat different, since the Emperor says that as long as the Pisans keep their oath of loyalty and of helping the empire against all its enemies, without fraud or deceit

M. M. FREJDENBERG, "Devolskij dogovor 1108 g. meždu Alekseem Komninom i Boemundom", *VV* 21, 1962, pp. 260-274. The word ἀμοιβαῖος (ANNE COMNÈNE, *Alexiade* XIII.xii.3, ed. Leib, III, p. 126) has been translated by Leib as meaning simply that a copy of the chrysobull was given to Bohemond. That is certainly a possible interpretation, and indeed plausible in context. However, a few years later (1111), Alexios's chrysobull to Pisa shows that in this period ἀμοιβαῖος can mean (as it does in this document) "reciprocal" (see MM III, p. 13). The second or third-hand rendition of the treaty of Devol in Anna Komnene leaves the issue in some doubt.

31. ANNE COMNÈNE, *Alexiade* XIII.xii.26, ed. Leib, III, p. 137.

32. ANNE COMNÈNE, *Alexiade* XIII.xii.19, ed. Leib, III, p. 134.

33. FULCHER OF CHARTRES, II.39, p. 524, reports that Alexios *iuravit* (to Bohemond) *super reliquias pretiosissimas*, to help the crusaders, while Bohemond *iuravit... pacem et fidelitatem*. However, this does not necessarily reflect the facts but rather a westerner's understanding of them.

34. Chrysobull to Venice, 1082, ZEPOS, I, p. 369.

35. Chrysobull to Venice, 1126: TAFEL-THOMAS, *Urkunden* (n. 6), I, p. 95.

36. Chrysobull to Genoa, 1169: MM III, p. 35.

(ἄνευ δόλου καὶ περινοίας τινός), his chrysobull would retain its force, a chrysobull that was sent as a reciprocal document to the Pisans' written statement, which had been confirmed by the oaths of their magistrates (ὁ παρὼν χρυσόβουλλος λόγος ἀμοιβαῖος ὢν τῆς ἐγγράφου συμφωνίας ὑμῶν τῆς διὰ τοῦ ὑμετέρου ὅρκου βεβαιωθείσης... ἀπεστάλη... (*hoc enim presens chrysobullum verbum, mutuum vestre scripte convenctioni per vestrum sacramentum confirmate... missum est...*).[37] Similar statements appear in Alexios III's chrysobull to Venice in 1198, which, however, adds that the privileges given by the chrysobull were granted as a donation (*ex gratia donata*).[38]

This is a key point. All of these documents, which show the substantive bilaterality more or less clearly, have a powerful unilateral aspect in form. First of all, they are confirmed by the oath of the magistrates of the various cities (or the Doge in the case of Venice), but the emperor took no oath. Secondly, the form remains that of the chrysobull, a pure act of imperial donation, and an imperial prerogative. Thus, these are bilateral agreements where the oath is unilateral; the distinction between the emperor and all others is preserved through this diplomatic form. The agreements are unilateral in form, but bilateral and synallagmatic in reality.[39] Both aspects are important.

By the late twelfth century, as the stability of the Komnenian system began to collapse under its own weight, there was further development of such agreements. The most striking developments of the period, in the matter under discussion, are in the realm of foreign affairs. The most interesting are those surrounding the Treaty of Adrianople (συμφωνία; *foedera pactis et concordia, conventio, compositio pacis*), which aimed to regulate relations between Isaakios II and Frederick Barbarossa (in February, 1190). This is a truly bilateral convention, in form and in substance. The two Emperors swore oaths through their representatives (Choniates says that "the Emperor and the King renewed their oaths"),[40] and there was an exchange of presents. Much more astonishing is the fact that there was a further sworn guarantee, by groups of subjects of the two emperors: 15,000 of Barbarossa's "milites" took this oath in the presence of imperial ambassadors. In exchange, in Constantinople, the Patriarch confirmed the treaty, while in the sacred precincts of Haghia Sophia

37. MM III, p. 13 (Greek text); ZEPOS, I, p. 464 (Latin text).

38. ZEPOS, I, p. 480.

39. L. BURGMANN, "Chrysobull gleich Privileg? Beobachtungen zur Funktion einer byzantinischen Urkundenform", in *Das Privileg im europäischen Vergleich*, B. Dölemeyer, H. Mohnhaupt, eds., I, Frankfurt 1997, pp. 78 ff, notes rightly that the treaties, in the form of chrysobulls, are stylized as the will of the Emperor. This goes so far that the recipients are presented as subjects of the Byzantine Emperor even when they are not. Note the dialectic relation between foreign and domestic developments: the chrysobull appears as a unilateral act in treaties with foreigners, because that was its usual form; in domestic relations, the substance then becomes similar to that of foreign treaties, but the chrysobull persists in its formal aspect of a unilateral act.

40. The reference is to the original agreements made between Frederick and Isaakios's representatives. They are called by Choniates πίστεις or ὅρκοι, the two terms being interchangeable here: NICETAS CHONIATES, *Historia*, ed. I. A. Van Dieten, Berlin-New York 1974, CFHB 11/1, p. 402. The agreements were clearly bilateral and secured by oaths.

"500 men of the marketplace and the court" (ἀπὸ τῶν ἀγοραίων καὶ τῆς βασιλείου αὐλῆς) swore that "the Emperor would keep the treaties inviolate."[41]

This extraordinary event undoubtedly owes much to the unusual political situation. It may well have occurred at the insistence of the Western Emperor. Yet it did not remain quite unique. In structural terms, it is not unlike the oath which all the inhabitants of the Empire of Nicaea – clergy, aristocrats, and people – had to swear in 1258, at the time of the coronation of Michael VIII and John IV at the behest of the Patriarch Arsenios, that essentially guaranteed the arrangements of joint rule with the further provision, to which the inhabitants swore, that they would rise against whichever Emperor acted against the arrangements.[42]

To recapitulate, bilateral, synallagmatic relations develop clearly in the late 11th century and continue in the 12th century. In foreign relations, on which we have concentrated so far, the agreement is made binding by an oath: unilateral in most cases, bilateral in the case of the agreement between Michael VII and Robert Guiscard in the beginning of the period, and between Isaakios II and Frederick Barbarossa at the end of the twelfth century.

The question then arises whether there were similar developments in the relationship between the emperor and his subjects. I will not deal with the question of the oath of all the subjects to the Emperor which, despite what has been argued to the contrary, remained episodic throughout the twelfth century, and was still sworn mainly to safeguard the succession.[43] On the other hand, the proliferation of acts of imperial donation, in the form of chrysobulls, to individuals, raises certain questions.

In the Komnenian period, chrysobulls were still treated as the Emperor's word; they never incorporated an oath. And they were issued at the Emperor's will, or, most often, at the request and upon the petition of the person who received them. They were a pure act of donation; the Emperor made a gift, he did not contract an obligation. When the Emperors made donations of land or revenues, that is what these ostensibly were, pure acts of donation, not part of a bilateral agreement, and not a result of an oath on the part of the beneficiary. No official document of this period contains any agreement where an oath of fidelity is involved, and where the grant of land is part of an agreement. The chrysobull is the most solemn word of the emperor, and grants of land through chrysobull preserve the emperor's absolute freedom of action. This is how things appear. But what of the substance?

41. Ansbert, *Historia de expeditione Friderici*, ed. A. Chroust, MGH, *ScriptRerGerm*, n.s., 5, Berlin 1928, p. 66: *quingenti homines meliores civitatis et imperii*. Note that in this case the form of the document was not, as far as we know, a chrysobull. In treaties with the Italians, even the ones that were clearly bilateral in substance, the chrysobull preserved the unilateral form all through the twelfth century. See, e.g. the chrysobull to Venice (1187), Zepos, I, 437ff. (*presente chrisobulo verbo imperii nostri firmo et inviolabili permanere debente in omnibus que continet*) and the treaty of 1192 with Pisa: Zepos, I, 457-68.

42. A. E. Laiou, "Peasant Rebellion : Notes on its Vocabulary and Typology", in *Ordnung und Aufruhr im Mittelalter*, M.-Th. Fögen, Frankfurt 1995, pp. 103-106 ; Svoronos, "Serment" (n. 1), pp. 111-12, 129, 139.

43. Only at the end of the period do we find the inhabitants of Constantinople swearing πίστιν and εὔνοιαν to Andronikos I, only to break their oath: Choniates, ed. Van Dieten, p. 350.

An early example of such chrysobulls is that issued by Alexios I in favor of Leon Kephalas (1082), confirming an earlier donation by Nikephoros Votaneiates. Alexios starts by saying that Kephalas has shown himself to be a faithful servitor and of true disposition to his lords (ὑπηρέτης πιστὸς καὶ ὀρθογνώμων τοῖς δεσπόταις), who kept toward them a sincere service (δούλωσιν), free of all duplicity (διπλόης πάσης ἀπηλλαγμένην). For that reason, Kephalas enjoys the benevolence (εὔνοιαν) of his masters. Kephalas, it is further said, is a grateful subject (εὐγνώμων... ὑπήκοος) and zealous in his faith to the Emperor (τὴν εἰς τὴν βασιλείαν μου πίστιν θερμότατος). As such, he has made a request (δέησιν), which the Emperor will honor, ordering by the present chrysobull that the donation (δωρεάν) granted to Kephalas by the previous emperor be confirmed, and adding further privileges. [44] This is, in form, a pure unilateral donation by the Emperor. However, it is worth noting the similarities in phraseology and concept with some of the documents governing international relations. Thus, the words ὑπηρέτης πιστός recalls the ἄνθρωπος πιστός and δοῦλος of the treaty of Devol; δούλωσις recalls the δουλείαν promised by Bohemond; πίστις appears in both these texts; ὑπήκοος reminds us of the ὑποταγή promised by Robert Guiscard, and of the ὑποχείριος that Bohemond proclaimed himself to be;[45] δωρεά appears in several texts, while Leon Kephalas' service without duplicity reappears as service *sine fraude et malo ingenio* in the chrysobull of Alexios III to Venice (1198). Quite apart from the phraseology, the relationship that appears here is bilateral: Kephalas has shown loyalty and good service, and as a result he receives imperial privileges. These, however, appear in the form of a donation. The chrysobull thus preserves the aspect of a free and unilateral donation, while in fact it is the result of a bilateral relationship. The form of the imperial chancery disguises the reality.

I am suggesting that, in the late eleventh century, we see similar developments both in the relations of the Byzantine Emperor with foreign powers, and in the relations between the Emperor and some of his subjects. Bilateral agreements are multiplying. But the fact that, on the imperial side, the agreement is incorporated in the traditional form of donation which is the chrysobull, preserves the fiction of the freedom of the Emperor and of the unilateral aspect of his munificence. Furthermore, no imperial oaths are given, with one exception, that of the chrysobull to Robert Guiscard. The chrysobull to Leon Kephalas is contemporary to that given to the Venetians in 1082, and predates the treaty of Devol. I am, therefore, arguing that the development is an internal, Byzantine one, not necessarily deriving from western influences, although those doubtless played a role in the long term.

44. P. LEMERLE, A. GUILLOU, N. SVORONOS, D. PAPACHRYSSANTHOU, *Actes de Lavra* I, Paris, 1970, no. 44 (March, 1082). The original donation may have contained similar words, although there is no way to know. *Ibid.*, n° 48, another chrysobull by Alexios I to the same person states that the confirmation of landed possessions, requested by Kephalas, was given as reward for his valiant fighting against Bohemond: οὐ προῖκα καὶ ἀμισθί ἀλλ' εἰς ἀνταμοιβὴν κόπων καὶτροπαίων τῶν παρ' αὐτοῦ ἐπιδεδειγμένων ἐν τῷ κάστρῳ Λαρίσσης... The reconstruction of the domains of Kephalas may be found *ibid.*, no. 65. See also CHEYNET, *Pouvoir et contestations* (n. 16), no. 120.

45. ANNE COMNÈNE, *Alexiade*, XIII.xii.1, ed. Leib, III, p.125.

As has already been suggested, the chrysobulls of the Komnenian period that were granted to individuals do not preserve traces of an oath on the part of the beneficiary. But, of course, the chrysobull would not necessarily incorporate such an oath if it had existed. Is it possible that oaths of loyalty were, in fact, given, but were preserved in separate documents, in the imperial archives, which have not survived? The existing evidence makes it legitimate to propose that bilateral and synallagmatic arrangements between the emperor and his subjects existed already in the late eleventh century.[46]

This hypothesis is perhaps given credence by the arrangements incorporated in two documents of the early fourteenth century. In 1319, when the city of Ioannina returned to the Byzantine Empire after the death of Despot Thomas, the emperor Andronikos II issued a chrysobull confirming the privileges of its inhabitants and adding new ones.[47] In his *prooimion*, the emperor recalled the parable of the prodigal son, and ascribed to his own philanthropy the privileges he was about to confer. In the course of the text, he mentioned the submission of the inhabitants, "with total loyalty" (μετ' εὐνοίας ἀκραιφνοῦς ὑποταγῇ). The document also makes it clear that the Emperor's representative and governor of Berat, the pinkernes Syrgiannes Palaiologos, had already promised, in writing, to the inhabitants the possession of certain lands as well as fiscal privileges.[48] The inhabitants, then, asked for an imperial chrysobull, the text we are analyzing. The document itself is in the good tradition of chrysobulls, a pure act of free and unilateral donation at the request of the beneficiaries; the emperor, through the chrysobull, "makes evident and promises" (δηλοποιεῖ καὶ ὑπισχνεῖται) the privileges.[49] A few oddities, such as the promise exacted by the inhabitants that the Emperor would not cede the city to anyone but would retain it in his possession, may be ascribed to the particularities of the political circumstances. No oath on either side is mentioned, an important point.

However, another document, dated a few years later but referring to the events of 1319, shows unequivocally that the chrysobull of 1319 had been part of a bilateral agreement complete with oaths on the part of the inhabitants. At that time (before or in February 1319), the inhabitants had sworn a solemn oath of fidelity to Andronikos II, even though subsequently they broke it and swore an oath to John II Orsini and his widow and son. In 1319, the inhabitants of Ioannina submitted themselves to the service of Andronikos II (ὑποταγέντες εἰς τὴν ὑποχειριότητα καὶ δουλοσύνην) and remained in submission, observing their oaths (ἐμμένοντες τῇ ὑποταγῇ αὐτῆς κατὰ τοὺς ἐπὶ τούτῳ γεγονότας ὅρκους παρ' αὐτῶν).[50] The convention with the

46. N. Oikonomidès, "Liens de vassalité dans un apanage byzantin du XIIe siècle", *ΑΕΤΟΣ, Studies in honour of Cyril Mango*, I. Ševčenko and I. Hutter, eds., Stuttgart and Leipzig 1998, pp. 257-63, suggests that there existed subinfeudation already in the 12th century, but in a limited number of cases. This shows an earlier appearance of feudal or quasi-feudal relationships than is usually admitted.

47. MM V, pp. 77-84. For the political circumstances, see D. M. Nicol, *The Despotate of Epirus*, Oxford 1957, pp. 82ff.

48. MM V, pp. 83-84.

49. MM V, pp. 79-80.

50. H. Hunger, O. Kresten, E. Kislinger, C. Cupane, *Das Register des Patriarchats von Konstantinopel, 2. Teil,* Vienna 1995 CFHB 19/2, no. 110 (July 1337-February 1338), pp. 96-98 (decision of the Patriarch John XIV Kalekas).

inhabitants of Ioannina, then, in 1319, had gone as follows: First, they had asked the Byzantine governor of Berat (Syrgiannes Palaiologos) to occupy the city, promising submission (ὑποταγήν).[51] At this point, or perhaps a little later, they took oaths of fidelity to the Emperor. Then, the governor, Syrgiannes, gave them certain privileges. They asked that the Emperor confirm both his overlordship and their privileges by chrysobull. Finally, the chrysobull was issued.[52] The arrangement is clearly bilateral and synallagmatic.

The important point is that the two halves of the agreement were registered in different documents. One was the oath of the inhabitants. It is not stated that it was a written one, but since every other agreement surrounding this affair was written, and since, almost twenty years later, the Patriarchal synod, which judged the matter of perjury, had clear views about the oath, we must assume that it existed in written form. The other document is the chrysobull, which records the benefices granted to the inhabitants of Ioannina. If we had only the chrysobull, and not the Patriarchal decision which mentions the other part of the agreement, we would not have known about the oath of fidelity.

The chrysobull of February 1319 for the city of Ioannina is misleading, in that it does not mention the oath of the inhabitants which formed part of the reciprocal agreement. One wonders whether the privileges and pronoia grants of the late eleventh and twelfth centuries were not also parts of bilateral, reciprocal agreements, of which only one, i.e., the chrysobull, survives. The terms used in the two documents concerning Ioannina, ὑποχειριότης, δουλοσύνη, ὑποταγή, μετ' εὐνοίας ὑποταγή, are very similar to those we find in the chrysobull of Kephalas, as well as in the texts of the late eleventh century which refer to foreign relations. Oaths of fidelity are not mentioned in this chrysobull. In pronoia grants of the mid-fourteenth century, too, it seems that the oath of fidelity and the grant were written down in two separate documents, of which the chrysobull preserved the traditional form.[53] Certainly, by 1319 there had been many developments, and the influence of western Europe had become much stronger. Nevertheless, it seems arguable that reciprocal arrangements between the Emperor and his subjects had begun much earlier, and must be dated to that seminal period, the late eleventh century, developing further during the period of the Komnenoi.

In the second half of the 11th century, as we have seen, there was a confluence of factors which caused bilateral agreements and sworn associations to proliferate.

51. According to the privilege, MM V, p. 79; according to the document that mentions their oath, they submitted themselves to the ὑποχειριότητα καὶ δουλοσύνην τοῦ... βασιλέως (*Register*, II, p. 96).

52. In a letter to Venice, the emperor Andronikos II wrote that the Despots of Epiros held their land *iuramento vassallagii*: G. M. THOMAS, R. PREDELLI, *Diplomatarium Veneto-Levantinum sive acta et diplomata res Venetas Graecas atque Levantis illustrantia, a. 1300*, I, Venice 1880, no. 77, p. 146; dated after September 27, 1319: DÖLGER, *Regesten,* no. 2426.

53. Compare P. MAGDALINO, "An Unpublished Pronoia Grant of the Second Half of the 14th Century", *ZRVI* 18, 1978, pp. 155-63, and the Ὀρκωμοτικὸν εἰς βασιλέα published by K. SATHAS, *Μεσαιωνικὴ Βιβλιοθήκη*, VI, pp. 652-53. There is, also, the oath mentioned by Moschopoulos, sworn to the Emperor, which will not be discussed here. On this, see SVORONOS, "Le serment" (n. 1), pp. 129-35.

Imperial power was weak, society was fluid, and there were new demands in terms of foreign relations. So there was a proliferation of horizontal links through oaths and other means. Vertical links cemented by oaths and bilateral contracts appear as well, most clearly in the case of Michael VII and Robert Guiscard, but also in the arrangements between Alexios I and Gregory Pakourianos.

Komnenian government, which I have called "the feudal authoritarianism of the twelfth century," [54] was very much based on grants of privilege, made by chrysobull. These did not ostensibly include oath-taking or mutual obligations. Reciprocal obligations thus remained formally weak, for the chrysobulls were couched in the language of acts of donation. The emperor did not contract obligations, and certainly took no oath, until the fourteenth century.

With the Komnenoi, we find the appearance of agreements that are bilateral in content, but unilateral in form. The illusion of imperial authority acting without preconditions and making unilateral free imperial donations was preserved into the fourteenth century by the persistence of the chrysobull as the diplomatic form in which the imperial part of a contract was presented. To my mind, it is a plausible proposition that the oath of fidelity was the other part of the agreement; however, that is not clearly attested until the fourteenth century. I have suggested that synallagmatic agreements appeared earlier and were stronger than we usually think, and that they go back to the late eleventh century and the early Komnenian period. At the same time, the force of the imperial tradition was so strong, that the free act of donation by the Emperor remained the dominant diplomatic form until the end; this both hides real changes from us and reflects a state tradition that hindered the full development of contractual links based on bilateral agreements. As so often in the Byzantine Empire, form disguises substance and in so doing becomes a constitutive element of its development; the tradition of form, the dynamic of substance are interactive parts of an intricate reality.

54. A. Laiou, "Law, Justice, and the Byzantine Historians: Ninth to Twelfth Centuries", in *Law and Society in Byzantium, Ninth-Twelfth Centuries*, A. Laiou and D. Simon, eds., Washington, DC 1994, p. 184.

INDEX

Terms that recur frequently in the texts, such as *Byzantium*, *Byzantines*, *Greeks*, *Romans*, have not been included in the index. Emperors are listed by their first name; other persons (where possible) by their last.

For Product Safety Concerns and Information please contact our EU representative GPSR@taylorandfrancis.com Taylor & Francis Verlag GmbH, Kaufingerstraße 24, 80331 München, Germany

Batch number: 10730818

Printed by Printforce, the Netherlands